BECOMING
METRIC-WISE

BECOMING METRIC-WISE

A Bibliometric Guide for Researchers

RONALD ROUSSEAU

LEO EGGHE

RAF GUNS

ELSEVIER

CP
CHANDOS
PUBLISHING
An imprint of Elsevier

Chandos Publishing is an imprint of Elsevier
50 Hampshire Street, 5th Floor, Cambridge, MA 02139, United States
The Boulevard, Langford Lane, Kidlington, OX5 1GB, United Kingdom

British Library Cataloguing-in-Publication Data
. A catalogue record for this book is available from the British Library

Library of Congress Cataloging-in-Publication Data
A catalog record for this book is available from the Library of Congress

ISBN: 978-0-08-102474-4 (print)
ISBN: 978-0-08-102475-1 (online)

For information on all Chandos Publishing publications
visit our website at https://www.elsevier.com/books-and-journals

Working together
to grow libraries in
developing countries

www.elsevier.com • www.bookaid.org

Publisher: Glyn Jones
Acquisition Editor: Glyn Jones
Editorial Project Manager: Charlotte Rowley
Production Project Manager: Debasish Ghosh
Cover Designer: Mark Rogers, Xiaojun Hu and Raf Guns

Typeset by MPS Limited, Chennai, India

CONTENTS

BIOGRAPHIES

Ronald Rousseau was born on August 14, 1949 in Antwerp, Belgium. He is married to Myrian Salembier with whom he has three children.

Rousseau obtained a Doctoral Degree in Mathematics (University of Leuven, 1977), the Habilitation degree in Mathematics (University of Leuven, 1983), and a doctorate in Library and Information Science (University of Antwerp, 1992). He received the Prize of the Belgian Academy of Sciences (1979) for his mathematical work.

He was a full-time mathematics professor at the engineering college KHBO (Oostende) and, over the years, taught different courses for the Education in Library and Information Science at the University of Antwerp (applied bibliometrics—knowledge representation—scientific communication, and research evaluation).

Together with Leo Egghe he wrote *Introduction to Informetrics* (1990), published by Elsevier. In 2001, they received the Derek De Solla Price Award for their work in scientometrics. He is a regular visitor of Chinese universities (with more than 50 Chinese co-authors) and became an Honorary Professor of Zhejiang University and of Henan Normal University. He is the former president of the International Society of Scientometrics and Informetrics (ISSI).

Rousseau is (co-)author of some 500 publications, most of them in journals covered by the Web of Science, but also in local journals (India, China) and journals for mathematics teachers (written in Dutch). His main interest is citation analysis and diversity measurement.

Leo Egghe was born on February 10, 1952 in Beveren, Belgium. He is married to Maria De Bock with whom he has three children.

Egghe has a Doctoral Degree in Mathematics (University of Antwerp, 1978), a Habilitation in Mathematics (University of Antwerp, 1985) and a Ph.D. in Information Science (City University London, 1989).

Egghe was Chief Librarian at the University of Hasselt in the period 1979–2017 and Professor in Library and Information Science at the University of Antwerp in the period 1983–2016 (teaching Information Retrieval and Informetrics). He was also visiting professor in several institutes in the world, among which the Indian Statistical Institute in

Bangalore, India several times. He coordinated development projects in information science in Kenya in the 1990s. Since 2017 he is retired.

Together with Rousseau he organized the first ISSI Conference at LUC, Belgium in 1987, and wrote *Introduction to Informetrics*, published by Elsevier. In 2001 they received the Derek De Solla Price Award for their work in scientometrics.

Egghe is (co-)author of almost 300 scientific publications, most of them in journals covered by the Web of Science. Among these are five books. He invented the g-index in 2006 (a generalization of the h-index) in an article in the journal *Scientometrics*, which is, at this date (2017) the most cited article in this journal. His main interest is the mathematical development of the theory of the Law of Lotka which resulted in a book on this Law in 2005, published by Elsevier.

In 2007, Egghe became the Founding Editor-in-Chief of the *Journal of Informetrics* (Elsevier).

Raf Guns was born on December 15, 1979 in Turnhout, Belgium. He is married to Caroline Van de Velde with whom he has three children.

Guns has a Master's Degree in Germanic Philology (University of Leuven, 2001) and in Library and Information Science (University of Antwerp, 2005). He obtained his Ph.D. in Library and Information Science (University of Antwerp, 2012) under the supervision of Ronald Rousseau.

He has worked for the Library and Information Science program at the University of Antwerp in various functions, including as coordinator, teaching assistant, doctor-assistant, and lecturer in ICT and knowledge organization. Since October 2015, he works as coordinator of the Antwerp branch of the Flemish Center for R&D Monitoring (ECOOM) and as a research administrator at the University of Antwerp's department of research and innovation.

Guns is (co-)author of about 35 scientific publications, mostly in journals that are indexed in Web of Science. In 2013, he was awarded the Emerald/EFMD Outstanding Doctoral Research Award. Since 2015, he has served as an editorial board member of the *Journal of Informetrics*.

PREFACE

This book has two origins, the first one being *Introduction to Informetrics* (1990), a book written by Leo Egghe and Ronald Rousseau, two of the authors of this new book, and a course, entitled *Scientific Communication and Research Evaluation*, taught by these two academics for many years as part of the education in Library and Information Science at Antwerp University (Belgium).

Introduction to Informetrics consisted of four parts: Statistics, aspects of operations research, citation analysis, and informetric models. Over the years, colleagues asked us to update its contents. As this book has a second origin, namely, our course, it is not really an update. Since none of the authors is a specialist in statistics, we decided to keep this part to the bare minimum. Techniques originating in operations research have not become mainstream in our field so that we do not cover this part anymore. The part on citation analysis has been kept and expanded while the part on bibliometric laws is reduced to one chapter, covering its basic aspects. A full account on the so-called "Lotkaian" aspects of the bibliometric laws has been written by Leo Egghe (2005). Besides this, we added—with respect to *Introduction to Informetrics*—chapters on scientific research and communication, publishing, research evaluation and networks. In view of recent developments in informetrics, a basic introduction to research evaluation and to networks was felt to be essential. Moreover, a timeline is provided as a (short) historical overview of the field.

For this new book, "new blood" in the person of a former doctoral student, Raf Guns, was more than welcome. His expertise is in networks and research evaluation, especially in the social sciences and humanities. Raf Guns is currently a coordinator at the Centre for R&D Monitoring at the University of Antwerp.

Quantitative methods to identify statistical regularities, as well as qualitative approaches to explain local deviations from global patterns are both essential for the study of the science of science. This way of thinking perfectly coincides with the ideas underlying the purpose of this book—namely to introduce the basics of bibliometrics and its applications to students and to a global audience of researchers from different backgrounds. We hope that this book is of help to educators preparing a course related to quantitative aspects of the information sciences. Yet, we hope in addition that researchers, scholars, and doctoral students interested in indicators and science policy will find many parts of this book interesting and useful.

The book is divided into 11 chapters and contains a reference list, preface, an appendix providing the names of the recipients of the Derek J. de Solla Price award, and some indexes. The reference list is, of course, not meant to be exhaustive. Moreover, we apologize to those colleagues who feel they have been unjustly omitted.

We thank our institutes, the former KHBO (Oostende), the University of Hasselt, the University of Antwerp, and KU Leuven for their interest and support. We thank in particular the teaching and supporting staff from the education in Library and Information Science at Antwerp University who, over a period of more than 30 years, created a pleasant working environment, sometimes in difficult external circumstances.

Ronald Rousseau, Leo Egghe and Raf Guns

ACRONYMS

A&HCI	Arts & Humanities Citation Index
ABP	article-based publishing
ABS	Association of Business Schools
AC-IE	Angewandte Chemie — International Edition
AF	audience factor
AIF	average impact factor
AIS	article influence score
ALM	article level metrics
APC	article processing charge
AR	acceptance rate
ARWU	Academic Ranking of World Universities
BCI	Book Citation Index
BOAI	Budapest Open Access Initiative
BRICK	Brazil—Russia—India—China—Korea
BRICKS	Brazil—Russia—India—China—Korea—South Africa
CAB(I)	originally, Commonwealth Agricultural Bureaux (International)
CERN	originally, Conseil Européen pour la Recherche Nucléaire
CPCI-S	Conference Proceedings Citation Index — Science
CPCI-SSH	Conference Proceedings Citation Index — Social Science & Humanities
CpP	citations per publication
CRIS	Current Research Information System
CRIStin	Current Research Information System in Norway
CRL	Center for Research libraries
CSS	Characteristic scores and scales
CWTS	Centrum voor Wetenschap en Technologie Studies = Centre for Science and Technology Studies
DCP	database citation potential (part of SNIP)
DEA	Data Envelopment Analysis
DIF	diachronous impact factor
DOAJ	Directory of Open Access Journals
DOI	digital object identifier
DORA	Declaration on Research Assessment
EIC	editor-in-chief
ESI	Essential Science Indicators
ESCI	Emerging Sources Citation Index
FTE	full-time equivalent
GDP	gross domestic product
GERD	gross domestic expenditure on R&D
GIF	global impact factor
GS	Google Scholar
HEEACT	Higher Education Evaluation & Accreditation Council of Taiwan
HTML	HyperText Markup Language
I3	integrated impact indicator

IC	Index Chemicus
ICMJE	International Committee of Medical Journal Editors
ICT	information and communications technology
IMRaD	Introduction, Methods, Results and Discussion
IPP	Information Production Process
IREG	International Rankings Expert Group
ISBN	International Standard Book Number
ISI	Institute for Scientific Information
ISO	is not an acronym; it refers to the International Organization for Standardization
ISSI	International Society for Scientometrics and Informetrics
ISSN	International Standard Serial Number
JASIS(T)	Journal of the American Association of Information Science (and Technology) later: Journal of the Association of Information Science and Technology
JCR	Journal Citation Reports
JIF	journal impact factor
JUF	journal usage factor
MIF	median impact factor
MNCS	mean normalized citation score
MOCR	Mean Observed Citation Rate
MOOCs	Massive Open Online Courses
NIF	Normalized Impact Factor
NPG	Nature Publishing Group
OA	Open Access
OAI	Open Archives Initiative
OAI-PMH	Open Archives Initiative - Protocol for Metadata Harvesting
OCLC	Online Computer Library Center
ODLIS	Online Dictionary for Library and Information Science
ORCID	Open Researcher and Contributor IDentifier
p-c matrix	publication-citation matrix
PAC	Probably Approximately Correct
PDF	Portable Document Format
PLoS	Public Library of Science
QS	Quacquarelli Symonds
RDCP	Relative Database Citation Potential (part of SNIP)
RQI	Review Quality Instrument
RR	rejection rate
SAIF	synchronous author impact factor
SCI(E)	Science Citation Index (Expanded)
SIR	SCImago Institutions Ranking
SJR	SCImago Journal Ranking
SNA	social network analysis
SNIP	Source Normalized Impact per Paper
SSCI	Social Science Citation Index
SSRN	Social Science Research Network
THE	Times Higher Education

UDC	Universal Decimal Classification
UK	United Kingdom
US(A)	United States (of America)
VABB (-SHW)	Vlaams Academisch Bibliografisch Bestand (voor de Sociale en Humane Wetenschappen) = Flemish Academic Bibliography (for the Social Sciences and Humanities)
WIF	Web Impact Factor
WoS	Web of Science

CHAPTER 1

Introduction

The term *metrics* has become one of the main topics of interest in science in general. The DORA declaration (DORA, 2012), the Leiden Manifesto (Hicks et al., 2015) and the Metric Tide report (Wilsdon et al., 2015) are just the tip of the iceberg of the discussions going on in top journals such as *Nature* and *Science* as well as in evaluation committees all over the world.

For this reason, all scientists should become knowledgeable about indicators used to evaluate them. They should know the publication-citation context, the correct mathematical formulae of indicators being used by evaluating committees, their consequences and how such indicators can be misused. In one word: they should become metric-wise (Rousseau & Rousseau, 2015, 2017). This is exactly the purpose of this book: To make scientists metric-wise. In this way readers will become aware of the evaluation techniques applied to their scientific output, making them stronger when being evaluated for funding, hiring and tenure.

1.1 METRICS IN THE INFORMATION SCIENCES

Information science is defined in the Online Dictionary for Library and Information Science (ODLIS) (Reitz, s.a.) as "The systematic study and analysis of the sources, development, collection, organization, dissemination, evaluation, use, and management of information in all its forms, including the channels (formal and informal) and technology used in its communication." Already in the 1930s, Otlet (1934) defined bibliometrics as the measurement of all aspects related to books and documents. Otlet, a Belgian documentalist, and one of the developers of the Universal Decimal Classification, introduced the idea of bibliometrics in his main work: *Traité de Documentation* (Treatise on Documentation). In this book, a general overview of the information sciences at that time, he covers a plethora of topics related to books, libraries and documentation. Among these he introduced the term "bibliometrics" or more precisely—as the book was written in French—"bibliométrie". This new

Becoming Metric-Wise
DOI: http://dx.doi.org/10.1016/B978-0-08-102474-4.00001-7
1

science makes use of measurements of library-related objects and facts, and leads to law-like relations. According to Otlet, bibliometrics must include single objects as well as groups of objects (and hence makes use of statistics). Relations between key aspects must give rise to indices. Moreover, sociometric aspects must be taken into account. As an example, Otlet mentions that one should measure how often a book or an author is read. Mathematics must find its place in this new field. Otlet observed that in his time scientific fields tended to use more and more mathematics (physics, chemistry, biology, sociology, economics) and regretted its total absence in library science. Clearly, his ideas preceded similar ones published by Pritchard (1969) by more than 35 years.

Indeed, unaware of Otlet's work, Pritchard (1969) wrote: "*Bibliometrics is the application of mathematics and statistical methods to books and other media of communication. It is the metrology of the information transfer process; its purpose is analysis and control of the process. In short: bibliometrics is the scientific study of recorded discourse*". Pritchard coined the term bibliometrics—or at least he thought he did—to replace the term "statistical bibliography" which had been in some use, but which was not popular, not very descriptive, and could be confused with bibliographies on statistics. Around 1948, Ranganathan proposed the term librametrics (*librametry*), but this proposal has never caught on outside India.

A related term, namely *scientometrics* (*naukometria* in Russian), a term proposed by Nalimov (Nalimov & Mul'chenko, 1969), is defined as the study of the quantitative aspects of science as a discipline or economic activity. It includes research evaluation and aspects of research policy. Yet, we note that nowadays the terms bibliometrics and scientometrics are used by many colleagues without any differentiation. As such, not trying to win a lost battle, we too will treat these two terms as synonyms.

The revolution in information and communications technology (ICT), including the rise of the Internet, changed the way scientists performed research and communicated their results. Consequently in 1979 the new term *informetrics* was proposed by Blackert and Siegel (1979) on the one hand, and by Nacke (1979) on the other. The term gained popularity by the organization of biennial international conferences of which the first was organized in 1987 in Belgium (Egghe & Rousseau, 1988, 1990). The foundation of the International Society for Scientometrics and Informetrics (ISSI) in 1993 under the impetus of Hildrun Kretschmer increased the popularity of the term.

According to Tague-Sutcliffe (1992) and Ingwersen & Björneborn (2004), informetrics is defined as the study of the quantitative aspects of information in any form, not just records or bibliographies, and in any social group, not just scientists. This definition has been formulated to stress that informetrics is broader than bibliometrics and other metrics that existed at that time. Yet, we think that nowadays this stress is not necessary anymore so we define informetrics as:

> *The study of the quantitative aspects of information in any form and in any social group.*

Although "any social group" implies that informetrics also covers nonscientific information, in practice most informetric studies focus on scientific and scholarly information and its context (producers, consumers, contents, etc.). In other words, most informetric research is also sciento-metrics or webmetric (digital) research. This will also be the focus of the present book. One may say that informetrics is situated on the intersection between applied mathematics and social sciences.

In the networked world in which we live nowadays, informetrics becomes more like webmetrics (Almind & Ingwersen, 1997; Barabási, 2003; Thelwall, 2004). Here webmetrics is defined as the study of the quantitative aspects of the construction and use of information resources, structures and technologies on the Internet drawing on bibliometric and informetric approaches. We admit that the difference between biblio-metrics and webmetrics is not always clear, but essentially we would say that using web sources is not webmetrics, but studying their use is.

On October 20, 2010 Jason Priem, Dario Taraborelli, Paul Groth, and Cameron Neylon published a manifesto (Priem et al., 2010) in which they stated that besides classical bibliometric metrics and usage statistics one needs alternative metrics—altmetrics—when evaluating scientists, results of scientific investigations and groups of researchers. They claimed that indicators should evolve with time and hence classical approaches using peer review, counting citations, judging journals by impact factors and so forth must be "extended" by modern, e-based approaches. Concretely, they pointed out that peer review and all citation-based approaches are too slow, and the journal impact factor (JIF) is for most purposes unacceptable.

Nowadays scientists apply Web 2.0 techniques to discuss problems and disseminate results. Written text is often accompanied by data sets, computer code and designs. Via Twitter and other social media scientific knowledge is distributed in snippets or nano publications. Finally, researchers often place new findings on their personal websites or in blogs and annotate others' work.

Altmetrics is a term referring to all metric techniques measuring new forms of performing, discussing or communicating science, especially through social media. It captures different forms of engagement with an article, a scientist or theory. A clear advantage of these techniques is the fact that they react on the spot and hence are able to map new tendencies and reactions. Not surprisingly journals such as *Nature* immediately reacted to this phenomenon (Piwowar, 2013).

This said, we think that the term altmetrics is a bad choice; its pronunciation resembles "old" metrics, what is alternative today will certainly not be alternative in 10 years, and finally altmetrics is just a special form of informetrics. Perhaps altmetrics should better be called social influmetrics (Rousseau & Ye, 2013) or social media metrics (Haustein, Costas, & Lariviére, 2015). Contemporary methods to describe and evaluate science should include new ways of science communication and the social implications of communicating and performing scientific results. Hence a multimetric approach is called for (Rousseau & Ye, 2013). Aspects of impact captured by altmetrics include (Lin & Fenner, 2013; Taylor, 2013):

> Viewed—*HTML or PDF views on a website, often this is a publisher's website but other websites may also provide view data.*
> Discussed—*in science blogs, Wikipedia, Twitter, Facebook, and similar social media.*
> Saved—*Mendeley, CiteULike and other social bookmark sites.*
> Recommended *(formal endorsement)—a metric used for example by F1000Prime.*
> Cited—*altmetrics also adopts citations in secondary and other knowledge sources, such as number of times a paper has been referenced by Wikipedia.*

If one has access to the data, one can make a distinction between "viewed by other scholars" and "viewed by the public." A similar distinction could be made for the other actions. Sometimes altmetrics is described as the metrics of the computerization of the research process. We do not agree with this as the step of including the computerization of the research process already happened when the term informetrics was introduced. Clearly altmetrics is a subfield of informetrics.

In standard citation studies, the citing population coincides with the cited population in the sense that authors cite authors. This clearly is usually not the case in altmetric studies. A tweeter can be just that. If altmetrics would be used in evaluation studies then one should realize that altmetric scores can easily be manipulated, and this much easier than citations. Blogs and tweets can be anonymous, while articles and hence citations rarely are, in the sense that the typical anonymous article is an editorial for which a journal's main editor takes responsibility. These examples imply that actions such as tweeting or blogging that lead to altmetric scores can easily become meaningless. The same holds for downloading. Yet, it seems that Mendeley scores and Google Book citations are the least susceptible to manipulation. Recent information on alternative metrics and a practical guide can be found in (Thelwall, 2017).

Finally, we agree with Glänzel and Gorraiz (2015) that download metrics should not be included within altmetrics but rather be considered as another type of metrics within the field of informetrics.

1.2 A SHORT OVERVIEW OF TOPICS STUDIED IN THE FIELD OF INFORMETRICS

In this section, we give a short answer to the question: "What are the topics studied in the field of informetrics?" We will provide a general outline without details. Precise definitions are provided further on in this book. One of the classical topics studied in the field deals with the so-called informetric (or bibliometric) laws. Although it is now established that many phenomena studied in the field can be described (at least approximately) by a power law all its consequences are not yet fully understood. Recall that these power laws occur in a size-frequency form (Lotka's law) or in a rank-frequency form (Zipf-Mandelbrot law). More than 10 years ago, Leo Egghe published a book describing the full development of the informetric laws (Egghe, 2005). Other forms of mathematical modeling (i.e., other than using power laws) are not so popular, but will probably gain more attention as they have the potential of modeling some phenomena better than do power laws. In this context, we mention the Weibull (Gorkova, 1988; Liang et al., 1996; Burrell, 2003), the stretched exponential (Laherrère & Sornette, 1998) or the generalized Waring distribution (Glänzel, 2009), but there are many more candidates.

Publication and citation analysis and its application in research evaluation exercises is, and will stay, the focus of most application-oriented scientometric research. In this context, publication and citation-based indicators play an ever-increasing role now that the world, or at least a large part of its scientists, has come to know the h-index (Hirsch, 2005) and related indicators (Egghe, 2006a,b,c; Jin et al., 2007). Indicators play also an important role in world rankings of universities, such as the Shanghai Academic Ranking of World Universities, the Times Higher Education World Universities rankings (in short: THE rankings), the Leiden ranking or the Cybermetrics Web Ranking. For more details on university rankings, we refer to Chapter 8, Research evaluation.

As the Web is a large and omnipresent network, it is no surprise that the use of network techniques is on the rise (Otte & Rousseau, 2002). Of course, we may not forget that citations as well as collaborations create a network between scientists, journals, countries and so on. In this global-ized, networked world, studies related to all forms of networking, collabo-ration and diffusion of ideas gain more and more significance. These huge networks need special visualization tools, making visualization a hot sub-field of informetrics (Chen, 1999, 2003, 2004; Boyack et al., 2005, 2006; van Eck & Waltman, 2007; Garfield, 2009; Klavans & Boyack, 2009; Yang et al., 2009). It has turned out that so-called maps of science (Boyack et al., 2005), showing the relative positions of scientific fields with respect to each other, are remarkably stable. This stability allows to "overlay" publications or references produced for a specific purpose against the background of a representation of global science (Rafols et al., 2010).

Managers and colleagues in the field of management science not only use informetric data and indicators for research evaluation and planning, but use the same techniques in patent and innovation studies (Gao & Guan, 2009; Guan & Gao, 2009). In this context one uses the term patentometrics. Similarly, innovation and knowledge transfer studies, e.g., between industry, government and academia, the so-called triple helix (Etzkowitz & Leydesdorff, 1995), make use of performance metrics (Independent Expert Group on Open Innovation and Knowledge Transfer, 2014).

1.3 INSTRUMENTS

This section explains—at least from a particular point of view—why a book like this is necessary. The point we want to make about biblio-metrics and informetrics is that one should not be satisfied with artefacts, but that one needs real instruments. What is meant by this? In order to perform research and research evaluations, instruments are needed. But what is an instrument? An instrument can be defined as an artefact plus a mental scheme (Vygotski, 1978; Drijvers & Gravemeijer, 2004). An artefact is just a thing. A typical example of an artefact is a previously unknown object found on an archeological site. No one knows its use. An artefact becomes an instrument when knowledge and understanding about the proper use of the artefact develops. This knowledge is called a mental scheme. For most people a computer once was an artefact; knowledge about how to use it makes it an instrument. Clearly with a complex artefact such as a computer, knowledge is often partial, so it often happens that the instrument is not used to its full capacity. Similarly, databases such as the WoS, Scopus and Google Scholar, mathematical formulae and statistical software are just artefacts. Only a mental scheme, i.e., thorough understanding of their functionalities, makes them into instruments fit for further research and for the evaluation of scientific research (Rousseau, 2005b).

Citation analysis, and in particular its applications in research evaluation, makes use of indicators, which, however are not perfect; but neither is peer review. Indicators may have inherent logical problems, such as the h-index which is not independent (see Subsection 7.3.3), may not be optimal in a statistical sense and/or are not applied in a rigorous way, such as the standard JIF (see Section 6.15); they depend on fields and always on the used database. In that sense, results based on scientometric indicators, but also on peer review, are never perfect but rather Probably Approximately Correct, borrowing a term introduced by Valiant (Valiant, 2013; Rousseau, 2016). That is the best one can do in any field which is not purely theoretical, and in particular in those fields which involve a human factor (Bernstein et al., 2000).

It is well-known that in some corners bibliometrics and the other metrics are not really popular. Titles such as "Scientometrics: A dismal science" (Balaram, 2008) and "Metrics: a long-term threat to society" (Blicharska & Mikusinski, 2012) are clear in this respect. May we suggest that, besides pointing to the misuse of some metric techniques, these statements may also indicate that some colleagues do not yet see informetric techniques as real instruments. We hope that this book helps in making artefacts into instruments.

1.4 OTHER METRICS AND THE LARGER PICTURE

Metrics not only exist in the information sciences. One also knows the terms biometrics, econometrics, archaeometrics, chemometrics, jurimetrics and a whole series of software metrics and sustainability metrics.

Yet, as observed in Zhang et al. (2013), in other fields metrics are often understood as statistical techniques, while in the information sciences statistical techniques are just a part of a more general notion. As stated above, this more general notion is in our view best described as informetrics.

Informetrics, and especially visualization techniques as used in informetrics, together with the sociology of science are important subdomains of the science of science, the scientific study of science itself.

1.5 MATHEMATICAL TERMINOLOGY

We end this chapter by providing some basic mathematical terminology and notation used throughout the book.

1.5.1 Numbers

We distinguish the following number sets (the term *set* is defined in Subsection 1.5.3).

The natural numbers, denoted as **N** or $\mathbb{N}$. This is the infinite set $\{0,1,2,\ldots\}$. If the number zero is excluded we write $\mathbf{N_0}$ or $\mathbb{N}_0 = \{1,2,3,\ldots\}$. These are the strictly positive natural numbers.

The set of integers, denoted as **Z** or $\mathbb{Z}$, consists of the natural numbers and their opposites, i.e., $\{0,1,-1,2,-2,\ldots\}$.

The set of rational numbers, denoted as **Q** or $\mathbb{Q}$, consist of all numbers that can be expressed as the quotient or fraction a/b of two integers, a and b, with the denominator b not equal to zero. The number a is called the numerator. If $b = 1$ the rational number is an integer.

We recall the following important relations:

If b and $d \neq 0$ then $\dfrac{a}{b} = \dfrac{c}{d} \Leftrightarrow ad = bc$

If b and d are strictly positive then $\dfrac{a}{b} < \dfrac{c}{d} \Leftrightarrow ad < bc$.

Finally we have the set of real numbers **R** or $\mathbb{R}$. Real numbers can be thought of as values that represent a quantity along a continuous line. Real numbers which are not rational numbers are called irrational numbers. The numbers $\pi \approx 3.14159$ and $\sqrt{2} \approx 1.4142$ are examples of irrational numbers. Irrational numbers never result directly from counting operations, but the real numbers, including the irrational numbers, are used when modeling informetric data. An important reason for using real numbers is that they contain all limits of sequences of rational numbers. Somewhat more precisely, every sequence of real numbers having the property that consecutive terms of the sequence become arbitrarily close to each other necessarily has the property that the terms in this sequence become arbitrarily close to some specific real number. In mathematical terminology, this means that the set of real numbers is complete.

For simplicity, and following famous mathematicians such as Donald Knuth (the inventor of TeX, the standard typesetting system for mathematical texts) we will further on only use the bold face notation for numbers, e.g., **N** and not the so-called blackboard bold, e.g., $\mathbb{N}$ in which certain lines of the symbol are doubled.

1.5.2 Sequences

We have already used the term sequence, but not yet defined it formally. A sequence is an ordered collection of objects. It should be observed that repetitions are allowed. Like a set, a sequence contains members, usually referred to as terms. An example of a sequence is $u = (1, 5, 12, 12, 17, 20)$. The number of elements (possibly infinite) is called the length of the sequence. The length of the above sequence u is 6. Formally, a sequence can be defined as a function whose domain is the natural numbers, with or without including zero. When the domain consists of the natural numbers the sequence is by definition infinitely long. In practical applications one may identify a sequence ending with infinitely many zeros with the finite sequence ending with the last nonzero element. The all-zero sequence is then not considered to be a finite sequence. Sequences are denoted as:

$$u: n \in \mathbf{N} \to u_n \in \mathbf{R} \quad \text{or} \quad (u_n)_n \text{ in short.}$$

A sequence is increasing if for all n: $u_n \le u_{n+1}$. It is strictly increasing if for all n: $u_n < u_{n+1}$. Similarly, a sequence is decreasing if for all n: $u_n \ge u_{n+1}$ and strictly decreasing if for all n: $u_n > u_{n+1}$.

A constant sequence is decreasing as well as increasing. The example sequence u is increasing but not strictly increasing.

1.5.3 Sets

Following Halmos (1960) we simply say that to define a set is to determine its members. In other words, a set X is determined if and only if one can tell whether or not any given object x belongs to X. Members of a set X are often characterized by possessing a common property. For example, one can consider the set of all prime numbers. More formally this set may be denoted as: $\{n \in \mathbf{N}$: n has exactly two divisors, namely itself and the number 1$\}$. By definition an object either belongs to a given set or it does not. If it belongs to a set it belongs exactly once to the set, and it does not matter in which order a set's members are listed. Sets are denoted using the following type of brackets $\{.\}$. Consequently the two objects $\{y, 7, *\}$ and $\{*, y, 7\}$ denote the same set.

CHAPTER 2

Scientific Research and Communication

It makes no sense to do research and not to communicate the results. Hence the publication of research results is an important duty for any researcher. Yet, it does not suffice to publish research: Whatever is published should be read as widely as possible. Research results are communicated and disseminated in various ways e.g., published in journals, in edited books, in monographs, presented at conferences, and circulated via blogs on the Internet. Research of great public importance may even be disseminated through television documentaries. In the context of scientific communication, there are thus three kinds of variables at play, namely documents, researchers, and cognitions, i.e., topics and ideas (Guns, 2013; Kochen, 1974).

2.1 KNOWLEDGE AND SCIENTIFIC RESEARCH

2.1.1 Tacit Versus Explicit Knowledge

According to Polanyi (1966) tacit knowledge is nonverbalized, intuitive, and unarticulated knowledge. It is knowledge that resides in a human brain and that cannot easily be codified or captured. Nevertheless it is one of the aims of the field of artificial intelligence, and in particular of expert systems, to include exactly this kind of knowledge. Explicit knowledge is that kind of knowledge that can be articulated in a formal language and transmitted among individuals. It is the kind of knowledge found in all types of scientific publications.

2.1.2 Scientific Research

This Subsection is largely based on information from Wikipedia: http://en.wikipedia.org/wiki/Science. Persons who spend their professional time doing science are called scientists or researchers. Note that here and further on in this work the word "science" refers not only to the natural and biomedical sciences, but also to applied science (engineering), the social sciences, and the humanities. Outsiders may ask: Why do research,

Becoming Metric-Wise
DOI: http://dx.doi.org/10.1016/B978-0-08-102474-4.00002-9
11

why publish research results? Is it for the benefit of humanity, out of curiosity, to increase one's social standing, to have an attractive and respected occupation, or in pursuit of recognition? We do not try to answer these questions as the answers are highly personal. Some may even do research in the secret hope of becoming famous like Einstein. However, getting rich is rarely a motivation for doing academic research.

Whatever one's field of inquiry one always has to deal with the "problem choice" the issue of choosing "good" research problems among a large amount of possibly interesting ones. Which criteria should one use to solve this question? Probably there is no general answer and being able to choose an interesting and soluble problem is just one of the characteristics that differentiates great scientists from good scientists.

Science is commonly viewed as an activity that leads to the accumulation of knowledge. Its main aim is to improve the knowledge of humanity by using scientific methods. The scientific method seeks to explain the events of nature in a logical and in most cases reproducible way (lab experiments must be reproducible but, e.g., the Big Bang is not). The use of such methods distinguishes a scientific approach from, for instance, a religious one, as supernatural explanations are never accepted in science.

Science can be described as a systematic endeavor to build and organize knowledge. Yet, performing scientific investigations differs in an essential way from following a recipe. It requires intelligence, imagination, and creativity. Research implies an inquiry process, including a problem statement, consideration of the significance of the problem, statement of the study objectives, research design, a clear and precise methodology, information about the reliability and validity of the results, appropriate data analysis, as well as a clear and logical presentation (Hernon & Schwartz, 2002).

Scientific investigations can be subdivided into different types. One distinction is between formal and empirical sciences. Formal sciences are not based on observations, but on logic and a set of axioms from which other statements (theorems) are deduced. The most important formal sciences are logic and mathematics, but theoretical computer science and formal linguistics are formal sciences as well. Most sciences are empirical sciences, including natural sciences, social sciences, and the humanities. While natural sciences study the material world and natural phenomena, the social sciences and the humanities investigate human behavior and societies. Being a scientist in the natural sciences usually leads to formulating testable explanations and predictions about the universe, followed by performing the actual experiments or trying to observe the expected phenomena (see further on when we discuss the work of Popper). Yet, there are exceptions such as large parts of cosmology or elementary particle physics (e.g., string theory) (Woit, 2006) for which there do not (yet) exist experiments. One may say that such theories belong to a region that is part of the formal sciences, but are geared towards becoming empirical theories.

Disciplines that use science, like engineering and medicine, are referred to as applied sciences. Different engineering fields apply physics and chemistry (and possibly other fields), while medicine applies biology. Some applied fields use basic knowledge from different fields, including the formal sciences, such as genetic epidemiology which uses both biological and statistical methods, or synthetic biology which applies, among others, biotechnology and computer engineering.

Another way of describing science is through Stokes' classification which involves Pasteur's quadrant (Stokes, 1997). Pasteur's quadrant is a label given to a class of scientific research methods that seek fundamental understanding of scientific problems, and, at the same time, seek to be eventually beneficial to society. Louis Pasteur's research is thought to exemplify this type of method, which bridges the gap between "basic" and "applied" research. The term Pasteur's quadrant was introduced by Donald Stokes in his book with the same title (Stokes, 1997). As shown in Table 2.1, scientific research can be classified according to whether it advances human knowledge by seeking a fundamental understanding of nature (basic research), or whether it is primarily motivated by the need to solve immediate problems (applied research).

The result is three distinct classes of research. Pure basic research (exemplified by the work of the atomic physicist Niels Bohr), pure applied research (exemplified by the work of the inventor Thomas

Table 2.1 Pasteur's quadrant

| | | Considerations of use? | |
		No	Yes
Quest for fundamental understanding	**Yes**	Pure basic research Bohr	Use-inspired basic research Pasteur
	No		Pure applied research Edison

Edison), and use-inspired basic research (exemplified by the work of Louis Pasteur). Actions that involve neither a search for fundamental understanding nor any considerations of use, can hardly be called "research"—hence the empty fourth cell.

Project leaders with a mindset belonging to the Pasteur quadrant are said to be the natural leaders of successful interdisciplinary work (van Rijnsoever & Hessels, 2011).

As we will occasionally refer to the nature of the scientific method we include a short description of the ideas of Karl Popper and Thomas Kuhn. According to Popper (1959) a scientific theory in the natural sciences must be empirical, which means that it is *falsifiable*. More concretely, a scientific theory leads to predictions. Falsification occurs when such a prediction (i.e., a logical consequence of the theory) is disproved either through observation of natural phenomena, or through experimentation i.e., trying to simulate natural events under controlled conditions, as appropriate to the discipline. In the observational sciences, such as astronomy or geology, a predicted observation might take the place of a controlled experiment. Popper stressed that if one singular conclusion of a theory is falsified the whole theory is falsified and must be discarded, or at least modified. If the hypothesis survived repeated testing, it may become adopted into the framework of a scientific theory. Yet, he writes:

> A positive decision can only temporarily support the theory, for subsequent negative decisions may always overthrow it. So long as a theory withstands detailed and severe tests and it is not superseded by another theory in the course of scientific progress, we may say that is has "proved its mettle" or that it is "corroborated" by past experience.
>
> **Popper, 1959.**

In addition to testing hypotheses, scientists may also generate a model based on observed phenomena. This is an attempt to describe or depict a phenomenon in terms of a logical, physical or mathematical representation and to generate new hypotheses that can be tested. While performing experiments to test hypotheses, scientists may have a preference for one outcome over another (called a confirmation bias), and so it is important to ensure that science as a whole can eliminate this bias. After the results of an experiment are announced or published, it is normal practice for independent researchers to double-check how the research was performed, and to follow up by performing similar experiments i.e., to replicate the original experiments. Taken in its entirety, the scientific method allows for highly creative problem solving (Gattei, 2009).

Another important aspect of Popper's philosophy, is his theory of the three worlds or universes:

First, the world of physical objects or of physical states, secondly, the world of states of consciousness, or of mental states, or perhaps of behavioural dispositions to act, and thirdly, the world of objective contents of thought, especially of scientific or poetic thoughts and works of art.

Popper, 1972.

Clearly the information sciences reflect on objects belonging to World 3. More information on the life and ideas of Popper can be found in Stokes, 1998.

When it comes to the nature of the scientific method, we also want to mention Thomas Kuhn's work (Kuhn, 1962) and his use of the term *paradigm*. A paradigm can be described as "a typical example or pattern of something" (http://www.merriam-webster.com/). Yet, when scientists use the word paradigm they mostly have in mind the set of practices that define a scientific discipline at a particular period of time, as proposed by Kuhn. More precisely in *The Structure of Scientific Revolutions* (Kuhn, 1962) he defines scientific paradigms as: "*universally recognized scientific achievements that, for a time, provide model problems and solutions for a community of practitioners.*" Kuhn saw the sciences as going through alternating periods of normal science, when an existing model of reality dominates, and revolution, when the model of reality itself undergoes a sudden drastic change. Paradigms have two aspects. Firstly, within normal science, the term refers to the set of exemplary experiments that are likely to be copied or emulated. (https://en.wikipedia.org/wiki/Paradigm). The choice of exemplars is a specific way of viewing reality: this view and the status of "exemplar" are mutually reinforcing. Secondly, underpinning this set of exemplars are shared preconceptions, made prior to (and conditioning) the collection of scientific evidence. In contrast to Popper, results in conflict with the prevailing paradigm (anomalies), are for Kuhn considered to be due to errors on the part of the researcher. It is only when conflicting evidence increases, that a crisis point is reached where a new consensus view is arrived at, generating a paradigm shift.

Popper's ideas can be said to be prescriptive while Kuhn's are more descriptive. Both originated from reflections on the natural sciences. For this reason we mention another model, originating from the social sciences, proposed by Van der Veer Martens and Goodrum (2006). This model has three types of factors: empirical factors, socio-cognitive factors and theoretical factors. The first and the last type have two aspects each so that there are in total five factors. These are:

applicability — constructivity — accessibility — connectivity — generativity

Concretely, these factors are related to the following questions:
- *Applicability* (the first empirical factor)
    Does this theory apply to a wide variety of phenomena?
    How salient are the phenomena? Or stated otherwise: How important are these phenomena?
- *Constructivity* (the second empirical factor)
    Is this theory constructed so as to facilitate its testing or replication?
- *Accessibility* (the only socio-cognitive factor)
    How easy is this theory to understand and utilize?
    How important is it to the discipline as a whole?
    What types of publication channel have carried it?
    How else has this theory been communicated?
- *Connectivity* (the first theoretical factor)
    How does this theory fit into existing theoretical frameworks?
    How closely is it tied to previous theories?
- *Generativity* (the second theoretical factor)
    Can this theory generate a new theoretical framework or new uses of earlier theories?

Although presented as a model for theories in the social sciences, we think that its applicability goes beyond the social sciences and hence can be applied to many other fields of investigation.

We note that the term *science* is also used to denote reliable and teachable knowledge about a topic, as in *library and information science, computer science* or *public health science.*

Because of increasing pressures and increasing needs for funds, science is, unfortunately, becoming more a race of all against all, instead of a joint human endeavor for the benefit of humanity. Yet, or maybe because of this, scientists form collaborating teams (often international groups) leading to an increase of multiauthored publications. Notwithstanding this caveat, the basic purpose of scientific research is still to benefit the community at large by trying to know the unknown, explore the unexplored and create awareness about new research findings.

2.1.3 Citizen Science

A relative newcomer in the realm of science is the citizen scientist and the terms citizen science or crowd science. This term refers to amateurs or networks of volunteers who participate in a scientific project, usually by collecting or analyzing data. It is a form of public participation in the scientific enterprise. It is said that such participation contributes positively to science-society-policy interactions and is a form of democratization of science. Newer technologies, often computer related, have increased the options for citizen science.

2.1.4 Open Science

Following the footsteps of movements like open source, open science is a movement that aims to make research and research output more accessible. By making data, software and publications openly accessible, researchers can increase the transparency and replicability of their research, both for colleagues and a wider audience. As such, open science and citizen science are related in bringing science to the general public.

2.2 SCIENTIFIC DISCOVERIES

2.2.1 Types of Scientific Discoveries: Koshland's cha-cha-cha Theory

In 2007 the journal *Science* published a posthumous essay in which Koshland, a former editor of *Science*, formulated the cha–cha–cha theory of scientific discovery (Koshland, 2007). Koshland proposed to subdivide scientific discoveries into three categories: charge, challenge and chance, hence the name cha–cha–cha theory.

A discovery belongs to the "Charge" category if the problem is obvious (e.g., cure cancer), but the way to solve it is not clear at all. The discoverer is he or she who sees what everyone else has seen, but thinks what no one else has thought before. A typical example, provided by Koshland, is Newton's discovery and explanation of gravity.

A discovery falls into the "Challenge" category if it is the response to an accumulation of facts or concepts that were unexplained. Often these facts were brought to the fore by individuals referred to as "uncoverers" by Koshland. An example is Einstein's theory of special relativity, a description of the relation between space and time, later extended by the so-called general relativity theory to include gravity. Einstein was guided to his investigations by the observed inconsistency of Newtonian mechanics with Maxwell's equations of electromagnetism. Hence his theory was a response to some unexplained facts. Solutions to important challenges may lead to paradigm shifts in the sense of Kuhn (1962).

Finally, a discovery may fall into the "Chance" category. Such discoveries are, however, not pure luck but "favor the prepared mind." Chance discoveries may also be said to be the result of a serendipitous finding. A well-known example belonging to this category is Fleming's discovery of penicillin.

Koshland stressed the fact that often the discoverer needs not one but a number of original discoveries until the discovery is complete. He further wrote that the cha-cha-cha theory is not only applicable to big discoveries, but also to small everyday findings. This encouraged us (Rousseau, 2007b) to see whether we could apply the cha-cha-cha theory to some findings in informetrics. We consider the application of an existing theory, concept or tool to a new situation as a "charge" discovery, as it means taking a (small) step that no one else has taken before. Our field is an applied field, hence for this reason most of our field's "discoveries" will fall into the "Charge" group. If someone just collects data and tries to find out which statistical distribution fits best, we consider this a "Chance" discovery, in particular if the resulting distribution turns out to be interesting and is confirmed later.

We next present some examples of discoveries in the information sciences and their corresponding cha-cha-cha category. The topics mentioned in these examples are discussed further on in this book.

- Problem: information retrieval across scientific disciplines;
  Discovery: Science Citation Index (SCI) (see Section 5.2);
  Discoverer: Garfield (1963);
  Category of discovery: charge (as the idea of a citation index existed already).
- Problem: evaluation of journals without the use of (subjective) peer review;
  Discovery: the journal impact factor;
  Discoverers: Garfield and Sher (1963), but based on ideas by others; see (Archambault & Larivière, 2007);
  Category of discovery: charge.
- Problem: finding a simple way for the evaluation of an individual scientist;

Discovery: the h–index (see Section 7.3);
Discoverer: Hirsch (2005);
Category of discovery: charge.
- Problem: finding a regularity in the scattering of scientific knowledge about a topic;
Discovery: Bradford's law of scattering (see Subsection 9.3.2);
Discoverer: Bradford (1934);
Category of discovery: chance (because he was actually searching for a way to compile a complete bibliography).
- Problem: proving the mathematical equivalence of the bibliometric laws;
Discovery: a mathematical proof (see Subsection 9.3.2);
Discoverer: Egghe (1985, 1990, 2005), based on partial work and suggestions of others, such as Fairthorne (1969), Yablonsky (1980), and Bookstein (1976, 1979, 1984);
Category of discovery: challenge.
- Problem: explanation of the ubiquity of Lotka's law (power laws);
Discovery: success-breeds-success (see Subsection 9.3.2);
Discoverer: de Solla Price (1976);
Category of discovery: charge, as it was an application of Simon's work (Simon, 1957) and the Yule process (Yule, 1925).
- Problem: a representation of relations between scientific authors;
Discovery: author cocitation analysis (see Subsection 5.10.3);
Discoverers: White and Griffith (1981);
Category of discovery: charge.
- Problem: structure of inlinks on the Web
Discovery: it follows a power law (=Lotka's law);
Discoverer: Rousseau (1997b, small sample); Michalis, Petros, and Christos Faloutsos (1999, large scale);
Category of discovery: chance (Rousseau); charge (or chance?) (Faloutsos).

Besides through discoveries, applied fields such as scientometrics make progress through developments such as, e.g., the Social SCI which was developed based on the SCI.

2.2.2 Replication Research

We add a few words on the opposite of scientific discoveries, namely replication research. First we make a distinction between replication and validation studies. A replication study in the proper sense means that one performs the same investigation, using the same experiments, materials, and tools as the original or one re-analyzes the original data. A validation study has the same purpose as the original, but one may use different data and do similar experiments with the purpose of coming to the same conclusions.

Replication research is not popular at all as it is not original and hence rarely leads to recognition by peers. For an inquisitive mind, it might also be less interesting. Yet, double-checking is an aspect of the scientific method as described by Popper. Normal science as we know it produces new findings. The more sensational, say unexpected or difficult to find, the higher the response inside and even outside the author's field. Yet, many publications are never or rarely cited and hence their content is never thoroughly checked after publication. As long as uncited is the same as unused no harm is done, except in an indirect way as clearly a lot of money may have been wasted. Unfortunately, unreplicable research, especially in the life sciences, is not rare at all (Begley & Ellis, 2012). For instance, scientists at Bayer reported that among 67 projects only 14 matched up with the published findings (Mullard, 2011).

A large-scale replication effort in psychology sought to replicate 100 studies published in reputable psychology journals in 2008 (Open Science Collaboration, 2015). While 97 of the original 100 studies reported statistically significant results, only 36 of the replications yielded significant results. Overall, many replications had far weaker results than the original studies.

Russell (2013) rightly states that reproducibility separates science from anecdote. Consequently, he argues that funding agencies should tie grant funding to replication attempts. He realizes that such a proposal may encounter objections, but provides answers to them. We refer the reader to the original article for more details.

We should mention also that scientometrics struggles with irreproducibility. Glänzel (1996) already warned that scientometric studies should be reproducible, and stressed that this can only happen if all sources, procedures, and techniques are properly documented. He further mentions that validation studies should be designed for detecting systematic errors and estimating random ones. Methodological validation studies must ensure that scientometricians really measure what is intended to be measured.

2.2.3 Shneider's Typology of Scientists

Shneider (2009) distinguishes four stages in scientific research and correspondingly four types of scientists based on the type of work they prefer.

Although in reality most scientists are probably a mixture of the four prototypes, many may prefer one of the four stages and scientific attitudes that go with them.

Shneider's four stages in scientific research.

Stage 1: Introduction of new subject matter, based on a new scientific language and often including new observations and/or experimental results. First stage scientists are not only those who discover new facts, but as stated above, can be among the first to study these new facts.

First stage scientists often need to be somewhat imprecise or inaccurate because not all necessary facts are known or properly understood. At this point the theory often contains uncertainty. Philosophical, aesthetic and cultural views, analogies and literature are instrumental to the first stage scientists' mode of thinking. Such scientists are real scientific pioneers.

Example: The double helix structure of DNA as proposed by Watson and Crick.

Stage 2: Development of major techniques. This includes the re-application of methods previously developed in another discipline (plus rethinking and adjustments to new tasks). The main characteristics of second stage scientists are ingenuity and inventiveness, an ability to implement ideas and a high risk-tolerance. Shneider mentions here that the two most noticeable changes to Newtonian mechanics were introduced by Joseph Lagrange and by William Hamilton. He considers both of them to be great second stage scientists.

Stage 3: Most of the actual data and useful knowledge is generated in stage 3. This includes the re-description of subject matter, creation of new insights and questions. Difficulties and unexplained phenomena often give birth to new first stage work. Most useful personal qualities of third stage scientists are being detail-oriented and hard-working. An extensive knowledge of philosophy or art is not required.

Example: Engineers and scientists such as Heaviside redefining their knowledge in mathematical terms in the 19th and early 20th centuries.

Another example is the work of Samuel Eilenberg and Saunders Mac Lane who introduced category theory as a general framework for all of mathematics.

Stage 4: Communication of knowledge; organization of knowledge.

These scientists write reviews and organize what is known. Without the fourth stage scientists, the explosion of new data generated at the third stage would be chaotic. Their work leads to the development of (more) applications. Fourth stage scientists use a broad spectrum of cultural and philosophical views. Their work serves to inspire new generations of scientists as they are often writers of influential books. They are not only good in understanding the facts, but are also well-informed and remember great amounts of necessary information which they combine with useful up-to-date scientific results.

Example: Simon Singh (PhD in particle physics) who wrote a book and made a documentary about the proof of Fermat's Last Theorem by Andrew Wiles.

The existence of these types of scientists or this type of work, leads to problems in research evaluation. Indeed: fourth-stage work is easily recognized, although not always appreciated, while "typical" research evaluation is geared towards third-stage research. Yet, it is more difficult to evaluate second-stage research and this becomes extremely challenging for first-stage work. The lack of methods to evaluate first-stage work will probably remain as even peers do not always recognize its potential.

As a consequence of these reflections, Shneider writes that it may happen that the development of a discipline virtually stops and this in any stage (least likely in the first stage). Then too much effort goes into the wrong research direction. Unfortunately, such cases might become self-supporting due to the present organization of the academic system in which people go where money goes, and money goes where people go. This leads to the formation of the scientific analog of economic bubbles. As a result, the number of people working in a field does not accurately reflect its actual promise. This is an important lesson to be remembered, especially by young scientists.

This subsection, and in particular mentioning stage four scientists, leads us to a subsection on scientific communication.

2.2.4 Scientific Communication

The term *scientific communication* refers to all forms of contact between researchers as part of their professional behavior. Scientific communication can be seen as part of a complex social system consisting of formal and informal components. It includes reading and studying manuscripts (published or not), downloading, criticizing (through direct contact, by e-mail, or by letters to the editor), mentoring (younger colleagues) and collaborating. Moreover, communication by scientists includes two other important aspects of the scientific profession: Communication with the public at large and communication with reviewing authorities, which may have no scientific background, or have only a background in a field totally different from the researcher whose work or working habits are reviewed.

As for scientific communication in journals and similar outlets, we note that already in the 1960s Price (1963) observed an exponential increase in scientific publications. Since then, this tendency has hardly declined. Scientific journals communicate and document the results of research carried out in universities and various other research institutions, serving as an archival record of science. The first scientific journals, *Journal des Sçavans* followed by the *Philosophical Transactions*, began publication in 1665. Since that time, the total number of active periodicals has steadily increased.

2.3 A TWO-TIER PUBLICATION SYSTEM
2.3.1 Types of Publications

We provide a short glossary of types of publications

Publication: what has been published, not necessarily peer-reviewed. Publications may involve a formal publisher or not. We define a formal publisher as a corporate entity or scientific society that produces and distributes something, such as a book or magazine, in printed or electronic form.

Edited book: A collection of chapters written by different authors, gathered and harmonized by one or more editors; conference proceedings are one type of edited books (Ossenblok et al., 2015).

Monograph: A book on a single topic, written by one or more authors.

Textbook or course book: A monograph written mainly for teaching purposes.

Enlightenment literature (popular-science books): Books, often monographs, written for a general audience.

A *scientific article* is a text written for a scholarly audience. It can be published in a scientific journal or as a chapter in an edited book and may describe original research, contain theoretical considerations or an overview of a part of the scientific literature.

A *peer-reviewed article* is an article of which the scientific quality has been checked by other scientists, so-called peers, before publication.

Preprint: This notion originally referred to a text accepted for publication, but nowadays the term preprint is also used for a technical report, a research manuscript or a working paper.

E-print = electronic preprint

Gray literature: The Fourth International Conference on Gray Literature (GL '99 Conference Program, 1999) defined gray literature as follows: "*That which is produced on all levels of government, academics, business and industry in print and electronic formats, but which is not controlled by commercial publishers.*" Working papers, technical reports, theses, preprints, technical handbooks, and government documents are examples of gray literature.

Technical reports are a form of gray literature. A technical report can be described as a document written by a researcher or group of researchers detailing the results of a project, often with the purpose to submit it to the sponsor of that project (based on: http://libguides.gatech.edu/c.php?g=53991&p=348582).

Although technical reports are very heterogeneous they tend to possess the following characteristics:

- they are published before the corresponding journal literature, if they end up in the formal literature at all;
- their content contains more technical details and jargon than the corresponding journal literature;
- technical reports are usually not peer reviewed;
- some reports may be classified or offer only restricted access.

Working papers: This is a term mostly used by economists and management scientists to refer to a prepublication version of a manuscript. Their departments often have numbered Working Paper Series. Working papers are generally provided for discussion before they are formally submitted for publication in a journal or an edited book.

In the context of research evaluation, one sometimes makes a distinction between citable publications and others. This distinction refers to the issue of including this publication in the denominator of the calculation of a journal impact factor or not (see Chapter 6: Journal Citation Analysis). As this distinction is made by a commercial database and is, at times, rather ad hoc it is better to make another distinction. White (2001) uses the terminology reference-heavy articles (normal articles, reviews, notes) and reference-light ones (editorials, letters to the editor, meeting abstracts, book reviews). The term "Notes," referring to short communications of a scientific character, has been removed from Thomson Reuters' databases in 1997. Besides these, journals also publish errata, retractions, corrections, updates, comments and author replies. Occasionally they may re-publish articles of exceptional importance, often with new comments. Most of these can be considered to be reference-light. Universities and research institutes sometimes publish advertisements which have the look and feel of real research articles, mostly in highly cited journals like *Nature* and *Science*. Although this is duly mentioned in these journals, this still might lead to confusion among some readers (Chen, 2015). Such advertisements may even get cited.

We like to mention that, contrary to textbooks for undergraduate students, journals are not meant to be repositories of the one and true knowledge (and according to Popper's views, textbooks aren't either). They should better be considered to be discussions amongst experts, who might disagree. Journals are a place where experts can exchange methods, results, opinions, calculations, observations, and the like.

2.3.2 Steps in the Publication Process

Once a researcher or a group of collaborating researchers, decides that they have obtained results that can be considered to form a coherent unit, they may want to make these results public. Most of the time this implies that a text—a first draft—describing their findings is prepared. As the title is the first aspect colleagues may see, statements made in the title should be correctly formulated and supported by the evidence presented in the article. Note that not all scientific results lead to a text: Research findings may also be communicated under other forms such as a computer program, an instrument, or a construction.

This first draft is often presented in an internal seminar. This provides researchers with immediate feedback. Departmental colleagues may also help to overcome challenges faced by researchers whose native language is not English (assuming that publication is intended for an international, English reading, audience). The revised text, referred to as a preprint, is then often put in a preprint archive, a so-called e-print archive or repository (discussed below). Friends and some colleagues, members of an invisible college, see Section 2.3.6, may even receive a version before the text is finished as an e-print, so that they can give early feedback (for which they will be acknowledged in the final version).

The arXiv (https://arxiv.org) is the best known repository for electronic preprints of scientific work, mostly covering papers in mathematics, physics, astronomy, computer science, quantitative biology, statistics, and quantitative finance. Yet, also informetric articles are accepted. In many fields of mathematics and physics, almost all scientific papers are self-archived in the arXiv. The arXiv was originally developed by Paul

Ginsparg, starting in August 1991 as a repository for preprints (later called e-prints) in physics and later expanded to include other fields. It was originally hosted at the Los Alamos National Laboratory and called the LANL preprint archive. Its existence has had a huge influence on the open access movement (see further Section 3.2). Nowadays, Cornell University is the main responsible for the arXiv's maintenance. Many other, smaller subject-specific repositories exist. E-LIS (http://eprints. rclis.org/), for instance, is a smaller archive for e-prints, postprints and reprints in library and information science. Besides early visibility, e-prints may lead to useful feedback from peers, sometimes even leading to corrections of errors.

The e-print version of a scientific paper is often submitted to a conference and, if accepted for presentation (oral or as poster), leads to more feedback, from a larger group of peers. If the research is not substantive then a version based on conference attendees' feedback may be published in the conference proceedings, ending the publication process.

If research is more substantive then an enlarged and revised version of the conference paper is submitted to a scholarly journal and, if considered within the scope of the journal, the (journal) peer review process is started. Of course, an author may skip one or more of the above stages and submit a manuscript directly for publication in a journal. In a cover letter the corresponding author must declare that the same paper has not been submitted for publication at the same time and that all authors have approved the manuscript and agree with its submission. We note that the corresponding author is that author who takes primary responsibility for communication with the journal during the manuscript submission, peer review, and publication process. They typically ensure that all the journal's administrative requirements are properly completed and submitted. Usually the submission needs some revision (if it is accepted at all) and when this is performed according to the comments of the reviewers and the editor, the article enters the publishing process and will be published (electronically, in print, or in both versions). The final version may or may not be made public for free (see further under Open Access, Section 3.2).

Simplifying the process, one may use the term two-tier communication model. In this model, the first tier consists of communication on the Internet for free (e.g., through publicly available repositories) while the second tier consists of formal publications (Zhao, 2005). The distinction between these two tiers is nowadays less clear, since "gold" open access publications are also freely available on the web.

2.3.3 Structure of a Research Paper and Major Steps Between Submission and Publication

Structure of a Research Article

An article has a title and usually shows its author(s) and address(es) in the byline under the title. This is followed by an abstract and, often, a set of keywords. The main part of the article typically follows the IMRaD structure, where IMRaD stands for Introduction, Methods, Results and Discussion. In some fields, a short literature review is expected, placed between the Introduction and the Methods section, while usually there is also a Conclusion after the Discussion chapter. Then there is room for acknowledgements and finally a reference list, sometimes followed by an appendix and supplementary online material.

Not all articles strictly follow this scheme, but the above is a general guideline. Describing methods should not be confounded with describing the results, while discussions of these results are for the discussion section, which, again, is not the same as stating a conclusion. Note that the main conclusion should also be part of the abstract.

Nowadays this abstract is often required to be a structured abstract. A structured abstract has a fixed structure, consisting of: Purpose, design/-methods/approach, findings, research limitations, implications, value and/or originality. On the one hand, this structure makes searching for information easier, but on the other hand it is obvious that prescribing to follow this structure is counterproductive for articles based on pure logical thinking or which are the result of a serendipitous observation.

Major Steps Between Submission and Publication

When the editorial office receives a submission it is first checked for formal completeness. Does the submission have a title; are authors, their institutes and addresses unambiguously reported; is there a corresponding author; have the roles of the authors been revealed (if this is a requirement); are there references; has supplementary information been submitted? Are figures and formulae clear and readable?

The editor checks if the article falls within the scope of the journal, otherwise it is immediately rejected (a so-called desk rejection, also see the next chapter). Nowadays many editorial offices submit submissions to a plagiarism detection system, before it is sent to one or more reviewers.

When receiving the reviewers' reports, the Editor-in-Chief (in short: EIC) reports their findings to the author(s). For those papers that have to be revised and resubmitted the EIC reviews the changes and checks if all comments made by the reviewers have been correctly addressed or replies contain convincing arguments against the statements of the reviewers. More details about this step are given in the next chapter where the role of the Editor-in-Chief and of the reviewers is discussed in more detail.

High quality journals used to revise the manuscript for English language and grammar. It is a pity that nowadays this is rarely done anymore, even for submitted monographs. Copy editors implement the journal's manuscript style or check if this has been done by the authors in an appropriate way.

The paper is typeset and proof-read by professional, preferably native English speaking, proof-readers (again it is assumed here that the work is meant for an international audience) who identify any typographical errors and highlight possible inconsistencies. Once this is complete the typeset proofs are sent to the corresponding author(s).

Either all authors receive typeset proofs, so-called galley proofs, from the publisher or the corresponding author makes sure that they do. When all authors agree on the final page-proof the work is ready to be published.

The article receives a DOI (a Digital Object Identifier) a code that uniquely identifies the article. For instance, the publication by Hirsch (2005) has DOI "10.1073/pnas.0507655102" and can be retrieved from https://doi.org/10.1073/pnas.0507655102. Nowadays the article is usually published online in a "preview" version. This version is exactly the same as the final version except that volume, issue and page numbers are not yet assigned.

Finally the article is published in a particular issue of a journal's volume and assigned page numbers. If a journal is published only electronically there is no reason to go through this "preview" step and the article is published immediately; it often has no page numbers, just an article number. A similar observation holds for journals that follow an article-based publishing strategy. This means that when accepted an article is immediately published in its final form, including volume, issue and page numbers.

2.3.4 Qualifying for Authorship

Returning to the issue of publishing, we consider the important question: What is an author? We next describe the guidelines as published in http://www.icmje.org/recommendations/browse/roles-and-responsibilities/ defining-the-role-of-authors-and-contributors.html. An "author" is generally considered to be someone who has made substantive intellectual contributions to a published study. An author must take responsibility for at least one component of the work, should be able to identify who is responsible for each of the other components, and should be confident in their coauthors' ability and integrity. In the past, editors and readers were rarely provided with information about the exact contribution of persons listed as authors or mentioned in the acknowledgments section. Nowadays, however, most journals publish information about the contributions of each person named as having participated in a submitted study. Moreover, they may ask for the name of a contributor who will act as a guarantor, this means the person who takes responsibility for the integrity of the work as a whole.

Another problem is the question of the quantity and/or quality of contribution that qualifies for authorship. The International Committee of Medical Journal Editors or ICMJE (http://www.icmje.org/recommendations/browse/roles-and-responsibilities/defining-the-role-of-authors-and-contributors.html) recommends the following four points as criteria for authorship:

1. substantial contributions to conception and design, acquisition of data, or analysis and interpretation of data.
2. drafting the article or revising it critically for important intellectual content.
3. final approval of the version to be published.
4. Agreement to be accountable for all aspects of the work in ensuring that questions related to the accuracy or integrity of any part of the work are appropriately investigated and resolved.

Authors should meet each of these four conditions. Acquisition of funding, pure data collection (but see below for a remark on biological field work), or general supervision of the research group alone does not constitute authorship.

All persons designated as authors should qualify for authorship, and all those who qualify should be listed. Authorship of big science investigations such as multicenter trials (in medicine); particle physics studies (as e.g., performed in CERN) or use of space ships or telescopes is often attributed to a group, using a group name such as e.g., the ATLAS collaboration (Aad et al., 2015). Also in cases of mega- (Kretschmer & Rousseau, 2001; Sen, 1997) or hyper-authorship (Cronin, 2001) all members of the group who are named as authors should, in principle, meet the above criteria for authorship. We think, however, that such groups are in fact a special case and one should leave decisions on authorship to the leaders of such groups instead. Indeed, in such cases membership does not lead to visibility. Some journals demand specific author contribution statements. In such cases information is required about who designed, directed, coordinated, provided conceptual guidance, provided technical guidance, planned, performed experiments, analyzed data, generated and characterized constructs, contributed, provided essential reagents, stem cells, tissues or other body parts (e.g., mice brains), commented on the design of experiments, and wrote documentation.

Davenport and Cronin (2001) proposed a three layer division of authors, depending on their contribution. They made a distinction between core, middle layer and outer layer tasks. This idea was taken up by Danell (2014) in an analysis of author contributions published in *Nature Neuroscience* (2012−2013). Table 2.2 shows this three-tier contribution taxonomy. Of course, the examples shown in Table 2.2 depend on the field. These tasks would mean little to a colleague in the formal sciences, for whom providing a clear and logical chain of thoughts, is a core task.

Obviously the division between core- and middle-layer tasks in a concrete investigation is open for discussion. Core tasks are mainly leadership tasks performed by principal investigators. This implies that often the most important intellectual contribution may come from middle layer authors. Sometimes even collecting data, as in biological field work, may need the most ingenuity. Although outer layer tasks generally do not qualify for authorship according to the ICMJE criteria, Danell (2014)

Table 2.2 A three-tier publication contribution taxonomy

Type of contribution	Examples of tasks
Core task	• Conception and design • Writing the manuscript
Middle layer tasks	• Conducting experiments • Data analysis • Interpretation of data • Project management
Outer layer tasks	• Obtaining funding • Providing samples/data • Providing technical assistance • Collecting data

found 13.8% of outer-layer contributors as coauthors in the papers he investigated.

Referring to the issue of mega-authorship we note that Piternick (1992) already discussed multiple authorship and pointed out an article in high energy physics with 246 authors. In 1993 an article with 972 authors (The GUSTO investigators, 1993) received the Ig Nobel prize for Literature because it had an average of one author per two words. This tendency for ever larger collaborating groups has not stopped as testified by an article published in 2015 describing the size of the Higgs boson (Aad et al., 2015). This article has 5099 authors (our count). Of the 33 pages, 24 contain the author list.

Increasing numbers of coauthors consequently led to an increasing number of related problems such as:

Responsibility of authors for the contents of the manuscript (an ethical problem).

Possible ghost writing (another ethical problem).

Honorary authorship (another ethical problem).

Restrictions on the number of authors listed by a journal (an editorial decision with possible consequences for some authors who become "invisible").

Appropriateness of using a group name (again making authors invisible).

How to allocate credit for publishing and for receiving citations (a problem related to evaluation, discussed further on in this book).

Contributors Listed in the Acknowledgments

All contributors who do not meet the criteria for authorship should be listed in an acknowledgments section. Examples of such persons are those who provided purely technical help, writing assistance, or a department chairperson who provided only general support. Of course funding and material support should also be acknowledged. If persons are acknowledged they must first give permission that their name is used in such an acknowledgement.

2.3.5 Collaboration

It is well-known that the fraction of articles with more than one author is increasing over the years. Smith (1958) and Price (1963) already observed this phenomenon. The rise in multiple authorship has been confirmed by Weller (2001, p. 121), Lipetz (1999), Schubert (2002) for authors in *Scientometrics* and Behrens and Luksch (2011) in mathematics.

Gordon (1980) proved that the probability of acceptance (of a submission to a journal) increases with the number of authors. Oromaner (1975) found an increasing relation between the number of authors and the number of received citations. Waltman, Tijssen, and van Eck (2011) studied coauthorship in terms of the average geographic distance of their institutes and found that this average has increased considerably over the past 30 years.

Given the rise of collaborative research, voices are raised to abolish the notion of authorship, and to replace it by the notion of contributor, implying a continuum of activities, instead of the notion of author, which implies a yes–no situation, see Rennie and Yank (1998). When supporting this model, colleagues often refer to end credits such as those used in the film industry. These credits list all the people involved in the production of a film, starting with the leading actors, the film director, and followed by the whole crew consisting of editors, writers, stand-ins, photographers, costume designers, set decorators, digital effects computer teams, prop masters, gaffers, and so on.

2.3.6 Invisible Colleges

Groups of colleagues that follow each other's work closely may be said to form a so-called invisible college. Modern use of this term was introduced by Price (1963, 1986). Yet, its original use dates from the 17th century when the Royal Society of London was founded. Members often did not belong to a formal institution and hence referred to themselves as an invisible college, because of their geographic proximity, regular meetings and shared interests (Zuccala, 2006). Price observed that although great artists and researchers are both intensely creative humans, the artist's creation is personal, while the scientist needs recognition by peers. For this reason scientists devised an informal mechanism to stay in (almost) daily contact with a group of peers. According to Price such an invisible college is composed at most of one hundred colleagues. Yet, Price just offered a rather vague description and not a precise definition. Studying the use of the term over the years led Zuccala (2006) to the following definition:

An invisible college is a set of interacting scholars or scientists who share similar research interests concerning a subject specialty, who often produce publications relevant to this subject and who communicate both formally and informally with one another to work towards important goals in the subject.

Note that nowadays geographic proximity plays no role (or maybe just a minor role) in the definition of an invisible college.

2.4 A THREE-TIER EVALUATION SYSTEM

Evaluation as such is discussed in later chapters, but here we already make a few observations. Besides the two-tier communication system—online preprint versions and formal publications, see 2.3.2—one may distinguish a three-tier evaluation system applied within the formal publication tier. This three-tier evaluation system consists of counting publications, counting usage e.g., downloads, and counting received citations. More about scientific evaluations can be found in Chapter 8, Research Evaluation.

2.4.1 Peer Reviewed Publications

Different aspects of publishing have been discussed in the previous sections, yet before documents are published and counted they must usually get past the peer-review-hurdle. Indeed, the oldest evaluation level among the three mentioned in this chapter is the peer review process of submitted journal articles. Nowadays, most journals are peer-reviewed, but some parts may not. Journals such as *Nature* have large sections that do not present original research, but are actually scientific journalism. These sections are written by the journal's editorial office or by paid freelance writers. According to Brown (2004) peer review—in general, not just for journals—can be defined as follows: "Scientific peer review is the evaluation of scientific research findings or proposals for competence, significance and originality, by qualified experts (peers) who research and submit work for publication in the same field." Peer review also takes place when evaluating grant applications, during promotion or tenure decisions of individual scientists; or when starting, evaluating or closing schools or departments. In the context of scientific publication activities peer review is further discussed in Chapter 3, Publishing in Scientific Journals.

2.4.2 Usage

The term *downloads* is clearly related to the age of electronic publications and as such its use is a relatively young development. Besides article downloads an electronic journal may also monitor article views and keep track of links to each article (Rousseau, 2002b). Of course, also the number of downloads in a repository of e-prints or postprints may be collected. In the era before electronic journals scientists browsed the contents of newly arrived journals, and if interested in a particular article made a photocopy. Maybe they would actually read the article and use it in their own research. In this series of events downloading of full-text articles can be compared to making a photocopy in the preelectronic days.

Collecting download numbers per journal, let alone per article is not obvious if the interested party is not the owner of the repository or the publisher of the journal. COUNTER, launched in 2002, an agreed international set of standards and protocols governing the recording and exchange of online usage data (http://www.projectcounter.org) is a partial solution for this. For more information about COUNTER we refer the reader to Conyers (2006), Davis and Price (2006), and Shepherd (2006). COUNTER is able to provide more and more reliable statistics for librarians and vendors, yet was originally designed to measure the use (views) of databases and certainly not of individual articles.

Based on their data COUNTER proposed a journal usage factor (JUF) for journals, which is nothing but the median number of downloads for articles in that journal during a given period of time. Note that COUNTER initially defined the JUF as an average in analogy of the journal impact factor which is an average number of citations per article (for details we refer to Chapter 6: Journal Citation Analysis). As this is a COUNTER metrics, downloads only refer to COUNTER-compliant online usage.

A report (CIBER Research Ltd., 2011) found no evidence that usage (as measured by an average) and citation impact metrics are statistically associated. The authors note that this is hardly surprising since author and reader populations are not necessarily the same. This is in particular the case for journals which have practitioners or students as their main readership. A similar remark about the relationship between downloads and citations was made by Davis (2011). As a result, the usage factor or other usage statistics add new evidence to our understanding of the structure and dynamics of the use of the scientific literature. It also opens up the possibility of developing new ways of looking at scholarly communication, with different journals occupying very different niches within a complex ecosystem. Some colleagues, however, claim that article downloads retrieved shortly after publication can predict future citations, but their strength of prediction is relatively low (Kurtz et al., 2005a,b; Schlögl & Gorraiz, 2010).

Knowing the number of downloads of articles published in a publisher's journals is of interest for the publisher as a means to evaluate the impact (mostly immediate impact) of its journals. Also downloads of e-prints in repositories are of interest for authors and publishers alike.

Indeed, the higher the visibility of articles, the higher the visibility of the journals in which the articles will be published. This is the main reason why (most) publishers allow this kind of prepublication. More about this and the relation with open access (see also next chapter) can be found e.g., in: Antelman (2004), Kurtz et al. (2005a,b), Brody, Harnad, and Carr (2006), Eysenbach (2006), Zhang (2006), Craig, Plume, McVeigh, Pringle, and Amin (2007), Kim (2011), Xia, Myers, and Wilhoite (2011), and Solomon and Björk (2012a,b). On the following site the reader may find what is allowed regarding prepublication and what is not: http://www.sherpa.ac.uk/romeo/ (organized per publisher).

It should be made clear that downloads (as an indication of usage) do not lead to visibility measurements comparable with citation results. For more on this we refer the reader to Bollen, Van de Sompel, Smith, and Luce (2005). An important point is that downloads are not influenced by delays in publication (of the citing articles). The first measures general interest in a particular new piece of knowledge; the second measures the incorporation of this knowledge into a new document. Most article downloads take place within the first months after publication (CIBER, 2011; Wan et al., 2010). Indeed, aging curves (see Chapter 9: The Informetric Laws) based on citations and on downloads have a different distribution over time. We finally recall that most altmetric indicators include a usage aspect.

2.4.3 Citation Analysis

With the advent of the SCI in 1963 (Garfield, 1963) a new evaluation level, based on received citations, came into existence. Of course, since the 19th Century it has become customary to refer to older work on which a publication was based. It was Eugene Garfield who realized the importance of these references, first as a tool for information retrieval via so-called: "citation pearl growing" or "citation cycling" and as a help for writing the history of a field or topic. However, Garfield and others soon realized that such a citation index could also be used as a tool for research evaluation. In its simplest form the idea was that the more citations received, the better the research. Such an approach is, of course, extremely naïve. Details about the proper use of a citation index for evaluation purposes are given in Chapter 8, Research Evaluation.

Citation indexes such as Scopus, the SCI, the Social Science Citation Index (SSCI), the Arts & Humanities Citation Index (A&HCI) and the Book Citation Index (BCI) and their availability on the Internet are discussed in Chapter 5, Publication and Citation Analysis.

CHAPTER 3

Publishing in Scientific Journals

In this chapter, we discuss three main topics: Editorship and peer review; open access (OA); and scientific misconduct such as fraud, plagiarism, the issue of retractions and the integrity of the publication record. This chapter deals with publishing in scientific journals; other forms of publishing were discussed in Chapter 2, Scientific Research and Communication Subsection 2.3.1.

3.1 EDITORSHIP AND PEER REVIEW

3.1.1 Peer Review

The term *peer* is used here in the sense of a scientific colleague. Peer review is the act, performed by a peer, of reading a scientific work or proposal and writing critical comments or a review on it. In this context, peers are also referred to as reviewers or referees. According to Csiszar (2016), peer review as we know it today originated in 1831 from a proposal of Cambridge professor William Whewell to the London Royal Society to publish reports on all submissions sent for publication in the *Philosophical Transactions*. Yet, after 2 years these reports became private and anonymous. The idea that reviewing had to be done to ensure the integrity of science came much later. According to Csiszar (2016) this happened near the turn of the 20th century. In this way, the editor and referees became voluntary gatekeepers with respect to the integrity of science. However, until late in the 20th century, submitted manuscripts were often only reviewed by the main editor and members of an editorial board. The journal *Nature*, for instance, only began external refereeing in 1973.

In this section, we focus on peer review of articles submitted for publication in scientific journals, conference proceedings, or book chapters. Of course, complete books are (or can be) peer reviewed as well (Verleysen & Engels, 2013) and peer reviews play a decisive role in research evaluations e.g., for hiring or tenure decisions, and in

Becoming Metric-Wise
DOI: http://dx.doi.org/10.1016/B978-0-08-102474-4.00003-0

distributing grant money based on proposals for scientific research. Most aspects of peer review discussed here also apply to these other situations, but this will not be the focus of this chapter. Peer review in research evaluations will be discussed in Chapter 8, Research Evaluation. In research evaluation by peer review, experts may be supported by citation-based evidence, but that is not possible for journal submissions. Peer review is the only possible way to evaluate a submission.

Peer review for journal submissions has two aspects: A summative one, leading to acceptance or rejection, and a formative one, leading to improvements of the original submission. Note though, that the role of reviewers is an advisory one and the editor-in-chief (EIC) is not obliged to follow their advice.

As peer review is performed by humans it is subjective and opinions about the content of a submission may differ. Indeed, reviewers sometimes show confirmation bias: this is the tendency to judge in favor of what is already known and against submissions that contradict a reviewer's theoretical perspective (Nickerson, 1998). Especially highly innovative research may encounter severe criticism. It is no surprise that many Nobel Prize winners can tell stories about the rejection of their prize-winning work (Campanario, 2009; Campanario & Acedo, 2007). Yet, assessment of research of potentially ground-breaking developments is, by its very nature, not straightforward. Authors claiming such breakthroughs should provide sufficient evidence, while editors should facilitate scientific debate on such claims.

Although the peer review system has a lot of problems, finding solutions is very difficult, see e.g., Hochberg et al. (2009) and a comment by de Mesnard (2010).

Complaints about peer review occur frequently e.g., see Santini (2005) for a very entertaining article in which fake reviews on famous computer science articles (Dijkstra, Codd, Turing, Shannon, Hoare, Rivest-Shamir-Adelman) and a fake performance review of Einstein (www.norvig.com/performance-review.html) are presented. In a systematic review on peer review in biomedical journals, Jefferson et al. (2002) concluded that editorial peer review, although widely used, is largely untested and its effects are uncertain. Yet, already 3 years earlier van Rooyen et al. (1999) had developed the Review Quality Instrument (RQI) to evaluate review reports. Since then, more studies of peer review, editorial and otherwise, and its effects have been published e.g., see Bornmann and Daniel (2005, 2009b), Langfeldt (2006), Sandström and Hällsten (2008), and Mulligan et al. (2013).

There are many different forms of peer review for journal submissions. Aspects to consider are postpublication or prepublication review? Who acts as peers? How many colleagues review one article? Possible answers to some of these questions are discussed further on.

3.1.2 The Editor-In-Chief and the Editorial Board

Each scientific journal has an Editor-in-Chief (EIC), sometimes also referred to as the main editor. Their main duties are:

- Handling peer review; possibly by sending submissions to section editors or sending directly to reviewers or referees.
- Rejecting submissions that are plagiarized, ghost-written, published elsewhere, or of little interest to readers i.e., do not fall within the scope of the journal.
- Contributing editorial pieces.
- Motivating and developing the editorial board and editorial staff.
- Ensuring final drafts are complete.
- Handling reader complaints and, if necessary, taking responsibility for issues after publication.

  Depending on the contract with the publisher, the EIC's duties may also include the following points:

- Cross-checking citations in text and examining references (although this is mainly the authors' responsibility).
- Cross-checking facts, spelling, grammar, writing style, page design, tables, figures and photos.
- Editing content and lay-out.

  It may happen that the last aspect is handled by the publisher's office.

Nowadays many of these points, including the act of submission are facilitated by an electronic editorial submission system. Such a system offers a whole range of facilities to authors, reviewers, and editors, smoothing the flow of editorial and submission handling. It includes templates for different types of letters, automatic e-mail forwarding, and so on.

In the large majority of cases, a manuscript is submitted to a journal where an editor takes charge of it. On the one hand, he or she may reject it immediately, typically because he or she judges the article to be out of scope, or because of linguistic reasons, such as incomprehensibility. On the other hand, the EIC may also accept some manuscripts without external reviewing, for instance, in the case of a well-known colleague being invited to write a contribution. Otherwise, the editor assigns one, two, three, sometimes even more reviewers. The EIC often has to search for the needle (the really exceptional contribution) in the haystack of submissions. Indeed, if a journal receives a flood of submissions it is impossible to send all of them out for review, so the EIC does not only make a reject-accept decision after peer review, but often before.

Nowadays many journals, including but not exclusively multidisciplinary journals, have several editors besides the EIC who, largely autonomously, take care of (sub)domains. For this (sub)domain they have the same authority and duties as an EIC.

It is of utmost importance for scientists' careers and the well-being of the journal that reviewers are chosen with care. This is one of the responsibilities of the EIC. Although the EIC is the final judge, his or her decision is based on the advice of the reviewers, sometimes chosen among the members of the editorial board.

This leads us to an aside on a journal's editorial board. Members of the board are usually important and frequent reviewers. It sometimes happens that they are responsible for their specialty and choose reviewers for submissions accordingly. One of their main tasks is to attract interesting manuscripts within the scope of the journal. Moreover, board members can influence their journals' receptiveness towards new topics and methods. In this way, they make sure their journal's content follows the field's research front. Occasionally they may also be responsible for a "special issue" on a timely topic. They also play a role in deciding the scope and future direction of the journal and may help in detecting fraud and plagiarism. Having members of different nationalities is often considered as an indication of the internationality of the journal itself. It must be admitted, though, that often some board members are honorary members, who have mainly been invited to increase the prestige of the journal. Yet, in a study on editorial board members of LIS journals, Walters (2016) found that journal citation impact is strongly correlated with board members' research productivity.

3.1.3 The Editorial Process

Fig. 3.1, based on (Weller, 2001), provides a complete scheme of the editorial process.

A distinction should be made between minor and major revisions. Resubmissions of manuscripts in the minor revision category are often handled by the EIC, who checks the revision and accepts or asks for a

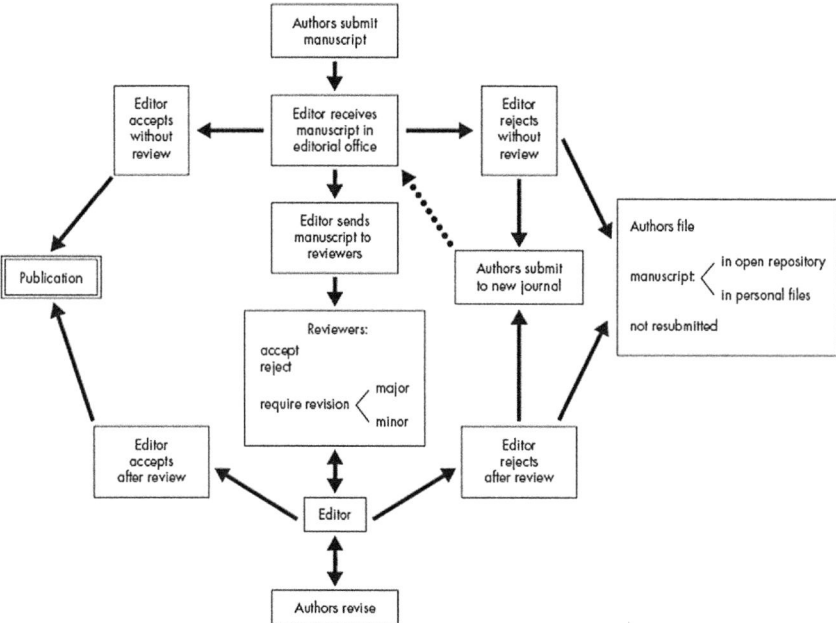

Figure 3.1 Path of a manuscript through the editorial peer review process; based on Fig. 1.1 in Weller (2001).

few new alterations. In most cases, major revisions are sent out for another round of review often to the same reviewers, but sometimes also to new ones. When an article is rejected, authors often resubmit (with or without revisions) to another journal. If after a number of attempts they remain unsuccessful, they may file their manuscript either in an open repository, so that their findings, although not formally published, are available to the field, or in their personal files, where the manuscript may either stay forever or may be a source of inspiration for later work.

It is unfortunate that the increase in submissions has made finding a colleague who is willing to review, a difficult task. Powell (2016) mentioned that in 2015 alone, the journal Public Library of Science (*PLoS*) *One* used 76,000 reviewers. Invited colleagues are often busy scientists and hence they decline to review or worse, they accept and that is the last one hears of them. Although it is quite acceptable to decline an invitation to review (scientists are not reviewers by profession), they should, however, realize that being an author includes being a reviewer and that the system is only in equilibrium if for each article one writes one should review at least two (and probably more) submissions (Wilson & Lancaster, 2006).

One of the reasons that scientists might decline to review a manuscript is that there is no reward system for reviewing. The only action taken by journals to thank referees is the (yearly) publication of a list of reviewers for the journal. For local (intra-university or intra-departmental) purposes the number of reviews and the type of journals could suffice to construct a review indicator. This number could then be incorporated in a local evaluation system. Wilson and Lancaster (2006) and Rousseau (2006e) even suggest an international referee factor. Yet, as long as the quality of the review is not taken into account, we do not see how this could be realized. Maybe the RQI proposed by van Rooyen et al. (1999) offers a solution. We feel that, however, reviewing does have some benefits, especially for younger scientists: reviewers get exposed to manuscripts and may acquire better writing skills, they come into contact with colleagues and journal editors, and if the review is not anonymous, reviewing may foster later collaborations.

3.1.4 Deontology of Authors, Editors, and Reviewers (De George & Woodward, 1994)

In this subsection, we present some deontological rules to which authors, reviewers, and editors must adhere. If these rules are violated, trust in the publication system may disintegrate.

Authors should:

- Submit original work.
- Use correct references (Liang et al., 2014).
- Not submit the same work to two or more journals at the same time.
- Not include information received confidentially e.g., as a referee, unless, of course, explicit approval has been obtained.
- Have contributed in a substantial way, see also Subsection 2.3.4.
- If an error has been found (by the author or by a colleague) contact the EIC and take action. This can be withdrawal of submission, retraction of a published article, submission of a correction or a *Letter to the Editor.*
- Most importantly, the integrity of science is the first responsibility of authors. Feynman (1974), for instance, points out that authors may not fool themselves, by taking a biased view on their results. They must include in their manuscript all the information that helps others to judge the value of their contributions.

Referees should:
- Decline the invitation to review if not sufficiently knowledgeable in the domain of the submission, if they are sure that they cannot finish the job within a reasonable time (say 1 month), or if there is a conflict of interest.
- Realize that each received document is confidential: its contents may not be used or diffused further.
- Try to review objectively and in a constructive way. No personal attacks or scorn should be present in a referee report: substantiated arguments should be used if one does not agree with contents.
- Only suggest to add references if these added references are really substantial for the reviewed manuscript. Under no circumstances can a long list of "referee's own" articles be suggested for addition.
- Try to come to a conclusion (not a decision, which is the task of the editor) whether, in their opinion, the paper should be published as is, revised before publication or rejected.
- Inform the editor at once if fraud or plagiarism is detected. Such accusations should, however, not be made public without further investigation.

Editors:
- One can be EIC of at most one journal; being a member of the editorial board of another journal is not a problem.
- An EIC must make decisions about submissions, not about authors.
- The content of each submission is confidential and hence the EIC can discuss submissions only with authors and reviewers, and possibly with the editorial board (for whom this too is confidential information).
- The EIC cannot use the contents of submissions for his or her own work, unless the author has given written consent.
- The EIC does not suggest adding references to the journal (unless these references are essential for the submitted manuscript). If he or she does the resulting citations are known as coercive citations (Martin, 2013);
- If the EIC submits their own work for publication in the journal, or submits work with which they have a special connection, then they must relegate all editorial power to a guest-editor, normally a member of the editorial board. An example how one's own articles should not be handled is given in Schiermeier (2008).
- If serious errors are found then the article must be rejected, publication stopped (if already accepted and the publication process can still be stopped), or the editor must make sure a correction is published.

In case of fraud, plagiarism or other serious misconduct a retraction note must be published stating the reason(s) for the retraction. These issues are further discussed in Section 3.3 of this chapter.

- Ethical problems must be clarified and may lead to rejection.
- Communication between reviewers and the editor is not disclosed to authors, and certainly not to the (scientific) public at large.

3.1.5 Review Systems

There exist several review systems with respect to the relation between authors and referees. We start with the two most common ones.

Single blind review, which is sometimes referred to as blind review or anonymous review. In this system, referees know the names of the authors, but not vice versa. This system protects the referee in case of a negative review and helps to maintain a pleasant atmosphere within the field. There are, of course, also disadvantages: for instance, the potential chance of intellectual theft increases. It, moreover, opens the door for conduct violating other deontological rules, such as personal attacks on authors. Yet, as referee reports are first read by the editor, such reports should not be forwarded and the reviewer should be made aware by the editor that such behavior is not tolerated. In library and information science this system is the one practiced the most. Weller (2001) writes that, over all fields, this system is applied in 60% of the cases.

Double blind review. In this system, authors do not know the reviewers and reviewers do not know the authors. In theory this procedure leads to an objective evaluation. In particular, one may expect that accepting based on the writer being a well-known figure will not occur. Yet, also here there are some problems. If one removes the authors' name, it is still easy to find out the writer(s) of the submission. For this reason, one usually requires that the authors remove all aspects that would make it possible to identify them. This means that all self-references must be deleted, and this is also the case for all acknowledgments of funding and sentences like, "In a previous article we ..." This places an extra burden on authors. Reading such a skeletal submission is not a pleasant task. Even then, if one of the authors is a well-known scientist in the field, an established reviewer can easily guess this colleague's identity by the type of research and language used. Another problem is that by blinding the authors and their laboratories, a reviewer cannot take the track record into account. Research groups with a reputation of mediocre research may rightly deserve extra scrutiny, but this is made impossible in this review system. According to Weller (2001) this system is applied in about one third of cases.

Open review. In this system, authors know reviewers and vice versa. A big advantage of this approach is that vindictive scientists cannot hide behind the cloak of anonymity. Yet, in an open review system, it would probably become even harder (than it already is) to find competent reviewers. Moreover, the idea of open peer review includes making review reports open—publishing them—to everyone. In this way the peer review process becomes fairer and completely transparent (Callaway, 2016).

As an aside, we mention that open peer review always happens for reviews of published books, but note that submitted book manuscripts are also reviewed by blind or double blind review. Models exist in which anything is (electronically) "published" and anyone may comment on it. In such models, authors and reviewers are not only known to each other, but to anyone who cares to read the submission. In these models, it is usually the case that, after a certain period, a final version is published which takes comments into account. Yet, this postpublication review model is, for the most part, still in the experimental phase. A mixed form is F1000prime (http://f1000.com/prime), which provides postpublication peer review for articles that are already published in peer-reviewed journals.

Signed review. It may also happen that authors are unknown to the referee(s) but not vice versa. One advantage of this system is that authors can easily contact reviewers and discuss problems. Yet, in any of the systems, reviewers may ask to be known to the authors, or sign their review. In any system where one of the parties is known to the other, the review becomes an opportunity to make an acquaintance, to exchange information, to invite for a talk, or for collaboration in a project.

In some journals, or for some conference proceedings, reviewers may read comments of other reviewers. This sometimes happens before a decision has been made, so that reviewers can change their opinion or sometimes after a decision has been made. In both cases, reviewers can learn from each other. Reviews can still be anonymous, so that one knows the content of a review, but not who wrote it, or reviewers may be known to each other. If reviewers are known to each other and can read their comments before a decision is made, this is a strong incentive not to take a review too lightly. Journal editors may send exceptionally well-written reviews to other reviewers (of the same submission) as part of a teaching activity as for scientists too, reviewing is a learning process.

Following Varn (2014), we note that a reviewer is not expected to replicate experiments, redo statistical analysis or go through all calculations in detail. The primary objective is to say whether the results are important enough to publish, more specifically, to be published in the journal to which it is submitted. The purpose of peer review is not to establish that the results in the submitted manuscript are surely correct. Instead, it does seek to determine whether the paper has obvious mistakes or omissions, is original, and is relevant to the journal. Peer review further checks whether the conclusions made by the authors are supported by the evidence presented, and whether the work is presented in a way experts in the field would understand. As for the issue of fraud, peer review is not the place to catch it, unless it was rather sloppily done. Indeed, who can say that an observation wasn't made?

3.1.6 Editorial Decision Schemes

We already mentioned that reviewers offer advice to the EIC who, in the end, has to accept or reject the manuscript. Now we take a closer look at how an EIC may proceed once he or she has received the suggestions of the reviewers. If one of the reviewers found a serious error, then the submission is rejected. Assume now that this is not the case and that the submission has been sent to two reviewers.

If the advice is YY (Y stands for yes: accept; N stand for no: reject) then the decision is accepted, and if it is NN the decision is rejected.

Decision schemes differ in the case of NY. In the clear-cut system used e.g., in the journal "Angewandte Chemie" (see Bornmann & Daniel, 2009b), this leads to a rejection. Otherwise, the EIC plays the role of a third reviewer and, hence, follows his or her own advice, or sends it to a third reviewer, who, possibly without knowing it, makes the decision, as the EIC follows a majority vote.

One may wonder if three reviewers are better than two. Schultz (2010) investigated 500 manuscripts submitted to *Monthly Weather Review.* In this journal, Schultz, being the EIC, chooses an editor, who then invites reviewers. This editor is free to choose of the number of reviewers. Schultz found that manuscripts were usually reviewed by two (61.2% of the time) or three reviewers (31.0% of the time). Occasionally a manuscript got zero, one, four, or five reviewers. Note that some editors strongly favor two reviewers and try to make a decision based on these two reports, while others select three reviewers from the start. Considering three cases, namely rejection when all reviewers recommend rejection, rejection when any reviewer recommends rejection, and rejection when the majority recommends rejection, he found that for this journal a manuscript was mostly rejected once one reviewer recommended rejection.

As is clear from Schultz' investigation one may also use three reviewers from the start. Then one must wait for the results and decide by majority rule. If one uses the clear-cut approach, then one just waits for one N or three Y. Yet, instead of waiting for three reports, one may try to decide on the basis of the two reports arriving first. Only when there is a difference of opinion, does one wait for the third review and decide by majority.

Realizing that selection processes are never faultless, Bornmann and Daniel (2009a) investigated the predictive validity of the manuscript selection process at *Angewandte Chemie International Edition* (AC-IE) and conducted a citation analysis for 1817 manuscripts that were accepted by the journal, or rejected but published elsewhere. They calculated the extent of type I error (defined here as accepted manuscripts that did not perform as well as or worse than the average rejected manuscript, hence their citation performance was overestimated) and type II errors (defined here as rejected manuscripts that performed equal to or above the average accepted manuscript for these submissions their citation performance was underestimated) of the selection decisions. They found for both types of errors 15% of wrong decisions. It should be observed that AC-IE is a very selective journal which publishes manuscripts only if two external referees consider the results of the study reported in the manuscript as significant and recommend publication in AC-IE.

Making type II errors (rejecting "good" manuscripts) is a missed opportunity for a journal. Moreover, setting the bar for acceptance too high inevitably leads to the rejection of good, and even excellent or breakthrough manuscripts.

Theoretically one may wonder if, assuming there were three referees, and one makes a decision when two reviews are received, what would be the difference when the third advice actually comes in second (and hence the one that was second previously is not taken into account). Concretely, Egghe (2010a), inspired by (Bornmann & Daniel, 2009b) studied the following two situations. The first one is the so-called 50-50 rule in which the editor randomly makes a Y decision in 50% of the cases (and hence a N decision in the other 50%) when he or she receives YN advice. The second one is the clear-cut case. It is further assumed that N and Y have an equal chance of occurring. It is shown that a decision is reversed in 37.5% of the cases in the 50-50 situation, and in 25% of the cases when the clear-cut rule is applied. Such changes are not to be ignored and illustrate the responsibility taken by an EIC. Yet, any choice of referees entails other possible outcomes. This is an inherent property of any decision scheme under variable conditions.

Luckily, Weller (2001) tells us that YY and NN each occur more than YN (in whatever order), and that NN occurs more than YY. This fact is confirmed in Bornmann and Daniel (2009b). This is good news for the editorial process: reviewers easily recognize weak or erroneous submissions.

We note that more than 25 years ago, Hargens (1988) already developed a model for the manuscript-refereeing process. This model included two variables: the journal's decision structure and the correlation between referees' evaluations of manuscripts. The rejection rates (RRs) (see Subsection 3.1.7 for a definition) obtained in his models corresponded to existing ones and hence he suggested that these variations suffice to explain observed variations in RRs. He concluded that space shortages cannot explain disciplinary variations in journal RRs. Finally, he proposed that actual RRs can be used as an indicator for consensus in a field.

Perakakis et al. (2010) propose a very experimental article evaluation system, in which, for instance, journals may compete to get an article published in their journal when it has received many good comments in an author-guided peer review system i.e., authors invite colleagues to write comments on their articles, placed in a repository. As authors may update their articles as many times as they want before publishing in a journal this would reduce the number of publications. Perceived importance of an article would be determined by actual comments and not by external factors, such as the impact factor of the journal in which an article is published.

Most scientists would agree with Mandavilli (2011) who wrote: "The peer review process isn't very good but there really isn't anything that's better." Yet, some like Macdonald (2015) clearly state that, especially for top journals, the peer review system cannot cope anymore. The reason for this statement is that these journals are flooded by submissions so that the large majority of them are desk-rejected (not rejected by peers). This behavior clearly favors established scholars working at top universities.

An overview of the peer review system can be found in Bornmann (2011).

3.1.7 Rejection Rate

The RR of a journal (over a certain period) is the ratio of the number of rejected manuscripts and the number of submitted ones (during that period). Similarly, the acceptance rate (AR) is the ratio of the number of accepted manuscripts and the number of submitted ones. Clearly, AR + RR = 1 for a given submission period. Most highly visible journals have high RRs of more than 90% (McCook, 2006). Actual RRs are field-dependent. Starting journals usually invite well-known colleagues to submit articles for their first issues, and hence have initial low RRs.

Sugimoto et al. (2013) note that, simple as these notions may seem, they are in reality not straightforward. Problematic issues are resubmissions counted as new submissions (and hence the original submission is counted as a rejection), the inclusion/exclusion of invited papers or special issues, an unclear timeframe used, and the inclusion/exclusion of book reviews. Moreover, if data are obtained by surveying editors they may try to bias the outcome in one or the other way.

Already in the seventies, Zuckerman and Merton (1971) examined disciplinary variation in RRs. They found substantial variation with RRs of 20–40% in the physical sciences, and 70–90% in the social sciences and humanities. They suggested two sources for the wide variation in RRs: differences in consensus between fields of scholarship, and differences in space shortages. Note though that this is a very old article and circumstances have changed quite considerably. Probably RRs in journals covered by the Web of Science (WoS) have increased considerably since this investigation.

Using Cabell's Directories of Publishing Opportunities, for which data are provided by editors, Sugimoto et al. (2013) found that statistically significant differences in ARs were found by discipline, country affiliation of the editor, and number of reviewers. In their study, including social health science, business, computer science, education and psychology, the health journals had the highest ARs (a median value of about 50%), while business journals had the lowest (a median of about 25%). Generally, journals with very high impact factors have low ARs, which may be explained by a reinforcement cycle consisting of authors trying to publish their work in journals with a high impact factor (even if not really appropriate) thereby reducing the AR. Such authors' unrealistic expectations lead to an inefficient and clogged publication system. Sugimoto et al. (2013) also found that OA journals had significantly higher ARs than nonopen access ones.

It is well-known that manuscripts that are rejected by one journal (through a peer review process) are often later accepted by another journal (again through a peer review process). This phenomenon is called *bouncebackability* by Cronin (2012). So it seems that there are no general criteria for acceptance or rejection. Acceptance and rejection may depend on individual perceptions (of reviewers and editors) and on local conditions, such as a shortage or abundance of manuscripts. In a review on the predictive validity of peer review, Bornmann (2010) concludes that editorial decisions (acceptance or rejection) reflect a rather high degree of predictive validity, if citation counts are employed as validity criteria. As such, peer review acts as a quality filter and as an instrument for the self-regulation of science.

In this context one may raise the question: What is *quality*? According to ISO 8402 quality is defined as the totality of features and characteristics of a product or service that bear on its ability to satisfy stated or implied needs. We will not try to define *research quality*, but just state that it is related, among other aspects, to research questions, experiments, data analysis, logic, and ethics.

3.1.8 Delays

The publication-citation system has some in-built delays. The most important ones are review(er) delay, publication delay, and citation delay.

Review(er) Delay

This is the delay between submission and receiving the final accept-reject decision. Although some delays may be due to the electronic system itself, these are negligible with respect to the delays occurring because the editor has to find peers, and most importantly, the delay due to reviewers. As explained above, one sometimes needs an extra referee. Yet, as most manuscripts need minor or major revision, authors are also responsible for a delay of weeks and sometimes months. Of course, this delay is not always entirely due to the authors. If reviewers have required additional data collection and analysis this may even take another year. When a manuscript is revised and resubmitted the whole review process starts all over again. Sometimes another revision is deemed necessary.

Although delays due to the reviewing process may take quite some time (from months to more than a year), Rousseau and Rousseau (2012) found that researchers are willing to wait more than a year to publish what they consider to be a high-quality paper in a journal with a high impact factor in the field.

Publication Delay

Publication delay in the strict sense is the time lag between acceptance and final publication. Previously when journals were printed this could easily take a year or even several years, in particular when the journal had a large backlog. In those cases, space shortage was the main culprit. Nowadays, printed journals may still have a large backlog, but they make articles available in electronic form as soon as possible. For purely electronic journals the delay between acceptance and publication is often less than a month. Authors hand in a manuscript that is largely ready for printing. This is sent to the publisher who prepares galley proofs. These are sent to the corresponding author(s) for verification. Once corrections are made the article is ready for online publishing.

Luwel and van Wijk (2012) observed that over a period of 15 years the time lapse between submission and publication for a selected group of engineering, medicine and library and information sciences became considerably shorter, sometimes even by 50%. As nowadays articles are first made available online the real time lapse is even shorter. However, these authors conclude that the competition between faster availability of recent results (publication delay) and easier access to the older literature did not lead to a reduced cited half-life for journals (we refer the reader to Chapter 6: Journal Citation Analysis, for an explanation of this term). Indeed, for many journals the cited half-life increased. Part of the explanation is that reduced publication delay is of the order of months, while availability of older literature is measured in years. Of course, another part of the explanation is that researchers actually make use of this older literature.

Citation Delay

The term citation delay can be defined in different ways, depending on the point of view. In any case it is a difference in time.

For the author and in view of the modern scientific system, citation delay can be defined as the time between submission of a final manuscript to a journal, and corresponding deposition in a repository on the one hand, and the first citation in a publication in any form on the other hand. This can be an accepted publication as included in a preprint server or a repository, but also, if this is not done, in a published article, book, or any other form of official publication.

For scientometric studies, one needs official data (and dates), hence citation delay is best defined as the time between publication and the time of actual publication of an article that cites the original one. Haustein, Bowman, and Costas (2015) propose using the online date as the official publication date of journal articles, where the online date is defined as the date on which the journal article is first made available on the publisher's website.

3.2 OPEN ACCESS (OA)

3.2.1 The Open Access Idea

The worldwide OA movement (a term coined around 2000) is a reaction to the fact that universities, research institutes, and other scientific institutions are confronted with huge increases in the price of journal subscriptions, leading to cancellations and hence nonavailability of scientific information. Moreover, high journal prices hit developing countries the most. The resulting pressures made university leaders and governments aware of the fact that their researchers produce the knowledge (for free) for which the libraries must pay publishers. In this context, it is often mentioned that the results of research done by taxpayer's money should be available to these same taxpayers, and this free of charge. According to the Budapest Open Access Initiative (BOAI, 2002) OA is defined as follows:

> By Open Access ... we mean free availability on the public Internet permitting any users to read, download, copy, distribute, print, search, or link to the full texts of articles, crawl them for indexing, pass them as data to software, or use them for any lawful purpose without financial, legal, or technical barriers other than those inseparable from gaining access to the internet itself. The only constraint on reproduction and distribution, and the only role for copyright in this domain, should be to give authors control over the integrity of their work and the right to be properly acknowledged and cited.

The goals of the BOAI can be achieved in different ways, leading to so-called Gold and Green OA.

3.2.2 Definitions: Gold and Green Open Access

The term "open access" refers to giving access to publications. In that context one makes a distinction between Green and Gold OA

(Poynder, 2009). This is a distinction based on who provides the access: the publisher (Gold OA) or the author (Green OA). In any case, the terms Green and Gold OA refer to immediate OA. We come back to this point in Subsection 3.2.6. What we have described in the previous subsection is Gold OA. Let us now describe the so-called Green OA.

The term Green OA refers to the following situation. Authors publish or want to publish in a subscription-access journal (otherwise we have Gold OA). Yet, they also deposit their manuscript in a repository or publish it in some other way online, making the content of their work freely accessible. Basically there are three types of repositories: institutional ones, topic-based ones, and general ones. The famous arXiv (http://arxiv.org) started as a repository for physics articles (hence a topic-based one), but soon expanded to include many other fields (and hence became a general one). E-LIS (http://eprints.rclis.org) is a repository for articles in the library and information sciences. Another famous, free, topic-based repository is PubMed Central (http://www.ncbi.nlm.nih.gov/pmc/). It archives publicly accessible full-text scholarly articles that have been published within the biomedical and life sciences journal literature.

An institutional repository is an online set of devices for collecting, preserving, and disseminating in digital form the intellectual output of a research institution. They are documentary systems whose contents are (usually) available on the Internet (exceptionally only on an Intranet, where there is no OA), consisting of scientific documents and related items such as articles (preprints and postprints), theses, reports, course notes, data sets, programs, graphical material, and so on. Most of these repositories use a common standard: the OAI (Open Archive Initiative), see (Van de Sompel & Lagoze, 2000). The OAI technical infrastructure, specified in the Open Archives Initiative Protocol for Metadata Harvesting (OAI-PMH), now version 2.0, defines a protocol for data providers to expose their metadata. OAI standards allow a common way to provide content, including that the content has metadata that describes the items in unqualified Dublin Core format.

Nowadays the majority of universities and research institutes support such repositories of scientific results obtained by their own researchers. They often replace the older "academic bibliographies." As such, besides making new research public, repositories also have an archival function.

3.2.3 Gold OA and Who Pays the Costs?

In the words of Subbiah Arunachalam the OA movement has as ultimate goal to "reach the unreached" (Arunachalam, 2002). These ideas led to a new business model for journals. Articles published in journals such as Biomed Central or the PLOS are freely available to anyone. Publishing costs, including maintenance of the journals' websites, are borne by authors or their institutes. Often, publishing costs are included when submitting an application for a project, so that it is actually the sponsor (often this means the government, through some agency) who pays. This has led to a dichotomy in publishing models: OA publishing and subscription access (sometimes also referred to as toll-access).

For some OA journals the author must pay the publication costs (they have to pay article processing charges, in short APCs), while others are completely free for authors. In such cases there is another sponsor who pays for the publication costs. Rodrigues and Abadal (2014) have shown that this model is paramount in Brazil and Spain. In these countries, alternatives to the "author pays" system are based on economic, technical, and political support for scientific journals by governments, universities, and associations. There also exist hybrid models which are embargoed or permanently priced journals, but in which the author(s) may pay the costs to make their article OA. Note that some society journals such as *Physical Review* had page charges already in the 1970s (and probably earlier). In this way access was made easier (i.e., cheaper) for society members.

3.2.4 Retrieving Articles

In the OA vision, scientists and their institutes (and not publishers) are responsible for making the scientific literature freely available. For this to happen having repositories does not suffice. The retrieval function must also be considered. When each university or research institute has its own repository these data sets become highly dispersed. In the case of repositories, this aspect is taken care of by harvesters such as: OAIster, Scientific Commons and Google Scholar. Moreover, cooperation agreements have been made. Examples are: Escholarship (University of California) and DARE (Digital Academic Repository) in the Netherlands. DRIVER (Digital Repository Infrastructure Vision for European Research), a European initiative to connect European repositories, offers retrieval in a user-friendly way and provide technical support for the development of new repositories (http://driver-community.eu). DRIVER resulted in

COAR (Confederation of Open Access Repositories; http://www.coar-repositories.org/).

Harvesters collect metadata made available through e-print servers (repositories) and hence make the contents of such repositories available worldwide. Note that most repositories have no, or only minimal, quality control. Yet, as documents in repositories are made available to anyone, anyone may read, interpret, discuss, and criticize their content. When documents are made public once they are finished they do not suffer reviewing delays.

If an article has been accepted for publication then one may replace the original version (the unreviewed manuscript) with the version accepted for publication. Most large publishers agree to this, sometimes after an embargo period of (at most) 1 year. Only when a submission is accepted one may speak of Green OA. Before that the manuscript has no authority whatsoever and could as well be placed on a scientist's personal webpage. Note that this does not mean that there do not exist extremely important and valuable manuscripts that have never been formally published. The most famous case probably being Perelman's proof of the Poincaré conjecture (only placed at the arXiv), which earned him the Fields medal and the one-million-dollar Millennium Prize, which, by the way, he both turned down.

The best known and probably largest list of OA journals is available at the Directory of Open Access Journals (DOAJ), a website maintained by the Infrastructure Services for Open Access.

3.2.5 Predatory Journals

The phenomenon of OA has given rise to so-called predatory journals and publishers. These are author-pays, open-access journals for which there is no or only a veneer of peer review. Such journals do not show author fees prominently on their websites or in e-mails that they send to authors soliciting manuscript submissions. Predatory publishers and journals only want to make a profit, by collecting APCs and have little concern for scientific integrity. The best-known watchdog on predatory publishers was Jeffrey Beall, who from 2008 till early 2017 compiled a list, known as *Beall's list* of potential, possible, or probable predatory open-access publishers and scholarly journals (Butler, 2013). Yet, not everyone agreed with Beall's methods and some journals have, after appeal, been removed from the list. Indeed, one may say that there is a thin line between predatory OA and low-quality OA journals. Early 2017 Beall removed his list from the Internet. Instead of Beall's list one may now use the DOAJ list as a "white" list of nonpredatory OA journals. Problems with predatory journals were nicely illustrated by Bohannon (2013), working for *Science*, who sent out a spoof paper (in slightly different versions with different—fictitious—authors) containing grave scientific errors and with the sensational conclusion that the author would prove subsequently that a certain molecule is effective against cancer in humans and animals. Papers were sent to OA journals largely taken from the DOAJ and many featuring on Beall's list. Of those versions that went through the whole editing process leading to acceptance or rejection, 157 were accepted and 98 were rejected. Many did not show any sign of external review which is good if the paper is rejected.

3.2.6 Delayed Open Access: An Oxymoron

In reality there are many cases in which full OA as stated by the BOAI is not granted, but rather in some restricted version. Sometimes reading is only permitted to humans, excluding the use of data mining software, and often the final published version is not free, but only a preprint version. According to the Budapest Initiative the term OA, whether Green and Gold, refers to immediate OA. Yet, many journals do not provide OA, but only so-called delayed OA (after an embargo period). This so-called delayed OA is one of the ways in which publishers (commercial or society) fight to retain control of their content. Many colleagues note that the term delayed OA is an oxymoron as OA is by the BOAI definition instantaneous. Laakso and Björk (2013) note that delayed OA journals constitute an important segment of the scholarly literature, even including a substantial proportion of high impact journals. At the moment, such journals include *Science*, *Proceedings of the National Academy of Sciences USA*, the *New England Journal of Medicine*, and *Cell*. From a practical point of view one may remark that even delayed OA is better than permanently priced access.

So, instead of delayed OA, one should just use the term Delayed Access (DA). This access can be provided by the publisher at the publisher's website, in which case one could use the term Gold DA, or by authors themselves (either because the publisher requests a delay, or because they themselves want to provide access only after some time). This could be called Green DA.

So there is Gold OA (immediate), Green OA (immediate), Gold DA, and Green DA. If desired, this can be further subdivided in terms of Gratis (free online access) and Libre (free online access plus re-use rights) OA and DA.

As official mandates by universities and governmental funding agencies are expected to increase self-archiving rates (Harnad et al., 2008), Harnad, Suber, and other OA-supporters urge institutes and funding agencies to demand immediate institutional deposit, irrespective of possible embargo periods. This would put the onus of complying on the fundee, threatened to lose further funding, or the university employee (professor, researcher), fearing to lose their job altogether.

3.2.7 The OA Impact Advantage

The debate surrounding the effect of OA started with a publication by Lawrence (2001), analyzing conference proceedings in the field of computer science. It seems obvious that the earlier an article is available the sooner it can be downloaded and consequently cited. In this way an advantage on similar research can be built up. Yet, if an author places only her better manuscripts in an OA repository, before it is published in a regular journal and it receives more citations than an average article, not placed in an OA repository and published in the same journal, then the reason for this difference in citations is not obvious. Is it because the article was OA? Was it because it was available earlier? Or was it because it was simply a better article? And if papers placed in OA repositories (Green OA) are generally the better ones, wouldn't that lead to the false conclusion that OA leads to more citations? Similarly, for Gold OA, if scientists are only willing to pay (assuming author-pays OA) for their best works, then naturally these receive on average more citations.

Early studies on the OA impact advantage include Antelman (2004), Harnad and Brody (2004), Kurtz et al. (2005a), and Eysenbach (2006). In all cases a citation effect was observed. Harnad and Brody claimed that physics articles submitted as preprint to ArXiv and later published in peer-reviewed journals, generated a citation impact up to 400% higher than papers in the same journals that had not been posted in ArXiv. Kurtz et al. (2005a) found in a study on astronomy evidence of a self-selection bias—authors post their best articles freely on the web—as well as an early view effect—articles deposited as preprints are published earlier and are therefore cited more often. The point is, which of the three causes led to the observed effect? In an attempt to answer this question Moed (2007) compared the citation impact of articles deposited in the ArXiv and subsequently published in a scientific journal, with articles published in the same journal and not deposited in the ArXiv. To discriminate between an OA effect and an early view effect he performed a longitudinal study over a period of 7 years. Author self-citations were excluded. His study provided evidence for a strong early view and quality effect. Correcting for these no sign of an OA effect was found. Note that Moed investigated the Green OA case. The next study investigates Gold OA.

3.2.8 Davis' Randomized Controlled Trial on Gold OA

If OA articles receive more citations, then the question is why? Davis et al. (2008) made an arrangement with a group of publishers to randomly pick some articles and make them freely accessible while other ones in the same issue were not. In total 36 journals in the sciences, social sciences, and humanities were involved. Neither authors, editors nor publishers were involved in this random assignment (otherwise it would not be random). They found that articles in OA received significantly more downloads and reached a broader audience (in the sense of more unique IP addresses) within the first year than subscription-access articles in these same journals. However, they found that OA articles were cited no more frequently, nor earlier, than subscription-access articles within a 3-year period. This finding contradicted many others. Yet, these others did not include the randomness feature. Davis et al. explained their result by social stratification. The best scientific authors are concentrated in a relatively small number of research facilities with excellent access to the scientific literature. They concluded that the real beneficiaries of OA are those who do not belong to this scientific elite: those who publish (and hence cite) less or not at all (students, practitioners, retired faculty).

In order to correct for selection bias, a new study by Gargouri et al. (2010) (including Harnad) compared self-selective self-archiving with mandatory self-archiving in four research institutes. They argued that, although the first type may be subject to a quality bias, the second can be assumed to occur regardless of the quality of the papers. They found that the OA advantage proved just as high for both, and concluded that it is real, independent and causal.

Moed (2012) mentioned that there is a bias when using citations in important, international journals covered by databases such as WoS or

Scopus, in the sense that scientists that publish in such journals almost surely have access to them. In such databases an OA advantage would not be visible. This leads to the question: "Is such an advantage more visible in lower impact or more nationally oriented journals than in international top journals?" As far as we know there is not yet an answer to this question. Finally we mention that when studying the OA advantage one must make a distinction between download advantage and citation advantage. Although both types of study depend on the used sets of databases or repositories, download data mostly have a more local character, reducing comparability between different observations.

Besides *OA* to research results, many researchers and policy makers strive for *Open Data*, the idea that the data on which research is based should also be freely available to everyone to reuse and republish without restrictions from copyright, patents or other mechanisms of control.

3.3 SCIENTIFIC MISCONDUCT: FRAUD, PLAGIARISM, RETRACTION AND THE INTEGRITY OF THE PUBLICATION RECORD

Although the term scientific misconduct is generally used, a more precise formulation can be found in (Fanelli, 2013). He proposes to redefine misconduct as distorted reporting: "any omission or misrepresentation of the information necessary and sufficient to evaluate the validity and significance of research, at the level appropriate to the context in which the research is communicated." He further writes that carefully crafted guidelines could make fabrication and plagiarism more difficult, by requiring the publication of verifiable details. These guidelines could help to uncover questionable practices such as ghost authorship, exploiting subordinates, introducing posthoc hypotheses or dropping outliers. If authors refused or were unable to comply, their paper (or grant application or conference talk) would be rejected.

If scientific misconduct occurs it are always scientists who exhibit this behavior. Hence they are the culprits. Yet, as mentioned in Fanelli's proposal, journals must play an essential role in applying best standards. They must constantly improve the transparency and rigor of the research they publish. This, unfortunately, means that they must put some measures in practice to avoid fraud and plagiarism and make sure that the share of the publication record for which they are responsible stays clean.

3.3.1 Plagiarism and Duplication

Plagiarism is defined as "the appropriation of another person's ideas, processes, results, or words without giving appropriate credit" (http://www.ori.dhhs.gov/definition-misconduct/), while duplicate publication is defined as an article that substantially duplicates another article without acknowledgment, where the articles have one or more authors in common (http://www.nlm.nih.gov/pubs/factsheets/errara.html).

COPE (Committee on Publication Ethics http://www.publicationethics.org.uk) was established in 1997 as a forum for publishers and editors. It provides help on ethical issues such as conflicts of interest, data falsification and manipulation, plagiarism, unethical experiments, priority disputes, and so on. Publishers united themselves in CrossRef (http://www.crossref.org) for the development of new technologies leading to faster publication and easier submissions. CrossRef is also responsible for CrossCheck, a software program to detect plagiarism, used by member publishers. Some publishers have their own services for imposing ethic behavioral, such as Elsevier's PERK (Publishing Ethics Resource Kit). Moreover, most universities use special software to detect plagiarism in theses.

Yet, duplication detection software such as CrossCheck should be an aid to human judgment, not a substitute for it. Human judgment should decide if copying methods sections almost verbatim is acceptable and within the domain of "fair use" (Samuelson, 1994). Zhang (2010) in a discussion of and introduction to CrossCheck seems to judge that copying from methods is rarely acceptable. The same diligence applies to republishing conference articles with little or no new facts or aspects, and to so-called self-plagiarism, discussed further on.

Chaddah (2014) makes a distinction among three types of plagiarism: text plagiarism (copying parts of an article without citing it), idea plagiarism (using someone else's idea or hypothesis, again without crediting the original source), and finally results plagiarism. In the last case, research has been done but presented as original instead of a replication and verification. He notices that plagiarism is not fraud, in which case data are fabricated or unfavorable outcomes removed from the results. He observes that in each of the events of plagiarism, papers should not be retracted, as they are scientifically correct, but a correction must be published giving credit where credit is due, and directly linked to the original paper and this in such a way that every download of the original paper automatically includes the correction. Idea plagiarism may occur accidentally, in the sense that one thinks that an idea is one's own, but it actually is someone else's. This may happen because one has not carefully checked the existing literature or even because one has heard or read about it, but forgot that one had, so-called cryptomnesia (Macrae et al., 1999).

So-called self-plagiarism is a delicate matter. Leaving purely legal aspects aside (for which we refer to Samuelson, 1994), we note that some colleagues place it on the same level as other forms of plagiarism, while others state that self-plagiarism does not exist. Of course, as pointed out by Chrousos et al. (2012) and by Cronin (2013) one cannot steal ideas from oneself, so linguistically the term "self-plagiarism" is an oxymoron. However, when re-using one's own material proper reference must always be given. It is unethical to claim ideas of others, and it is unethical to give the impression that one presents an idea for the first time when this is not the case. This corresponds to the definition stated at the beginning of this section. According to Errami and Garner (2008) duplication, duplicate submission and repeated publication (self-plagiarism) are clearly on the rise. As such they urge journal publishers to use automated means to detect duplicate publications.

Re-publishing parts of one's work often happens when an article published as part of conference proceedings is later published as a journal article. As conference proceedings play an important role in engineering and computer science this point was investigated by Zhang and Jia (2013). They found that in this field most editors were willing to accept submissions derived from a conference paper provided that a substantial amount of the content had been changed (usually expanded). Concretely, they often required 30% new content, but some even went as far as 75% new content. Moreover, such submissions were again submitted to peer review. So, although a software tool such as CrossCheck would signal a large overlap in content, this is not considered self-plagiarism. That said, writing in a repetitive style is usually not good for one's reputation, unless one addresses a totally different audience.

Duplicate publication, in the sense of publishing the same article twice, is another matter. Duplicate publication is only allowed with full permission of the publisher of the first version.

3.3.2 Fraud

Full-blown fraud is discussed in Glänzel (2010), including, among others, the case of J.H. Schön in the field of semiconductors. This scientist received several important prizes before it was found out that his publications were fraudulent. Accusing a colleague of fraudulent behavior, even if true, is not easy and may harm the career of the whistle blower. Three case studies illustrating different ways of whistleblowing were shown in Yong et al. (2013).

An interesting case brought out by Labbé (2010) showed how it is possible to manipulate automatic rankings and write nonsensical articles, which however, look quite impressive to an outsider. To do this he used Scigen (http://pdos.csail.mit.edu/scigen) an automatic generator of articles, including references, in computer science. These so-called articles were written by the fictitious author Ike Antkare. By including references to articles indexed in Google Scholar and by extensive cross-referencing he was able to give Ike Antkare a Google Scholar h-index (a well-known bibliometric indicator, see Chapter 6: Journal Citation Analysis and Chapter 7: Indicators) of 94, making him one of the most visible scientists in the field.

While doing this he found out that this method had been used by some persons to get papers accepted at IEEE conferences (Labbé & Labbé, 2013). This finding led Springer and IEEE to remove more than 120 papers from their subscription services, as reported in Van Noorden (2014).

In view of such cases it would be best if all collaborators on a project carry out verification tests (in case the collaboration involves lab work) before submitting the work. Indeed, the fact of being an author carries responsibilities, concretely with respect of the validity of published work. Yet, direct verification is not always feasible and there has to be trust in scientific collaboration, otherwise the science system would break down. Trust not only applies to collaboration, but also in the publication system itself. It simply is impossible to redo all experiments that lead to the results one uses for one's own work.

Misrepresentation and deliberate over-interpretation of results, although not data fabrication, are other forms of scientific misconduct. This also applies to failing to disclose conflicts of interest.

3.3.3 Fake Reviews

A recent form of fraud consists of faking reviews in order to get one's papers accepted. This is done as follows: Authors suggest real researchers as reviewers, but provide fake e-mail addresses. These e-mail addresses lead to one of the authors or an accomplice. When these researchers are then approached to perform the review they of course accept and write a glowing review (in reality the accomplice does). In 2017, Springer had to retract 107 articles with faked reviews published in *Tumor Biology*, a journal included in the WoS and the Journal Citation Reports (Stigbrand, 2017), but these articles are not the only ones that were retracted for this reason.

3.3.4 Retractions

According to the COPE, retraction should be reserved for publications that are so seriously flawed (for whatever reason) that their findings or conclusions should not be relied upon (Wager et al., 2010). Retraction is then the measure taken to safeguard the integrity of the scientific literature. Retractions can result from honest mistakes, sloppy work, or incompetence. Yet they can also result from plagiarism and fraud.

According to Amos (2014) plagiarism accounts for about 10−17% of all retractions, while duplicate publication accounts for another 14−17%. Other articles in her study were retracted for reasons of human error, or were not mentioned. She further observes that unethical publishing practices cut across all nations.

Although retracted articles should play no role anymore in scientific research and consequent publications, Neale et al. (2010) could provide a categorization of the use of articles affected by scientific misconduct not just retracted ones. They considered 102 articles from the biomedical literature officially identified as resulting (at least partially) from scientific misconduct. Of these 102 articles, 86 were cited at least once after retraction. Next they performed a content analysis of a stratified random sample of size 603 among the 5393 articles citing these tainted articles. Only 17 (or 2.8%) of the 603 included a reference to the corrigendum, i.e., retraction, erratum, or comment. Luckily, it turned out that none of these articles retracted as the result of misconduct had affected clinical practice.

Conrad (2015) worries about false discoveries (in physics, but his thoughts apply to many other fields: how many possible steps that might lead to cures for cancer have been announced?). Pressure to be first let scientists announce "results" they, or another team, have not confirmed yet. Conrad also note that making data public increases the risk that these data are used by scientists who do not know how they were obtained or are not familiar with restrictions of the instruments used to collect these data. Placing preliminary results (that are later found to be wrong) in the arXiv may even lead to giving credit to scientists who do not deserve this. Conrad concluded that academic metrics need to be devised that distinguish citations of discredited claims so that it is not more advantageous to state and retract a result than to make a solid discovery. He notes that competition between universities, journals and scientists may lead to it being better to be first but wrong, than scooped but right.

Fanelli (2014) wrote that the rise in retractions over the past years does not signify a surge in misconduct. On the contrary, retractions should be interpreted as evidence for the commitment of editors and scientists to remove invalid results from the literature. As such it reflects growing scientific integrity. Too many academics and journalists conflate retractions with the falsification of results. Moreover, despite growing pressures on scientists, retractions account for less than 0.02% of annual publications. In another comment, Fanelli (2016) proposes the notion of self-retraction as a neutral term for *honest retraction* and simply defined as a retraction note signed by all coauthors. Besides the terms *correction* and *retraction* Ronald (2016) proposes the terms notice of concern and error alert for self-reported amendments to articles that are less clear-cut.

Meanwhile, there are so many retractions for whatever reason (fraud or error) that it is possible to study the consequences for—possibly innocent—coauthors. Mongeon and Larivière (2014) found that retractions generally have consequences for the career of coauthors mostly in terms of scientific output. Consequences affect first authors more than others and are, of course, much more important in cases of fraud than in cases of error.

3.3.5 A Note on Irreproducibility

Failure to replicate does not necessarily prove that the original research is fraudulent or even unsound. A replication attempt may fail simply because something was done differently. Indeed, there may be a lot of procedural subtlety in the original research, which is not conveyed in the journal article. Moreover, scientists sometimes do this deliberately in order to be certain that those using their results make contact with them and their original contribution is recognized as such. Of course, this too is a form of unethical behavior.

We end this chapter and this section on scientific misconduct by the following observation. In a discussion on the work on cell-induced stress and revealed misconduct in two publications on this topic (Cyranoski, 2014) Alan Trounson said that "Reputation in science is everything. Once gone, it's extremely hard to get back." Cyranoski added that this statement applies not only to individual scientists, but also to journals and institutions. Besides this, retractions also lead to a substantive monetary loss to the science system. Concrete figures can be found in Stern et al. (2014).

Martin (2013) published a statement about all forms of distorted reporting while Zhang (2016) provides an excellent guide on plagiarism and all related problems.

CHAPTER 4

Statistics

4.1 INTRODUCTION

Statistical analysis can be subdivided into two parts descriptive statistics and inferential statistics. In descriptive statistics, one summarizes and graphically represents data of a sample or a whole population. In inferential statistics, one not only collects numerical data as a sample from a population but also analyzes it and, based on this analysis, draws conclusions with estimated uncertainties (i.e., by using probability theory) about the population. It goes without saying that in order to measure aspects of scientific communication and to evaluate scientific research, scientists use statistical techniques. Although hundreds of books have been written on statistics, few deal explicitly with statistics in the framework of information and library science. A basic introductory text for library professionals is Vaughan (2001), while Egghe and Rousseau (2001) is more elementary. One quarter of *Introduction to Informetrics* (Egghe & Rousseau, 1990) is devoted to statistics. Ding et al. (2014) contains a practical introduction to recent developments in informetrics, including statistical methods.

The term *population* refers to the set of entities (physical or abstract ones) about which one seeks information. The publications of scientists forming a research group, of scientists in a country, of scientists active in a scientific domain; of articles included in Scopus and published during the year 2015, are all examples of populations.

In order to investigate a population, the investigator collects data. If it is possible, the best option is to include the whole population in this investigation. Yet, it is often impossible to collect data on the whole population, so the statistician collects a representative sample. This means that a subset is collected in such a way that it provides a miniature image of the whole population. If, moreover, the sample is large enough, then a diligent analysis of the sample will lead to conclusions that are, to a large extent, also valid for the whole population. Such conclusions must be reliable, which includes that the probability to be correct must be known.

Classical inferential statistics draws samples from a population and then tries to obtain conclusions that are valid for the whole population (with a

Becoming Metric-Wise
DOI: http://dx.doi.org/10.1016/B978-0-08-102474-4.00004-2

specified level of confidence). In informetrics there often are no samples, but one tries to draw conclusions based on an observed population e.g., all journals included in Scopus. Does this make sense? We will not answer this question, but refer to Section 4.14 for some useful references related to this question.

This chapter is subdivided into two main parts. In Part A, we describe some techniques from descriptive statistics, while in Part B we discuss inferential statistics, including a short introduction to the normal distribution and a few nonparametric tests. Although we will not consider parametric tests, we nevertheless briefly introduce the normal distribution as it is near-impossible to talk about statistics without in some way involving the normal distribution e.g., when talking about z-scores. Multivariate techniques are beyond the scope of this introductory book. For these we refer the reader to specialized literature.

PART A. DESCRIPTIVE STATISTICS

4.2 SIMPLE REPRESENTATIONS

4.2.1 Nominal Categories

If a sample or the whole population can only be subdivided into groups without any relation, we have nominal categories. The only measurement we can perform is counting how many items there are in each category. For example, when describing the journals used by scientist S to publish his research results over a certain period of time we have nominal data such as: 2 articles are published in journal J_1, 1 article in journal J_2, 10 articles in J_3 and 5 articles in J_4. The number of articles published by the authors of different countries during a given period of time is the result of a counting activity performed on nominal data (countries). A binary scale (yes-no) is a special case of a nominal scale.

Counting results for nominal data can be represented by bar diagrams. Categories c_j, $j = 1, \ldots, k$ are represented on the horizontal axis, while the height of the corresponding bar is proportional to the absolute or relative frequency (which is the same here) of the items in category c_j. It does not matter in which order categories are shown on the horizontal axis, but placing them according to the obtained counts in an obvious option.

For example, if we consider the number of publications in the year 2000 included in the Web of Science with at least one author from England, Northern Ireland (the Web of Science writes *North Ireland*), Scotland and Wales, we may represent these by the following bar diagram (Fig. 4.1).

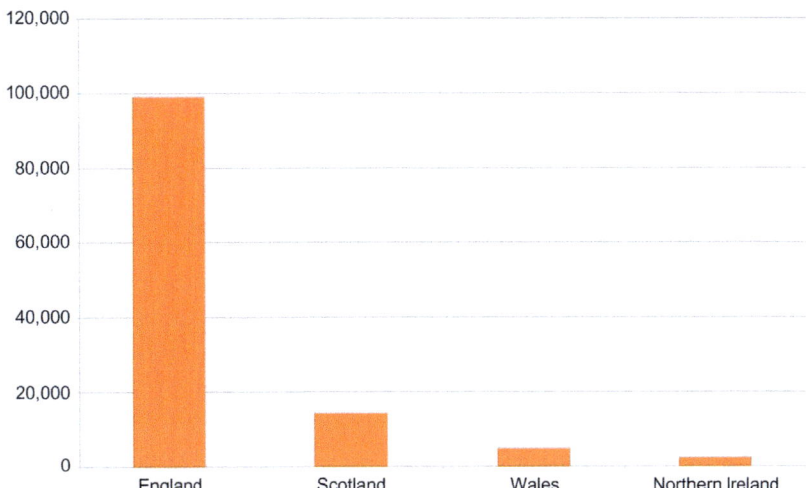

Figure 4.1 Bar diagram.

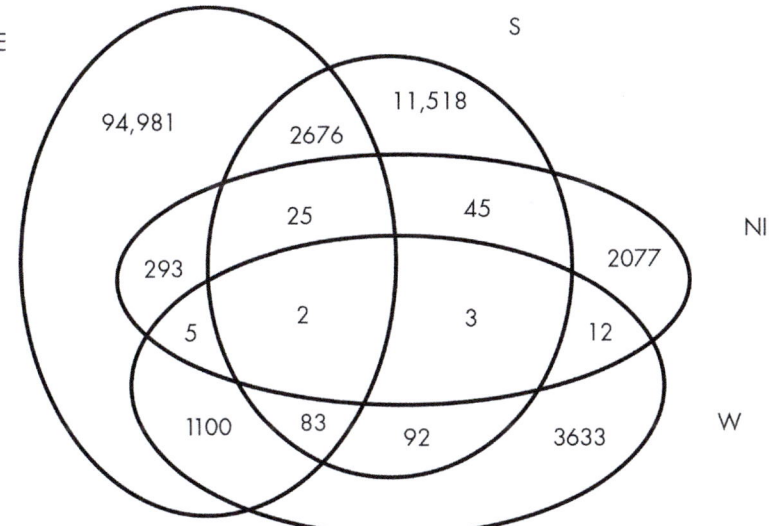

Figure 4.2 Inter-country collaboration and total publications for the United Kingdom in the year 2000 (WoS data). E: England, NI: Northern Ireland, S: Scotland; W: Wales.

For a small (2 to 4) number of possibly overlapping nominal categories, counting results can be represented in Venn diagrams. Applying this approach to the year 2000 data from the United Kingdom we obtain Fig. 4.2. Now we can not only show how many articles there are with at least one author from each of the four countries, but show exactly how many publications there are resulting from inter-country collaborative work (Fig. 4.2).

4.2.2 Ordinal Scales

In a set of chemistry journals some may belong to the top 10% of their field (in the Web of Science), they can be indexed in the Web of Science, but not belong to the top 10% of its category, or they cannot be indexed in the Web of Science. In this example, one may say that there is a natural ranking between these three categories of journals, but nothing more can be said based on this information. Also, in such cases, one uses bar diagrams, but now the order in which categories are placed on the horizontal axis is fixed in a natural way and before data are collected. Data collected over time or time series have a natural order (time) and are usually represented following this natural order, leading to visualizations of time series.

4.2.3 Interval Scales

Suppose one considers a scientist and collects all their publications and for each of these, the number of received citations. One could consider this a measurement (counting the number of received citations) on nominal categories, namely the different publications, and represent them by bar diagrams. Yet, this would not be very illuminating. A better approach would be to show how many publications (or the relative frequency of publications) that are cited zero times, once, twice and so on. Yet, when citations are counted fractionally (for details on fractional counting we refer the reader to Chapter 5: Publication and Citation Analysis) this approach makes no sense and one has to collect how many publications receive a fractional count result lying in the intervals [0, 1[, [1,2[, and so on, ending with one or more intervals with lengths larger than one. In other applications, intervals have other widths and do not have to start with zero. The main point is that these intervals may not overlap. Bringing data together in classes is sometimes called binning and the resulting classes or intervals are then referred to as bins. The difference between the smallest value (in the previous example dealing with citations this would probably be zero) and the largest one is called the range (R) of the observations.

If there are k classes of equal width, denoted as W, and the first class begins at the smallest observation minus $W/2$, while the last one ends at the largest observation $+ W/2$, then the class width is equal to $R/(k-1)$.

Indeed, following this construction we have that $kW = (R + W)$, or $(k - 1)W = R$, hence $W = R/(k - 1)$. Yet, in practice this simple construction is not always possible and one needs one or two rest classes e.g., every observation smaller than a given number (the upper bound of the first interval), and everything larger than the lower limit of the last interval. Next, one determines how many observations belong to each of the classes leading to an absolute frequency distribution. A graphical representation of the resulting frequency distribution is called a histogram.

The classical histogram is the counterpart of a bar diagram. Instead of drawing a bar, one draws a rectangle, centered on the mid-point of a bin (or class). The bins are specified as adjacent, nonoverlapping intervals of a variable. Histograms using relative frequencies provide a rough idea of the density of the population from which data have been collected. Note that, for such density histograms, relative frequencies must be represented by areas, not by heights.

A density histogram usually has one top (then it is said to be unimodal) and is either approximately symmetric or skewed. If there is a long elongated tail on the right-hand side, the histogram is said to be right-skewed, and if the long tail is to the left, it is left-skewed. Most histograms encountered in informetrics are right skewed. For instance, there are many scientists publishing relatively few articles and few scientists publishing a large number of articles. This leads to a right-skewed distribution. If data originate from two sets with different characteristics this leads to a bimodal histogram.

Instead of drawing rectangles, one may connect the midpoints of the upper parts of the rectangles. These are then connected with the midpoint of the first empty class on the left and the first empty class on the right. The resulting curve is called a frequency polygon. When the histogram represents relative frequencies, then the area under the frequency polygon is one.

4.2.4 An Illustration

Table 4.1 shows (fictitious) publication and citation data of a scientist during a given publication and citation window. This scientist has published a total of 30 articles and the table shows how many articles have received zero citations, how many one citation and so on. The following column shows relative frequencies and the last column shows **cumulative** relative frequencies (see also Subsection 4.4.1).

Table 4.1 Fictitious publication and citation data of a scientist

# citations	# publications	Relative number of publications	Cumulative values	# citations	# publications	Relative number of publications	Cumulative values
0	10	0.333	0.333	6	1	0.033	0.933
1	6	0.200	0.533	7	0	0	0.933
2	4	0.133	0.667	8	1	0.033	0.967
3	4	0.133	0.800	9	0	0	0.967
4	1	0.033	0.833	10	1	0.033	1.000
5	2	0.067	0.900	11	0	0	1.000

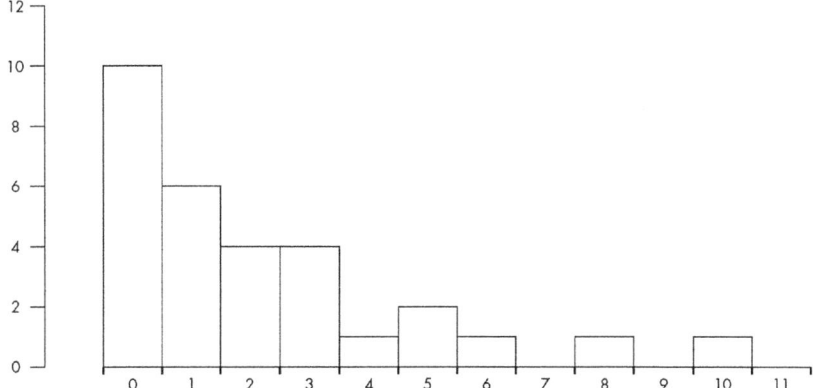

Figure 4.3 Histogram of the data shown in Table 4.1; absolute values on the vertical axis.

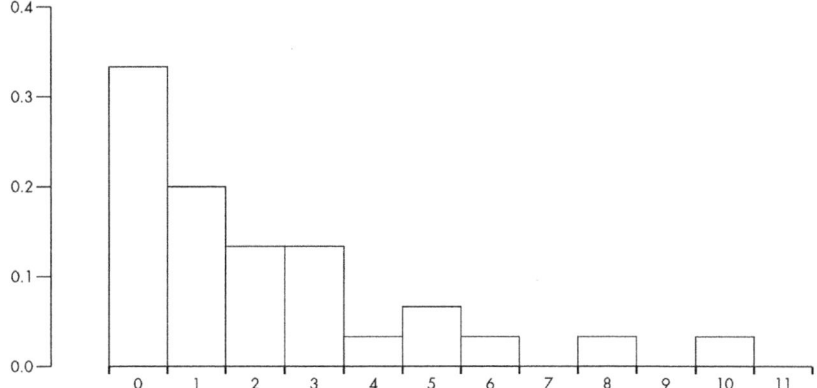

Figure 4.4 Histogram of the data shown in Table 4.1; relative values on the vertical axis.

Fig. 4.3 is a histogram of the data from Table 4.1, using absolute values, while Fig. 4.4 shows relative values. This only changes the vertical axis. Fig. 4.5 shows the same data represented as a frequency polygon. Note that the total area of the rectangles shown in Fig. 4.4 is equal to one. Similarly, the area under the polygon is equal to one.

4.3 MEASURES OF CENTRAL TENDENCY

The term "measures of central tendency" refers to quantities trying to summarize a complete table of observations by one number.

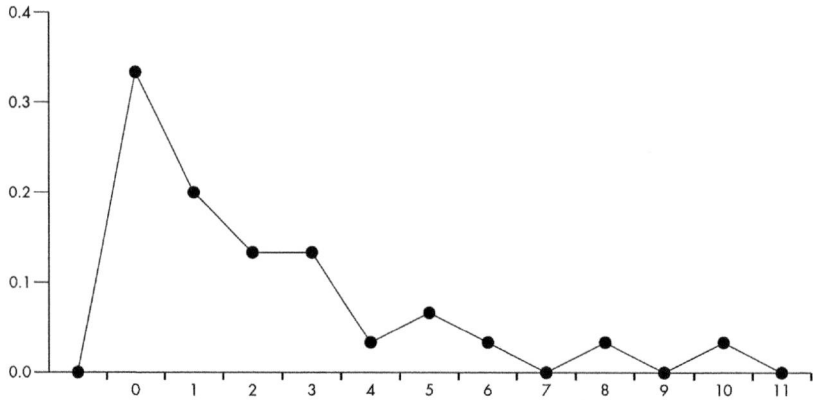

Figure 4.5 Data shown in Table 4.1 represented as a frequency polygon.

4.3.1 The Arithmetic Average

The arithmetic average or mean, of a sequence of values $(x_i)_{i=1,\ldots,n}$ is denoted $\bar{x}$ and defined as:

$$\bar{x} = \frac{1}{n}\sum_{i=1}^{n} x_i \tag{4.1}$$

The famous Journal Impact Factor, discussed in Chapter 6, Journal Citation Analysis, is actually an average number of received citations. If data are only given by a frequency table and m_j is the mid-point of the j-th class, then the average is obtained—approximately—by:

$$\bar{x} = \frac{1}{n}\sum_{j=1}^{k} f_j m_j \tag{4.2}$$

where k is the number of classes and f_j is the number of elements in the j-th class.

4.3.2 The Geometric and the Harmonic Mean

Given a sequence of strictly positive values $(y_i)_{i=1,\ldots,n}$ then its geometric mean is defined as

$$\sqrt[n]{y_1 \cdot y_2 \cdots y_n} \tag{4.3}$$

Its harmonic mean is:

$$\frac{n}{\sum_{j=1}^{n} \frac{1}{y_j}} \tag{4.4}$$

Normalizing is often done by dividing by the arithmetic mean. In some cases, however, scientists preferred normalizing by a geometric mean such as D'Souza and Smalheiser (2014). We draw the attention of the reader to the requirement that in (4.3) all numbers must be strictly positive. Indeed, once one number is zero the geometric mean is zero too and becomes virtually meaningless. We further note that the geometric mean can be rewritten as the antilog (an exponential function) of the arithmetic mean of the logarithms of the data. Concretely:

$$\exp\left(\frac{1}{n}\sum_{j=1}^{n}\ln(y_j)\right) = \exp\left(\sum_{j=1}^{n}\frac{\ln(y_j)}{n}\right) = e^{\frac{\ln(y_1)}{n}}.e^{\frac{\ln(y_2)}{n}}.\cdots.e^{\frac{\ln(y_n)}{n}}$$

$$= e^{\ln\left(y_1^{1/n}\right)}.e^{\ln\left(y_2^{1/n}\right)}.\cdots.e^{\ln\left(y_n^{1/n}\right)}$$

$$= y_1^{1/n}.y_2^{1/n}.\cdots.y_n^{1/n} = (y_1.y_2.\cdots.y_n)^{1/n} = \sqrt[n]{y_1.y_2.\cdots.y_n}$$

(4.5)

This expression can be approximated by:

$$\exp\left(\frac{1}{n}\sum_{j=1}^{n}\ln(y_j+1)\right) - 1$$

(4.6)

which has the advantage of being applicable when zeros occur, as is the case for citation data. Formula (4.6), applied to journal citation data is proposed in Thelwall and Fairclough (2015) as an alternative for the standard journal impact factor, which is an arithmetic mean. In Subsection 6.7.3 we will show that when the geometric mean is used, the average and the global impact factors of a set of journals coincide.

The revised source–normalized impact per paper indicator (Waltman et al., 2013), see Chapter 6: Journal Citation Analysis, formula (6.17), makes use of harmonic means. An important harmonic mean is the F-score used in information retrieval. It is defined as the harmonic mean of recall (REC) and precision (PREC), where recall is the number of retrieved and relevant items divided by the number of relevant items in the database, and precision is the number of retrieved and relevant items divided by the number of retrieved items. Hence we have:

$$F = \frac{2}{\frac{1}{REC} + \frac{1}{PREC}}$$

(4.7)

If O_1 and O_2 are the two overlap measures introduced in Egghe and Michel (2002) then their geometric mean is the Salton measure, while their harmonic mean is the Dice coefficient. For a proof and a definition of these terms we refer the reader to Egghe and Rousseau (2006b).

4.3.3 The Median

The median of a sequence of observations is determined as follows: Rank all observations from smallest to largest. If the number of observations is an odd number, then the one in the middle is the median. If the number of observations is even, then the median is the average of the two middle observations.

For example:

The median of 10, 12, 13, 20, 30 is 13, while the median of 10, 12, 13, 20, 30, 50 is 16.5.

The average can be heavily influenced by a few outliers. Hence the median provides a more robust alternative. For example, the average of (1,3,5,10,21) is 8 (influenced by 21 which is an outlier for this set of numbers); its median is 5.

If values are symmetric with respect to the average, then the median coincides with the average.

With regard to the median, we include some food for thought or challenges for the reader. These are included to illustrate that even simple notions may have unexpected outcomes. This serves as a warning that the more complicated research indicators discussed further on do not always lead to intuitively obvious results.

Is it possible that for a finite sequence of numbers average and median coincide, but that the sequence is not symmetric with respect to the average? The answer is yes: try to find an example yourself.

A sequence of numbers is given and its median is determined. Now add a number to this sequence (not to each number of the sequence) which is strictly larger than the median. Is it possible that the median of this new sequence stays the same?

Yes. Consider the sequence (1,0,3,2,2). Its median is 2. Now we add the number 10, leading to the sequence (1,0,3,2,2,10). Its median is still 2.

Another question. A sequence of numbers is given and its median is determined. Now add to this sequence a number which is strictly larger than its mean. Is it possible that the median of this new sequence is smaller than the median of the original sequence?

Yes. Consider the sequence (10,10,10,0,0). Its median is 10 and its mean is 6. We add the number 8, leading to (10,10,10,0,0,8). The new median is 9.

4.3.4 The Mode

When dealing with nominal data (classes are just names with no inherent order, such as names of scientists, or countries) or in cases where only a small number of values is possible, one may use the mode as a measure of central tendency. The mode is the value that occurs the most. In the case of classes there may be a modal class this is the class occurring with the highest frequency. In such cases, the midpoint of the modal class is the mode.

4.4 CUMULATIVE DISTRIBUTIONS AND THE QUANTILE FUNCTION

4.4.1 The Observed Cumulative Distribution

The value of an observed or empirical cumulative distribution in a point x, given the n observations $x_1, \ldots, x_n$, is the number of observations x_j smaller than x, divided by the total number of observations, n. This observed cumulative distribution will be denoted as $\widehat{F}_n(x)$. The index n refers to the number of data (not necessarily different ones) and the "hat" refers to the fact that it is an observed rather than a theoretical distribution. A cumulative distribution can be represented as an increasing step function.

Suppose we have observed the values 1, 2, 3, and 4, each exactly once. What is the observed cumulative distribution $\widehat{F}_n(x)$? The number 1 is the smallest value we have observed. Hence, $\widehat{F}_n(x) = 0$ for $x < 1$. We see that $\widehat{F}_n(1) = 1/4$ and for every x in $[1, 2]$. $\widehat{F}_n(x)$ stays equal to $\frac{1}{4}$. Clearly, $\widehat{F}_n(2) = 2/4$, $\widehat{F}_n(3) = 3/4$ and $\widehat{F}_n(4) = 1$. This empirical function is constant on each half-open interval between these points and for $x \geq 4$ $\widehat{F}_n(x) = 1$. Fig. 4.6 illustrates the result of this procedure.

4.4.2 The Quantile Function

Now we ask: Given the percentage p, which real number x has p as its cumulative frequency? Consider for example, $p = 0.25$, then we are interested in that observation such that 25% of all observations is smaller than or equal to x. For $p = 0.5$ we are interested in the observation situated in the middle. In mathematical terminology, this is the problem of finding an inverse function of the cumulative distribution function. However, as for empirical [= observed] distributions, this function is a step function and hence not one-to-one (not injective), one has to agree on a precise

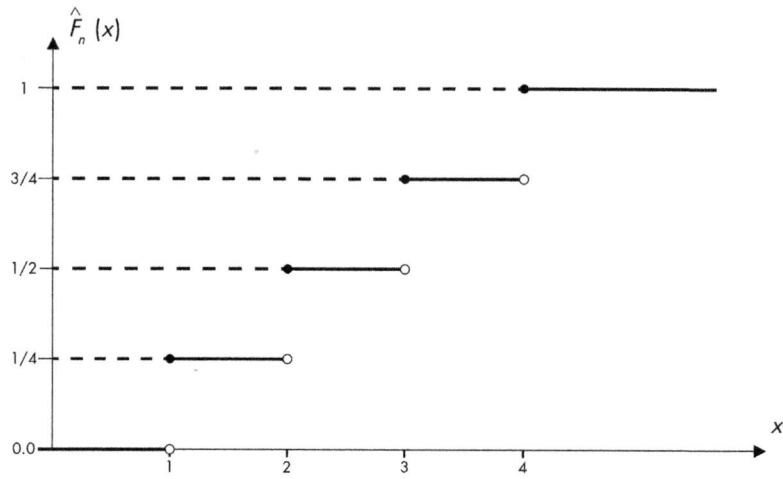

Figure 4.6 An empirical cumulative distribution.

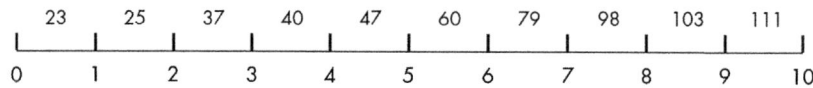

Figure 4.7 Illustration of the first procedure to obtain quantiles (first example).

(and somewhat arbitrary) method. As a consequence, there exist many, slightly different, procedures (Hyndman & Fan, 1996). This "inverse" function is called the quantile function, denoted as $\widehat{Q}_n(p)$. Here, as before, the index n denotes the number of data. If $p = 0.25$ the resulting value is the first quartile: for $p = 0.5$ it is the median (or second quartile) and for $p = 0.75$ it is the third quartile. When $p = 0.1$, 0.2, ..., 0.9 this leads to decile values, and $p = 0.01$, 0.02, ..., 0.99 lead to percentiles.

Next we provide two procedures to calculate quantiles by hand, but recall that most of the time this operation is performed with the help of software and that different procedures may lead to different outcomes.

Procedure 1
One places the observations in increasing order as illustrated in Fig. 4.7.

What is the first quartile $\widehat{Q}_{10}(0.25)$? 25% of 10 is 2.5. This value is situated under the third box. The value in this box, here 37, is said to be the first quartile. Similarly the third quartile is obtained by taking 75% of 10, which is 7.5. The value 7.5 is situated under the eighth box, hence the third quartile is 98. We already know how to calculate a median, but

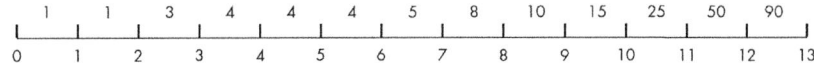

Figure 4.8 Illustration of the first procedure to obtain quantiles (second example).

we illustrate it also using this procedure as there is a slight difference. 50% of 10 is 5. This value is exactly situated between two boxes above the line. In that case one takes the average of the values in these two boxes. Here this leads to $(47 + 60)/2 = 53.5$.

Consider now the somewhat more difficult situation where we have 13 observations: 1,1,3,4,4,4,5,8,10,15,25,50,90. These are illustrated in Fig. 4.8.

Again we start with the first quartile: 25% of 13 = 3.25. This value is situated under the 4th box. This box happens to contain the value 4. Hence the first quartile is 4. Similarly, 75% of 13 = 9.75. This value is situated under the 10th box, which contains the number 15. Hence, 15 is the third quartile. Finally, we check if we find the median: 50% of 13 = 6.5. This value is under the 7th box, leading to a median = second quartile equal to 5.

We point out that this method can also be used to determine deciles, percentiles and any quantile in general. For example, the 16th percentile of the data shown in Fig. 4.8 is 3. Indeed: 16% of 13 = 2.08; this value is situated under the third box. Hence the 16th percentile is 3.

Procedure 2

This method uses interpolation. Values above the line are assumed to be placed exactly in the middle of the box. We illustrate it for the situation shown in Fig. 4.8.

What is the first quartile? The observation 3, placed in the middle of the third box, corresponds to 2.5/13 = 0.1923; observation 4 placed in the middle of the fourth box corresponds to 3.5/13 = 0.2692. We want the value corresponding to 0.25. Using some simple mathematics, we find that 0.25 corresponds to 3.750. Concretely, one calculates: $3 + [(0.25 - 0.1923)/(0.2692 - 0.1923)].(4 - 3) = 3.75$. This is the first quartile. See Fig. 4.9. Clearly, this value differs from the one obtained by the first procedure.

The median or second quartile is clearly 5. Finally, we determine the third quartile. The observation 15, placed in the middle of the tenth box, corresponds to 9.5/13 = 0.7308; observation 25 placed in the middle of the eleventh box corresponds to 10.5/13 = 0.8077. We want the

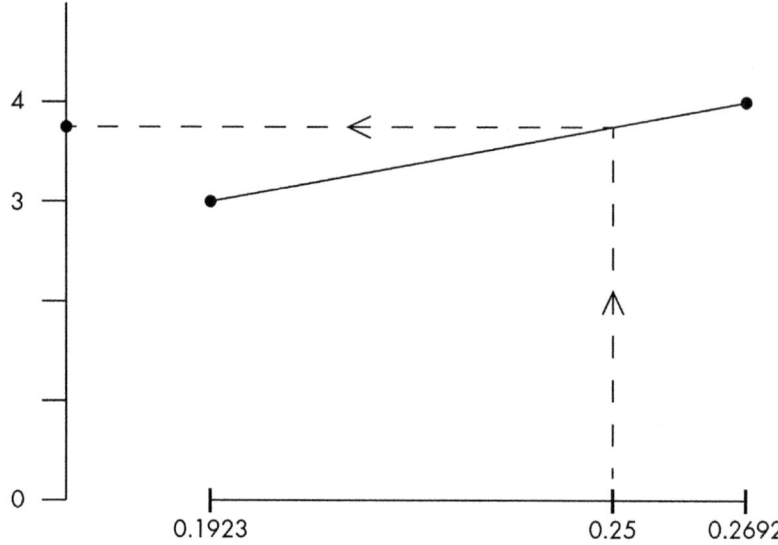

Figurre 4.9 Illustration of the second procedure to obtain quartiles (second example).

value corresponding to 0.75, which corresponds to 17.497, obtained as: $15 + [(0.75 - 0.7308)/(0.8077 - 0.7308)].(25 - 15)$. This is the third quartile. This method can also be used to calculate any decile, percentile or quantile.

The reader may observe that applying the second procedure to the first example, shown by Fig. 4.7 yields exactly the same result as the first procedure.

We recall that quantiles are usually obtained using a software program. This program will probably use a more sophisticated method than the two procedures illustrated here. Only the median is—most of the time—calculated in the same way.

Finally, for more mathematically educated readers, we note that one often defines the quantile function corresponding to the observed cumulative distribution $\widehat{F}_n(x)$ as $\widehat{Q}_n(p) = \inf\{x{:}p \leq \widehat{F}_n(x)\}$.

4.5 MEASURES OF STATISTICAL DISPERSION

Observations with the same mean can have totally different characteristics, depending, for instance, on how observations are dispersed around the mean. Fig. 4.10 shows two frequency curves with the same mean.

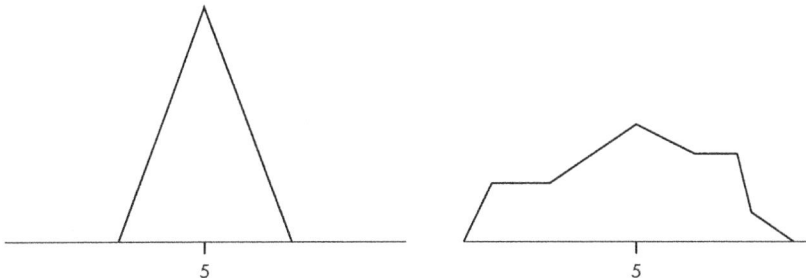

Figure 4.10 Two frequency curves with the same mean.

Although they have the same mean, their characteristics are totally different, but the areas under the curves are the same. This dispersion is measured through measures of statistical dispersion.

4.5.1 The Standard Deviation and the Variance

The best-known measure of dispersion is the standard deviation, denoted
by s. The standard deviation of the sequence $(x_i)_{i=1,\ldots,n}$ (the whole population) is defined as:

$$s = \sqrt{\frac{1}{n}\sum_{i=1}^{n}(x_i - \overline{x})^2} \tag{4.8}$$

Note that s is never negative. The square of s, denoted s^2, is the variance. It is also known as the second moment about the mean. If data are
only given by a frequency table, then the standard deviation is calculated—approximately as follows:

$$s = \sqrt{\frac{1}{n}\sum_{j=1}^{k}f_j(m_j - \overline{x})^2} \tag{4.9}$$

where k is the number of classes, m_j is the midpoint of the j-th class and f_j
is the number of elements in the j-th class.

4.5.2 The Range

The difference between the largest and the smallest observation is called
the range. This number too is a (simple) measure of dispersion.

4.5.3 The Interquartile Range

The interquartile range (IQR), defined as the difference between the third and the first quartile, is a robust measure of dispersion:

$$IQR = \hat{Q}_n(0.75) - \hat{Q}_n(0.25) \qquad (4.10)$$

4.5.4 Skewness

In Section 4.2.1 we already introduced the term skewness in an intuitive way. Now we provide a formula to measure skewness. This expression is known as Pearson's moment coefficient of skewness, in short skewness.

Skewness, denoted as Sk, is calculated using the following formula (m_2 and m_3 denote the second and third moment about the mean; n is the number of data):

$$Sk = \frac{\sqrt{n(n-1)}}{n-2} \frac{m_3}{(m_2)^{3/2}} \text{ with } m_3 = \frac{1}{n}\sum_{i=1}^{n}(x_i - \overline{x})^3$$

$$\text{and } m_2 = \frac{1}{n}\sum_{i=1}^{n}(x_i - \overline{x})^2 \qquad (4.11)$$

The factor $\frac{\sqrt{n(n-1)}}{n-2}$ is used to reduce bias when skewness is calculated from a sample. If data are left-skewed, skewness is negative and when it is right-skewed it is positive. If a distribution is symmetric, or when mean and median coincide, then the skewness coefficient is zero, but the opposite does not hold: zero skewness does not imply symmetry or that the mean is equal to the median. Formula (4.10) was used in Rousseau (2014b) to measure skewness in journal citations.

4.6 THE BOXPLOT

4.6.1 The Five-Number Summary

The five-number summary of a sequence of data consists of the smallest observation, the first quartile, the median (=second quartile), the third quartile and the largest observation. These five numbers provide a summary of the statistical characteristics of a sequence of data.

4.6.2 Boxplots

A boxplot is a convenient way of graphically depicting the five-number summary, and may even provide more information. It consists of a box

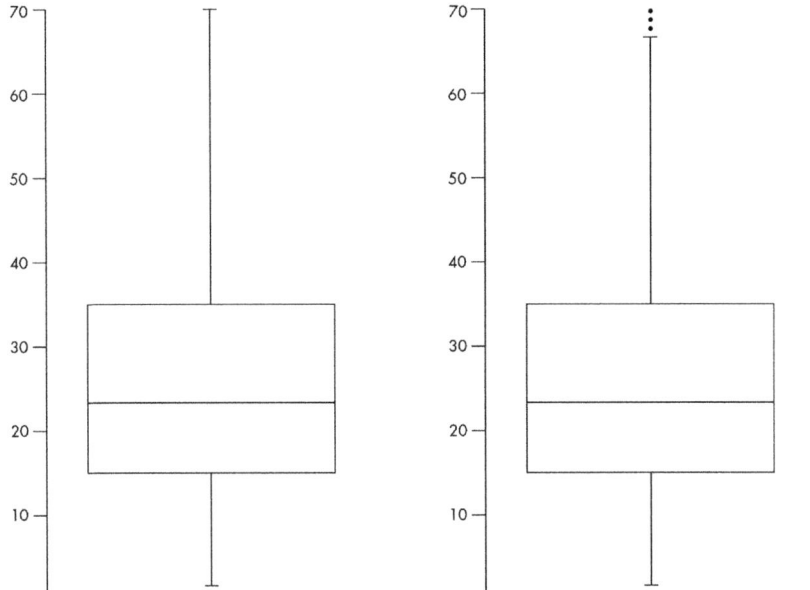

Figure 4.11 Examples of boxplots.

with a line inside, see Fig. 4.11. The bottom and top of the box are always the first and third quartiles, and the line inside the box shows the median. Boxplots have lines extending vertically from the boxes (these are called whiskers) indicating variability outside the upper and lower quartiles. For this reason such boxplots are also known as box-and-whisker diagrams. One often ends the whiskers at the 5th and 95th percentile and denotes the remaining data, considered as outliers, by dots.

4.7 SCATTERPLOTS AND LINEAR REGRESSION

4.7.1 Regression

Metric variables can be represented in a scatterplot. Such a scatterplot is a mathematical diagram using Cartesian coordinates to display values for a sequence of data. Their positions are determined by two coordinates: the *abscissa*, which is the value of the variable determining the position on the horizontal axis and the *ordinate*, which is the value of the other variable determining the position on the vertical axis. Usually the abscissa determines the independent variable, while the ordinate represents the dependent variable. When the independent variable is *time*, the scatterplot represents evolution of a variable over time.

It is possible to determine a best fitting line for a scatterplot. If the independent variable is denoted as x, and the dependent one as y, then this best fitting line has the equation

$$y = a + bx \tag{4.12}$$

a is called the intercept and b is called the slope. When the slope is positive the line is increasing and when it is negative the line is decreasing. When b is zero, y is constant. The best fitting line through the scatterplot $(x_i, y_i)_i$ is obtained as follows:

$$b = \frac{\left(\frac{1}{n}\sum_{i=1}^{n} x_i y_i\right) - \bar{x}.\bar{y}}{\left(\frac{1}{n}\sum_{i=1}^{n} x_i^2\right) - (\bar{x})^2} \tag{4.13}$$

and

$$a = \bar{y} - b.\bar{x} \tag{4.14}$$

A best fitting line, often called a regression line, can always be calculated, even if the scatterplot has no linear appearance at all. For this reason, a measure of the quality of the fit of the regression line to the scatterplot is calculated. This measure is called the Pearson correlation coefficient.

4.7.2 Pearson Correlation

The Pearson correlation coefficient is given as:

$$r(x, y) = \frac{b.s_x}{s_y} = \frac{\left(\frac{1}{n}\sum_{i=1}^{n} x_i y_i\right) - \bar{x}.\bar{y}}{\sqrt{\left(\frac{1}{n}\sum_{i=1}^{n} x_i^2\right) - (\bar{x})^2} * \sqrt{\left(\frac{1}{n}\sum_{i=1}^{n} y_i^2\right) - (\bar{y})^2}} \tag{4.15}$$

As standard deviations s_x and s_y are always positive, this equation shows that the correlation coefficient and the slope of the regression line have the same sign. Of course, neither the calculation of a regression line, nor that of the correlation coefficient is usually done by hand. One uses a software package or a pocket calculator.

Using the correlation coefficient, a best fitting line can be rewritten, more symmetrically, as:

$$\frac{y - \overline{y}}{s_y} = r(x, y) \, \frac{x - \overline{x}}{s_x} \tag{4.16}$$

It can be shown that $-1 \le r(x,y) \le +1$. If r is about zero there is no linear relation between the variables x and y. If r is close to -1 or $+1$ there is a strong linear relation. For values between 0 and 1 the linear relation is more or less strong and positive; for values between -1 and 0 the linear relation is similarly more or less strong and negative. Note that it is possible that a weak linear relation corresponds to a strong nonlinear relation, e.g., an exponential one.

4.7.3 Spearman Correlation

The Pearson correlation coefficient measures a linear relation and can be highly sensitive to outliers. In such cases one prefers the Spearman correlation, which is a robust measure of association. It is determined by ranking each of the two groups (from largest to smallest or vice versa, this does not matter). In case of ties, an average rank is used. The Spearman correlation coefficient is then calculated in exactly the same way as the Pearson correlation, but using ranks instead of the real observations. Also, the interpretation of the Spearman correlation differs from Pearson's. Pearson correlation coefficient is a measure of linearity, while Spearman's is a measure of monotonicity i.e., it determines whether or not the order between the variables is preserved. Of course, a perfect linear relation is monotone, but the opposite does not hold.

It can be shown that the Spearman rank correlation coefficient R_S can be calculated as:

$$R_S = 1 - \frac{6 \sum_{i=1}^{n} d_i^2}{n(n^2 - 1)} \tag{4.17}$$

where d_i denotes the difference in ranking for the ith item and n is the number of items studied.

4.8 NONPARAMETRIC LINEAR REGRESSION

Nonparametric linear regression is a distribution-free method for investigating a linear relationship between two variables Y (dependent, outcome) and

X (predictor, independent). After a study of possible alternatives, Dietz (1989) recommends the following nonparametric regression estimators:

For the slope, she recommends the Theil estimator β_M, which is the median of the sequence of $N = \binom{n}{2}$ sample slopes (assuming all $x_j, j = 1, \ldots, n$ are distinct):

$$S_{ij} = \frac{y_j - y_i}{x_j - x_i};\quad i < j,\ x_i \neq x_j \tag{4.18}$$

For the intercept, she recommends the median of all $y_j - \beta_M.x_j$, $j = 1, \ldots, n$.

An example

Consider the points (0,5), (1,1),(2,3), (3,3.5), (4,3.5), (5,5), (6,7).

The parametric linear regression line has equation $y = 0.518\,x + 2.304$, with $r = 0.567$. This line is heavily influenced by the first point with coordinates (0,5). The nonparametric regression line (thicker line) has equation: $y = 0.833\,x + 0.833$. Fig. 4.12 clearly shows that this line follows the general trend much better than the parametric one.

4.9 CONTINGENCY TABLES

The relation between two nominal variables (with a small number of characteristics) can be represented in a contingency table. A contingency table is created by counting how often each combination of characteristics

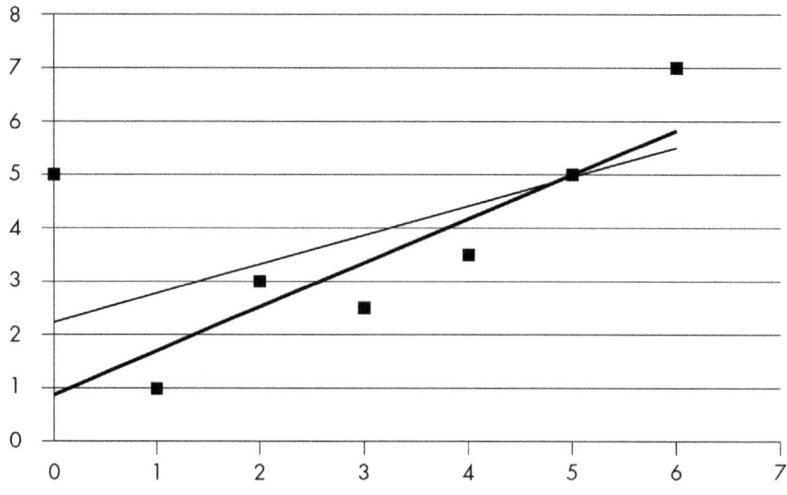

Figure 4.12 Parametric and nonparametric regression lines.

Table 4.2 Articles published on the topic of dust storms (Jin & Rousseau, 2008) 1972–2007

Fields	China	USA	Other countries	Total
Meteorology	106	126	289	521
Environmental sciences	83	77	192	352
Geosciences	61	52	113	226
Total	250	255	594	1099

Table 4.3 Expected values for Table 4.2

	China	USA	Other countries	Total
Meteorology	118.5	120.9	281.6	521
Environmental sciences	80.1	81.7	190.3	352
Geosciences	51.4	52.4	122.2	226
Total	250	255	594	1099

occurs, or by providing a value for the combination of two characteristics, see Table 4.2. One, moreover, adds row and column totals. The act of creating a contingency table is called cross tabulation. The example shown in Table 4.2 is based on (Jin & Rousseau, 2008) where we assume that each article belongs to exactly one cell.

One may consider the question whether values of the two variables are independent or not. For this purpose, a new table is drawn so that each cell contains its row total multiplied by its column total divided by the total N (here 1099). This leads to the following table of so-called expected values (Table 4.3).

Note that totals are not completely correct due to rounding-off errors. How these tables are used in a statistical test will be explained in Subsection 4.13.1.

4.10 THE LORENZ CURVE AND THE GINI INDEX

4.10.1 The 80/20 Rule

The 80/20 rule is a rule-of-thumb which states that the top 80% of actions are provided by 20% of the actors. In a research group, it would mean that 80% of the group's publications result from 20% of its members. In a library, it would mean that 80% of all misshelved books occur on 20% of the shelves (top and bottom ones are good candidates). Of course, the 80/20 rule is just a rule-of-thumb, in reality one encounters perhaps an 85/15 ratio or a 70/30 one. Nevertheless, the 80/20 rule is a well-known rule between percentiles which shows, in a cogent way, how relatively small groups or causes are responsible or determine a much larger part of the consequences. We will next discuss a graphical tool to illustrate the exact relation.

4.10.2 The Lorenz Curve

Consider a set of N scientists and let $X = (x_i, i = 1, \ldots, N)$ be the sequence of numbers of publications they (co-) authored (using whole counting) during a given period of time. We assume that these authors are ranked from most active to least active. Let $s_j = \sum_{i=1}^{j} x_i$ be the j-th partial sum and hence $s_N = TOT$ the total number of publications (with possible double counting if scientists collaborated) of this group of scientists; s_0 is set equal to 0. Now plot the points $\left(\frac{k}{N}, \frac{s_k}{TOT}\right)_{k=0,\ldots,N}$ and connect them by line segments to obtain a curve joining the origin (0,0) with the point (1,1). This curve is known as the Lorenz curve (Lorenz, 1905). If all scientists had published the same number of articles, the Lorenz curve would be a straight line. Otherwise the curve is concave and situated above this straight line. Fig. 4.13 provides an illustration of a Lorenz curve. We note that the Lorenz curve can be considered a normalized cumulative relative frequency curve.

It is now easy to read a $100y/100x$ rule from this curve, where one can choose $100y$ (80 for example). The more a Lorenz curve approaches the diagonal, the more balanced the situation represented by it. A real 80/20 relation indicates a very unbalanced situation. Yet the point (0.2, 0.8) is just one point on a Lorenz curve (possibly) and hence the whole curve contains much more information than just giving a $100y/100x$ relation.

We note, though, that Lorenz curves of two situations may intersect and then it is not immediately clear which of the two situations is the more balanced or the more unequal. In such cases one uses a measure of inequality. A simple one is the coefficient of variation, defined as the standard deviation divided by the mean and denoted as V. Another measure of inequality is the Gini coefficient, discussed next.

4.10.3 The Gini Coefficient (Also Known as the Gini Index) (Gini, 1909)

We observed that the lower the Lorenz curve, the smaller the inequality. Hence once uses the area between the Lorenz curve and the diagonal as a measure of inequality. More precisely, the Gini index, denoted as g, is

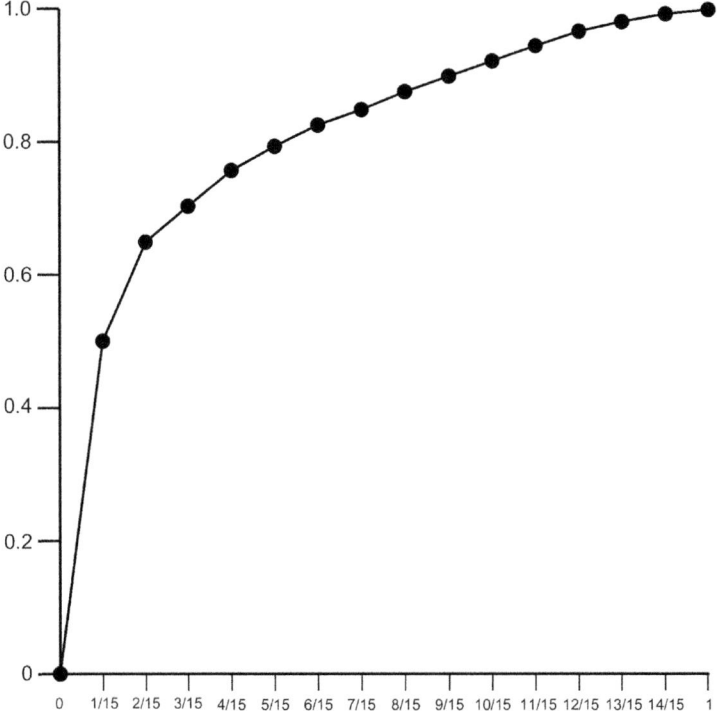

Figure 4.13 A Lorenz curve.

equal to twice this area. The Gini index of the diagonal is zero and when one item takes a larger and larger share of the whole (TOT) the corresponding Gini index becomes closer and closer to one. The formula to calculate a Gini index of an ordered sequence $X = (x_j)_j$ of length N is:

$$g(X) = \frac{1}{N}\left(N+1 - \frac{2}{TOT}\sum_{j=1}^{N} jx_j\right) \qquad (4.19)$$

In most applications outside informetrics (economy, ecology, demography), the Lorenz curve is represented as a convex curve, by ranking data from smallest to largest. If this is done, then the Gini index is calculated as follows:

$$g(X) = \frac{1}{N}\left(N+1 - \frac{2}{TOT}\sum_{j=1}^{N}(N-j+1)\ x_j\right) \qquad (4.20)$$

Of course the obtained value is the same as above. The formula is slightly different because the data are ranked in the opposite way.

Finally, the Lorenz curve and the Gini index are also used when one is interested in diversity, for instance the diversity of journals shown in a reference list. Also then the Gini index can be used, but as diversity is seen as the opposite notion of inequality, the Gini diversity index is calculated as one minus the Gini inequality index. For the Gini diversity index the diagonal leads to the value 1 (largest diversity).

4.11 APPLICATIONS IN INFORMETRICS

In this section we provide a list of possible applications of descriptive statistics.

- number of publications per author, where authors are all members of the same institute, or working in the same domain;
- number of authors per publications, again studied per domain, or over time;
- number of coauthors per publication (per domain, over time);
- ages of references;
- time between publication and received citations; as a specific case one has studied the time to first citation, see Subsection 9.4.2;
- number of references (per journal, per domain);
- number of collaborations between institutes or countries or sectors (e.g., industry − government collaborations);
- number of downloads per article, per journal;
- number of received citations (a specific average is called the journal impact factor, see Chapter 6: Journal Citation Analysis);
- number or fraction of uncited articles (over time, per journal, per author);
- fraction of citations older than n years (where n can be any natural number).

PART B. INFERENTIAL STATISTICS

4.12 THE NORMAL DISTRIBUTION

Classical statistics is based on the normal distribution. Although most distributions observed in informetric applications do not have a normal distribution, we cannot completely do without this basic function. For this reason we briefly recall its main definitions and features.

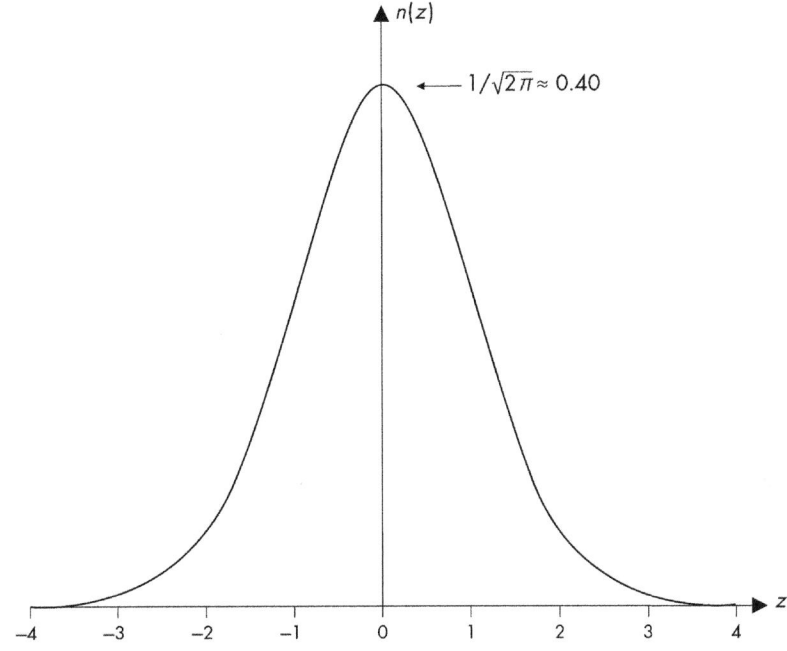

Figure 4.14 Standard normal pdf.

The normal distribution is best-known through its probability density function (pdf) which has the well-known bell-form, see Fig. 4.14. Such a pdf can be considered as a continuous, theoretical form of a histogram.

The mathematical equation of the general normal pdf is:

$$f(x) = \frac{1}{\sigma\sqrt{2\pi}} e^{-\frac{(x-\mu)^2}{2\sigma^2}} \tag{4.21}$$

This function has two parameters: μ and $\sigma > 0$. For each value of these parameters, one has another normal pdf. It can be shown that the mean or average of a normal pdf is μ and its standard deviation is σ. Moreover, this function is symmetric with respect to its average. The relation between the general normal pdf, with variable x, and the standard normal pdf, with variable z is $z = (x - \mu)/\sigma$. Clearly the standard normal distribution has mean 0 and standard deviation equal to 1, see Fig. 4.14.

The distribution function of a normal distribution is given in Fig. 4.15. Note that this is not a discrete function and not an observed function, but a theoretical, continuous function.

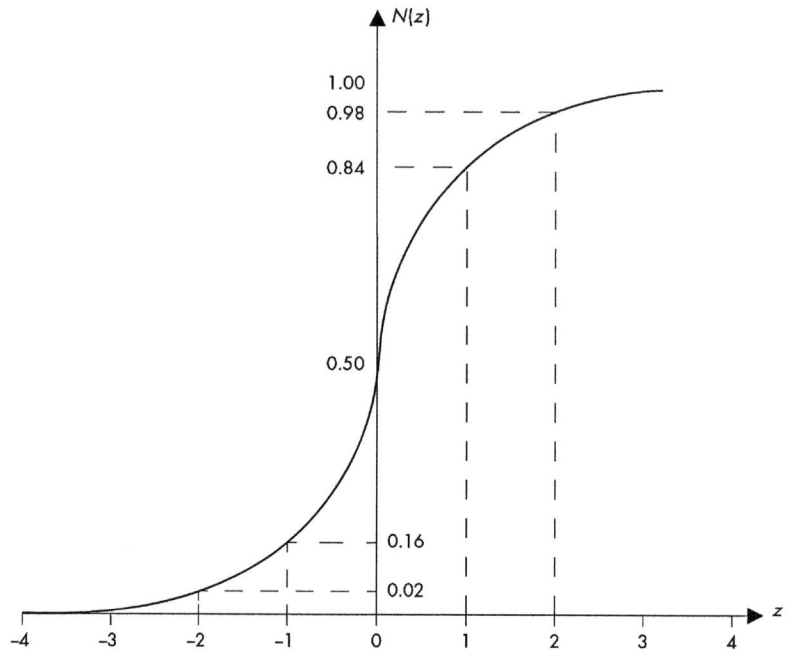

Figure 4.15 Standard normal distribution function $N(z)$.

The relation between the normal distribution function F and its pdf $f(x)$ is given by the fact that the area under the pdf from $-\infty$ to u is equal to the value of $F(u)$. As F has limiting value $(u \to +\infty)$ equal to 1, the area under a normal pdf is always one.

The standard normal distribution is denoted as $N(0,1)$. It is this function which is shown in Fig. 4.14. Important areas, i.e., values for $N(z)$ are given in Table 4.4. A general normal distribution function is denoted as $N(\mu, \sigma^2)$. Note that is customary to use the variance (σ^2) as a parameter here and not the standard deviation (σ).

It follows from the symmetry property of the function N that for every z,

$$N(z) = 1 - N(-z) \tag{4.22}$$

4.12.1 The z-score

The z-score of a value from a normal distribution is the corresponding value for the standard normal distribution. Assume that one has the value 39 in a normal distribution with parameters $\mu = 25$ and $\sigma^2 = 49$. The corresponding

Table 4.4 z-Values and corresponding N(z)-values

z	0	1.282	1.645	1.960	2.326	2.576
N(z)	0.5	0.9	0.95	0.975	0.99	0.995

z-score is obtained by subtracting the average and dividing the result by the standard deviation. This leads to a z-score of $(39-25)/7 = 2$.

Using z-scores is a way of comparing data from different normal distributions.

4.13 HYPOTHESIS TESTING

We only discuss two nonparametric tests: the chi-square test for independence and homogeneity in tables and the Mann-Whitney U-test for equality of distributions. We assume that the reader is already familiar with basic hypothesis testing such as the z- or the t-test.

Nonparametric tests are designed to avoid assumptions inherent in more common tests. Usually such assumptions assume that variables are normally distributed or are distributed according to a distribution that is related to the normal distribution. For instance, the standard test on the difference between two means assumes that the distribution of the means follows a t-distribution (a distribution which very much resembles the normal distribution) and that data are sampled from continuous distributions with the same variance. These assumptions are rarely met for informetric data.

4.13.1 Test of Independence in Contingency Tables

This subsection is largely taken from Egghe and Rousseau (1990, [I.3.5.3]). A contingency table, as discussed in Section 4.9, is a multiple classification. Items under study are classified according to two criteria, one having m categories and the other having n. Hence the contingency table is an $m \times n$ matrix. Cell frequencies are denoted as O_{ij} and $\sum_{i,j} O_{ij} = N$. Cell frequencies obtained under the assumption of independence, see Table 4.3, are the expected values, denoted as E_{ij}. These are compared with the observed frequencies O_{ij}. Then the quantity

$$\sum_{i=1}^{m}\sum_{j=1}^{n}\left(\frac{\left(O_{ij}-E_{ij}\right)^2}{E_{ij}}\right) \tag{4.23}$$

is said to be χ^2-distributed (read: chi-square) with $(m-1)(n-1)$ degrees of freedom. This expression clearly is a sum of relative squared differences. It can be shown that the χ^2-distribution with k degrees of freedom is the distribution of a sum of the squares of k independent standard normal variables explaining the meaning of the so-called "degrees of freedom". If the expected frequencies can only be computed by estimating h population parameters, we have a χ^2-distribution with $(m-1)(n-1)-h$ degrees of freedom. We omit the proofs.

If expected cell frequencies (not the observed ones!) are too small (in practice <6) we have to combine categories. For small tables it is recommended to apply Yates corrections for continuity. This means that one uses

$$\sum_{i=1}^{m}\sum_{j=1}^{n}\left(\frac{\left(|O_{ij}-E_{ij}|-0.5\right)^2}{E_{ij}}\right) \tag{4.24}$$

instead of formula (4.23). The χ^2-value for the data in Table 4.2, without Yates' correction, is:

$$\chi^2 = \frac{(106-118.5)^2}{118.5} + \frac{(120.9-126)^2}{120.9} + \frac{(281.6-289)^2}{281.6} + \frac{(80.1-83)^2}{80.1}$$

$$+ \frac{(81.7-77)^2}{81.7} + \frac{(190.3-192)^2}{190.3} + \frac{(51.4-61)^2}{51.4} + \frac{(52.4-52)^2}{52.4}$$

$$+ \frac{(122.2-113)^2}{122.2} = 4.607$$

This variable has 4 degrees of freedom.

Now we use a software tool to find out what the probability is that a χ^2-distribution with 4 degrees of freedom has a value of 4.607 or smaller. This is called its P-value. In this case the P-value is 0.33. When the P-value (P) is smaller than 5% (this is just a conventional value, sometimes one uses 1% or 10% as the test level) one rejects the null hypothesis of independence. As this is not the case here, there is no reason to reject the null hypothesis. Note that to apply this test observed cell frequencies must be absolute frequencies, not relative frequencies, fractions or percentages. Also, categories must be mutually exclusive so that data cannot be allocated to more than one cell.

Table 4.5 Number of publications of information scientists at university A and university B

A	B	B	A	B	A	B	A	B	B	B	A	B	B	A	A	B	A
5	8	11	12	14	16	17	19	22	26	38	40	51	57	61	76	90	105
1	2	3	4	5	6	7	8	9	10	11	12	13	14	15	16	17	18

First row: affiliation.
Second row: number of publications.
Third row: rank (from lowest producer to highest).

4.13.2 Mann-Whitney U-test for Equality of Distributions (Mann & Whitney, 1947)

This test is also known as the Mann-Whitney-Wilcoxon test. It is a two-sample rank test. This nonparametric test has as null hypothesis that two samples come from the same population (or they come from two populations with the same statistical properties). The alternative is often formulated as a one-sided test: one population has larger values than the other one. The following explanation is largely taken from Egghe and Rousseau (1990). Suppose we are interested in the question whether information scientists at university A are more productive than information scientists at university B. One may assume that outputs differ, but the question is whether these differences can be attributed to chance fluctuations. Therefore we consider their publication lists over the past 8 years. Results are shown in Table 4.5. Note that eight information scientists work at university A and ten at university B. For the moment we assume that all scientists have a different output, hence there are no ties.

The test is derived from the following line of reasoning. If the publication outputs of the information scientists at these two universities differ strongly, the lower numbers of publications will mainly be found for scientists at one university and the higher numbers for the others. In the most extreme case. the lowest ranks will all be assigned to one group and the highest to the other. If the first group has m members and the second one n members and if the members of the second group all publish more than those of the first, then the sum of the ranks of the second group, denoted by T2 will be at its maximum. This maximum sum is equal to $nm + n(n + 1)/2$. Indeed, in this extreme case the members of the second group occupy ranks $m + 1$ up to $m + n$. The sum of these ranks is equal to the sum of the first $m + n + 1$ natural numbers minus the sum of the first m natural numbers. This is:

$$\frac{(m+n)(m+n+1)}{2} - \frac{m(m+1)}{2} = \frac{m^2 + mn + m + nm + n^2 + n - m^2 - m}{2}$$

$$= mn + \frac{n(n+1)}{2}$$

(4.25)

If the ranks of these two groups are mixed, $T2$ will be smaller than this maximum. This is the basic idea for considering the statistic $U2$ calculated as:

$$U2 = mn + \frac{n(n+1)}{2} - T2 \tag{4.26}$$

$U2$ is small when groups differ greatly and large when groups differ little. A symmetry argument shows that $U2$ can be large when the ranks of the elements in the second group are the lowest, but in this case the roles of the first and the second group are interchanged. The null hypothesis of this test is that both groups do not differ. Consider

$$U1 = mn + \frac{m(m+1)}{2} - T1 \tag{4.27}$$

where $T1$ is the sum of the ranks of the elements in the first group. In practice one uses $U = \min(U1, U2)$. However, one does not have to calculate $U1$ and $U2$ as it is easy to show that their sum is mn. Indeed:

$$U1 + U2 = 2mn + \frac{m(m+1)}{2} + \frac{n(n+1)}{2} - (T1 + T2)$$

$$= 2mn + \frac{m(m+1)}{2} + \frac{n(n+1)}{2} - \frac{(m+n)(m+n+1)}{2} = mn$$

(4.28)

Applying this procedure to Table 4.5 with $m = 8$ and $n = 10$ yields $T1 = 80$ and $T2 = 91$, and thus $U1 = 36$ and $U2 = 44$ (and we note that $36 + 44 = 8*10$). So we use the value 36.

If m and n are large (say at least 10), then U is approximately normal with mean $mn/2$ and a variance of $nm(n + m + 1)/12$. Standardizing leads to:

$$\frac{U - \frac{mn}{2}}{\sqrt{\frac{mn(m+n+1)}{12}}} \sim N(0; 1) \tag{4.29}$$

This expression means that the expression on the left-hand side is distributed as the standard normal distribution (the normal distribution with mean 0 and variance 1). It is now possible to apply a standard normal (parametric) test (a so-called z-test), see e.g., Egghe and Rousseau (2001). For smaller values of m and n, one has to use dedicated software (or printed tables).

In case there are ties, one uses as rank the median rank of all outputs with the same rank. In such cases statistical software automatically applies a correction for ties. Huber and Wagner-Döbler (2003) provide a handy spreadsheet when using the Mann-Whitney test in case there are ties and no statistical software package is available. Note that their formulae are slightly different from ours as their U is our T. We followed the original notation from Mann and Whitney.

Finally we mention that if the two populations under study with distribution functions F_1 and F_2, can be assumed to be continuous and the alternative is stated as a shift in location (i.e., $F_1(x) = F_2(x + \delta)$), this means that the two distributions have the same shape. Under these circumstances, a rejection of the null hypothesis can be interpreted as showing a difference in medians.

4.14 CONCLUDING REMARKS ON STATISTICS

For an elementary introduction to issues on parametric and nonparametric statistical inference we refer the reader to Egghe and Rousseau (2001) and Vaughan (2001).

It has recently come to the attention of scientists that statistics are sometimes misused and that the traditional method of hypothesis testing may lead to invalid or useless conclusions (Ioannidis, 2005; Schneider, 2012, 2013, 2015; Vidgen & Yasseri, 2016). Three points are important here: Not reporting effect sizes, not reporting statistical power and the misuse of P-values. A Bayesian approach (the "traditional" method is then referred to as the frequentist approach) may be the solution to the last problem. Yet, we consider these topics to be outside the scope of this book. Moreover, when working with a "complete population" statistical significance tests are irrelevant as there is no sampling error. In these circumstances, one must use the techniques provided by descriptive statistics. Yet, such populations often change over time, and as such they too can be considered to be samples. Discussions of this point can be found in issue 10(4) of the *Journal of Informetrics*.

CHAPTER 5

Publication and Citation Analysis

In this chapter we introduce publication and citation analysis in general. Details on the use of citations for journals and derived indicators will be studied in the following chapters. A large part of this chapter is based on Egghe and Rousseau (1990, III.0–III.4). Sections including mathematical concepts contain clarifications through worked out examples.

5.1 PUBLICATION AND CITATION ANALYSIS: DEFINITIONS (ROUSSEAU, 2008)

5.1.1 Publication Analysis: A Formal Definition

Publication analysis is a subfield of informetrics. In this subfield scientists study frequencies (numbers) and patterns related to the act of publication. Publication studies are performed on the level of documents (articles, contributions to edited books, monographs), authors, universities, countries and any unit that might be of interest.

Counting the number of articles published in a given journal during the year Y by authors of country C is a basic aspect of publication analysis. A less elementary aspect is, e.g., by-line country correspondence.

5.1.2 Definition: By-Line Country Correspondence

Two articles A_1 and A_2 exhibit the phenomenon of by-line country correspondence if the sets of countries occurring in the by-line of articles A_1 and A_2 are the same.

Note that we consider sets of countries: if country C_1 occurs two times in article A_1 and once in article A_2 then this is considered the same as when country C_1 occurs once in article A_1 and four times in article A_2. We require that the set of countries in the by-lines are the same.

By-line country correspondence is an equivalence relation in the set of all nonanonymous articles (assuming that each author has at least one country name in their address). Belgium-France-the Netherlands is one name of such an equivalence class. This equivalence class consists of all articles such that at least one author has an address in Belgium, at least one author has an address in France, at least one author has an address in

Becoming Metric-Wise
DOI: http://dx.doi.org/10.1016/B978-0-08-102474-4.00005-4

the Netherlands, and none of the authors has an address outside these three countries.

Besides by-line country correspondence, other forms of publication-related similarities may be distinguished such as coauthorship, collaboration between institutes or cooccurrence of title words.

Similar to publication analysis, we define citation analysis as follows.

5.1.3 Citation Analysis: A Formal Definition

Citation analysis is a subfield of informetrics. In this subfield scientists study frequencies (numbers) and patterns related to giving (reference behavior) and receiving (being cited) citations. Citation studies are performed on the level of documents (articles, contributions to edited books, monographs), authors, universities, countries, and any unit that might be of interest.

5.1.4 Scientific Achievements Weave Citation Networks

Scientific research is a social and cumulative process, although it may occasionally be interrupted by a totally new and original approach, a so-called new paradigm (Kuhn, 1962). One may confidently say that nowadays not a single scientific discovery or other scientific activity occurs in splendid isolation. New results are always connected to work of predecessors. Citations reflect this social and cumulative aspect by connecting the past with the present, hence functioning as a bridge to the future. Citations are an intrinsic part of the progress and development of all sciences. Related to the aspect of functioning as a bridge between past and future we recall from Price (1970) and Egghe and Rousseau (1990, p. 204) that—on document level —a citation is the acknowledgment that one document receives from another, while a reference is the acknowledgment that one document gives to another. So *reference* is a backward-looking concept (given to an older document), while *citation* is a forward-looking one (received from a younger one).

5.1.5 Scientific Contributions and the Act of Citing

Contributions to scientific knowledge are mostly crystallized as scientific articles or as a monograph. Yet, one should not forget that there are many more types of scientific or technological contributions such as: software programs, data themselves (as published in data repositories), blueprints, patents, new scientific instruments, constructions (such as spacecrafts or the storm-surge barrier (Delta Works) in the Netherlands), schemes, and even new ways of thinking. All these are essential scientific accomplishments. In this chapter about publication and citation analysis we do not concern ourselves with these other scientific results, although many colleagues do study patents and patent citations see e.g., Trajtenberg (1990) and Guan and Gua (2009). When, however, one performs an evaluation exercise (see Chapter 8: Research Evaluation), these other forms of scientific results should not be overlooked (Jansz & Le Pair, 1992).

When considering publishable scientific results, one deals with new facts, new hypotheses, new theories, new theorems or proofs of theorems, new explanations, new thinking schemes or a new synthesis of known facts, as in a review. In each of these examples a transition took place from an "old" situation to a "new" one. Often this transition occurs in the head of the investigator or group of investigators, with or without the help of instruments. In the beginning only the investigators themselves know that a step has been taken, outsiders are not yet aware of the new situation. When the "new" finding or hypothesis is made public, scientific tradition and deontology require that authors refer to those colleagues and publications that inspired them. The new finding must be placed in its proper framework. The authors do this by making their starting point clear. The old situation is described by mentioning (=citing) the concepts, methods and discoveries of predecessors helping them or serving as a source of inspiration to develop the new findings. In other words, the author recognizes an intellectual debt to a group of documents and their authors by citing them. Here *citing* means mentioning them in the proper context and providing an explicit and correct bibliographic description as part of a reference list (or footnote, an older habit still persisting in the humanities). The older articles are cited by the new one.

As an aside we note that a similar process takes place when a new web page is designed and links are made to already existing web pages. Yet, citing articles or linking to web pages are different actions. For instance: a reference always has a date, while web pages rarely do. On the level of citing articles there is a clear direction, namely from the citing article to the (older) cited one. Indeed, if article A cites article B then rarely article B will cite article A, but see Rousseau and Small (2005) for a rare and rather special exception of a so-called Escher staircase. Web links may go in both directions, but the same can be said about citations between authors, journals, and other groups of articles.

5.1.6 Criticism on Citation Analysis

MacRoberts and MacRoberts (1989, 2010) noted that many influences on the content of articles stay unmentioned. As an example they quote the field of biogeography. Observations in this field often end up in floras. When these floras are used in analytical studies they are rarely cited and the observations on which they are based are certainly not. The point made by MacRoberts and MacRoberts is that being uncited or rarely cited is not the same as being unused or of little interest.

5.1.7 Citation Networks

Articles are connected to other ones by citations. These citation links lead to a directed and possibly weighted network of citations (for more on networks, see Chapter 10: Networks). Hence, one can derive citation networks of articles, journals, authors, universities, countries and many more. Scientific authors may also be connected by coauthorship, cocitation and bibliographic networks (see further for a definition of these notions). The term network theory is often used when one has applications in mind, while the term graph theory is more used in a purely mathematical context. Yet, this distinction is not very strict and these words may be used interchangeably. Needless to say network theory plays a basic role in citation analysis. Some aspects of network theory will be studied in Chapter 10, Networks. Price (1965), Xhignesse and Osgood (1967), and Garner (1967) were among the first to study the citation relation as a graph.

5.1.8 Applications of Publication and Citation Analysis

We mention three main application areas of publication and citation analysis (Hu et al., 2011).
- Information retrieval: returning to the origin of the citation network, or finding related or subsequent articles. In information retrieval this method is called citation pearl growing or cycling.
- Research evaluation: contributing to the evaluation of scientists, research groups, institutes and universities, and groups of countries. Note the word "contributing" as research evaluation can never be based on publication and citation indicators only.
- Study of science: research related to the structure of publication and citation networks. This can be done by tracing the origin of an idea or the relations between subfields. Garfield already applied citation analysis when tracing the history of the breaking of the genetic code,

referring to this type of application as historiography (Garfield, 1979). A recent variation of this idea is the idea of reference publication year spectroscopy, see e.g., Marx et al. (2014). Another interesting example is provided in Liu and Rousseau (2012) where it is shown that citations to the key article that led Charles K. Kao to the 2009 Nobel Prize in physics (Kao & Hockham, 1966) reflect the evolution of the field of fiber optics, including alterations between periods in which academic research dominated and periods in which technical-application oriented research dominated.

5.2 CITATION INDICES: GENERALITIES

5.2.1 Definition of a Citation Index

A citation index is a structured database of all reference items in a given set of documents.

In modern terms a citation index can be described as the result of an automatic text mining exercise performed in scientific publications.

5.2.2 History of the Science Citation Index

Eugene Garfield is without any doubt the father of modern citation analysis. In 1960 he founded the Institute for Scientific Information (ISI, Philadelphia, PA, USA) and thanks to a research project of US$300,000 (1961 dollars) he published the Genetics Citation Index in 1963, followed by the first Science Citation Index (SCI). This first SCI described the publications of the year 1961 in a set of 613 selected journals, leading to a total of 1.4 million references. In small print, namely 5 point (pt) type letters for author names and cited articles; 3.5 pt type for citing articles (and recall: the point is about is 0.35 mm), it consisted of five volumes. The history of the development of this very first SCI is described by Paul Wouters in his doctoral dissertation (Wouters, 1999).

The SCI was a yearly publication (with the possibility to buy quarterly editions) which was followed in 1973 by a Social Science Citation Index (SSCI) (covering the year 1972) and in 1978 by the Arts & Humanities Citation Index (A&HCI). In 1976, the first volume of the Journal Citation Reports (JCR) was published, as a volume (volume 9) of the 1975 SCI. The JCR is online available for data beginning in the year 1997. The JCR makes use of the data leading to the citation indices and shows data referring to journals as a whole. It is discussed in more detail in the next chapter. Since 1988, the citation indices became available on CD-ROM and since 1997 it became possible to consult these citation indices via the Internet in the Web of Science (WoS). The year 2009 saw the inclusion in the WoS of the Conference Proceedings Citation Index Science (CPCI-S) and the Conference Proceedings Citation Index Social Science & Humanities (CPCI-SSH). More than 20,000 journals are covered, but not all are described in the JCR. In the year 2011 Thomson Reuters (the then owner of the WoS) launched a Book Citation Index (BCI) (Adams & Testa, 2011). By including books, Thomson Reuters hoped to provide a better coverage of the social sciences and the humanities. In 2015 Thomson Reuters launched the Emerging Sources Citation Index (ESCI), extending the set of publications in the WoS to include more publications of regional importance and in emerging scientific fields. The company claims that ESCI will also make content important to funders, key opinion leaders, and evaluators visible in the WoS even if it has not yet impacted an international audience. ESCI journals do not receive an impact factor, but are evaluated regularly and those qualified will be transferred to the WoS and hence, will receive an impact factor.

The SCI has been expanded retrospectively and goes back nowadays to the beginning of the 20th century (existing since 2005). The subdatabase *Century of Science* describes the period 1900—1944, while also the period 1945—1960 has been included retrospectively.

The Institute of Scientific Information was bought in 1992 by Thomson Scientific & Healthcare, and became known as Thomson ISI. Thomson Scientific itself became part of the Thomson Reuters Corporation. In 2016 Thomson Reuters sold its Intellectual Property & Science Business, which included the WoS, to Onex and Baring Asia. In this way the WoS and several other databases such as InCites and the Derwent World Patents Index became part of Clarivate Analytics.

More information about the use of the WoS is provided in Section 5.15.

5.2.3 Competitors for Thomson Reuters

Until the year 2004, ISI and later Thomson Reuters held a monopoly position of global citation indices (there were only a few small or local initiatives). However, in 2004 the situation changed when Elsevier launched Scopus. Nowadays Scopus provides a complete description of articles in more than 22,000 journals and goes back for most journals to the year 1996. In Section 5.16 we provide a more complete description of Scopus. Via SCImago and also via the CWTS Journal Indicators (http://journalindicators.com) Scopus describes complete journals in a similar way as the JCR (see Chapter 6, Journal Citation Analysis).

That same year (2004) Google launched a beta version of Google Scholar (GS). Also this database provides citation data, but its most significant disadvantage is that it is unclear which journals or websites are covered and which are not, see further Section 5.17.

Since the end of the 1980s regional databases have been installed (first in China). These databases cover the scientific production (or part thereof) of a country or region. One finds several regional databases in China (see Jin & Wang, 1999; Su et al., 2001; Wu et al., 2004), Japan, Taiwan, South-America (SciELO), Russia, India and Spain. Such databases mainly, but not exclusively, cover journals published in a local language (Chinese, Japanese, Spanish, Portuguese, Russian). As commercial databases will never cover the complete scientific literature, such local or regional databases are a necessary complement.

5.2.4 Advantages of a Citation Index

What are the advantages of a citation index with respect to an index covering a specific literature, such as medicine or mathematics? (Garfield, 1979).

- Citations and hence, on a higher level, citation indices represent topic relations.
- Authors are the best qualified persons to link their article with those written by other scientists. They do this better than professional indexers.
- Citation indexes are not influenced by specific systems of subject description.
- A citation index is by construction multidisciplinary.
- A citation index is not influenced by semantic problems, occurring when the same word means something different in different fields or when the same property is described by different terms.

Finally an important advantage in the beginning years was the speed with which a new version of the SCI was made (a new version every 3 months, with yearly compilations). Nowadays, as the publishing process is done electronically this advantage has largely ceased to exist.

5.3 CITING AND REASONS TO CITE

White (2001) considered the question: When does an author cite a document? He came up with four essential steps.

1. Authors must know that the document exists.
2. Authors must possess sufficient bibliographical information to cite properly.
3. Authors must judge that the cited document bears on what they are writing.
4. Finally, authors must judge that the cited document carries enough weight to cite it.

Hence, the four steps outlined by White lead to the question: When does a known document carry enough weight to be cited?

Ideally, researchers should cite those articles whose ideas, theories or research have directly influenced their work. But, why do scientist really cite? If reasons for citing are a mere coincidence or are of semi-fraudulent nature, then citations cannot be used to describe relations between fields or for studying other aspects of the science of science. If that were the case citations could not be used in research evaluation exercises. Hence, studying reasons for citing is an important topic in the field.

5.3.1 A List of Acceptable Reasons to Cite

The following list is based on Garfield (1965) with some expansions.
• Describing a method.
• Providing the origin of an idea.
• Giving credit to a colleague or a group of colleagues.
• Providing background information.
• Reporting the most important article related to an idea or subfield.
• Convincing the reader that the article is of importance (Gilbert, 1977).
• Correcting an earlier publication (one's own or that of others).
• Showing that one disagrees with a certain thesis or result.
• Establishing (one's own) priority.

5.3.2 A List of Less Acceptable Reasons to Cite

This list is based on (Thorne, 1977):
• Showing that one builds on work by an important scientist (while this is not really the case).

- Citing mainly the important journals in one's field, or in general including the famous triad: *Nature, Science*, and the *Proceedings of the National Academy of Sciences of the United States of America*.
- Supporting one's point of view, and "forgetting" to mention the opposite view.
- Citing oneself, one's doctoral supervisor or lab director (without real necessity).
- Applying "you scratch my back and I'll scratch yours" or expressed with a more academic term: *reciprocal altruism* (Trivers, 1971).
- Social consensus; an unspecified and vague perception of a consensus in the field, see also (Bavelas, 1978).
- Strongly preferring fellow countrymen or close acquaintances.
- Citing articles published in the journal where one intends to submit one's article, this to increase the chance to be accepted.

5.3.3 What Happens in Reality?

If citations were given only for the reasons mentioned in Thorne's list, then citations would be useless for research evaluation. At best they could be used for a study of the sociology of scientists. The first person who effectively asked researchers why they included certain articles in their reference lists was Terrence Brooks (1985). From his study it emerged that citing to convince readers of the importance of the article occurred the most this is persuasion, the reason proposed by Gilbert (1977). Disagreement with other scientists and pointing out errors occurred the least. Indeed, when scientists observe (unimportant) errors they usually just ignore them. We mention here that Bornmann and Daniel (2008) reviewed about 40 studies of citing behavior.

How and why bibliometricians cite was investigated by Case and Miller (2011). The idea was that bibliometricians know the meaning of citing (it is their profession) and hence it was hypothesized that their citation behavior was different from other scientists. This was confirmed to some extent. It was found that bibliometricians mostly cited a concept marker (a genre). This agrees with the idea, discussed further on, of articles becoming concept symbols.

As reasons to cite may be somewhat field-dependent or may depend on cultural factors it may be interesting to study such reasons per field or per country or region. This is what Mengxiong Liu (1993) and Ma and Wu (2009) did in the case of Chinese scientists. Yuxian Liu (2011) argued that the overarching reason for citing is "interestingness": An author cites a certain publication because it is of interest for the citing publication, see also (Liu & Rousseau, 2013). Indeed, most reasons for citing— acceptable or not—can be described using the term *interestingness*. In this sense, interestingness can also be considered as *perceived relevance* (Poole, 1985; White, 2001). Somewhat similarly, citing may be viewed as a kind of voting (Doyle et al., 1996), whatever the reason for the vote.

5.4 CITATION CLASSIFICATION SCHEMES

5.4.1 The Moravcsik-Murugesan Classification of Citations

Moravcsik and Murugesan (1975) proposed a classification such that a citation always belongs to one of two alternatives. Four sets of alternatives were considered:

- Conceptual (reference is made to an idea, a concept or a theory) or operational (reference is made to a method, tool or technique).
- Organic (=essential) or perfunctory (not essential, ceremonial).
- Evolutionary (building on previous ideas) or juxtapositional (an alternative viewpoint is proposed).
- Affirmative or negational.

Moreover, Moravcsik and Murugesan observed that many citations are redundant. This means that there are many references included that all make more or less the same point. This may happen when one provides relevant background information. Instead of referring to one or two standard reference books or reviews one provides a long series of books or articles. These references are not all redundant or perfunctory, but taken as a whole, the majority among them is perfunctory. The main result drawn from their sample of high energy physics was that 41% of the citations fell in the perfunctory category.

5.4.2 The Chubin-Moitra Classification Scheme

The work of Chubin and Moitra (1975) was a more or less direct response to Moravcsik and Murugesan. Although they recognized the value of an approach to citation analysis based on an inspection of the contents of an article, they recommend a mutually exclusive classification scheme. This approach leads to a tree structure, see Fig. 5.1.

In this scheme affirmative citations are either essential or supplementary. Essential citations are further categorized as basic if the references

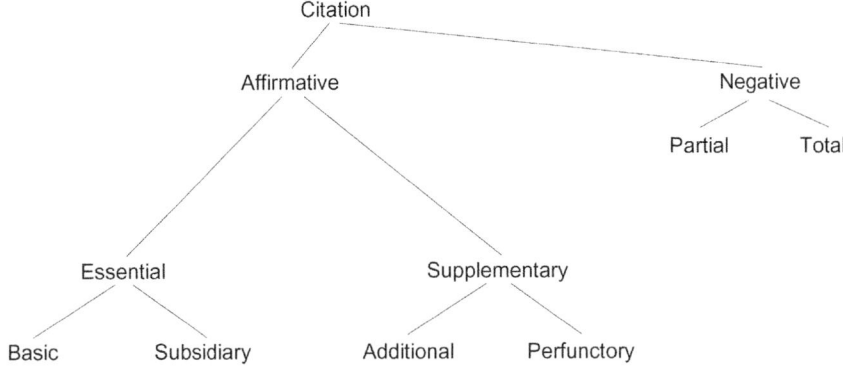

Figure 5.1 Chubin-Moitra scheme.

paper is central to the reported research: It is a reference on which the citing article really depends. If a specific method, tool or mathematical result is not directly connected to the subject of the paper, but is still essential to the reported research it is categorized as a subsidiary citation. Supplementary citations provide additional information when the referenced paper contains an independent supportive observation (idea or finding) with which the citer agrees. Included in the perfunctory category are papers referred to as related to the reported research without additional comment. Finally, the division of negative citations into partial and total needs no further comment. Using this classification scheme Chubin and Moitra found 20% perfunctory citations and about 5% negative citations, none of which was totally negational.

5.4.3 White's Synthesis

Admittedly, the difference between essential—subsidiary and supplementary—additional is in practice difficult to make. Hence we agree with White's (2001) synthesis, leading to four citation contexts:

- Perfunctory-positive: pointing to related studies, providing background, invoking a prestigious name.
- Perfunctory-negative: justifying a study by pointing to omissions in prior studies.
- Organic-positive: discussing previous research in detail; acknowledging concepts, methods, hypotheses introduced in earlier research; pointing to research results which are essential for the author's research.
- Organic-negative: showing errors in previous publications; refuting the conclusions of earlier research.

White (2001) places this scheme in a "principle of least effort" perspective. Perfunctory-positive citations do not require a lot of effort. Perfunctory-negative ones require more effort as they must be carefully put in context. The creation of context for organic-positive ones is the major part of writing an article. Organic-negative citations really require a lot of effort. One must carefully create a context in which to justify an attack and explain why previous studies fell short. As, moreover, one risks making enemies, it is no surprise that these citations occur the least.

White's synthesis could even be taken one step further leading to influential (organic) and noninfluential (perfunctory) paper-reference pairs. Zhu et al. (2015) point out that author impact measures such as citation counts and the h-index, journal impact measures such as the JIF and other applications of citation analysis such as citation network studies, tracking the spread of ideas, recommender systems and so on could be based on influential citations only. They propose a supervised learning approach to split influential from noninfluential citations.

Another synthesis is that by Baumgartner & Pieters (2003). These authors discern five categories: application/use, affirmation/support, negation, review and perfunctory mention. In this classification the first three categories represent a higher level of impact than the last two. In a study on marketing journals Stremersch et al. (2015) found 53% of review type citations, 32% of perfunctory citations and only 15% of citations belonging to the higher impact categories. They further investigated the relation between citation counts and challenging commonly held beliefs. The highest levels of citations occurred for papers with a moderately high level of challenging commonly held beliefs.

Considering reasons for citing, especially in view of their use in research evaluations, one encounters the normative versus social constructivist point of view (Baldi, 1998). The premise of the normative theory of citations is, broadly speaking, that the more frequently a scientific publication is cited, the more important it is for the advancement of knowledge. Citing is performed to give credit where credit is due (Merton, 1942). The social constructivists, however, believe that the contemporary position of science is the outcome of a negotiation process in which one party convinces the other by using many persuasive techniques in reporting research. MacRoberts and MacRoberts (1987), two major proponents of the social constructivist view on citing, have argued that persuasion, not a desire to give credit where credit is due, is the major motivation for citing. White (2004) pointed out that the issue is not the ordinary claim that scientists write to persuade their readers and, in doing so, use citations as a rhetorical device. The persuasion hypothesis, rather, is the much stronger idea that persuasion in science and scholarship relies on a form of manipulation similar to that used in commercial advertising (Davis, 2009; Nicolaisen, 2008).

5.5 AUTHORS AND THEIR CITATION ENVIRONMENT

White (2000, 2001) defines four groups of authors that are related to a given author, referred to as the ego.

The first group simply consists of all coauthors of the ego. Within this group coauthors can be ranked depending on the number of times they copublished with the ego.

The second group consists of the ego's citees: all authors that are cited, at least once, by the ego. These can be ranked by the number of times they were cited. This set is referred to as the ego's citation identity.

The third set consists of authors that are cocited with the ego. This means that articles by these authors occur (at least once) in a reference list together with an article of the ego. They may be called the ego's cocitees. Together they form the ego's citation image. These were described e.g., in (White & McCain, 1998). Again this set can be ranked according to the number of times a colleague is a cocitee with the ego.

Finally, the fourth set consists of citers who refer to the ego in their publications. Because these authors create an ego's citation image White (2001) calls them the citation image makers of the ego. Authors can be ranked according to the number of times they cite the ego. Fig. 5.2 illustrates the citation image, citation identity and the set of citation image makers for an ego (E). Dots in this figure may refer to the same person as scientists may belong to one, two or all three of these sets. The group of coauthors is not shown.

These four sets are time-dependent in membership as well as in the frequencies associated with them. Obviously, the second and the fourth group may include the ego himself. Yet, if an article by the ego is cocited with another article by the ego then one may say that the ego is cocited with himself, and hence belongs to his citation image. So, also the third group may include the ego. In "Authors as citers over time" White (2001) discusses in detail the citation identities of eight information scientists (Bates, Borgman, Cooper, MacRoberts, Small, Spärck Jones, Swanson, and Paul Wilson). In practice, the ranked lists making up an

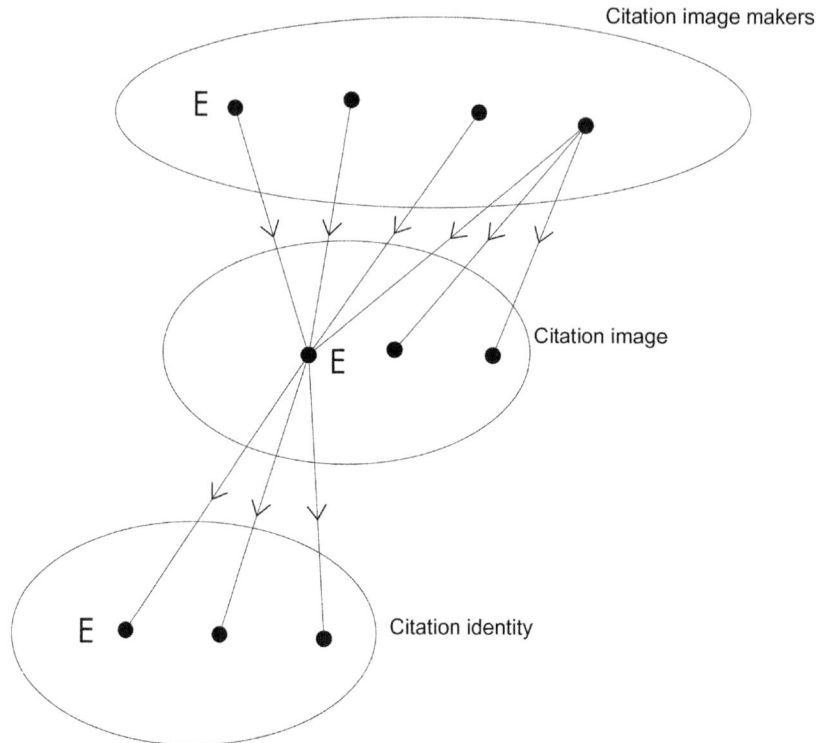

Figure 5.2 The ego (E), the Ego's citation identity, the Ego's citation image and the Ego's citation image makers.

ego's citation identity tend to begin with the ego himself. It further consists of those colleagues that are cited often- are recited – and ends with a
long list of unicitations (authors that are cited exactly once by the ego).
Clearly, the study of author recitations connects to the study of author
citation networks. Such networks can be considered as a special type of
social networks (see Chapter 10: Networks). The intersection between
the image and the identity set consists of self-citations, actually author
self-citations, see Subsection 5.6.2.

From these examples (and using common sense) one can easily
describe an author's citation identity. For a theoretical informetrician it
may consist of:

- Oneself.
- One's team (students, research group).
- One's formal organization (department).
- One's invisible college.

- One's other colleagues; more precisely colleagues studying the same topics and sharing the same research interests (other theoretical informetricians).
- One's larger membership group, such as a professional society (ASIS&T, ISSI).
- The research field at large (all information scientists).
- All scientists and the culture in which one is embedded (one may occasionally cite a Nobelist, a well-known writer or philosopher, an editor of a journal which is totally outside one's own field).

We note that recitation may also occur within one article, but such synchronous recitation is not what was studied by White (2000, 2001). Recitation within one article can be used to weight received citations (Rousseau, 1987).

5.6 DIFFICULTIES RELATED TO COUNTING

5.6.1 Problems Related to Publication and Citation Counts (Egghe & Rousseau, 1990)

We provide a list of problems or difficulties occurring when counting publications or citations. Some of these problems are related to providing correct credits to actors.

- Self-citations, of authors, journals, countries, . . . This point is discussed in the next subsection.
- How to assign credits in the case of multiauthored articles. Also this point is discussed further on.
- Homonyms (different persons with the same name). Many persons with the same full name, or with the same name and initials happen to work in the same field or at the same university. To differentiate between them additional information is necessary, such as a complete publication list, detailed institutional affiliation, or names of (frequent) coauthors. This problem is especially large in Eastern countries (China, Japan, Korea) (Cornell, 1982) and India. A solution for this problem consists of providing a persistent digital identifier that distinguishes a scientist from each other colleague. At the moment the best known author identifier is ORCID (Open Researcher and Contributor ID; available at https://orcid.org/), which consists of 16 characters. It provides a persistent identity to humans, similar to the way a digital object identifier uniquely identifies a digitally accessible object. Clarivate Analytics' ResearcherID can be considered (although

not strictly) a special subset of ORCID. Virtual International Authority File is another international authority file, mainly used by National Libraries and by OCLC. Moreover, MathSciNet, the online version of Mathematical Reviews, maintains a name authority file.

- Synonyms (different names referring to the same person). Citations will be scattered unless a unique name is used for an author. Examples of such "synonyms" are author names with a variable number of initials, with or without a middle name, a woman's maiden name and her married name, different transliterations of nonwestern languages and misspellings. A famous example in the field of informetrics is given by the different forms of Derek J. de Solla Price's name. This problem as well can be solved by using ORCID or a similar unique identifier.

- Synonyms do not only exist for persons but also for journals or even countries (Congo vs Zaire; Russia, the Russian Federation and the larger (former) Soviet Union). In addition to variations in the abbreviated form of a given journal title, journals merge, split, change titles and may appear in translations (Garfield, 1975).

- Which sources should one use: only journals (and which type(s) of journal publications), or does one include books and/or conference proceedings? As the type of used sources can influence the results of a citation analysis (especially in the social sciences and the humanities) the choice and the number of sources should depend on the purpose of the analysis.

- Implicit citations. Most citation analyses only consider explicit citations for the simple reason that most databases only give information on this kind of citations. Yet, the A&HCI includes some implicit citations too. Implicit citations are frequently found in the form of eponyms, discussed further on.

- Which periods to use? When counting publications, one needs to determine a time period called the publication window: only publications published in this window are counted. When counting citations to publications, we need a publication window as well as a citation window, i.e., the time period during which citing publications are published. As there may be large variations in citation counts from one year to another, citation data should not be too restricted in time.

- Variations in the number of references, and hence the number of citations per field. Publications and referencing practices depend strongly on research specialties. As a consequence variations between citation counts also strongly depend on research fields. This may lead to difficulties in cross-disciplinary comparisons.

- Which database should one use: the WoS or Scopus? Or maybe GS? Is it advisable to use a local database or a local database combined with an international one? Recall that none of the international databases is complete (and even local ones are not). Because the coverage of databases tends to vary with disciplines, this reinforces the previous point: the number of citations in a poorly covered field may in reality be much higher than what one can deduce from one single database.
- Dominance of English in the sciences. English is the lingua franca of the sciences. As a consequence papers published in English are preferred for citations (Liang et al., 2013). This means that if two papers make the same point and one of them is written in English and the other one in another language, the one written in English will receive the most citations.
- Bias in favor of the United States, bias at the expense of developing countries. In the eighties Cronin (1981) found that US authors cited American works for 95% of the time, a percentage which is much larger than the US' share of publications. We do not know if this is still the case, but expect that it is not. Bias at the expense of developing countries is related to the Matthew effect on the level of countries (Bonitz, 1997; Bonitz et al., 1997). Note though, that almost all countries exhibit an own-country preference, in the sense that they cite articles coauthored by countrymen relatively more than expected from the share of the own country's publications.
- Gender bias. Ferber (1986) claims that researchers tend to cite a larger proportion of authors of their own sex than of the opposite one. This has substantial consequences in fields where men are the large majority. A numerical calculation illustrating this fact can be found in Rousseau (2006a). Gender issues in scientific evaluation are briefly discussed in Subsection 8.13.5.
- Papers containing important ideas will not necessarily continue to be highly cited. Once an idea is widely known in its field citing the original version is deemed unnecessary, e.g., Einstein's theory of special relativity. This phenomenon (no longer citing the original source) has been termed *obliteration by incorporation*. It has recently been studied in McCain (2012).
- Errors in databases. Citation analysis cannot be more accurate than the raw material, usually the databases, they use. In turn, these databases cannot correct every mistake made by writers when compiling

reference lists. Copying mistakes from earlier reference lists occurs all too often (Liang et al., 2014).

As it is in practice impossible to include all influences (through publications) in a reference list, citations always undercount scientific influence.

5.6.2 Self-Citations

The term self-citation has been used with different meanings. If the citing paper has one or more authors in common with the cited paper one usually describes this as a self-citation. Yet, one could, more precisely make a distinction between different authors. Indeed, if an article written by A and B is cited in an article written by B, then this certainly is a self-citation for author B, but what about author A? One could make a distinction here between a self-citation on article level (then this is a self-citation) and a self-citation on author level (then this is a self-citation for author B and not for author A).

References to articles published in the same journal as the one in which the citing article appears are called journal self-citations. This type of self-citation is discussed further on in Chapter 6, Journal Citation Analysis. When citations are used for evaluation purposes then citations of articles authored by people working in the same research group or department as the citing author are also called "self-citations," see e.g., Moed et al. (1985a).

This leads to a hierarchy of self-citations:
- Author self-citations.
- Article self-citations.
- Research group self-citations.
- Country self-citations (in the context of own-country preference).

Besides these different forms of self-citations there are, of course, citations by outsiders (the remaining ones). Clearly in terms of diffusion of scientific knowledge this group is the most important one, while author self-citations may reflect no diffusion effect (possibly only from one author to a coauthor).

Tagliacozzo (1977) conducted a systematic study of author self-citations in the areas of physiology and neurobiology. The main conclusions were that only few articles do not include self-citations, and the numbers of author self-citations per article are widely distributed. Moreover, authors are inclined to cite their own work more abundantly than the work of any other single author. This observation coincides with the fact that the ego leads the citation identity list. Self-citations refer to a more recent group of publications than other citations do. This recentness of author self-authors might indicate the high degree of continuity in the work of individual scientists. One of the important findings of Tagliacozzo is that self-citations are more often repeated in the same article than other citations. If we assume that repetition of the same reference in the text of an article is an indication of the significance of the cited work for the citing work then the set of self-citations clearly stands out as having a particular prominence among the other references. Contrary to expectation, the results of the study showed no significant relationship between the size of the bibliography and the extent of self-citing. There was, moreover, also no significant relationship between the amount of self-citing and the productivity of the author.

Lawani (1982) distinguishes two genera of author self-citations: synchronous and diachronous self-citations. An author's synchronous self-citations are those contained in the references the author gives (those studied by Tagliacozzo; self-citations on article level which are not on author level do not play any role here), whereas diachronous self-citations are those included in the citations an author receives (and these include self-citations on article level). The synchronous self-citation rate, or better, the self-citing rate of an author over a given period is the ratio of this author's self-citations divided by the number of references given during this period. Note that these references (to oneself or to others) do not need to be different, and usually are not. The diachronous self-citation rate, or better, the self-cited rate of an author over a given period is the ratio of this author's self-citations divided by the total number of received citations during this period. For example, if an author writes a paper with 20 references, 4 of which refer to the author's own work, then the self-citing rate is $4/20 = 0.2$. If he receives during one month 30 citations, 10 of which originate from his own work, then the self-cited rate is $10/30 \approx 0.33$.

Besides an author's self-citing and self-cited rate on may also define and study a research group's, a journal's or a country's self-citing and self-cited rate.

Lawani (1982) indicates the practical implications of high or low self-citing and self-cited rates. High self-cited rates may be an indication of poor research (the author is mainly cited by himself). On a more positive note, White (2001) writes that a high self-cited rate may indicate intellectual isolation. Moreover, a researcher's self-citing rate may be high, but if this is combined with a low self-cited rate this may suggest that the researcher is a productive, key figure in his research specialty.

A journal's self-citing and self-cited rates can be obtained from data available in the JCR.

Porter (1977) found that it does not matter whether one includes author self-citations or not, at least when using citation analysis to study science subfields or any other large unit. Glänzel et al. (2004) point out that author self-citations are an organic part of the citation network. They can be measured and modelled and consequently, significant deviations of reference standards can be determined.

5.6.3 Coauthorship and Counting Contributions

We will now turn to the difficult problem of coauthorship and its influence on counting contributions (of authors, institutions, countries). Usually, scientists consider each article with their name in the by-line as one of their articles. For an outsider, however, this is not so straightforward. The productivity of author A who wrote four articles on her own, is certainly larger than that of author B who wrote four articles in collaboration with three colleagues (during the same period).

Generally speaking there are nowadays five major approaches for counting contributions depending on the number and/or position of authors in the by-line:

- First author count (also called straight count) in which only the first author receives a credit.
- Major contribution count in which the first author(s) and the corresponding author(s) (if different) receive a credit. One either gives a full credit (one) to each major contributor; or credits are fractionalized over major contributors.
- Complete or normal count, giving each contributing author a full credit.
- Complete-normalized fractional counting in which each coauthor receives $1/n$ credits for an article with n authors.
- Other methods for fractional counting are proposed in the literature, among which harmonic counting is the most interesting one, see further.

Counting methods can be subdivided into four groups, according to two times two criteria. The first makes a distinction between giving credit to each author and sometimes giving no credit to some authors.

The second one assigns credits as whole numbers or allows for fractions, in which case the sum of all fractional credits is one. Table 5.1 illustrates this two-fold distinction.

Harmonic counting (i.e., giving credit according to a harmonic progression) was originally suggested by Hodge and Greenberg (1981). This proposal went virtually unnoticed until it was re-proposed by Hagen (2008). In this proposal, the author ranked at the i-th place in the author by-line receives a credit equal to

$$\frac{\frac{1}{i}}{\left(1 + \frac{1}{2} + \frac{1}{3} + ... + \frac{1}{n}\right)} \tag{5.1}$$

Hagen (2010) proposed to adapt this formula in cases where it is shown that the last author played a special role, e.g., it is the corresponding author. In that case the first and the last author could receive an equal credit. We note that any method, such as this, that uses the order in which authors are placed in the byline is only valid if this order really represents the importance of the contribution, with a possible exception for the last author. Complete-normalized counting and harmonic counting are examples of fractional counting: the sum of credits of all coauthors always equals one.

Giving only the first author a full credit (first author count) is an easy method. When, however, alphabetical order is applied, this method makes no sense (unless, maybe, for very large units, as when comparing the contributions of countries). Lindsey (1980) notes that the straight count procedure should be considered a sampling strategy. As such, it should be examined in terms of representativeness. On author level this method presupposes that the set of papers on which a scientist's name occurs first (including solo-authored papers) is a representative sample of all that scientist's papers. In this context we also mention that Zuckerman (1968)

Table 5.1 Counting methods

	Each contributor receives some credit	Some contributors may not receive any credit
Credits are natural numbers	Complete or normal count	First author count; Major contribution count
Credits may be fractions, summing to one	Complete-normalized fractional counting; Harmonic counting	Fractionalized major contribution count

and Garfield (1982) found that eminent scientists received nearly twice as many citations as secondary authors in the sense of not being the first author than as primary ones. This shows that eminent scientists have been systematically ceding first authorship to their junior collaborators. This practice was termed *noblesse oblige* by Harriet Zuckerman. Nowadays there is probably little noblesse included as very often the hard work and sometimes the main idea comes from the first author, while the last one (the eminent scientist) plays a more supervising role. Anyway, we are convinced, with Lindsey (1980), that there is neither strong empirical evidence nor theoretical rationale to support using straight counts.

Giving each author a full credit favors authors who often collaborate. For this reason this method is sometimes referred to as inflated counts. Especially in cases of mega- or hyperauthorship, say 50 authors or more it does not seem right that each author receives a full credit.

Major contribution count seems more correct, but still some contributors receive no credit. The habit of giving first and corresponding authors a special treatment has led to the strange (i.e., mathematically illogical) phenomenon of several first authors and/or several corresponding authors. Hu (2009) showed that in the *Journal of Biological Chemistry* this phenomenon occurred in about 8% of the articles in 1999 and increased to about 26% in 2008.

Adjusting credits to all authors seems the best method. If no information is given one should use complete-normalized counting, while when it is known that authors are listed in order of importance harmonic counting, (possibly adapted for the role of the last author) seems the best solution. Of course, also here mega-authorship leads to a practical problem.

Note that all methods except complete count and major contribution count, assign a unit credit to one article. Complete counts assign a credit of n (if there are n authors) to one article and major contribution count gives as many credits as there are major contributors. Of course, it is also imaginable that each major contributor receives a fraction of a credit in such a way that also for this method one article leads to a total of one credit.

It is easy to understand that different counting methods may lead to different rankings among authors (rankings according to the number of articles to which they contributed). We provide an illustration.

Determine from Table 5.2 the credits received by each author separately (authors A, B, C, D, E, F) and their publication rank by using first

Table 5.2 Data for the author credit problem

Art 1 A–B–C–F	Art 2 A–C–B–D	Art 3 C–E	Art 4 D	Art 5 C–D

Table 5.3 Solution of the problem

	Credit (first author count)	Rank	Credit (normal counts)	Rank	Credit (fractional)	Rank
A	2	1	2	3	$(1/4) + (1/4) = 0.5$	3
B	0	4	2	3	$(1/4) + (1/4) = 0.5$	3
C	2	1	4	1	$(1/4) + (1/4) + (1/2) + (1/2) = 1.5$	2
D	1	3	3	2	$(1/4) + 1 + (1/2) = 1.75$	1
E	0	4	1	5	$1/2$	3
F	0	4	1	5	$1/4$	6

Source: Data in Table 5.2. One could also give an average rank, but that is not essential here. In that case first author count leads to three authors at rank 5 (instead of rank 4).

author counts, normal counts and complete-normalized (fractional) counts. Authors are given as in the by-line of their articles.

The solution is given in Table 5.3.

Counting contributions of universities or countries is even more complicated. One method consists of giving an equal credit for every address that occurs in the by-line, irrespective of the number of collaborators with that address.

An example

Assume that an article has three authors: one from country C_1 and two from country C_2, belonging to the same department. The author from country C_1 is first author, while one of the other authors is corresponding author.

Applying First Author Count gives one credit to country C_1, and no credits to country C_2.

Applying major contribution count gives one credit to country C_1 and one credit to country C_2; or alternatively (when normalizing), half a credit to each country.

Applying Normal Counts gives country C_1 one credit, but now country C_2 receives two credits.

Applying fractional counting (we illustrate the two main cases).

Using complete-normalized counting assigns 1/3 of a credit to country C_1 and 2/3 of a credit to country C_2 (based on the number of authors). If this information is not available (which used to be the case in the WoS before 2008) then one assigns credits based on the institutional addresses. Then country C_1 and country C_2 each receive one half of a credit.

Harmonic counting gives country C_1 $1/(1 + 1/2 + 1/3) = 6/11$ credits and country C_2 $(1/2)/(1 + 1/2 + 1/3) + (1/3)(1 + 1/2 + 1/3) = 3/11 + 2/11 = 5/11$ credits. Again, if this information is not available then C_1 receives $1/(1 + 1/2) = 2/3$ credits and country C_2 1/3 of a credit.

Obviously the way in which credits are assigned can influence the outcome and hence country rankings to a large extent. This has been stressed by Gauffriau and Larsen in several publications see e.g., Gauffriau and Larsen (2005a,b). Although assigning credits based on the number of contributing authors of a given country (possibly taking the author rank in the by-line into account), is the only correct way, it is only since 2008 that this is possible in the WoS. Before that time WoS records just gave a list of authors and a list of institutes (including the country of the institute).

Counting citations leads to the same problems as counting publications. Yet, one may say that the problem is doubled as one may study citations given and citations received, and the problem occurs in the two directions. Citations are assigned according to the contributions of each author. If an article with 4 authors received 10 citations, complete-normalized counting assigns 2.5 citations to each author. If, however, one has used first author count, then those ten citations are assigned to the first author, and the other ones do not receive any citation credit.

5.7 A NOTE ON EPONYMS

It is sometimes said that eponyms present the highest form of scientific recognition. An eponym is a thing, a theorem or a method named after a person. Well-known examples are Newton's Laws, Kepler's laws, Pascal's triangle, the periodic table of Mendeleev, the Erlenmeyer flask, Einstein's relativity theory or Alzheimer disease. In the field of informetrics we know the laws of Bradford, Lotka, Zipf and the Hirsch index (all discussed further on). Yet, some remarks are in order. First, to eponymize is naming things after persons, rather than scientific content. Second, many eponyms are given to the wrong person (but this also happens for citations). In this context one uses the term palimpsests. Zipf was not the first to observe or describe the regularity that bears his name (Rousseau, 2002a) and Pascal's triangle was known to Jia Xian (c. 1010–1070) in China and to Omar Khayyam (1048–1131) in Persia. We even have Stigler's law (Stigler, 1980) which states that no scientific discovery is named after its original discoverer (of course, Stigler's law was not discovered by Stigler).

5.8 THE ETHICS OF CITING

Citing is also an ethical question. Citing an article, and consequently, its authors is recognizing an intellectual debt. Honesty requires that this is effectively done. Not citing on purpose is a form of dishonesty, sometimes referred to as idea-plagiarism (Chaddah, 2014). Yet not trying to retrieve who was first or who discussed a topic in depth is a form of laziness that takes from others something they deserve. As with most ethical problems it is difficult to draw a line. Which references should one include in a reference list and which are considered not influential enough for one's research? Moreover, related to the retrieval question: Should a western scientist ask a specialist to search in Russian, Persian, Chinese, or Japanese language databases? And should one expect Russian, Iranian, Chinese, or Japanese colleagues to search through English, French, or Spanish language databases?

Kelly P. Downing in (Sills, 2014) warns against not checking original sources and hence perpetuation of invalidated ideas or misinterpretation of data.

The more citations play a role in evaluations of scientists the more not citing takes away from colleagues not only honor or prestige, but also money and possibly progress in their career.

5.9 CITATION NETWORKS AND THE MATHEMATICS OF CITATION

5.9.1 Generalities on Citation Networks or Graphs

When document d_i cites document d_j this can be represented by an arrow linking a node representing d_i to a node representing d_j (see Fig. 5.3).

In this way the documents of a collection D form a directed graph or network, which is called a citation network. Using a so-called adjacency matrix is another way of representing a citation network. In this representation one considers a matrix (a table consisting of rows and columns). In this adjacency matrix a 1 is placed in the cell for which the row corresponds to

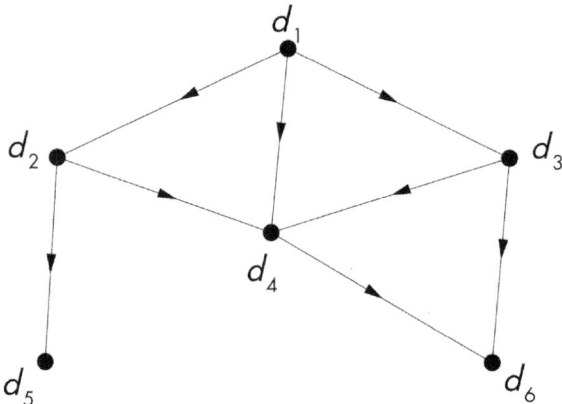

Figure 5.3 A citation network.

Table 5.4 The adjacency matrix of Fig. 5.3

	d_1	d_2	d_3	d_4	d_5	d_6
d_1	0	1	1	1	0	0
d_2	0	0	0	1	1	0
d_3	0	0	0	1	0	1
d_4	0	0	0	0	0	1
d_5	0	0	0	0	0	0
d_6	0	0	0	0	0	0

Table 5.5 Representation of the network of Fig. 5.3 by a list of outlinks

Citing document	Cited document
d	d_2, d_3, d_4
d_2	d_4, d_5
d_3	d_4, d_6
d_4	d_6

the citing document d_i and the column to the cited document d_j. Fig. 5.3 and Table 5.4 illustrate this, where an arrow means "cites."

Of course, it is also possible to reverse the arrows to obtain the graph of the relation "is cited by." The adjacency matrix of this new graph is merely the transpose (exchange rows and columns) of the adjacency matrix of the citation network of the "cites" relation. Another representation consists in just listing all outlinks, see Table 5.5. As a real-world citation network is often very sparse (many empty cells in the matrix) this third method is often a parsimonious representation.

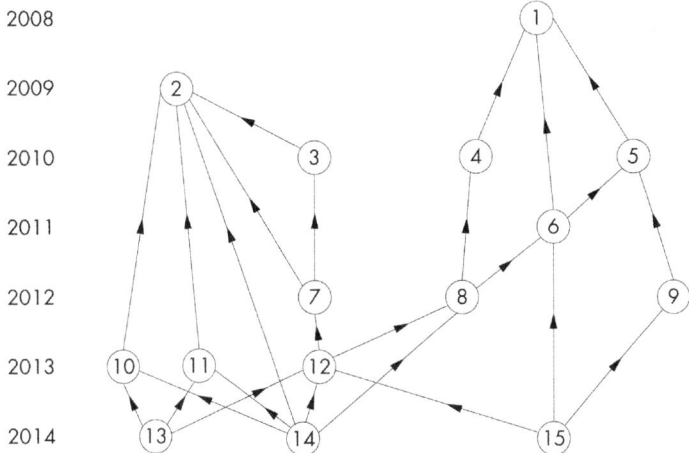

Figure 5.4 A citation network representing the conflation of two ideas. *Based on (Cawkell, 1974).*

In Fig. 5.4 circles representing articles are arranged in horizontal rows by year of publication, with the most recent year (2014) at the bottom. As it is a citation graph an arrow means "cites." From this graph deductions can be made without any knowledge of the exact subject content (Cawkell, 1974). Paper number 2 has had a considerable impact upon later work, since it has been heavily cited (directly and indirectly). Papers 13 and 14 are probably rather similar in subject content as they contain common references to articles 10, 11, and 12 (they are bibliographically coupled, see Section 5.10). Before the year 2013 the articles in Fig. 5.4 formed two disconnected groups. In that year articles 7 and 8 were cocited by article 12 (the notion of cocitation will also be explained in Section 5.10). The relation between the two groups was consolidated the next year, as for instance, articles 8 and 12 were cocited by articles 14, and article 6 by 13 and 15. This observation implies that the relatedness between the two groups was first perceived by the author(s) of article 12.

5.9.2 Mathematical Theorems About Citation Graphs

Theorem 1 (Kochen, 1974, p. 17): Let d be any document and let $C(d)$ be the set of all references in d; similarly, let $C^{-1}(d)$ be the set of all documents from which d received a citation. If d_0 is now a fixed document then

$$d_0 \in \bigcap_{d \in C(d_0)} C^{-1}(d) \qquad (5.2)$$

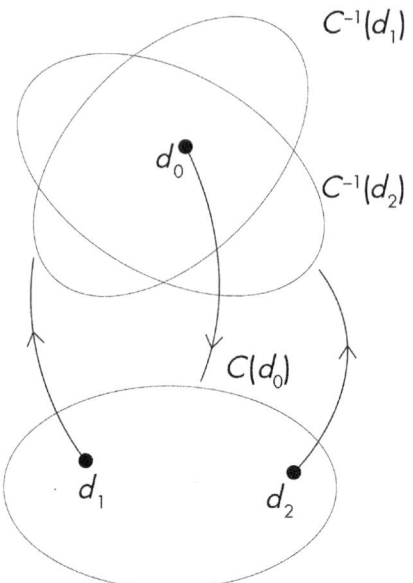

Figure 5.5 An illustration of Theorem 1.

The proof of this theorem is obvious once we understand the mathematical formalism. Formula (5.2) merely states that when we form the collection of all documents cited by d_0 (this is d_0's reference list, denoted as $C(d_0)$), and we pick any document d in this collection, then d_0 belongs to the set of all documents that cite d. See also Fig. 5.5.

The next result is somewhat more intricate, but also more important as it leads to the notion of *cycling*. We note that a directed graph, such as a citation graph, is said to be weakly connected if for any two vertices or nodes there is a path of edges joining them, ignoring the directions of the edges (see also Section 10.1).

Theorem 2 (based on Kochen (1974, p. 18)): If the citation graph of a nonempty set D of N documents is weakly connected then, for any d_0 in D:

$$D = \bigcup_{j=0}^{N-1} C_j \qquad (5.3)$$

where $C_j = \bigcup_{d_j \in C_{j-1}} \left(C(d_j) \cup C^{-1}(d_j) \right)$, $j > 0$ and $C_0 = \{d_0\}$.

Proof.: Pick any document d_0 in D and recall that $C(d_0)$ is the set of all references of d_0 and $C^{-1}(d_0)$ the set of all documents that cite d_0. Then C_1 is the set of all documents which either cite d_0 or are cited by d_0. By the requirement of weak connectedness, C_1 is not empty unless D is equal to the singleton $\{d_0\}$, in which case the theorem is proved. So we can proceed and form C_2. By Theorem 1 we know that d_0 belongs to C_2.

To show that $\cup_{j=0}^{N-1} C_j$ is equal to D we suppose that some d in D does not belong to $\cup_{j=0}^{N-1} C_j$. This assumption leads to a contradiction: as there is a path, necessarily finite, joining d to d_0 there is a number $j \leq N-1$ such that $d \in C_j$.

This theorem yields an algorithm for obtaining all the documents in a given collection, provided the collection is reasonably homogeneous, so that its citation graph is weakly connected. Moreover, if D is a large computer file, then the algorithm provides a procedure for exploring the core of a topic (take d_0 to be a core document) and moving further and further towards the boundaries. This method is known as "cycling." A mathematical discussion of cycling can be found in (Cummings & Fox, 1973; Garner, 1967).

The following results provide useful insight into the structure of a citation

Theorem 3 (Kochen, 1974, p. 21): *The average number of references per document times the number of documents in a collection under investigation is equal to the average number of citations to a reference item in the collection times the total number of different references.*

Proof.: Let C be the citation matrix of the collection under investigation. Then $c_{ij} = 1$ if document d_i cites reference r_j and $c_{ij} = 0$ if it does not; note that the index i refers to citing document i, while the index j refers to cited document j. The columns of this citation matrix contain only those documents that are cited at least once by the documents in the collection. On the one hand, if there are n source documents, the average number of references per document is:

$$\frac{1}{n} \sum_{i=1}^{n} \left(\sum_{j=1}^{p} c_{ij} \right) \tag{5.4}$$

Here p denotes the total number of different references and $\sum_{j=1}^{p} c_{ij}$ is the number of references contained in d_i. The citation matrix is an (n,p) matrix. Then the average number of references per document times the number of documents is equal to:

$$\sum_{i=1}^{n} \left(\sum_{j=1}^{p} c_{ij} \right) \tag{5.5}$$

which is the total number of 1's in the citation matrix. On the other hand, we see that the average number of citations to a document in the collection is

$$\frac{1}{p} \sum_{j=1}^{p} \left(\sum_{i=1}^{n} c_{ij} \right) \tag{5.6}$$

where $\sum_{i=1}^{n} c_{ij}$ is the number of citations received by the j-th reference from documents in the collection. Then, the average number of received citations times the total number of different references is also equal to the number of 1's in the citation matrix. This proves the theorem.

An application. Assume that you have a $(20,120)$ citation matrix and you know that the average number of references per document is 10.

How many documents are there in this collection? And what is the average number of received citations for the references in this collection?

From the dimensions of the citation matrix we know that the collection contains 20 documents (and that there are 120 different references).

The average number of citations is then equal to $(1/120) \times (10 \times 20) = 5/3 \approx 1.67$.

5.9.3 The Publication and Citation Process Described by Matrices

Although this section is useful for performing or checking some calculations, it may safely be skipped by those readers who are not really familiar with matrix calculations. In Subsection 5.9.1 we have shown how a citation matrix is written and how it is related to a citation network. In this section we will show how notions such as the number of articles, number of references in a given paper or the number of references common to two articles can be obtained (automatically) from such a matrix. Similarly, starting from an author-article matrix we will derive the number of authors, the number of contributions of a particular author and the number of common contributors. This section is based on (Krauze & McGinnis, 1979).

Assume that an (m,n) matrix C, with elements c_{ij}, is a citation matrix. This means that $c_{ij} = 1$ if article i cites document j and that $c_{ij} = 0$ if this is not the case. Recall that c_{ij} denotes the element, entry or cell (three terms used here as synonyms) situated at the intersection of the i-th row and j-th column.

We know from the dimensions of the citation matrix that we consider a collection of m articles, citing in total n different documents. Mathematical relations become easy if one knows how to multiply matrices. Readers who know this or are not interested may safely skip the next paragraph.

Matrices and how to Multiply Them

Let A and B be matrices. Let A be an (m,n)-matrix and let B be a (k,l)-matrix. The dimensions of a matrix can be any couple of strict positive natural numbers. An $(m,1)$ is a column matrix (or column vector); an $(1,l)$-matrix is a row matrix (or row vector); an $(1,1)$-matrix is just a number. If one or both of the dimensions of a matrix P is known to be one, then the corresponding 1 is not written: one writes $P_{j,1}$ simply as P_j (or p_j, using the convention to write a matrix with a majuscule and its entries with the corresponding minuscule). For further use we note that if C is a matrix then C^t is its transpose. This means that rows and columns have been interchanged. If C is an (m,n)-matrix then C^t is an (n,m)-matrix and $(C)_{ij} = c_{ij} = (C^t)_{ji}$.

First we note that the matrix multiplication $A * B$ is in general not the same as $B * A$. It might even occur that one of these two multiplications is possible (is defined), while the other one is not. Indeed $A * B$ is defined only if $n = k$; similarly $B * A$ is only defined if $l = m$. Assuming that $A * B$ is defined, hence that A is an (m,n) —matrix and B is an (n,l)-matrix then the resulting matrix $C = A * B$ has dimensions (m,l). The element c_{ij} of the matrix C is then defined as: $c_{ij} = \sum_{k=1}^{n} a_{ik} \cdot b_{kj}$. This is all one has to know to understand matrix multiplication.

An example: If $A = \begin{pmatrix} 1 & 0 \\ -1 & 2 \end{pmatrix}$ and $B = \begin{pmatrix} 0 & 1 & -1 \\ 4 & 6 & 10 \end{pmatrix}$ then $A * B = C = \begin{pmatrix} 0 & 1 & -1 \\ 8 & 11 & 21 \end{pmatrix}$.

Let $D = \begin{pmatrix} 1 \\ 2 \\ 0 \end{pmatrix}$ and suppose that we want to calculate $D^{t*}D$. First we note that this multiplication is mathematically possible as the number of columns of D^t is equal to the number of rows of D. The result of this matrix multiplication is: $\begin{pmatrix} 1 & 2 & 0 \end{pmatrix} * \begin{pmatrix} 1 \\ 2 \\ 0 \end{pmatrix} = 1 + 4 + 0 = 5$ (this is a (1,1)-matrix or a number, sometimes referred to as a scalar when matrices, vectors and numbers (scalars) are used in the same context).

Note that also D^*D^t exists. This is a (3,3)-matrix obtained as follows:

$$\begin{pmatrix} 1 \\ 2 \\ 0 \end{pmatrix} * \begin{pmatrix} 1 & 2 & 0 \end{pmatrix} = \begin{pmatrix} 1 & 2 & 0 \\ 2 & 4 & 0 \\ 0 & 0 & 0 \end{pmatrix}$$

Using matrix multiplication we now prove four propositions showing how to derive the number of references of a given article, the number of articles written by a given author, the number of citations received by a given paper and the number of coauthors of a given paper, when a larger article-article matrix C or an author-article matrix W is given.

Proposition 1: Given the citation matrix C, the number of references of a given article d_i is $\sum_{j=1}^{n} c_{ij} = (C * U)_i = (C * C^t)_{ii}$, where U is the column vector completely consisting of 1's.

Proof: This result is easy to see since the C matrix consists of zeros and ones, ones if the corresponding cell is occupied and zero otherwise. Keeping the row i fixed $\sum_{j=1}^{n} c_{ij}$ is just the number of ones in the i-th row. This is the number of times document d_i has a reference, or the total number of references of document d_i.

Now $C * U$ is an $(m,1)$ matrix, i.e., a column vector. $(C * U)_i$ is the i-th element of this column vector. It is equal to: $(C * U)_i = \sum_{j=1}^{n} c_{ij} U_j = \sum_{j=1}^{n} c_{ij} 1 = \sum_{j=1}^{n} c_{ij}$.

Similarly $(C * C^t)_{ii} = \sum_{j=1}^{n} (C)_{ij}.(C^t)_{ji} = \sum_{j=1}^{n} c_{ij} c_{ij} = \sum_{j=1}^{n} c_{ij}$. The last equality follows from the facts that $1^2 = 1$ and $0^2 = 0$.

Next we consider an author-article matrix W.

Assume that the (m,n)-matrix W, with elements w_{ij}, is an author-article matrix. This means that $w_{ij} = 1$ if author i has authored (as sole author or as coauthor) article j, and zero if this is not the case. The following proposition is just a re-interpretation (in a different context) of the previous one.

Proposition 2: The number of articles of a given author a_i is $\sum_{j=1}^{n} w_{ij} = (W * U)_i = (W * W^t)_{ii}$, where U is the column vector consisting completely of 1's.

The proof is exactly the same as that of Proposition 1. The only difference is that C is replaced by W. Clearly similar propositions hold with other matrices. This shows the power of mathematics. One proof holds in all similar circumstances; only the interpretation is different.

Proposition 3: The number of citations received by a given paper r_j is $\sum_{i=1}^{m} c_{ij} = (U^t * C)_j = (C^t * C)_{jj}$

Similarly we have Proposition 4.

The number of coauthors of paper j is $\sum_{i=1}^{m} w_{ij} = (U^t * W)_j = (W^t * W)_{jj}$

Again the same calculations prove Propositions 3 and 4. We prove Proposition 4 as an example.

Proof: The matrix W consists of zeros and ones, ones if the corresponding cell is occupied and zero otherwise. Keeping the column j fixed $\sum_{i=1}^{m} w_{ij}$ is just the number of ones in the j-th column. This is the number of times paper r_j has an author, or the total number of authors of paper r_j.

Now $U^t * W$ is an $(n,1)$ matrix, i.e., a column vector. $(U^t * W)_j$ is the j-th element of this column vector. It is equal to:

$$(U^t * W)_j = \sum_{i=1}^{m} (U^t)_i w_{ij} = \sum_{i=1}^{m} 1.w_{ij} = \sum_{i=1}^{m} w_{ij}.$$

Similarly $(W^t * W)_{jj} = \sum_{i=1}^{m} (W^t)_{ji}.(W)_{ij} = \sum_{i=1}^{m} w_{ij} w_{ij} = \sum_{i=1}^{m} w_{ij},$ where, again, this last equality follows from the facts that $1^2 = 1$ and $0^2 = 0$.

5.10 BIBLIOGRAPHIC COUPLING AND COCITATION ANALYSIS

5.10.1 Bibliographic Coupling

Bibliographic coupling and cocitation are two notions used to describe mutual relations in a citation network. Until now we studied relations that can be described as Cit(A;B), i.e., A cites B. In this section we move up one level of abstraction and study relations of the form Cit(A;B,C) and Cit(A,B;C). Cit(A;B,C) stands for A cites B and C, while Cit(A,B;C) stands for A and B cite C.

If Cit(A,B; C) holds, i.e., articles A and B both cite article C then we say that A and B are bibliographically coupled. The term bibliographic coupling has been formally introduced by Kessler (1962, 1963) but the idea dates from somewhat earlier (Fano, 1956). Indeed, using the same underlying mathematical relation as for bibliographic coupling, Fano pointed out that documents in a library could be grouped on the basis of use rather than content.

Articles A and B may have other articles, besides C, occurring in their reference list. The number of articles that their reference lists have in common is called the bibliographic coupling strength, see Fig. 5.6. Using the terminology of set theory we can say that the bibliographic coupling strength of two articles is the number of elements in the intersection of their reference lists.

The relative bibliographic coupling strength is the number of common items divided by the number of items in the union of their two reference list. This notion was introduced in Sen and Gan (1983). The relative bibliographic coupling strength is actually a Jaccard index (Jaccard, 1901).

In the language of set theory bibliographic coupling, bibliographic coupling strength and relative bibliographic coupling strength are

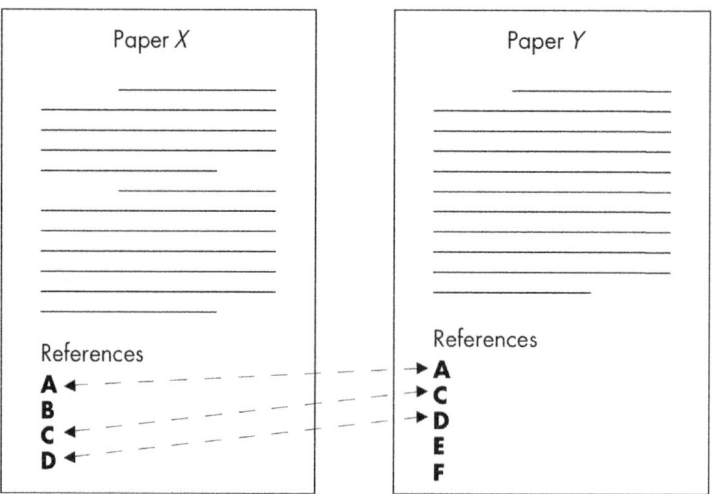

Figure 5.6 Bibliographic coupling between papers X and Y and cocitation (between e.g., papers A and B).

defined as follows. Let X and Y be two documents. If $R(X)$ denotes the set of papers in the reference list of document X and $R(Y)$ the set of papers in the reference list of Y then $R(X) \cap R(Y)$, the intersection of $R(X)$ and $R(Y)$, is the set of papers belonging to these two reference lists. If this set is nonempty then X and Y are bibliographically coupled. The number of elements in this intersection, denoted as $\#(R(X) \cap R(Y))$ is the bibliographic coupling strength of X and Y. The relative bibliographic coupling strength frequency can easily be defined using the notation of set theory. It is:

$$\frac{(R(X) \cap R(Y))}{(R(X) \cup R(Y))} \tag{5.7}$$

We note that the bibliographic coupling strength of two documents is at most equal to the length of the smallest reference list of the two. The bibliographic coupling strength of two documents is fixed once the most recent one of the two is published, but the number of documents to which a given document is bibliographically coupled may increase over time and has no theoretical limit.

Bibliographic coupling is a symmetric relation: if document d_1 is bibliographically coupled to document d_2 then automatically document d_2 is bibliographically coupled to document d_1, and this with equal absolute and relative coupling strength. One may agree, as in (Egghe & Rousseau, 1990) that a document is bibliographically coupled to itself, making the bibliographic coupling relation reflexive. Yet, this relation is not necessarily transitive: If d_1 and d_2 are bibliographically coupled and also d_2 and d_3 are bibliographically coupled then there is no reason to conclude that d_1 and d_3 are bibliographically coupled (readers can easily provide an example themselves). Contrary to what is claimed in (Egghe & Rousseau, 1990, p. 238) the relation *is* transitive if it is known that documents d_1, d_2, and d_3 have exactly one reference.

Kessler (1963) saw bibliographic coupling in the first place as a retrieval tool. Knowing that a paper P_0 is relevant to a user's search, an automatic retrieval system would also retrieve (or suggest to retrieve) all papers that are bibliographically coupled to P_0. This idea has been taken up by the WoS as a suggestion to expand the search with closely related papers (by bibliographically coupled papers with a high coupling strength).

Kessler remarks that a paper's set of articles with which it is bibliographically coupled can be considered its "logical references." This might be particularly true at the moment of its publication.

The major theoretical criticism of the concept of bibliographic coupling comes from Martyn (1964). He contends that a bibliographic coupling unit is not a valid measure of relationship because the fact that two papers have a common reference is no guarantee that both papers are referring to the same piece of information.

Finally, using the notation of Subsection 5.9.3 we note that the bibliographically coupling strength between documents d_i and d_j, with C the citation matrix of the field including d_i and d_j is given by:

$$\sum_{k=1}^{n} c_{ik}c_{jk} = (C * C^t)_{ij} \tag{5.8}$$

Indeed, terms in the sum on the left hand side are zero or one. The value one only happens in the case that document k is cited by document d_i and by document d_j. These occurrences are added, yielding the bibliographic coupling strength. Finally $(C * C^t)_{ij} = \sum_{k=1}^{n} (C)_{ik} \cdot (C^t)_{kj} = \sum_{k=1}^{n} c_{ik}c_{jk}$. To make this less abstract, we include a concrete example. Consider a matrix M. Its columns denote references and its rows articles (Art1, Art2, Art3, and Art4). A value 1 in cell (k,l) means that article k has article l among its references; a zero value in cell (k,l) means that this is not the case.

$$M = \begin{pmatrix} 1 & 1 & 1 & 1 & 1 \\ 0 & 0 & 1 & 1 & 0 \\ 1 & 0 & 0 & 0 & 1 \\ 0 & 1 & 1 & 1 & 0 \end{pmatrix}.$$

Its transpose M^t is:
$$\begin{pmatrix} 1 & 0 & 1 & 0 \\ 1 & 0 & 0 & 1 \\ 1 & 1 & 0 & 1 \\ 1 & 1 & 0 & 1 \\ 1 & 0 & 1 & 0 \end{pmatrix}$$

The multiplication $M * M^t$ gives the bibliographic coupling matrix of the articles Art1 to Art4. This matrix is symmetric by definition.

$$M * M^t = \begin{pmatrix} 5 & 2 & 2 & 3 \\ 2 & 2 & 0 & 2 \\ 2 & 0 & 2 & 0 \\ 3 & 2 & 0 & 3 \end{pmatrix}.$$

Checking, we see that the value 3 in cell (1,4) indicates that articles 1 and 4 have a bibliographic coupling strength equal to 3. This is indeed the case (see matrix M). The values on the diagonal show the number of references of each article.

We propose the following (somewhat tricky) exercises on bibliographic coupling and relative bibliographic coupling.

Article A has 9 references; the relative bibliographic coupling of articles A and B is 7/13. How many references does article B have?

Solution

There are 7 references in the intersection of the two reference lists, hence there are 2 references in A which are not references of B. Hence there are 4 references of B which are not references of A. Consequently B has 11 references.

Try now to solve the following exercise. Article A has 6 references; the relative bibliographic coupling of articles A and B is 0.1666667 (rounded). How many references does article B have? Hint: there are six different solutions.

Solution

We must realize that the number 0.1666667 is equal to $1/6 = 2/12 = 3/18 = 4/24 = 5/30 = 6/36 = 7/42 = \ldots$ Writing these fractions we see the exact number of references in the intersection of the two reference lists. As A has a total of 6 references 7/42 (referring to the case of 7 references in the intersection) cannot occur. This reasoning leads to six different solutions presented in Table 5.6. Note that, for the first problem, there was a unique solution, contrary to the second one.

Table 5.6 Solution of the bibliographic coupling problem

Number of articles in A's reference list, not belonging to B's reference list	Joint references	Number of articles in B's reference list, not belonging to A's reference list	Length of B's reference list
5	1	0	1
4	2	6	8
3	3	12	15
2	4	18	22
1	5	24	29
0	6	30	36

5.10.2 Cocitations

A Soviet information scientist (Irina Marshakova) and an American one (Henry Small) independently proposed the same variation on bibliographic coupling. Small (1973) and Marshakova (1973) both suggested cocitation of documents as a method of measuring relationships between documents.

Two documents are said to be cocited when they both appear in the reference list of the same document. That is, if the relation Cit(A;B,C) holds, documents B and C are cocited. The cocitation frequency is defined as the frequency with which two documents are cited together. Thus, while bibliographic coupling focuses on groups of papers which cite the same source document, cocitation focuses on references which frequently come in pairs (see Fig. 5.6). In the Soviet (Russian) literature bibliographic coupling is said to be retrospective while cocitation is called prospective coupling (Marshakova, 1973).

Alternatively, by using the language of set theory, one can define the cocitation frequency of two documents X and Y as follows. If $S(X)$ is the set of papers citing document X and $S(Y)$ is the set of papers citing document Y then $S(X) \cap S(Y)$, the intersection of $S(X)$ and $S(Y)$, is the set of papers citing X and Y. If this set is nonempty then X and Y are cocited. The number of elements in this intersection, denoted as $\#(S(X) \cap S(Y))$ is the cocitation frequency of X and Y. Of course, to be precise one must also mention a citation window. It makes quite a difference if one studies cocitation over 1 year or over a decade.

The relative cocitation frequency can easily be defined using the notation of set theory. It is:

$$\frac{\#(S(X) \cap S(Y))}{\#(S(X) \cup S(Y))} \tag{5.9}$$

Of course the notions of bibliographic coupling and cocitation can be used for any type of documents (not just journal articles) such as books. The cocitation strength of two documents can never decrease.

Bibliographic coupling and cocitation of articles are not equivalence relations as they are not transitive in general. This is somewhat unfortunate as an equivalence relation leads to natural groups (equivalence classes). As there are no natural groups and obtaining nonoverlapping groups of related documents is highly desirable, groupings are obtained in a subjective manner, for instance by using a clustering algorithm, see e.g.,

Small (1986, 1993). Subjectivity enters in the choice of clustering algorithm and in the choice of a threshold value.

Similar to the case of bibliographic coupling we use the notation of Subsection 5.9.3 and matrices to describe the cocitation strength of two documents d_i and d_j with C the citation matrix of the field including d_i and d_j. This value is given by:

$$\sum_{k=1}^{m} c_{ki}c_{kj} = (C^t * C)_{ij} \tag{5.10}$$

Terms in the sum on the left hand side are zero or one. The value one only happens in the case that documents d_i and d_j are cited by document d_k. These occurrences are added, yielding the cocitation strength. Finally $(C^t * C)_{ij} = \sum_{k=1}^{m} (C^t)_{ik}.(C)_{kj} = \sum_{k=1}^{m} c_{ki}c_{kj}$.

Martyn's (1964) criticism on bibliographic coupling also applies to cocitation analysis. The fact that two papers are cocited does not imply that they contain similar pieces of information. Probably David Edge was the strongest opponent of cocitation analysis without human judgment. In his two papers *Why I am not a cocitationist* (Edge, 1977) and *Quantitative measures of communication in science: a critical review* (Edge, 1979) he expresses the view that quantitative methods such as cocitation analysis have only limited use. Among other objections he emphasizes the need to be able to see individual variations. It is often because individual scientists and groups do not share the consensus view, as shown by cocitation maps, that crucial innovative decisions are made.

Next we propose an exercise on bibliographic coupling and cocitation.

Consider articles A, B, C, and D. Their reference lists are shown in Table 5.7. Determine the order in which these articles are written. Next, determine the bibliographic coupling of each two articles and their relative bibliographic coupling. When this is done, determine the cocitation frequency and relative cocitation of each pair of articles occurring in at least one reference list. Article D does not belong to any reference list, and hence is not considered for this part (one may say that its cocitation frequency with any of the other articles is zero).

Solution

Among these articles article A was written first, followed, in this order, by articles C, B, and D. Indeed, A is in the reference list of C (and hence

Table 5.7 Data for the bibliographic coupling and cocitation problem
Articles

A	B	C	D
E	A	A	A
F	C	K	B
G	E	E	E
H	F	F	F
			G
			K

Table 5.8 Solution of the bibliographic coupling problem

Pair	Bibl. coupling	Relative bibl. coupling
A–B	2	2/6
A–C	2	2/6
A–D	3	3/7
B–C	3	3/5
B–D	3	3/7
C–D	4	4/6

Source: data in Table 5.7.

Table 5.9 Solution of the cocitation problem

Pair	Cocit	Rel cocit	Pair	Cocit	Rel cocit
A–B	1	1/3	C–F	1	1/4
A–C	1	1/3	C–G	0	0/2
A–E	3	3/4	C–H	0	0/2
A–F	3	3/4	C–K	0	0/3
A–G	1	1/4	E–F	4	4/4
A–H	0	0/4	E–G	2	2/4
A–K	2	2/3	E–H	1	1/4
B–C	0	0/2	E–K	2	2/4
B–E	1	1/4	F–G	2	2/4
B–F	1	1/4	F–H	1	1/4
B–G	1	1/2	F–K	2	2/4
B–H	0	0/2	G–H	1	1/2
B–K	1	1/2	G–K	1	1/3
C–E	1	1/4	H–K	0	0/3

Source: data in Table 5.7.

is older than C); C belongs to the reference list of B (and hence is older than B) and B is in the reference list of D.

Bibliographic coupling results are shown in Table 5.8.

Result for cocitation frequencies are shown in Table 5.9.

5.10.3 Applications of Bibliographic Coupling and Cocitation Analysis

Cocitation analysis and bibliographic coupling can be applied to many types of actors: authors, journals, countries (via their authors' affiliations), and so on. The most-studied type of cocitation analysis is Author Cocitation Analysis or ACA in short. ACA is most often used to analyze the intellectual structure of a scientific field. It was introduced by White and Griffith (1981). In 1990 Kate McCain published a technical overview of ACA, which became a standard for this particular application (McCain, 1990). She distinguishes four steps:

- In the first step one constructs the raw cocitation matrix (expressing how often two authors are cocited during a particular citation window, in a given database).
- Next this matrix is transformed into a proximity, an association or a similarity matrix.
- In the third step one applies multivariate statistical analysis. The technique applied in this step is often MDS (multidimensional scaling), cluster analysis, factor analysis or correspondence analysis (statistical techniques not studied in this book). This results in a two-dimensional map on which authors that are often cocited are represented in each other neighborhood. If this technique is successful authors with similar research interest form groups.
- In the last step one proposes an interpretation of the results.

In early applications of this four-step approach Pearson's correlation coefficient was used to obtain a similarity matrix. However, Ahlgren, Jarneving, and Rousseau (2003) have shown that it is possible that the Pearson correlation coefficient may lead to results leading to the opposite of what is desired (or what is logical). This observation is nowadays generally accepted leading to the use of Salton's cosine measure instead of the Pearson correlation coefficient. Moreover, Leydesdorff and Vaughan (2006) and later Zhou and Leydesdorff (2016) pointed out that one should start from the citation matrix and directly obtain a normalized cocitation matrix, where normalization can be performed by the cosine similarity.

Bibliographic coupling is used in a similar way as cocitation analysis, but is less popular. It seems that results are somewhat more difficult to interpret (cf. step 4). Yet, the WoS applies bibliographic coupling in its *Related Records* link (McVeigh, 2009).

5.11 TRI-CITATIONS

In (Small, 1974) the author defined tri-citation as follows. Let $S(X)$ be the set of papers citing document X, $S(Y)$ the set of papers citing document Y and $S(Z)$ the set of papers citing document Z, then the tri-citation frequency of documents X, Y, and Z is $\#(S(X) \cap S(Y) \cap S(Z))$. The relative tri-citation frequency can then be defined as

$$\frac{\#(S(X) \cap S(Y) \cap S(Z))}{\#(S(X) \cup S(Y) \cup S(Z))} \tag{5.11}$$

Similarly one may consider author tri-citation where $S(A)$ denotes all authors citing author A. Marion (2002) and McCain (2009, 2010) applied this approach with one specific restriction: they hold one author fixed, leading to a specific context (provided by the author who is kept unchanged) for the cocitation of the two other ones.

5.12 HIGHLY-CITED DOCUMENTS BECOME CONCEPT SYMBOLS

Garfield (1970) and Small (1978) have shown that highly-cited articles or books become symbols for the idea (or ideas) contained in them. In this way the act of citing becomes a form of labelling. The fact that this is actually possible is another argument in favor of citation analysis (and hence of citation indexes). Small (1978) investigated to which extent highly-cited articles in chemistry were cited for the same reason. He found many examples of high uniformity (the article was almost always cited for the same reason). He also found that such highly-cited articles are often included in groups of redundant citations. He concluded that such highly-cited articles become symbols for the concept with which they are associated: they become concept symbols or concept markers. From this investigation we may conclude that references can be seen as a part of the symbol language of science. We finally note that if an article and hence its author is always associated with a certain concept, this may lead to eponymisation.

Moreover, Susan Cozzens (1982, 1985) found that the meaning of a scientific document can be different for different groups, and may even change over time.

5.13 CITATION GENERATIONS

In the past little attention has been paid to different citation and reference generations. Although admittedly a complex issue, we think that taking more than one generation into account reveals better the structure of the network underlying progress in science. In particular, when studying a publication's contribution to the evolution of its field or to science in general, taking only direct citations into account, tells only part of the story. This has been pointed out in (Hu et al., 2011) where it is explained how citation generations can be studied from different angles. In this section we bring this line of reasoning to the attention of the reader. We start with the notion of a multiset.

5.13.1 Multisets

The notion of a multiset generalizes the notion of a set (Jouannaud & Lescanne, 1982). In a multiset an element can occur several times. Hence, $\{a,a,b,b,b\}$ may denote a multiset. As it is the case for sets, the order plays no role in a multiset, hence $\{a,a,b,b,b\} = \{b,a,b,a,b\}$. More formally a multiset may be defined as a couple consisting of a set X, and a function m from X to the natural numbers, such that $m(x)$ denotes the number of times x belongs to the multiset. As an example, the multiset $\{a,a,b,b,b\}$ is formally denoted as *(A,m)*, where

$$A = \{a, b\} \quad \text{and} \quad m{:}A \to \mathbf{N}{:} \begin{cases} a \to 2 \\ b \to 3 \end{cases}$$

5.13.2 Definition: Citation Generations in a Uni-Directed Citation Network

By the term *uni-directed citation network* we mean a citation network which has the property that if there is a directed link between node A and node B (in this order), then there is certainly no link between node B and node A (in that order). Consequently this notion applies to citation networks between single articles, but not to a network of journal citations (at least not in the usual sense).

We consider now a set of publications (the target group), for instance all articles coauthored by scientist S during a given period of time. This target group is called generation zero. Publications that cite generation zero publications or publications that cite publications citing generation zero publications and so on, build up higher order forward generations. These are called forward generations as one goes forward in time, hence these articles come later. Similarly, publications cited by the target group build up backward generations. However, there are many ways to define these other generations. Indeed, besides backward and forward generations, we have two times two types of definitions, denoted here using the symbols G^s, G^m, H^s, and H^m. Focusing on forward generations, they are defined as follows.

The first distinction is between disjoint and possibly overlapping generations. Beginning with the zero-th generation $G_0 = H_0$ we make the following distinction:

- Generation G_n contains all publications that cite at least one generation G_{n-1} publication and that do not yet belong to G_k, $k = 0, \ldots, n - 1$.
- Generation H_n contains all publications that cite at least one generation H_{n-1} publication.

Generations of type G_n are disjoint, while generations of type H_n usually are not.

The second distinction is between sets and multisets:

- A generation is a set: an element belongs to it or not, and this exactly once.
- A generation is a multiset: an element may belong to it several times.

This leads to four definitions of forward generations: Generations of type G, considered as sets, hence denoted as G^s, and considered as multisets, denoted as G^m; generations of type H, considered as sets, denoted as H^s, and considered as multisets, denoted as H^m. We, moreover, require that if an element belongs more than once to a multiset then it must be connected to the zero generation through different paths (this is a specification with respect to Hu et al. (2011)). Backward generations are defined in a similar way. The difference is that backward generations are determined by references (cited publications), while forward generations are determined by citing publications. Forward generations are indicated by adding a positive index, such as G_n^m, n being a positive natural number, while backward generations are indicated by a negative whole number, such as H_{-n}^s, where again n is a positive natural number. Note that the zero generation is always a set (not a *proper* multiset) and $G_0 = H_0$.

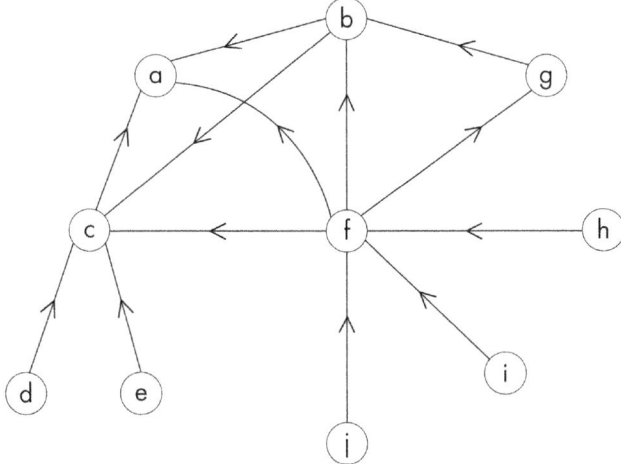

Figure 5.7 Generational structure.

5.13.3 An Illustrative Example

Consider the generational structure shown in Fig. 5.7; all publications are articles.

Using Fig. 5.7 we illustrate the difference between these definitions of generations.

Description of the citation network:

Let A = {a,b} be the target set; articles b, c, and f cite article a; article b moreover cites article c; articles d, e, and f cite article c; besides articles a and c, article f also cites articles b and g; article g cites article b; and finally, articles h, i, and j cite article f. We now describe the generations.

As sets we have:

$$G_0 = \{a, b\}$$

$$G_1^s = \{c, f, g\}$$

$$G_2^s = \{d, e, h, i, j\}$$

and

$$H_0 = \{a, b\}$$

$$H_1^s = \{b, c, f, g\}$$

$$H_2^s = \{b, f, g, d, e, h, i, j\}$$

$$H_3^s = \{f, g, h, i, j\}$$

$$H_4^s = \{f, h, i, j\}$$

$$H_5^s = \{h, i, j\}$$

There are now five generations, nodes h,i,j belong to the second, third, fourth as well as the fifth generation, because they can be linked to the target set in two, three, four, and five steps.

This illustrates the difference between overlapping and nonoverlapping generations.

As multisets however we have:

$$G_0 = \{a, b\}$$

$$G_1^m = \{c, f, f, g\}$$

$$G_2^m = \{d, e, h, i, j, h, i, j\}$$

Article f belongs twice to the first generation (as multisets) because it is linked to the target set via a and also via b. Finally:

$$H_0 = \{a, b\}$$

$$H_1^m = \{b, c, f, f, g\}$$

$$H_2^m = \{b, f, f, f, g, d, e, h, i, j, h, i, j\}$$

$$H_3^m = \{h, i, j, f, h, i, j, g, f, h, i, j\}$$

$$H_4^m = \{h, i, j, f, h, i, j\}$$

$$H_5^m = \{h, i, j\}$$

Because these overlapping multisets are not easy to see we provide a full explanation.

$H_1^m = \{b, c, f, f, g\}$, obtained from $b \to a$; $c \to a$; $f \to a$; $f \to b$; $g \to b$

$H_2^m = \{b, f, f, f, g, d, e, h, i, j, h, i, j\}$, is obtained from $b \to c \to a$; $f \to b \to a$; $f \to c \to a$; $f \to g \to b$; $g \to b \to a$; $d(e) \to c \to a$; $h(i,j) \to f \to b$; $h(i,j) \to f \to a$

$H_3^m = \{f, f, g, h, i, j, h, i, j, h, i, j\}$, is obtained from $f \to b \to c \to a$; $f \to g \to b \to a$; $g \to b \to c \to a$; $h(i,j) \to f \to g \to b$; $h(i,j) \to f \to c \to a$; $h(i,j) \to f \to b \to a$

$H_4^m = \{f, h, i, j, h, i, j\}$, is obtained from $f \to g \to b \to c \to a$; $h(i,j) \to f \to b \to c \to a$

and finally: $H_5^m = \{h, i, j\}$ is obtained from: $h(i,j) \to f \to g \to b \to c \to a$

This illustrates the use of multisets.

The oldest example we know of a scientometric article that shows explicitly how to calculate influences of several generations is (Rousseau, 1987). In that article we explained an algorithm, based on the so-called Gozinto theorem, to calculate the influence of backward generations on a target article. Generations are considered as sets, but an element is used in the calculation as often as it is cited. The article further used the idea of weighting citations based on their location in the article and the frequency of occurrence.

5.14 DELAYED RECOGNITION AND SLEEPING BEAUTIES

The term *sleeping beauty* (van Raan, 2004b) refers to a paper whose importance is not recognized for several years after publication (it is asleep) and then suddenly (kissed by a prince?) receives recognition and accrues many citations (they live happily ever after?). Although the term *sleeping beauty* in this context dates from the early 21st century, the phenomenon of delayed recognition or premature discovery has been observed much earlier (Garfield, 1980, 1989). Van Raan proposed three dimensions along which delayed recognition can be measured: the length of the sleep, the depth of the sleep, i.e., the average number of citations per year during the sleeping period, and the intensity of being awake referring to the number of citations received after the awakening time. Braun et al. (2010) focused on the role of the prince. Articles playing the role of the prince are among the first citing articles, are themselves at least fairly cited and have a considerable relative number of cocitations with the sleeping beauty. In a few cases the "kiss" was actually a self-citation. Examples of sleeping beauties in ophthalmology were studied by Ohba and Nakao (2012) determining the three factors proposed by Van Raan.

Yet, the original fairy tale does not begin with the sleeping period. Indeed, the *Sleeping Beauty* in the story is a lively princess (the article receives some citations) and then pricks her finger on a spindle and falls asleep. Li and Ye (2012) found examples of articles that went through all stages of the story, referring to them as *all-elements-sleeping-beauties*. Hence, it might be better to restrict the term sleeping beauty to all-elements-sleeping-beauties, or for emphasis, real sleeping beauties, and keep the terms delayed recognition and premature discovery for the situation studied by van Raan. Li and Ye (2012) refer to the time line of citations during the sleeping period as the heartbeat spectrum. Such heartbeat spectra are also studied in Li et al. (2014).

Du and Wu (2016) propose four requirements for a paper to act as a Prince: (1) to be published near the year in which the Sleeping Beauty starts to attract a lot of citations; (2) be a highly cited paper itself; (3) receive a substantial amount of cocitations with the Sleeping Beauty, and (4) during a certain period around the awakening the annual number of citations of the Prince is higher than that of the Sleeping Beauty. They further point out that sometimes there is more than one Prince and the author of the Sleeping Beauty paper can be the author of the paper that plays the role of the Prince.

Although being a sleeping beauty sounds like a yes/no situation, it is clear that delayed recognition is not a clear-cut phenomenon and a sleeping beauty in the eyes of one person may not be one in the eyes of a colleague. To solve this problem Ke et al. (2015) turned delayed recognition or being a sleeping beauty into a time-dependent continuous phenomenon by defining a beauty coefficient at time T, denoted as B(T). Let $c(t)$ denote the citation curve of an article, i.e., $c(t)$ is the number of citations received in year t (or generally in period t, as the unit of time can be a month, or some other time period). The publication year is year $t = 0$ and t takes values between 0 and T. Let c_m be the maximum number of received citations, for which we assume that it happened in year t_m. The line connecting $(0, c(0))$ and (t_m, c_m), which we refer to as the recognition line, denoted as $y(t)$, has equation:

$$y(t) = \frac{c_m - c(0)}{t_m} t + c(0) \tag{5.12}$$

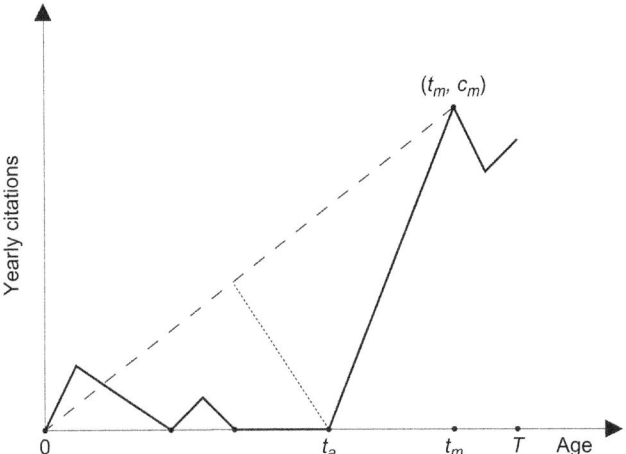

Figure 5.8 Recognition line for a sleeping beauty. *Based on (Ke et al., 2015).*

where $c_m = c(t_m)$ is assumed to be strictly positive. If $c_m = 0$ then $B(T) = 0$. If $t_m = t(0)$ then $B(T)$ is not defined.

Otherwise,

$$B(T) = \sum_{t=0}^{t_m} \left(\frac{\frac{c_m - c(0)}{t_m} t + c(0) - c(t)}{\max\{1, c(t)\}} \right) \qquad (5.13)$$

The calculation of $B(T)$, according to Ke et al. (2015), is illustrated in Fig. 5.8.

The numerator of a term in $B(T)$ is equal to the—signed—difference between the recognition line and the citation value. As the denominator of this term is equal to the number of citations (unless this number is zero, in which case the denominator is 1) each term in the sum determining $B(T)$ is a relative value.

If $c(t)$ has a concave trajectory then $B(T)$ is negative.

If $c(t)$ is linear then $B(T)$ is close to zero.

If $c(t)$ is convex then $B(T)$ is positive.

In the discussion that follows we assume that each term in the sum determining $B(T)$ is nonnegative. Then the following properties hold.

- All else staying the same, $B(T)$ is increasing when c_m increases.
- All else staying the same, $B(T)$ decreases when $c(t)$, with t fixed and different from 0 or t_m, increases as the numerator decreases and the denominator increases.

The awakening time

Ke et al. (2015) also propose a formula to determine the awakening time (assuming a mainly convex trajectory, as in Fig. 5.8). For each point $(t, c(t))$, $t < t_m$, they determine the distance to the recognition line, given as d_t:

$$d_t = \frac{\left| (c_m - c(0))t - t_m(c(t) - t(0)) \right|}{\sqrt{(c_m - c(0))^2 + t_m^2}} \tag{5.14}$$

The time t_a for which d_t is at a maximum is then called the awakening time (see Fig. 5.8). We observe that the awakening time is more stable than $B(T)$ which may fluctuate more. This is especially true when an article is a clear sleeping beauty. The fact that sleeping beauties in the general sense are not as rare as thought before (Ke et al., 2015) is another warning that research evaluation based on short-term citation metrics should be considered with caution.

5.15 A SHORT DESCRIPTION OF THE WEB OF SCIENCE

The WoS used to be a part of Thomson Reuters' Web of Knowledge. This term is not used anymore. Instead, the same platform has been renamed WoS. The original WoS database is called WoS Core Collection. The Journal Citations Reports (JCR), Essential Science Indicators (ESI), and InCites Benchmarking & Analytics were Thomson Reuters' analytical databases, but they became part of a new platform called InCites.

Besides the WoS Core Collection, which includes the SCI, the SSCI, the A&HCI, the CPCI-S, the Conference Proceedings Citation Index — Social Science & Humanities (CPCI-SSH), the Book Citation Index — Science (BCI-S), the Book Citation Index — Social Sciences & Humanities (BCI-SSH), the ESCI, Current Chemical Reactions and Index Chemicus (IC), the WoS contains: Current Contents Connect, BIOSIS Citation Index, Biological Abstracts, BIOSIS Previews, the Data Citation Index, Derwent Innovations Index, CAB Abstracts, CAB Global Health, the Chinese Science Citation Database, INSPEC, FSTA-Food Science & Technology Abstracts, Medline, KCI: the Korean Journal Database, the Russian Citation Index, SciELO Citation Index and Zoological Record.

Since 2016 all these databases have moved to Clarivate Analytics.

Although the WoS Core Collection goes back to 1900 the part that is actually available to a researcher depends on the contract which his working unit (university, research institute, company) has with Clarivate Analytics. In the year 2011 Thomson Reuters launched a BCI, in 2012 the Data Citation Index and in 2015 the ESCI, extending the set of publications in the WoS to include more publications of regional importance and in emerging scientific fields.

Thomson Reuters itself claimed that articles published in more than 20,000 journals are included in the WoS (McVeigh, 2010). Yet, exact numbers change each year and objective values are hard to find.

Document retrieval in the WoS can be done by searching on topics, authors, group names (as author), address, conference, language, document type, funding agency and grant number. It is also possible to adapt publication years. Only searching in one of the subdatabases, e.g., A&HCI, is possible too. Yet, professionals prefer *Advanced Search*. Searching in this mode allows more refined queries than in basic search. When using *Advanced Search* prefixes such as AU = (for an author search) or TS = (for a topic search) are used in queries. Note that a topic search is performed in the title, abstract and keyword sets, but for publications before 1991 no abstracts and keywords are available. This may lead to an artefactual jump in the number of retrieved publications on a certain topic (Pautasso, 2014). Also Boolean combinations are available, using AND, OR, NOT, and SAME (to be used in the same record field). We suggest always using *Advanced Search*. We note that Clarivate Analytics applies some automatic lemmatization and unification of English and American language (Rousseau, 2014a).

If one is interested in citations one must perform a *Cited Reference Search*. Basic retrieval options are: cited author, cited work and cited year(s).

Once a search has been performed the WoS provides a number of useful tools.

Results can be viewed ranked according to:
- Date (this is the default) shown antichronologically.
- Times cited (useful for determining an h-index yourself).
- Recently added.
- Usage count.
- First author.
- Source title.
- Publication year.
- Conference title.

If the result of a query contains not more than 10,000 results it is possible to ask for a *Citation Report*. This report shows on the right-hand side:

- The total number of retrieved records (also available on the original screen)
- The total number of citations
- The average number of citations per item
- The h-index

It is possible to retrieve citing articles (note the difference between the number of citations and the number of citing articles), with or without self-citations (where Clarivate Analytics determines what is a self-citation and what is not). Two histograms (left and in the middle) show:

- The number of publications per year.
- The number of received citations, per year (normally this graph is increasing as citations are shown for all publications on the left).

All results are ranked (as a default) according to the number of received citations; a thick line delimits the h-core. The default can be changed leading to a ranking according to first author (alphabetically), publication year and so on.

Besides producing a citation rapport the WoS also allows to "analyze" the results. Analyzing is possible for at most 100,000 items. When analyzing results are ranked from most to least (but depending on a chosen smallest number):

- Authors.
- Conference.
- Country or region.
- Document type.
- Funding agency.
- Grant.
- Institution name (university, . . .).
- Language.
- Publication year.
- Source (often journals, but also conference proceedings).
- Subject area (the JCR journal subject areas).

5.16 SCOPUS

Scopus contains descriptions and abstracts of articles from more than 22,000 peer-reviewed journals published by more than 5000 different publishers (including 2600 open access journals). This database also contains conference reports (5.5 million conference articles), 350 book series and quality-selected web sources. Scopus' content expanded considerably since June 2009. It also covers a large number of journals from the Arts & Humanities.

Scopus contains about 50 million records, among which:

- 29 million referring to articles published since 1996
- 21 million older records

Scopus contains historical material from the American Chemical Society, Springer / Kluwer, the Institute of Physics (IOP), the American Physical Society, the American Institute of Physics, the Royal Society of Chemistry and the journals *Nature* (going back to 1869) and *Science* (going back to 1880).

Finally Scopus contains articles 'in press' from 3850 journals. These journals are published by Cambridge University Press, Elsevier, Springer Nature, Karger Medical and Scientific Publishers and the IEEE. It has 100% coverage of all Medline titles.

In Scopus it is possible to see the percentage of uncited articles of a journal.

5.17 GOOGLE SCHOLAR (GS)

Informetric data from GS can be consulted via *Publish or Perish*. This program was developed by Anne-Wil Harzing and can be found at: http://www.harzing.com/pop.htm. It is described and its use illustrated in Harzing (2010). Publish or Perish is a software program that can easily and freely be installed on one's computer. It finds and analyses citations using GS as source. The following indicators are calculated for a given set of articles:

- The total number of publications.
- The total number of received citations.
- The average number of citations per publication.
- The average number of citations per author.
- The average number of articles per author.
- The average number of citations per year.
- The h-index and some variants.
- The g-index.
- The number of authors per article.

Moreover, GS Metrics provides the following indicators for journals:

- The h5-index: this is the h-index restricted to publications in the latest 5 complete calendar years.
- The h5-core: the core corresponding to the h5-index.
- The h5-median: the median citation value of the items in the h5-core.

5.18 COMPARISONS

Many colleagues performed investigations comparing GS, Scopus and the WoS. Because of unique features related to each of these databases a general consensus, see e.g. (Meho & Yang, 2006) for one of the earliest studies, is that the three databases complement each other.

Vieira and Gomes (2009) compared Scopus and the WoS as to differences for some typical (Portuguese) universities. They agree with the general consensus, mentioning that some high impact documents were found in only one of the two databases. Yet, documents included in both databases were generally the most-cited ones. Bar-Ilan (2010) studied a difficult case, namely a book, which is cited under many different forms. She carefully searched for variants in all databases, removed duplicates and made a thorough analysis of unique citations. She concluded that for this particular case the coverage of the WoS and Scopus was quite comparable and that GSs coverage was surprisingly good—it found the most unique citations and was more accurate than she expected. More generally, Kousha et al. (2011) assessed the citation impact of books studying Google Books, GS and Scopus. They found that, especially in book-oriented disciplines such as the arts and humanities online book citations could better support peer review for research evaluation than Scopus citations. Based on their investigations Amara and Landry (2012) urge those that perform assessments in Canadian business schools to complement WoS data by GS data.

Meho and Yang (2007) compared the WoS, GS and Scopus to assess the extent to which the results of a citation analysis depend upon the data source, using the task of ranking the faculty of a library and information science school. Their findings showed that GS was probably too difficult to use for a large-scale citation analysis and that the other two gave similar results overall. Yet, as mentioned above they came to the consensus view that using all databases in conjunction gives the fairest results. Fields which emphasize conferences, such as computer science and computational linguistics are best served by including GS results. Yet, studies with wider disciplinary coverage showed that the coverage of GS is variable and can be unreliable for some subdisciplines (Kousha and Thelwall, 2007).

Leydesdorff (2012) compared publication trends for China, the USA, EU-27, and smaller countries as derived from the WoS and Scopus. Compared with an earlier version of the WoS interface he found that China no longer grew exponentially during the 2000s, but linearly. Consequently, the cross-over of the lines for China and the US was postponed in time with respect to predictions based on an exponential growth. He concludes that besides the dynamics in publication trends, one also has to take into account the dynamics of the databases used for predictions.

5.19 FINAL REMARKS

Citation data made available by Clarivate Analytics or Scopus (Elsevier) are behind a paywall. As a consequence informetric papers can rarely comply with requirements of making data open because of the license restrictions on which their results are based. One may wonder why they are not freely available for everyone. Expertise is needed to handle and interpret them, not to collect them. Hence, it is not surprising that voices have been raised to consider citation data as part of the commons and placed in an open repository (Shotton, 2013).

As a cautionary note ending this chapter we would like to point out that numbers of citations can certainly not be equated to scientific originality, let alone to the mark of geniality. The larger the audience the higher the citation potential, and conversely, the smaller the audience the smaller the chance to get cited. Moreover, paradigm changing discoveries have notoriously limited early impacts (Wang et al., 2013) because the more a discovery deviates from the current paradigm the longer it takes to be appreciated by the community. In the context of citation analysis, we also notice the phenomenon of superspecialization: some topics (e.g., in pure mathematics) are studied by only a handful of scientists. Articles and scientists dealing with these topics can never become highly-cited on an overall scale. Moreover, like any human endeavor also science knows topics that are temporarily "en vogue" and hence articles dealing with these topics receive—temporarily—much more citations than expected (than deserved?), see e.g., Rousseau et al. (2013) for the case of the h-index.

CHAPTER 6

Journal Citation Analysis

6.1 SCIENTIFIC JOURNALS

Most scientists agree that there are top journals and journals of lower standing. We can further distinguish between general journals, say multi-disciplinary ones, and specialized ones. Over the years, science has become more and more specialized, resulting in a relative decrease in the number of general journals. This specialization is also visible in most fields and is not a recent development at all. Just as an example we mention the journal *Physical Review* which split in 1970 into *Physical Review A* (dealing with atomic, molecular, and optical physics), *Physical Review B* (condensed matter and materials physics), *Physical Review C* (nuclear physics), and *Physical Review D* (particles, fields, gravitation, and cosmology). A fifth member of the journal, *Physical Review E*, was launched in 1993 dealing with statistical, nonlinear and soft matter physics. The best known multidisciplinary journals with a long history are *Nature, Science*, and the *Proceedings of the National Academy of Sciences USA* (in short, *PNAS*). These three journals are also top journals. *Current Science* (India) and the *Science Bulletin* (formerly *Chinese Science Bulletin)* (China) are general journals of a more local interest. Recently, the phenomenon of electronic-only journals, combined with the phenomenon of open access journals covering all sciences, or at least a large part of them, has given rise to new, general mega-journals. Prototypes of such mega-journals are *PLOS ONE* (Public Library of Science One) and *Scientific Reports*, but *PeerJ* (restricted to the biological and medical sciences) falls into this category as well.

Each field has its own top journals. It is not surprising that scientists try to publish in one of their field's top journals. As a consequence, these journals receive large numbers of submissions, their editors can easily reject many and—if they make good choices—increase the impact of their journals. This self-reinforcing mechanism is an example of the Matthew effect (discussed further on in Chapter 9: The Informetric Laws). Because of the rise of citation indexes, and in particular the Journal Citation Reports (JCR) (see further Section 6.13), the vague criterion "reputation" has increasingly been replaced by "receiving many

Becoming Metric-Wise
DOI: http://dx.doi.org/10.1016/B978-0-08-102474-4.00006-6

Table 6.1 A complete p-c matrix of a hypothetical journal

Year of publication		1	1	2	2	2	3	3	3	4	4	4	4
Articles		A	B	C	D	E	F	G	H	I	J	K	L
Number of citations received in year 1		1	0										
Number of citations received in year 2		4	2	2	1	1							
Number of citations received in year 3		6	2	1	4	6	3	0	0				
Number of citations received in year 4		8	1	0	5	9	3	1	2	4	1	2	3

citations in the short term." In this way, well-known (=heavily cited) scientists publish mainly and preferably in well-known (=heavily cited) journals.

The best known—and most criticized—criterion for a journal's visibility is the journal impact factor (JIF). This indicator and related ones are discussed in this chapter. Note that here we consider the JIF as the result of a specific mathematical formula. At this point we do not go into details about the way databases such as the Web of Science (WoS) apply this formula.

6.2 THE PUBLICATION-CITATION MATRIX PER ARTICLE

6.2.1 A Complete Publication-Citation Matrix

A complete publication–citation matrix (in short, p-c matrix) of a journal contains all citation information for each of its articles. Table 6.1 provides an example in which we consider a fictitious journal publishing, for simplicity's sake, very few articles. We note that all citations come from a given pool of citing articles (Ingwersen et al., 2001).

The numbers in Table 6.1 mean the following: the number 6 in the column starting with 2E, means that article E, published in year 2, received 6 citations in year 3.

6.3 THE PUBLICATION-CITATION MATRIX OF A JOURNAL AND THE GARFIELD-SHER (1963) IMPACT FACTOR: INTRODUCTION

When one is interested in knowing a journal's impact factor, the number of citations received by each individual article plays no role: all articles published in a particular year are brought together. For this purpose Table 6.1 is replaced by Table 6.2. This type of table contains all data needed to calculate impact factors (see further).

Table 6.2 The matrix needed to determine an impact factor (derived from Table 6.1)

Year of publication	1	2	3	4
Number of articles	2	3	3	4
Number of citations received in year 1	1			
Number of citations received in year 2	6	4		
Number of citations received in year 3	8	11	3	
Number of citations received in year 4	9	14	6	10

The purpose of Table 6.2 is to show that it can easily be derived from the complete p-c matrix (Frandsen & Rousseau, 2005; Ingwersen et al., 2001). Information about individual cited or citing articles is not necessary. Only the number of publications (per year) and the total number of received citations per year by all publications matter.

The first row of Table 6.2 gives the publication year, while the second one shows the number of published articles in each of these years. For simplicity we assume that each article is taken into account when calculating a JIF. In reality, only some types of articles are. These are referred to as being "citable." Editorials, meeting abstracts, book reviews and similar publications are considered "uncitable." We go into some more details about this in Section 6.13. The following rows in Table 6.2 are citation rows. The table shows, for instance, that in year 3 this journal received 8 citations for articles published in year 1. Moreover, this journal received in year 3, 3 citations to articles published in the same year.

Starting from such a p-c matrix a plethora of impact factors and even types of impact factors can be defined. An important difference is that between synchronous and diachronous impact factors (Ingwersen et al., 2000, 2001). The standard Garfield-Sher impact factor for journals, denoted as JIF_2, is a synchronous impact factor based on one citation year and two publication years (Garfield & Sher, 1963). An example: the Garfield-Sher impact factor of the journal represented in Table 6.2 in the year 4 is obtained as:

$$JIF_2(4) = \frac{14 + 6}{3 + 3} \approx 3.33$$

It is this impact factor which is published on a yearly basis in Thomson Reuters' (now Clarivate Analytics) JCR, a statistical byproduct of the WoS, see further. A precise definition follows in Section 6.4.

6.4 SYNCHRONOUS IMPACT FACTORS

6.4.1 Definition of the Journal Impact Factor

Next we consider a larger p-c matrix, based on (Frandsen & Rousseau, 2005).

Table 6.3 is structured in the same way as Table 6.2. We see, for instance, that this journal received in the year 2011 20 citations for articles published in the year 2009. In 2015 it received 6 citations to articles published in that same year (2015).

The Garfield-Sher impact factor of this journal for the year 2013 is:

$$JIF_2(2013) = \frac{13 + 25}{30 + 25} = 0.691 \tag{6.1}$$

In general, the Garfield-Sher JIF_2 for the year Y is defined as:

$$JIF_2(Y) = \frac{CIT(Y, Y-1) + CIT(Y, Y-2)}{PUB(Y-1) + PUB(Y-2)} \tag{6.2}$$

The symbol $CIT(Y,X)$ in formula (6.2) refers to the number of citations received in the year Y by articles published in the year X. It is assumed that the pool of citing journals is known and that it is also clear about which journal J one is talking. Otherwise one may write $CIT_J(Y,X)$. Similarly,

Table 6.3 A fictitious publication-citation matrix

Year	2009	2010	2011	2012	2013	2014	2015	2016
# publications	15	20	25	30	35	35	40	40
# citations received in the year 2009	10							
# citations received in the year 2010	15	10						
# citations received in the year 2011	20	14	10					
# citations received in the year 2012	30	20	14	8				
# citations received in the year 2013	25	25	25	13	8			
# citations received in the year 2014	20	22	30	20	12	8		
# citations received in the year 2015	17	18	25	26	18	11	6	
# citations received in the year 2016	15	16	20	22	25	17	10	6

$PUB_J(Z)$ denotes the number of articles published in journal J in the year Z. Again one may omit the index J if it is clear about which journal one is talking, or when it does not matter. JIF_2 is a synchronous impact factor. The term "synchronous" refers to the fact that all citations used to calculate it were given (hence received by the journal) in the same year. Stated otherwise, these citations can be found in reference lists of articles published in the same year. Besides a 2-year JIF one can define an n-year synchronous impact factor in an analogous way (Rousseau, 1988a):

$$JIF_n(Y) = \frac{\sum_{i=1}^n CIT(Y, Y - i)}{\sum_{i=1}^n PUB(Y - i)} \qquad (6.3)$$

We observe that if $n = 2$ in formula (6.3) one obtains the standard Garfield-Sher impact factor, formula (6.2). Citation data needed to compute a synchronous impact factor are found in the same row of a p-c matrix (Ingwersen et al., 2001). In case the journal is included in the JCR one can find all necessary data by opening the "Cited Journal" view in the file corresponding with the year Y. Since edition 2007 Thomson Reuters' JCR also provides 5-year synchronous impact factors for journals, i.e., taking $n = 5$ in formula (6.3). We will return to this point.

Besides Clarivate Analytics (formerly Thomson Reuters) other databases also show JIFs (though usually not called as such). SCImago, for instance, based on data from the Scopus database, shows a Cites/Doc (2 years) indicator. The Chinese Science Citation Database (CSCD), the China Scientific and Technical Papers & Citations (CSTPC) and the China National Knowledge Infrastructure (CNKI) database in China provide 2-year synchronous impact factors for Chinese scientific journals. In the calculation of these impact factors only journals available in these databases are used (hence these JIFs are based on different pools) (see Jin & Wang, 1999; Jin et al., 2002; Rousseau et al., 2001; Wu et al., 2004).

6.4.2 An Example and a Warning

Let us calculate the standard impact factor of journals J and J' for the year Y. Data necessary for this calculation are shown in Table 6.4. Which journal has the highest impact factor?

$JIF_2(J) = \frac{30 + 30}{10 + 10} = 3.0$ and $JIF_2(J') = \frac{60 + 60}{30 + 30} = 2.0$. Hence journal J has the highest impact factor. Now we add, to both journals, 25 uncited articles

Table 6.4 Fictitious citation data

	J	J′
Pub(Y-1)	10	30
Pub(Y-2)	10	30
Cit(Y,Y-1)	30	60
Cit(Y,Y-2)	30	60

(say that we had forgotten to include the uncited articles). Then the new impact factors are: $JIF_2(J) = \frac{60}{45} = 1.333$ and $JIF_2(J') = \frac{120}{85} = 1.418$. Now journal J' has the highest impact factor. Assume now that, instead of 25 uncited articles we add 27 uncited articles to journal J' and keep the 25 uncited ones for journal J, then the new impact factor for journal J' is $JIF_2(J') = \frac{120}{87} = 1.379$. So, by adding more uncited articles to J' than to J the impact factor of J' has become higher than that of J. This might seem rather contradictory, but this result is just a consequence of the fact that the impact factor is a ratio (Rousseau & Leydesdorff, 2011).

A simple question. Journal A is heavily related to journal B and hence articles in journal A often cite articles in journal B. Yet, because of the special way in which peer review is handled in journal A, the time between submission of a manuscript and actual publication (if accepted) is at least 156 weeks (36 months). What is the contribution of journal A to the JIF of journal B? Answer: journal A has no influence at all on the JIF of journal B. This is an extreme example showing that publication delays of one journal may influence the JIF of other journals (Shi et al., 2017).

6.5 DIACHRONOUS IMPACT FACTORS

Besides synchronous JIFs also diachronous ones exist. In order to make a distinction we denote these as JDIF (Frandsen & Rousseau, 2005; Ingwersen et al., 2001). The 2-year diachronous impact factor of the journal represented in Table 6.3 in the year 2012 is:

$$JDIF_2(2010) = \frac{13 + 20}{30} = 1.1 \tag{6.4}$$

Starting with the publication year (which is often done and seems more logical) this becomes:

$$JDIF_2^0(2010) = \frac{8 + 13}{30} = 0.7 \tag{6.5}$$

The general formula for calculating an n-year (shifted) diachronous JIF in the publication year Y is:

$$\text{JDIF}_n^s(Y) = \frac{\sum_{i=s}^{s+n-1} \text{CIT}(Y+i, Y)}{\text{PUB}(Y)} \qquad (6.6)$$

where $s = 0,1,2, \ldots$ denotes a possible shift with respect to the publication year Y.

Citation data needed to calculate a diachronous impact factor can always be found in the same column of a p-c matrix. The term "diachronous" refers to the fact that the data needed to calculate it refer to different years: one has to "move through time" (dia = through and chronos = time in ancient Greek). The diachronous JIF as calculated by formula (6.6) for a given year Y is increasing in n (more precisely, nondecreasing) and reflects an evolution over time.

The time interval used to calculate an impact factor, be it synchronous or diachronous is called the citation window.

One may also calculate a relative diachronous JIF by dividing $\text{JDIF}_n^s(Y)$ by n leading to: $\text{JDIF}_n^s(Y)/n$. This indicator will usually, after an initial increase, decrease over time.

The 1-year journal diachronous impact factor without a time shift, $\text{JDIF}_1^0(Y)$, is called the journal immediacy index. It is one of the indicators provided in the JCR.

6.6 MORE ON PUBLICATION-CITATION MATRICES AND IMPACT FACTORS

We note that the data shown in p-c matrices do not necessarily have to refer to a journal. Any set of articles, for instance those published by a research group during a given publication year, can be represented in a similar matrix.

A diachronous impact factor can be calculated for one-off publications such as a conference proceedings or an edited book. This was done by Rousseau (1997a) for *Informetrics 87/88* and *Informetrics 89/90* (Egghe & Rousseau, 1988, 1990), the proceedings of the first and second scientometrics and informetrics conference (which later became the ISSI conferences). The pool for this calculation were all journals included in the WoS (at that time), expanded with all proceedings volumes of this conference series. A 4-year citation window was used. This approach also provides an example of a case where the citation pool is expanded.

Concretely: the data in the WoS were augmented by all references used in the ISSI conference proceedings. Next we provide a scheme to go beyond the standard synchronous and diachronous impact factor calculations.

6.6.1 A General Framework for Calculating Impact (Frandsen & Rousseau, 2005): A First Proposal

Calculations of the impact of groups of articles can be made more robust when allowing for publication and citation windows consisting of more than 1 year. If the analyzed unit, for instance a research group, only publishes a small amount of articles a year, then an analysis based on several years is clearly called for.

We now introduce the following notation:

n_p represents the length of the publication window.

n_c represents the length of the citation window.

Y_p is the first (oldest) year of the publication period.

Y_c is the first (oldest) year of the citation period.

Using these notations we denote the general impact factor of a set S of articles by $IF_S(n_p, n_c, Y_p, Y_c)$, and define it by:

$$IF_S\left(n_p, n_c, Y_p, Y_c\right) = \frac{\sum_{i=0}^{n_p-1} \sum_{k=0}^{n_c-1} CIT(Y_c + k, Y_p + i)}{\sum_{i=0}^{n_p-1} PUB(Y_p + i)} \qquad (6.7)$$

Formula (6.7) is similar to the diachronous impact factor. Sums run from the first year in the publication period and in the citation period till the last one (the most-recent one). Yet, it may also represent a synchronous Garfield-Sher impact factor for journal J as follows: $IF_J(2,1,Y-2,Y)$. The diachronous $JDIF_2^0(Y)$ of journal J is then, in this notation, $IF_J(1,2, Y,Y)$. Similarly $JDIF_n^1(Y)$ for journal J is $IF_J(1,n,Y,Y+1)$. The immediacy index of journal J becomes: $IF_J(1,1,Y,Y)$.

Table 6.5 shows the data used for the calculation of $IF_S(2,3,Y,Y)$, while Table 6.6 shows those needed for the calculation of $IF_S(3,3,Y, Y+2)$. These tables are taken from (Frandsen & Rousseau, 2005).

Some of these generalized impact factors were used in Moed et al. (1985a) and de Bruin et al. (1993). The approach explained here can be used if all citation and publication data are known till and including the year $Y+n_c-1$. An obvious disadvantage of this approach is that publication years are treated differently, in terms of used citation years. The next approach tries to remediate this by treating publication years on an equal footing.

Table 6.5 Data used for the calculation of $IF_S(2,3,Y,Y)$

Year	Y-1	Y	Y+1	Y+2	Y+3
Publ.	x			x	x
Cit. Y-1	x	-	-	-	-
Cit.Y	x		-	-	-
Cit.Y+1	x			-	-
Cit.Y+2	x			x	-
Cit.Y+3	x	x	x	x	x

The symbol − is placed in cells where no values are possible (an article is assumed not to be cited before it is published), the symbol x is placed in cells for which data may exist, but these are not used for the calculation illustrated here.

Table 6.6 Data used for the calculation of $IF_S(3,3,Y,Y + 2)$

Year	Y-1	Y	Y+1	Y+2	Y+3	Y+4
Publ.	x				x	x
Cit. Y-1	x	-	-	-	-	-
Cit.Y	x	x	-	-	-	-
Cit.Y+1	x	x	x	-	-	-
Cit.Y+2	x				-	-
Cit.Y+3	x				x	-
Cit.Y+4	x				x	x
Cit.Y+5	x	x	x	x	x	x

6.6.2 A General Framework for Calculating Impact (Frandsen & Rousseau, 2005): An Alternative

Using the same symbols as in the previous section we now introduce an alternative generalized impact factor, denoted as $AGIF_S(n_p, n_c, Y_p, Y_c)$, and defined by:

$$AGIF_S\left(n_p, n_c, Y_p, Y_c\right) = \frac{\sum_{i=0}^{n_p-1} \sum_{k=0}^{n_c-1} CIT(Y_c + i + k, Y_p + i)}{\sum_{i=0}^{n_p-1} PUB(Y_p + i)} \qquad (6.8)$$

Table 6.7 Data used for the calculation of $AGIF_S(3,3,Y, Y+2)$

Year	Y-1	Y	Y+1	Y+2	Y+3	Y+4
Publ.	x				x	x
Cit. Y-1	x	-	-	-	-	-
Cit.Y	x	x	-	-	-	-
Cit.Y+1	x	x	x	-	-	-
Cit.Y+2	x		x	x	-	-
Cit.Y+3	x			x	x	-
Cit.Y+4	x				x	x
Cit.Y+5	x	x			x	x
Cit.Y+6	x	x	x		x	x
Cit.Y+7	x	x	x	x	x	x

Table 6.7 shows the data used for the calculation of $AGIF_S(3,3,Y, Y+2)$, also taken from (Frandsen & Rousseau, 2005).

Counting starts from the first year in the publication and in the citation period. Using this notation it is easy to express diachronous impact factors. Indeed, $JDIF_2^0(Y)$ of journal J is now denoted as $AGIF_J(1,2,Y,Y)$, and $JDIF_n^1(Y)$ can be written as $AGIF_J(1,n,Y,Y+1)$. The immediacy index becomes $AGIF_J(1,1,Y,Y)$.

Table 6.8 provides an example for the case of the average number of citations, 2 years after publication, calculated for a 4-year publication window, starting in the year Y.

This type of averages has been used by Liming Liang when calculating so-called rhythm indicators (Liang, 2005).

6.7 REMARKS ABOUT JOURNAL IMPACT FACTORS

6.7.1 Expanding or Restricting the Citation Pool

JIF calculations need a citation pool from which citations are harvested. This pool is often the whole WoS or the complete Scopus database. Yet, the original pool can be restricted or expanded, or both. One may, e.g., restrict the pool to all journals belonging to a certain discipline or group of disciplines (however determined). This may be the discipline to which

Table 6.8 Data used to calculate $AGIF_S(4,1,Y,Y+2)$

Year	Y-1	Y	Y+1	Y+2	Y+3	Y+4
Publ.	x					x
Cit.Y-1	x	-	-	-	-	-
Cit.Y	x	x	-	-	-	-
Cit.Y+1	x	x	x	-	-	-
Cit.Y+2	x		x	x	-	-
Cit.Y+3	x	x		x	x	-
Cit.Y+4	x	x	x		x	x
Cit.Y+5	x	x	x	x		x
Cit.Y+6	x	x	x	x	x	x
Cit.Y+7	x	x	x	x	x	x

the journal belongs, leading to discipline impact factors (Hirst, 1978; Kim, 1991) or, another discipline leading to the study of import/export ratios (Rinia et al., 2002). One could imagine that one wants to study the impact of a journal on so-called top publications by restricting the pool to the journals *Science* and *Nature*.

The citation pool may also be expanded. This is necessary if one wants to calculated a JIF or JDIF for a journal that is not covered by the WoS or Scopus and one wants to include journal self-citations (Stegmann, 1999). Then the pool must be expanded by including the journal that is not covered by the database one uses. Recall that a journal self-citation occurs if an article published in journal J_1 cited another article which was also published in journal J_1.

If one uses the journal itself as the citation pool then one obtains a journal self-impact factor. Usually the self-impact factor is lower than the one obtained by using the whole database as a pool. Indeed, the denominator is the same in both cases, while the numerator is only the same in the highly improbable case that a journal only receives citations from articles published in the journal itself.

6.7.2 Normalization

If we consider the subject category *Family studies* in the JCR for 2014, we see that the highest impact factor in this category is 2.833. That is more than 11 times less than 31.427, the highest impact factor in the subject category *Neurosciences*. For comparison, the latter category also has a journal with impact factor of 2.833, which is ranked 123rd. This example illustrates that impact factors cannot be compared across fields, because different fields have different citation habits (number of references, age of references) and are not always covered as well in international databases. Hence, if one wants to compare impact factors across fields, normalization is called for. Normalizing JIFs with respect to a field or domain is done in two fundamentally different ways: normalization on the cited side or normalization on the citing side (Moed, 2010; Zitt & Small, 2008). The normalization process goes through the following steps.

1. One determines an average number of citations per article (in other words: an impact factor is calculated).
2. One determines the field or domain to which the journal belongs. This is a problem in itself on which we do not dwell further now.
3. The actual normalization step:
   a. Normalization on the cited side. In this approach a journal's field is determined by some classification scheme. Then one determines the average number of citations in the journals' field or domain and applies a correction based on this average. The simplest way to do this is by taking the ratio of the journal's impact and that of its field.
   b. Normalization on the citing side. Here a journal's field is determined by the journal itself (see further when we discuss the audience factor and the source-normalized impact per paper (SNIP) indicator). One determines the average number of references in the journal's field or domain (a kind of citation potential). Then a correction factor is determined based on this citation potential.

Normalization on the cited side is done in the MOCR (Mean Observed Citation Rate) (Braun & Glänzel, 1990), the earlier CWTS crown indicator (van Raan, 2004a) and the MNCS (Mean Normalized Citation Score) indicator (Waltman et al., 2011a,b). Normalization on the citing side is done when calculating the audience factor (Zitt & Small, 2008) or the SNIP index, in its original and revised version (Moed, 2010; Waltman et al., 2013). Most of these indicators are discussed further on in this chapter or in this book.

6.7.3 Meta-Journal Indicators (Egghe and Rousseau, 1996a,b)

Indicators such as the JIFs presented above are actually indicators for sets of publications and corresponding citations. So, it is also possible to calculate an impact factor for the field of mathematics, chemistry or information and library science, as examples.

For a set of journals, J_i, $i = 1, \ldots n$, one can define the global impact factor (GIF) as:

$$\text{GIF} = \frac{\sum_{i=1}^{n} C_i}{\sum_{i=1}^{n} P_i} = \frac{\mu_C}{\mu_P} \tag{6.9}$$

where C_i denotes the number of citations received by the i-th journal (over a given citation window) and P_i denotes the number of publications in the i-th journal (during a given publication window). This is essentially the same formula as that used for an impact factor of a journal. It is also equal to the average number of citations per journal (μ_C) divided by the average number of publications per journal (μ_P).

Yet, one might also calculate the average impact factor (AIF) of this same set of journals:

$$\text{AIF} = \frac{1}{n} \sum_{i=1}^{n} \frac{C_i}{P_i} \tag{6.10}$$

The difference between the two is essentially a matter of weighting and hence of perspective. If one uses geometric means instead of arithmetic ones then GIF(geometric) becomes $\dfrac{\sqrt[n]{C_1 \cdots C_n}}{\sqrt[n]{P_1 \cdots P_n}}$ while AIF(geometric) becomes $\sqrt[n]{\dfrac{C_1}{P_1} \cdots \dfrac{C_n}{P_n}}$, which means that in their geometric form GIF and AIF coincide (Egghe & Rousseau, 1996b).

Normalization is further discussed in the context of indicators and research evaluation.

6.7.4 Citable Publications

In the standard JIF_2 only the number of so-called citable articles is used for the calculation of the denominator, while citations to all publications in the journal are included in the numerator. Corrections, meeting abstracts, book reviews, obituaries and short letters to the editor rarely receive a large number of citations (Hu & Rousseau, 2013), and are for this reason not included in the calculation of the denominator. An argument for this practice is that otherwise journals would be "punished" for publishing these otherwise useful types of publications. It is, however, not always clear if a publication is "citable" or not, in particular for multidisciplinary journals who have a lot of article types. The recently introduced CiteScore index (see Section 6.16) ignores this distinction and considers all journal publications as citable.

6.8 THE H-INDEX FOR JOURNALS

The h-index was originally introduced as a lifetime citation indicator for individual scientists (Hirsch, 2005). We come back to the original version in the next chapter. Yet, it was soon recognized that, being an indicator based on publications and citations, it could also be applied to journals (Braun et al., 2005). Today's h-index of journal J for the publication year Y is determined as follows. One collects all publications in journal J in year Y and determines the number of citations received by each of these publications (until the day of the data collection) in the used database. This list is ranked according to the number of received citations. Then the h-index of this journal and for the publication year Y is the largest natural number h such that the first h articles have received each at least h citations. As this value may change day by day it is an instantaneous indicator. Besides the h-index described here, one may calculate a journal h-index based on all the journal's publications (since its inception; this is similar to a scientist's career h-index). It is also possible to calculate an index for the same publication and citation window as for the standard synchronous JIF. This has been mentioned explicitly in Liang and Rousseau (2009).

Returning to Table 6.1 we extract the data necessary to calculate the h-index of this journal using the periods of this table. This is shown in Table 6.9.

The h-index can now be calculated from Table 6.10 where articles are ranked according to the number of received citations. Clearly, this h-index is equal to 5.

Table 6.9 The p-c matrix required to calculate the h-index of the (fictitious) journal represented by Table 6.1

Articles	A	B	C	D	E	F	G	H	I	J	K	L
Citations received during the period: year 1—year 4	19	5	3	10	16	6	1	2	4	1	2	3

Table 6.10 Ranked table for the calculation of the
h-index of a journal

Rank	Received citations
1	19
2	16
3	10
4	6
5	5
6	4
7	3
8	3
9	2
10	2
11	1
12	1

6.9 INDICATORS THAT TAKE THE IMPORTANCE OF THE CITING JOURNAL INTO ACCOUNT

One could argue that a citation received from an important journal carries more weight than a citation received from a less important journal (whatever the words "important" and "unimportant" may stand for). Based on an idea from Kochen (1974) this was elaborated by Pinski and Narin (1976). In this approach citations are weighted by the impact of the citing journal. In this way these colleagues were the first to break through the "equally weighted citations" wall.

The underlying idea of their approach is the calculation of an eigenvector associated with the largest eigenvalue of a linear mapping (or equivalently, a matrix). It is this idea that has been re-invented (with some clever adaptations) by Brin and Page (1998) and applied to links on the Internet, leading to the Google algorithm also known as the PageRank algorithm.

Determining eigenvalues and eigenvectors of large matrices is not straightforward. Pinski & Narin proposed the so-called "power method," a well-known numerical algorithm.

6.9.1 A Short Description of the Pinski-Narin Algorithm

Let $C = (C_{i,j})$ be a citation matrix. In our case $C_{i,j}$ denotes the number of citations given by journal i to journal j. Let S_i be the number of references in journal i. We construct a new matrix $M = (M_{i,j})$, where

$M_{i,j} = C_{i,j}/S_i$. If W_i is the influence weight of journal i (the new type of impact factor) then W_i is determined by the requirement:

$$W_i = \sum_{j=1}^{N} M_{ji} W_j \qquad (6.11)$$

hence taking the weights of the journals into account. This may look like a circular reasoning as the W's are calculated from the W's. Yet, this is not really true. It is known (Langville & Meyer, 2006) that this equality means that W_i is the i-th component of the solution of the matrix equation

$$W = M^t W \quad \text{or} \quad M^t W = 1W \qquad (6.12)$$

The symbol superscript t in this equation represents matrix transposition, i.e., replacing rows by columns and vice versa. This equation only determines the direction of the eigenvector W. A unique solution is determined by an extra—normalization—requirement. Pinski and Narin normalized in such a way that the average value of the components of W is equal to 1. An equation of the type (6.12) is called an eigenvector equation. The reason for this name is that matrix M^t maps the vector W to a multiple of itself (*eigen* is German for *self*). In this particular case this multiple, called the eigenvalue, is equal to 1.

Basic mathematical (algebraic) methods cannot solve eigenvector equations for large matrices. For this reason one applies approximate, iterative methods such as the power method. In its basic approach one proposes a solution for W consisting completely of ones. Substituting these in the left-hand side of (6.12) leads to a better approximation. Then this new approximation is substituted in the left-hand side of (6.12) and so on, until subsequent approximations do not change anymore (more precisely the first decimals do not change anymore).

In order to apply the Pinski-Narin algorithm to a real network some adaptations are needed and choices must be made, leading to several variants of the basic algorithm. These include the Eigenfactor Score, the article influence score (AIS) and the SCImago Journal Rank. The Eigenfactor Score is a practical realization (Bergstrom, 2007; Bergstrom et al., 2008) based on the journal status proposed by Bollen et al. (2006).

It is rather difficult to imagine what an eigenvector score means, but the following story comes close. A "random journal surfer" randomly chooses a journal, and an article in this journal, again at random. Then he or she randomly chooses a reference in this article. Then he or she moves to this reference's journal and the whole procedure is repeated millions of times. The relative number of times this "random journal surfer" visits a journal is this journal's eigenfactor. Clearly one needs an extra rule in case a reference list is empty or does not contain a single suitable item. One must also take precautions against infinite loops.

The AIS is a measure for the influence of a journal, normalized in such a way that the average journal in the database has an AIS-value of 1 (details are provided in Subsection 6.9.2). If a top journal has an AIS of 12 this means that the average article in this journal has 12 times more influence than the average article in the database. As all citation measures also this measure is field dependent. In 2012 the journal with the highest AIS in the JCR was *Reviews of Modern Physics* with a value of 32.565. Among the 85 journals in the category *Information Science and Library Science* only 8 had an AIS value larger than 1.

6.9.2 Calculating the Eigenfactor Score and the Article Influence Score

In a previous section we explained the Pinski-Narin approach and pointed out that in practice some adaptations are needed. Here we go into the practical calculation of the Eigenfactor Score and the AIS as described in http://www.eigenfactor.org and Franceschet (2010a). For the mathematical principle we refer the reader to Langville and Meyer (2006). Let $C = (C_{ij})$ be a journal citation matrix for the year Y. The aim is to find the Eigenfactor Score for each journal described by this citation matrix. The value C_{ij} in the matrix cell of the i-th row and j-th column denotes the number of references given in journal i in the year Y to articles published in journal j during the previous 5 years. This matrix is clearly not symmetric: in general $C_{ij} \neq C_{ji}$ (although equality may happen occasionally for some i and j). Moreover, C_{ii} is set equal to zero, i.e., journal self-citations are omitted. Next we introduce the article vector a. The components of a, a_i, are equal to the number of articles published in journal i during the previous 5 years (the citation window), divided by the total number of articles published by all journals represented in C, during the same 5-year period. Hence, the component a_i represents the relative publication contribution of journal i in the journal network under study. A dangling node (journal) i is a node that does not cite a single other journal of the network. In a next step matrix C is transformed into a normalized matrix $H = (h_{ij})$. In this matrix rows (journals) not corresponding to dangling journals are divided by the row totals (so that the new row totals are always equal to one). Rows of dangling journals are replaced by the article vector *a*. Next one defines a new matrix *P* as:

$$P = \alpha H + (1 - \alpha)A \qquad (6.13)$$

where *A* is a matrix consisting of the same rows, each consisting of the article vector. The Greek letter α represents an adaptable parameter. In the calculation of the Eigenfactor Score α is taken equal to 0.85. The occurrence of this parameter implies that, by adapting α, an infinite number of eigenfactors is feasible. Let now π be the eigenvector of *P* for which the equality $\pi = \pi P$ holds (hence, with corresponding eigenvalue equal to 1). This vector π is called the *influence* vector. It contains the scores used to weight the citations in *H*. Finally, the eigenfactor vector *r* is obtained as:

$$r = \frac{\pi H}{\sum_i (\pi H)_i} 100 \qquad (6.14)$$

The Eigenfactor Score of journal *j* is the *j*-th component of this vector. It can be considered as the sum of all normalized citations received from citing journals, weighted by the Eigenfactor Scores of these citing journals. Eigenfactor Scores are normalized in such a way that their sum (for the whole citation database) is equal to 100.

The AIS of a journal is equal to its Eigenfactor Score divided by the number of articles published during the 5-year publication window and normalized in such a way that the average value for the whole database is equal to 1. Hence the AIS of a journal is a normalized Eigenfactor Score per published article.

The SJR (SCImago Journal Ranking) indicator, as made available in SCImago Journal & Country Rank, is also a variant on the Pinski-Narin or Google approach. González-Pereira et al. (2010) refer to this class of indicators as prestige indicators. Also the SJR indicator is directly inspired by the journal status as described in (Bollen et al., 2006).

6.9.3 Advantages of the Eigenfactor Score and Related Journal Indicators (Franceschet, 2010b)

- Citations are weighted according to the importance of citing journals. Hence, the Eigenfactor Score and related indicators can be considered prestige indicators, see also Gonzalez-Pereira et al. (2010), while the class of synchronous or diachronous impact factor are rather popularity scores.
- The AIS takes the length of reference lists into account. Hence receiving a citation from a journal with short reference lists is considered

more important than receiving a citation from journals with long reference lists (typically review journals).

- A 5-year publication window is used, while the classical JIF uses a 2-year publication window.
- These indicators use information from the whole network and not just from directly citing journals.
- Journal self-citations are not used.
- They are based on a solid mathematical theory of matrices and eigenvalues.
- The method satisfies an axiomatic uniqueness property (Palacios-Huerta & Volij, 2004).
- These indicators embed citation analysis in the field of (social) network theory where eigenvector centrality is one of the basic centrality measures (Bonacich, 1972, 1987). Networks are discussed in Chapter 10, Networks.

6.10 CORRELATIONS BETWEEN JOURNAL INDICATORS

Most journal indicators are highly correlated with the standard JIF and other journal indicators. In Rousseau & Stimulate 8 Group (2009) a comparison has been made between values for the JCR JIF, the SJR, the Eigenfactor Score, the AI score and the h-index as provided by Scopus (using 77 randomly selected journals). Table 6.11 shows the results. Yet, high correlations do not mean that these indicators do not contain unique, new information (West et al., 2010).

Similarly, González-Pereira et al. (2010) found a Spearman rank correlation of 0.93 and a Pearson correlation of 0.86 between the SJR and a 3-year synchronous impact factor for 27 subject areas (in SCImago), and values of 0.91 (Spearman) and 0.89 (Pearson) for 295 specific subareas.

Table 6.11 Pearson correlations between journal indicators for the year 2006: (Rousseau & Stimulate 8 Group, 2009)

Indicators	JIF	SJR	Eigenfactor	AIS	h
JIF	1.00	0.915	0.827	0.918	0.869
SJR	—	1.00	0.731	0.813	0.760
Eigenfactor	—	—	1.00	0.827	0.951
AIS	—	—	—	1.00	0.855
h	—	—	—	—	1.00

As a disadvantage of PageRank type of indicators we note that they enforce the Matthew effect for journals (see Subsection 9.3.2 for a discussion of the Matthew effect).

6.11 THE AUDIENCE FACTOR

This indicator was introduced in 2008 by Michel Zitt with the help of Henry Small (Zitt & Small, 2008). It is defined as follows. Consider the journal J as a citing journal in the year Y. This journal has published articles containing reference lists going back in time. Let now $m_J(Y, Y_0)$ denote the average number of references of articles published in journal J during the publication window $W(Y, Y_0) = [Y - Y_0, \ldots, Y - 1]$ $(Y_0 > 0)$. This publication window contains the so-called active references of J (as older references are not taken into account). Now each reference is weighted by a function depending on $m_J(Y, Y_0)$, namely $w_J(Y, Y_0) = m_S(Y, Y_0) / m_J(Y, Y_0)$, where $m_S(Y, Y_0)$ is the average number of active references in the whole database (representing all sciences). In fields with shorter reference list such as mathematics, these weights are larger than in fields that generally have longer reference lists.

The audience factor of journal J_0 in the year Y, denoted as $AF_{J_0}(Y)$, is defined as

$$AF_{J_0}(Y) = \frac{\sum_J w_J(Y, Y_0) \cdot c_{J,J_0}(Y, Y_0)}{\alpha_{J_0}(Y, Y_0)} \tag{6.15}$$

The symbol $c_{J,J_0}(Y, Y_0)$ represents the number of citations received by journal J_0 from journal J in the year Y for articles published (in J_0 of course) during the publication window $W(Y, Y_0)$; and $a_{J_0}(Y, Y_0)$ denotes the number of articles published by journal J_0 during the period $W(Y, Y_0)$.

It is clear that when all weights w are equal to one, one obtains a standard synchronous impact factor.

Properties of the audience factor are:
- It does not depend on a field's propensity to cite.
- It does not depend on citation speed, i.e., the period between the moment of citing and the moment of publication.
- It is independent of any journal classification scheme.

A variant of this definition, proposed in (Zitt & Small, 2008) consists of replacing $m_J(Y, Y_0)$ by $m_F(Y, Y_0)$ defined as the average number of references in articles published in the field (or domain) F to which journal J belongs. Again the average is determined over the publication window

$W(Y,Y_0)$. The advantage of this approach is that journals with short reference lists such as most trade journals (journals geared towards professionals in a discipline) are not anymore favored with respect to other journals in the same field. A disadvantage of this approach is that the audience factor becomes dependent on the used journal classification scheme.

6.12 THE SNIP INDICATOR (MOED, 2010, 2016; WALTMAN ET AL., 2013)

6.12.1 Definition of the SNIP Indicator

The SNIP-indicator, where SNIP stands for Source Normalized Impact per Paper, was introduced by Moed in 2010 (Moed, 2010) and is available, in revised form, in Elsevier's Scopus database. The idea of a source normalized approach is to correct for differences in citation practices between scientific fields. This is done by taking the length of the reference lists of citing papers into account. The underlying idea is that it is better to receive one citation among 10, than to receive one citation among 70. Other advantages are that scientific fields do not depend on a journal (as do the JCR categories) but depend on articles' references. Consequently this approach can also be used for multidisciplinary journals such as *Nature* and *Science*. By its construction it corrects for differences in citation habits.

The original SNIP indicator was defined as a ratio, namely the ratio of a raw impact per paper (RIP) and a relative database citation potential (RDCP):

$$\text{SNIP} = \frac{RIP}{RDCP} \tag{6.16}$$

The raw impact (RIP) is very similar to the standard JIF as available in the WoS but is calculated over 3 years while the JIF is calculated over a citation window of 2 years. Only publications of article type, conference papers and reviews (as defined in Scopus) are taken into account in the calculation of the SNIP.

The denominator RDCP is defined as the ratio of the journal's DCP (Database Citation Potential) and the median DCP of the database. The DCP-value of a journal is determined by the following procedure. First, a journal's subject field is determined. This subject field is defined as the set of all publications in the year of analysis with at least one reference to the journal (going back no more than 8 years). Then the DCP value of a journal equals the average number of references in the publications in the subject field of the journal, counting only recent references, i.e., references to publications that appeared in the three preceding years in journals covered by the database. As a mathematical formula DCP can be written as follows:

$$\text{DCP} = \frac{r_1 + r_2 + ... + r_n}{n} = \frac{1}{n} \sum_{j=1}^{n} r_j \qquad (6.17)$$

In this formula, n denotes the number of publications in the journal's subject field; r_j denotes the number of references in the j-th publication that appeared in the three preceding years in journals covered by the database. Such reference items are called active references.

6.12.2 The New SNIP Indicator

Waltman et al. (2013) pointed out that the original SNIP indicator had some properties which a good indicator is not supposed to have, namely:

1. It may happen that an additional citation leads to a decrease of the SNIP-value.
2. Nonconvexity: if two journals merge (are considered as one whole) then one would expect a new SNIP-value between the original two SNIP-values. However, this does not have to be the case. This is a convexity issue, see also Ramanana-Rahary et al. (2009) for a discussion of convexity issues in scientometric evaluations.

For these reasons Waltman et al. (2013) proposed a revised SNIP index. Its most significant modifications with respect to the original one are:

- Database citation potential (DCP)-values are calculated as harmonic rather than arithmetic averages.
- The calculation of DCP values takes into account not only the number of active references in citing publications but also the proportion of publications with at least one active reference in citing journals.
- The distinction between DCP and RDCP is abandoned, in other words the median DCP value does not play a role anymore.

We provide now some details about the new SNIP. The basic formula is SNIP = RIP/DCP in which the RIP-value of a journal is the same as in the original version. The DCP-value is a harmonic mean:

$$\text{DCP} = \frac{1}{3} \cdot \frac{n}{\frac{1}{p_1 r_1} + \frac{1}{p_2 r_2} + ... + \frac{1}{p_n r_n}} \qquad (6.18)$$

where the r_j's have the same meaning as before, namely the number of references in the j-th publication. The p_j's are new entities. Consider the jth publication in the subject field of a journal and consider then all publications that appeared in the same journal and the same year as the selected publication. Then p_j is the proportion of these publications that have at least one active reference. The underlying idea, according to Waltman et al. (2013) for using these new variables is that without including p_j, the source normalization mechanism may fail to completely correct for differences between low and high citation density fields.

We further note the following points related to the DCP calculation.

1. Only peer-reviewed publications of the type article, conference paper and review are considered (as was the case for the original SNIP).
2. The subject field of a journal consists of all publications in the year of analysis that refer to a publication in the journal in the three preceding years (not 8 anymore). Moreover, duplicate publications are now allowed (they were not).
3. The multiplication by 1/3 ensures that the average SNIP-value for all journals in the database is close to one.

The authors make the following comments on the selection of citing journals:

- journals that have changed titles are considered as one (this is typically not the case in the WoS).
- trade journals are excluded.
- journals that did not publish continuously during four consecutive years are excluded.
- journals with less than 20% of the publications in the year of analysis having at least one active reference are excluded.

We now have another look at the formulae, beginning with $\text{SNIP} = \frac{\text{RIP}}{\text{DCP}}$.

$\text{RIP} = k/m$, where k is the number of received citations and m is the number of publications during the used citation and publication windows. We already know that:

$$\text{DCP} = \frac{1}{3} \cdot \frac{n}{\frac{1}{p_1 r_1} + \frac{1}{p_2 r_2} + \dots + \frac{1}{p_n r_n}} \qquad (6.18)$$

Combining these two formula yields:

$$\text{SNIP} = \frac{3}{m} \sum_{j=1}^{n} \frac{1}{p_j r_j} \qquad (6.19)$$

Clearly SNIP decreases when any r (a number of references) increases.

This formula can be understood as follows: the revised SNIP is a journal's average number of citations per publication (division by m), where each citation is weighted inversely proportional to both the number of active references in the citing publication, and the proportion of publications with at least one active reference in the citing journal. The first problem mentioned in relation to the original SNIP-index, is solved as adding one citation clearly increases the new SNIP. Also the second problem is solved. For this we refer the reader to Waltman et al. (2013). These authors also show that indeed SNIP corrects for differences between citation potentials.

6.12.3 Comments

Waltman et al. (2013) observed some problems inherent in the formula for the original SNIP indicator and proposed a revised version that solves these problems. Yet, the price that has to be paid for this is that its calculation has become more complicated. The harmonic mean is less intuitive than the arithmetic mean or the median; the proportion of publications that have at least one active reference is introduced as a new parameter, and several ad hoc decisions have been made, for instance the decision to exclude journals with less than 20% (why 20, not 15 or 10%?) of the publications in the year of analysis having at least one active reference. Yet, as Elsevier—Scopus is using the modified SNIP since October 18, 2012 this new version is the only "official" one. Moed (2016) expresses doubts about the necessity of the changes that have been made on his original version. He concludes that none of the two indicators is superior to the other as they are both based on plausible statistical assumptions. He notes that the modified SNIP calculation strongly emphasizes the requirement to comply with certain consistency criteria, while the original SNIP can be interpreted as a correction to a subject field bias in the classical JIF as calculated in the WoS. Moreover, Mingers (2014) points out that, by using a harmonic mean the new SNIP result can be significantly dependent on the dispersion of the number of references as well as their volume. He sees no justification for this procedure as the point of normalization is to make allowance for the volume of activity not its degree of variability. A large part of this discussion of the SNIP-index and its revision is taken from (Rousseau, 2013).

Finally, JIFs, however calculated, can only have a minor or restricted meaning in evaluations for fields where conference proceedings, contributions in edited books or monographs play an important role.

6.13 CLARIVATE ANALYTICS' JOURNAL CITATION REPORTS

The first edition of the JCR dates from 1976 (Garfield, 1976). It was added to the Science Citation Index 1975 as volume 9 and covers the scientific literature of 1974. We note that before the official launch of the JCR a preliminary version had been available as computer printouts based on 1969 data. This explains why one finds use of the JCR in the literature, before the year 1976 (Inhaber, 1974). At first the JCR were printed as a volume of the SCI and the SSCI (but with considerable delay), later they became available on microfiches, then on CD-ROM and more recently as part of the InCites platform. The A&HCI has no accompanying JCR.

The complete matrix of all journal citation relations is very sparse, and hence consists largely of empty cells. Any given journal does not cite the large majority of the other journals in the database (this observation holds for any database of this type, not only for the JCR). If a journal cites another one exactly once this is usually not shown in the JCR. Taking this restriction into account, approximately 97% of all cells in a journal-journal citation matrix are empty (Leydesdorff & Jin, 2005).

6.13.1 WoS Categories

Journals included in the JCR are assigned to subject categories (SCs) of science, including a category Multidisciplinary Sciences. In this mixed group one finds top journals such as *Science, Nature* and the *Proceedings of the National Academy of Sciences USA*, but also journals with a much lower impact factor such as *National Academy Science Letters — India* and the *Johns Hopkins APL Technical Digest*. One of the categories in the social sciences is Information Science and Library Science. Assignment of journals to categories is not unequivocal as journals may be assigned to more than one subject category. This is illustrated in Table 6.12.

This table shows that more than 40% of all journals are assigned to more than one subject category. Overlap between subject categories is a form of cooccurrence. This aspect has been used by (Morillo et al., 2003)

Table 6.12 Division of journals over JCR SCIE subject categories (for the year 2015)

6 SCs	6 journals
5 SCs	25 journals
4 SCs	172
3 SCs	820
2 SCs	2765
1 SC	4989

to study interdisciplinarity, in the sense that the number of categories to which a journal belongs can be used as a basic measure of journal interdisciplinarity.

6.13.2 Indicators Available in the JCR

In this section we present a brief overview of the indicators available in the JCR. The JCR provides yearly values of the following indicators: total number of received citations (in that year), the standard JIF, the 5-year synchronous impact factor, the immediacy index, the number of published articles, the cited and citing half-life, the Eigenfactor Score and the AIS. Very often, and maybe somewhat surprisingly, there is not much difference between a ranking of all journals in a subject area based on JIF (2) and on JIF(5) (see Campanario, 2011; Garfield, 1998; Leydesdorff, 2009; Rousseau, 2009a).

We have not yet given the definition of the cited and the citing half-life in the year Y. Informally, the *cited half-life* of a journal in the year Y is the median age of articles from this journal that were cited in year Y. Roughly speaking, a *cited half-life* of 7 years in the year 2014 means that the articles published in this journal during the period (2008−2014) received half of this year's citations. For the citing half-life the term *received citations* must be replaced by *references given*. It has been observed that the term half-life is actually a misnomer (Broadus, 1953; Száva-Kováts, 2002) as in the scientific literature the term half-life implies an exponential function. The terms *median age of cited articles* and *median age of references* (or of citing articles, if cited items which are not articles are not taken into account) would be better. As the cited and citing half-life are actually given with one decimal we provide some more information about their calculation.

Consider, as an example the following data for a journal in the JCR 2012 (Table 6.13).

This journal received 2138 citations in the year 2012; 15 were for articles published in the year 2012 itself, 92 were for articles published in the year 2011 and so on. Note that when the same article has been cited several times it is counted more than once. We see that after 6 years the journal has received 49.2% of all its citations. Hence, the time after which exactly 50% of all citations is received lies between 6 and 7. We use linear interpolation to find the exact number. Using linear interpolation means that it is assumed that citations are spread evenly over the year. The

Table 6.13 Table illustrating the calculation of the median cited age

Cited year	2012	2011	2010	2009	2008	2007	2006	2005	2004	2003	Earlier
Rank	1	2	3	4	5	6	7	8	9	10	
# citations received in 2012	15	92	210	267	287	180	200	171	191	123	402
Cumulative number	15	107	317	584	871	1051	1251	1422	1613	1736	2138
Cumulative percentage	0.7	5.0	14.8	27.3	40.7	49.2	58.5	66.1	75.4	81.2	100

difference in citations between year 6 and year 7 is $1251-1051$ corresponding to a difference in percentage points of 9.36. The difference between 49.2 (actually 49.16) and 50.00 is 0.84. Hence we need another 0.84/9.36 of a year to reach 50%. This is 0.09 years. Hence the median age of cited articles of this journal is 6.09 or rounded to one decimal 6.1 year. This is how cited and citing half-lives are calculated in the JCR.

Consider now the slightly changed Table 6.14.

Yet one could make another point. The journal represented by Table 6.14 has a median cited age of exactly 6. What is the average age of the 198 articles published in the year 2007 and cited in the year 2012? One would expect them to be, on average, 5 years old. Indeed, if all citations were received on the last day of the year 2012 and if all cited articles were published on the first day of the year 2007 than these articles would be almost 6 years old. If however, all citations were received on the first day of the year 2012 and all cited articles were published on the last day of the year 2007 then these articles would be slightly more than 4 years old. On average such citations refer to articles that are 5 years old (Rousseau, 2006b). So, the median cited age (as calculated in the JCR) refers to articles that are on average half a year less old than this median cited age. We think that it would be more logical if the time line as presented in the JCR were shifted over one half year. The point we want to make here is that an article cited in the year Y (here 2012) and published in the year $Y-5$ (here 2007) is not, on average, 5 1/2 years old as suggested by the second row of Table 6.10 (assuming a uniform distribution of citations over the year), but only five (on average), as explained above. Even then, there is still a problem for the first year, but for this technical issue we refer the reader to (Rousseau, 2006b).

One of the points of discussion about the Garfield-Sher JIF is that the numerator takes all citations into account (received within the citation window) while the denominator only counts "citable documents." This leads to two problems: the first is that the notion of a "citable document" is not precisely defined (although it always includes "normal articles" and reviews), and the second one is that in some journals "noncitable documents" receive quite a lot of citations (for instance some editorials or letters to the editor). In this context such citations are sometimes referred to as "for-free-citations." We return to this point in the sections on impact factor manipulation (see Section 6.15) and on CiteScore (Section 6.16).

The JCR provides the data used to calculate the indicators shown in its database. This includes, for instance, the number of citable publications and

Table 6.14 An illustration of a problem with half-life calculations

Cited year	2012	2011	2010	2009	2008	2007	2006	2005	2004	2003	Earlier
Rank	1	2	3	4	5	6	7	8	9	10	
# citations received in 2012	15	92	210	267	287	198	182	171	191	123	402
Cumulative number	15	107	317	584	871	1069	1251	1422	1613	1736	2138
Cumulative percentage	0.7	5.0	14.8	27.3	40.7	50.0	58.5	66.1	75.4	81.2	100

the number of citations received by each journal by all documents published in the two previous years. Note though that these numbers are not the same as those one can retrieve oneself in the WoS. Thomson Reuters (nowadays, Clarivate Analytics) claimed that the numbers shown in the JCR are more accurate as they are derived from a cleaned version of the WoS. This means that, most of the time, the official JIF is higher than one an outsider would calculate based on the WoS (Wu et al., 2008). The JCR also provides the number of review articles and the number of other citable documents for each journal. This is interesting information as reviews generally receive more citations than other publications and hence review journals (journals that publish—almost—exclusively reviews) have generally higher impact factors than journals which publish no or much less reviews.

Yet, also here there is a problem in the sense that Clarivate Analytics uses its own definition of a review. It may happen that the authors state in the title or abstract that they wrote a review but that this article is not classified as a review in the WoS or in the JCR (Colebunders & Rousseau, 2013).

The JCR provides even more detailed information shown under the cited journal data or the citing journal data for journal J. The cited journal table provides detailed information about journals, and other sources, citing journal J; their names and the publication year(s) they have cited. This information covers a 10 year period. Cited older volumes are brought together under *rest*. There is a lower bound for the number of citations (usually 2). All sources citing journal *J* just once (if the lower bound is 2) are brought together as *all others*. As expected (see Chapter 9: The Informetric Laws) *all others* is always very high in the list, as informetric data such as these are very skew with a long tail. Yearly totals are shown on top of the detailed table. The citing journal table is constructed in a similar way. We note that a journal usually cites itself a considerable amount of time. Hence a journal is usually ranked high, i.e., having a small rank, in these tables and this in the cited as well as the citing data list.

Recall that data taken from the cited journal table (top line) are needed in case one wants to calculate a diachronous impact factor.

6.14 STRUCTURE OF THE SCIMAGO DATABASE

The SCImago database for journals is freely available at http://www. scimagojr.com/journalrank.php. SCImago uses Scopus data for these rankings. The SCImago Group was founded by Félix de Moya Anegon, who later became an external consultant for the group.

The default view of the SCImago website shows journals ranked according to the SJR. The SCImago Journal Ranking is an indicator calculated for all Scopus journals, which is similar to PageRank or to the Eigenvector Score. The following indicators are also available for each journal J: the journal h-index (calculated for the period since 1996); the number of published documents (during the year Y shown on upper right hand side, the number of documents published during the previous 3 years $(Y - 3$ to $Y - 1)$; the number of references in journal J in the year Y, the number of received citations in the year Y for articles published during the publication window $[Y - 3; \quad Y - 1]$; the number of "citable documents" (these are: normal articles, review articles and conference contributions); cites/per docs (2 year); the average number of references; country. Viewing journals per subject category one sees the quartile, according to the SJR, to which this journal belongs.

Scopus distinguishes 295 specific subfields, grouped in 27 subject areas (among which an area called "General," including the journals *Nature* and *Science*). All journals are assigned to four large categories: Life Sciences ($>$4300 journals), Physical Sciences ($>$7200 journals), Social Sciences ($>$5300 journals) and Health Sciences (about 6800 journals).

The following information is provided per journal:

Country—subject area—subject category or categories (in this database too a journal may belong to several subject categories)—the quartile (calculated per subject category) to which this journal's SJR belongs—publisher—coverage (period)—ISSN—h index.

A number of graphs related to a journal can be viewed.

- SJR versus cites/doc (2 year) over a period of 10 year (if available)
- Number of citations versus number of (journal) self-citations (over a period of 3 year) again shown over 10 years.
- The same information, now per document.
- The synchronous impact factor (cites per doc) using a 3 and 4-year publication window.
- International collaboration = percentage of documents containing addresses in different countries.
- The relation between citable and noncitable documents.
- Percentages and numbers of cited and noncited documents.

SCImago also provides a country ranking, see http://www.scimagojr.com/countryrank.php

In this subdatabase one can view a ranking over the period [1996, Y], or separately by year. The following indicators are available:

- Total number of published documents.
- Total number of citable documents.
- Total number of received citations (ending in Y).
- Total number of journal self-citations (ending in Y).
- Citations per document (ending "today").
- The country h-index

Finally SCImago also provides a ranking per institute: the SCImago Institutions Ranking (SIR), see http://www.scimagoir.com/

This report contains a list of research institutes and organizations. Their research over a 5-year period is described in terms of output, collaboration and scientific impact. All data come from the Scopus database. Research institutes and organizations from more than eighty countries are ranked. They are classified according to five sectors: government (such as CNRS (France) and CAS (China)), higher education, health, companies and other.

Elsevier owns the Scopus database which covers over 22,000 titles from over 5000 publishers (2016 data). Each journal in the database is assigned to one or more subject classifications, using their "All Science Journal Classification" (ASJC) codes (referring to entities similar to WoS' subject areas). A list of ASJC codes can be found at: http://www.scopus.tk/2016/06/asjc-code-list.html

6.15 PROBLEMS RELATED TO IMPACT FACTORS (MOED, 2005A; STOCK, 2009; VANCLAY, 2012)

We first note that some of these problems are related to the database used, e.g., coverage, some are related to the mathematical formula used to calculate the JIF, and some are related to the specific way in which Clarivate Analytics calculates the JIF.

1. Not all academic journals are indexed in the WoS or Scopus. This is a problem of coverage.
2. Which publications are "citable?" "Normal" research articles are always considered to be citable as are reviews, but other types of publications are often considered at an ad hoc basis. This may lead to bias in favor of journals that publish many *letters to the editor* or *editorials*, and—sometimes—have earned a reputation for the quality of published letters or editorials.

3. Generally speaking review journals have a higher impact factor than journals which publish few reviews. In fact, these two types of journals are incomparable. Because reviews tend to receive more citations, journals tend to increase the number of reviews they publish, see e.g. (Colebunders et al., 2014) for some medical fields.

4. Databases do not treat all fields, all regions and all languages in the same way.

5. Databases are not error-free.

6. Impact factors can be manipulated by editors.

   a. One manipulation method is forcing authors to cite recent articles published in their journal (Wilhite & Fong, 2012). These dealings can be made futile if one removes journal self-citations from the calculation of a journal's impact factor. Yet, highly specialized fields have sometimes just one main journal and removing journal self-citations from the calculation of the impact factor of these journals would marginalize them even more. As most authors consider coercive citation as inappropriate, cf. Chapter 3, Publishing in Scientific Journals, and prestige reducing (for the editor as well as for the journal) (Wilhite & Fong, 2012) one might hope that this practice would eliminate itself.

   b. A more subtle form of impact factor manipulation is by using citation cartels. This means that a group (a cartel) of editors agrees to preferentially cite each other's journals. This is most easily done in editorials, but also coercive citations can be used in this way. As a prospective author is asked to cite other journals this is less conspicuous. An example of such a cartel was revealed by Davis (2012).

7. Impact factors are, essentially, an average number of citations. However, the distribution of citations to individual publications is skewed and, hence, the impact factor can sometimes yield misleading results. An extreme example of this occurred for the journal *Acta Crystallographica A*. Whereas this journal typically has a JIF of about 2, it rose to, respectively, 49.926 and 54.333 in the years 2009−2010, almost completely due to one single, very highly cited paper.

8. In calculating the JIF Clarivate Analytics does not seem to check if an item mentioned in a reference list really refers to an existing article: they just check the name of the journal (is it the journal for which a JIF is calculated?) and the publication date of the article as mentioned (is the publication date mentioned one of the 2 years required in the calculation of the JIF; not if this date is correct) (Vanclay, 2012).

Vanclay (2012) published an article which was very critical for Thomson Reuters and the way the standard impact factor is calculated. Colleagues, including some working for Thomson Reuters (Pendlebury & Adams, 2012) got the opportunity to react (positively or negatively) to his memorandum.

We think that citations in editorials should not be counted when calculating the JIF. As editorials are very rarely highly cited (Rousseau, 2009c) this illustrates the fact that such references hardly ever support high level arguments.

A simple solution to some of the problems related to the calculation of the JIF is using a median instead of an average. This approach has recently been applied by the Nature Publishing Group (NPG) as announced by EIC Philip Campbell and Sowmya Swaminathan, head of editorial policy, in an anonymous editorial (Anonymous, 2016). The median impact of a journal for the year Y is the median number of citations that articles published in the years $Y-2$ and $Y-1$ received during the year Y. NPG used only genuine articles or reviews for the calculation of the median impact.

6.16 CITESCORE INDEX

On December 8, 2016 Elsevier launched the CiteScore index, a journal indicator serving the same purpose as the JIF, but calculated in a slightly different way.

The first difference is, of course, the used database. The CiteScore index makes use of the journals covered by Scopus. The second is the different way in which a journal's impact is calculated. The CiteScore index is a 3-year synchronous indicator (while JIF is a 2-year one). Finally, and this makes a huge difference for some journals, while not affecting others, the CiteScore index divides by all published items, not just the so-called "citable" ones. For journals such as the *Lancet*, *Science* or *Nature* this makes quite a difference.

6.17 WHO MAKES USE OF BIBLIOMETRIC INDICATORS? (STOCK, 2009)

- Journal editors and publishers.

  They use impact factors as marketing tools. Journals' impact factors and especially their increase are prominently displayed on journals' webpages. Note that, as databases tend to increase and reference lists tend to become longer, there are more journals that increase their impact factor than journals that show a decrease.

- Librarians.

    Impact factors may be an element in buying or deselection decisions. Yet, for two reasons impact factors are not that important for librarians. First, impact factors are related to global use and importance, but librarians must work for local researchers and students. Local use may be considerably different from global use, language being one factor. Secondly, big publishing companies propose large packets (so-called big deals) and it is difficult to change their content.

- Librarians new style and research administrators.

    Åström and Hansson (2013) point out that in many countries, especially in Scandinavian countries, librarians organize bibliometric activities as a way to redefine their role within the university and increase their status. Informing users, i.e., researchers, about bibliometric indicators, such as the JIF, and their use for research evaluation is one aspect, while actually providing bibliometric analyses as background for evaluations and funding policies is another one. Other universities have created special functions, say research administrators, to perform these tasks.

- Authors who want to know the top journals or rising stars in their field. Sometimes evaluation committees make a difference between publishing in journals with a high impact factor, a medium one or a journal not included in the WoS. Let us already say that comparing actual received citations with a benchmark value in the same field would be much better (whatever the venue in which the article is published), and actually reading the article and making up one's own mind would be better still (assuming the member of the evaluation committee is an expert in this particular field).

- Some scientists, in particular informetricians.

    For them indicators, such as impact factors are a form of measurement. Results inform about relations within the network of academic journals. Studying correlations between rankings based on different indicators is one aspect of such studies.

6.18 RANKING JOURNALS (ROUSSEAU ET AL., 2015; XU ET AL., 2015)

Once an indicator has been constructed, journals can be ranked according to this indicator. Yet, using bibliometric indicators is not the only possible method to rank journals. Generally speaking, existing ranking methods can be classified as peer review based, citation (or indicator) based or a combination of the two.

6.18.1 Peer Review Based Approach

In this approach, the assessment of scientific journals in a particular field or subfield is undertaken by a group of scholars working in the same area. In most cases a survey or questionnaire is designed to collect opinions from professors or academic administrators (Chandy et al., 1991). The peer review based approach is expected to produce a valid assessment because experts (not just any scientist) judge the quality of a journal based on their experience and accumulated impressions of the quality of the published papers that they have read or reviewed. However, it is unclear on what criteria experts base their judgments. Thus, it is not clear how or even whether assumed quality criteria are measured in any of these rankings. More to the point, these quality criteria are rarely made explicit nor are their relative weights in the overall assessment. One may say that journal rankings based on peer review are reputation rankings while the citation based approach, discussed next is a visibility or influence based approach (Christenson & Sigelman, 1985). Christenson and Sigelman also found that scholars in sociology and political sciences tended to establish reputations that stick and are not re-evaluated in light of recent publications.

A comprehensive list of the advantages and disadvantages of the expert survey ranking method is provided in Table I of Serenko and Bontis (2013), which we reproduce here with some adaptations.

Advantages of expert survey journal ranking:

a. Suitable for rankings on all levels, in particular for local and regional journals.
b. Suitable for rankings in new disciplines.
c. New journals can be included.
d. This approach is widely accepted.
e. It reflects the multifaceted opinion of a representative group.
f. It is difficult to manipulate by outsiders.

Disadvantages of expert survey journal ranking:

a. Subjectivity as experts may be influenced by their personal research interests and those of leading figures.
b. Familiarity bias: respondents assign higher values to journals they are familiar with.

c. Identity concerns: if respondents fear that their identity would become known they might follow the general opinion; similarly they might favor journals of which they are an editorial board member.

d. Rater fatigue if they have to rate long lists of journals.

e. Path dependency: lists to be ranked are built upon older lists so that some journals stay on these lists for ever (this also holds for the citation based approach).

f. Underrepresentation of practitioners and journals aiming at this group.

g. Order bias: the order in which journals are presented to raters may have a confounding effect on their rankings.

Most of these disadvantages can be avoided by taking the necessary precautions when soliciting expert opinions.

6.18.2 Citation Based Approach

The citation based approach is the most-used approach to produce journal rankings. Moreover, a variety of citation based indicators have been applied for journal evaluations. Several studies employed total citations (Liebowitz & Palmer, 1984) or average citations (Doyle & Arthurs, 1995) in specified evaluation windows. Moreover, one sometimes emphasizes selected citations. Tahai and Meyer (1999), e.g., produced the SMJ99 management journal ranking based on citations that were received from the top 17 journals in the field using a 2-year window. Among these citation based indicators, the JIF received by far the most attention. The JIF assigns identical weights to all received citations, regardless of the prestige of citing sources (papers, authors, journals or conferences). The concept of weighted citations (Kochen, 1974; Pinski & Narin, 1976) is, after its conversion to Google's PageRank, applied for journals as the Eigenfactor (Bergstrom, 2007), the SJR index (http://www.scimagojr.com/journalrank.php) or, in a normalized form, as the AIS and used, as such, for journal rankings.

The well-known h-index (Hirsch, 2005) has also been used in the assessment of academic journals as suggested by Braun et al. (2005, 2006). These authors moreover claimed that the h-index is a more robust index than the JIF. However, the h-index only counts the publications in the h-core and ignores all the rest. Also the g-index (Egghe, 2006a,b,c) has been applied for journal rankings (Bontis & Serenko, 2009; Serenko & Bontis, 2009).

A comprehensive list of the advantages and disadvantages of the journal ranking method based on citation impact measures is provided in Table II of (Serenko & Bontis, 2013) which we republish here with some adaptions.

Advantages of the citation indicator method for ranking journals:

a. The method is more objective than using peer review or experts' opinions as it involves the actual use of a large group of scientists.
b. There exist many citation based indicators, which may be combined in the most appropriate manner.
c. Over the years citation based indicators have obtained a wide acceptance for journal rankings.

Disadvantages of the citation indicator method for ranking journals:

a. Citation behavior differs between fields and hence comparison between fields is not valid. Moreover, multidisciplinary journals cannot really be included in journal rankings.
b. Some indicators, such as the JIF (being an average), are highly influenced by the skewness of citation data.
c. Citations may be manipulated by journal editors.
d. Citation impact is generally low for new or niche journals.
e. Retracted articles may be included in citation counts.
f. All databases contain errors.
g. If a journal is not included in the database used for the ranking exercise it cannot be ranked.
h. Path dependency (Truex et al., 2008). This means that authors have the tendency to use and re-use journals studied and ranked by predecessors. This is even true for the WoS as a whole, a point discussed in (Rousseau & Spinak, 1996).
i. Most citation indicators do not make a distinction between citing sources (but eigenvector related methods do).
j. Different citation indicators or different weightings in composite measures may lead to different rankings.

Most of these disadvantages apply to any use of citation measures, not just for journal rankings.

6.18.3 Combination of the Two Approaches

When applying this approach, journal quality assessments and rankings are generated through a combination of the two approaches listed above. Often initial journal rankings are generated based on bibliometric information and later reviewed and adjusted according to experts' opinions. This approach is widely used for local journal evaluations and, moreover, often applied in research institutes as a standard for staff promotion. Among them, the Association of Business Schools (ABS) journal quality guide, produced by the ABS has attracted much attention among business schools. In the ABS journal ranking a total of more than 800 selected journals from 22 fields are rated from 4 (indicating the highest quality) to 1 (for the lowest quality). Opinions from experts including journal editors and researchers, and information on journal impact and journal submissions are considered to produce the final journal ranking. Serenko and Bontis (2013) provide a ranking of knowledge management and intellectual capital academic journals combining an expert survey with journal impact methods.

6.18.4 Other Journal Ranking Indicators

Finally, several other types of indicators suggested for journal ranking purposes can be found in the literature. We mention the following:

Brown (2003) developed a download metric to rank journals in the area of accounting and finance. Download frequencies of articles were obtained from the Social Science Research Network.

Holsapple (2008) proposed the publication power approach for identifying a group of most-important (he uses the term "premier") journals in a field. This method takes into account the actual publication behavior of all full-time, tenured faculty at leading universities (the benchmark researchers) over a given (recent) period of time. The publication power of a journal is then defined as the product of its publishing intensity and its publishing breadth. Here, a journal's publishing breadth is defined as the number of benchmark researchers who have published at least one article in this journal, and the journal's publishing intensity is the sum of the number of times this journal has been the publication outlet across all benchmark researchers. By definition, the publishing breadth is never larger than the publishing intensity. This method has been applied in (Serenko & Jiao, 2012) to provide a ranking of Information Systems (IS) journals in Canada.

Ending this section we note that, whatever the method used, this does not need to lead to a—complete—ranking of journals. Often a classification in first tier, second tier and so on is sufficient, and often more sensible. A three-tier classification is, for instance, applied in the Norwegian model (Sivertsen, 2010), see Subsection 8.9.1.

6.19 THE MEDIAN IMPACT FACTOR

A group of colleagues from Thailand proposed a new kind of impact factor, the cited half-life impact factor, or better median impact factor, in short MIF (Rousseau, 2005a; Sombatsompop et al., 2004). In this approach the actual form of the journal citation curve is taken into account, making this impact factor better suited for a comparison of impact among fields and subfields. It is defined as follows:

$$\text{MIF}_J(Y) = \frac{\text{TOT}_J(Y)/2}{\text{CPUB}_J(Y - X, Y)} \tag{6.20}$$

In this formula, $\text{TOT}_J(Y)$ denotes the total number of citations received by journal J in the year Y; $\text{CPUB}(Y - X, Y)$ denotes the cumulative number of publications in the journal J, during the period $[Y - X, Y]$, where X denotes the median cited age (see Subsection 6.13.2). As citations are collected in the same year (Y) this is a synchronous impact factor.

An example: the MIF(2003) for the journal *Scientometrics*.

The total number of citations received by the journal *Scientometrics* in the year 2013 was 5129. Hence TOT = 5129 and thus TOT/2 = 2564.5. Further data can be found in Table 6.15. For simplicity we used as number of publications the number of so-called citable items according to the WoS.

The median is attained somewhere between the 6th and the 7th year. The cumulative number of citations received by articles published during

Table 6.15 Data for the calculation of *Scientometrics* MIF(2013)

Year	2007	2008	2009	2010	2011	2012	2013
# publications	129	128	189	226	217	254	255
Cumulative number of publications (going back to the past)	1398	1269	1141	952	726	509	255
Number of citations received in the year 2013	305	307	382	566	558	513	84
Cumulative number of citations (going back to the past)	2715	2410	2103	1721	1155	597	84
Cumulative percent of citations (going back to the past)	52.93	46.99	41.00	33.55	22.52	11.64	1.64

Source: Taken from (Rousseau, 2005a).

the first 6 most recent years is 2410. As $(2{,}564.5 - 2{,}410) = 154.5$ and 154.5 is 0.51 of 305, the median citation age is 6.51 (rounded in the JCR to 6.5). The number of articles published during the most recent 6 years in *Scientometrics* is 1269 (see row three of Table 6.15). Finally, $0.51 \times 129 = 65.79$ is added to this number, yielding 1334.79. This is the denominator for the calculation of the MIF. It is concluded that the 2013 MIF of *Scientometrics* is $2564.5/1334.79 = 1.921$, a value which is smaller than the corresponding $JIF_2(2.274)$ for 2013 and also smaller than its 5-year JIF (2.294).

6.20 MATHEMATICAL PROPERTIES OF THE DIACHRONOUS AND THE SYNCHRONOUS IMPACT FACTOR

In this section we illustrate how one can make elementary mathematical considerations related to indicators.

6.20.1 Elementary Considerations on Impact Factors

As an example we first use the diachronous impact factor. Recall that this indicator is defined as:

$$JDIF_n^s(Y) = \frac{\sum_{k=s}^{s+n-1} CIT(Y, Y + k)}{PUB(Y)} \tag{6.6}$$

Clearly, when one or more of the citation data increases, and all other data stay the same, then the JDIF increases. The same happens when the number of publications decreases. If all citation data are multiplied by the same factor, say a, then the JDIF also increases by this same factor: JDIF $\rightarrow$ a.JDIF. Similarly, when the number of publications increases by a factor b then the JDIF becomes (1/b).JDIF. If $a = b$ then the JDIF stays invariant. Note though that thinking in percentages is more difficult. If each citation data increases by 10% then $a = 1.1$ and JDIF also increase by 10%. If however PUB increases by 10% then $b = 1.1$ and $(1/b) = 0.91$. Hence an increase of PUB by 10% leads to a decrease of the JDIF by about 9% (and not 10%!).

What happens if citations come from different pools of citing articles? We first assume that the total pool of citing articles is subdivided into two disjoint pools. We denote by CIT_j $(j = 1{,}2)$ the number of citations given by journals belonging to pool j $(j = 1{,}2)$, and use a similar notation for the JDIF. Hence $JDIF_j$ ($j = 1,2$) denotes the diachronous impact factor calculated exclusively with respect to pool j. Then we have the following simple decomposition:

$$JDIF^s_n(Y) = \frac{\sum_{k=s}^{s+n-1} CIT_1(Y, Y+k) + \sum_{k=s}^{s+n-1} CIT_2(Y, Y+k)}{PUB(Y)}$$

$$= JDIF^s_{n,1}(Y) + JDIF^s_{n,2}(Y)$$

$$(6.21)$$

because the pools are disjoint.

Clearly, if the global pool is subdivided into m disjoint subpools then the decomposition takes the following form:

$$DIF^s_n(Y) = \sum_{j=1}^m DIF^s_{n,j}(Y). \tag{6.22}$$

What happens if we have m possibly overlapping pools, as in the case of JCR's journal categories?

A citing journal may belong to 1, 2, ..., m pools, making the situation difficult to oversee. For two overlapping pools the answer is relatively easy:

$$DIF(Y) = DIF_1(Y) + DIF_2(Y) - DIF_{1,2}(Y) \tag{6.23}$$

where, to simplify the notation, we have omitted the length of the citation window (n) and the offset period (s). The index 1,2 refers to the journals in the intersection of pool 1 and pool 2. For the general case (m possibly overlapping pools) we refer the reader to Rousseau (2005b).

6.20.2 A Property of the Basic Journal Citation Model

Next we prove that in the basic journal citation model, explained below, the 3-year synchronous impact factor is always larger than the 2-year JIF. This calculation is taken from Rousseau et al. (2001).

It is generally agreed that synchronous citation curves are unimodal graphs, having a mode at the year two or later. This is in accordance with Price's theory on the immediacy effect (Price, 1970). At the mode the curve levels off, so that $c(3)$ is larger than the average of $c(1)$ and $c(2)$, where we denoted the number of citations given in year Y to documents

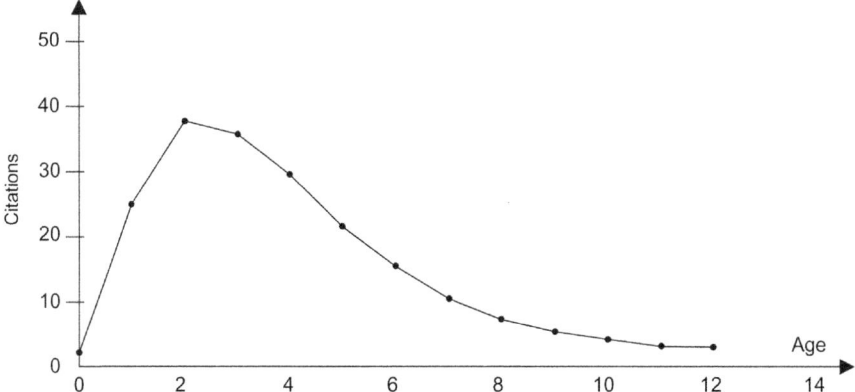

Figure 6.1 Typical synchronous citation curve: relationship between the number of articles cited in the target year and their age.

published in the year $Y - k$ (recall that we study synchronous citation curves) by $c(k)$. Fig. 6.1 is an illustration of a typical synchronous citation curve. The "age" axis represents the age of cited articles for a given target year; the "citations" axis represents the number of articles cited in the target year.

In this typical, "basic" model we further assume that the number of publications does not decrease in time. This means that we assume that $p(3) \leq p(2) \leq p(1)$, where e.g., $p(2)$ denotes the number of items published in the year $Y - 2$, while $p(3)$ denotes the number of articles published in the year $Y - 3$, i.e., 3 years ago. The assumption that sources, e.g., journals, increase their production over time is a very natural one.

The following theorem is a consequence of this basic model.

Theorem: In the basic model $\text{JIF}_3 > \text{JIF}_2$.

Proof. We have to compare

$$\text{JIF}_2 = \frac{c(1) + c(2)}{p(1) + p(2)} = \frac{\mu_c(2)}{\mu_p(2)}$$

where $\mu_c(2)$ and $\mu_p(2)$ denote the average number of citations, respectively publications, over a 2-year period, with:

$$\text{JIF}_3 = \frac{c(1) + c(2) + c(3)}{p(1) + p(2) + p(3)} = \frac{\mu_c(3)}{\mu_p(3)}$$

Now, the 3-year impact factor, JIF_3, will be larger than JIF_2 if

$$JIF_2 < JIF_3$$

$$\Leftrightarrow \frac{c(1) + c(2)}{p(1) + p(2)} < \frac{c(1) + c(2) + c(3)}{p(1) + p(2) + p(3)}$$

$$\Leftrightarrow c(1)(p(1) + p(2)) + c(1)p(3) + c(2)((p(1) + p(2)) + c(2)p(3)$$
$$< (p(1) + p(2))c(1) + (p(1) + p(2))c(2) + (p(1) + p(2))c(3)$$

$$\Leftrightarrow (c(1) + c(2))p(3) < (p(1) + p(2))c(3)$$

$$\Leftrightarrow \frac{c(1) + c(2)}{c(3)} < \frac{p(1) + p(2)}{p(3)}$$

Dividing both sides of the last inequality by 2 yields equation (*) below:

$$\frac{\mu_c(2)}{c(3)} < \frac{\mu_p(2)}{p(3)} \quad (*)$$

The assumptions $p(3) \leq \mu_p(2)$ and $c(3) > \mu_c(2)$ entail that

$$\frac{\mu_c(2)}{c(3)} < 1 < \frac{\mu_p(2)}{p(3)}$$

so that inequality (*), and hence the inequality $JIF_3 > JIF_2$ is always satisfied. This shows that JIF_3, the impact factor calculated over a 3-year period is, in the basic model, always larger than JIF_2, the "standard" or Garfield–Sher impact factor.

6.21 ADDITIONAL INFORMATION

Additional information about impact factors and their use in citation analysis can be found in: Todorov and Glänzel (1988), Stegmann (1999), Wilson (1999), Egghe and Rousseau (2002), Glänzel and Moed (2002), Moed (2005a), Nicolaisen (2008) and Bar-Ilan (2008). Rousseau (2002b) discusses aspects of journal evaluation and concludes that a whole battery of indicators is necessary, see also (Haustein, 2012). In the same vein, Bar-Ilan (2012) proposes journal report cards.

Regional citation indices, such as the already mentioned Chinese ones and SciELO often provide a derived database of local impact indicators (Jin et al., 2002). Also Publish or Perish (Google Scholar) provides means to search per journal.

In this chapter we focused on the classical citation- based journal indicators. Yet, all methods known as altmetrics can, of course, also be applied to journals. This remark holds true also for download data which are typically collected for journals, see e.g. (Bollen et al., 2005). We should also mention that multidisciplinary journals such as *Nature*, *Science* or *PLoS One* do not lead themselves to the application of most journal indicators, as their content crosses the borders between many fields. Such journals should be considered as sets of articles, each of which to be considered on their own merit.

Journals with a high impact factor attract a lot of attention, and hence, one may expect that a Matthew effect comes at play, increasing the impact factor. Yet, it is very difficult to prove this as many factors determine the citedness of an article, besides the journal in which it was published. In order to find out, one should theoretically publish the same article at the same time in different journals to determine the influence of the impact factor on citedness. This is, of course, normally not possible, but Perneger (2010) and Shanahan (2016) found a case where the same text was published in different journals, namely the case of biomedical reporting guidelines. As they are not scientific publications, but rather recommendations for authors, reporting guidelines are often published simultaneously to encourage wider adoption and dissemination. Perneger and Shanahan found that the number of citations received by the same publication was moderately strongly correlated to the JIF. Shanahan (2016) also found a strong positive correlation between the number of citations and the number of article accesses. Bornmann and Leydesdorff (2017) investigated and confirmed the skewness of the journal citation distribution. They found though that among all factors that may have an effect on resulting article citedness (number of cited references, number of authors, number of pages, JIF) the JIF has the strongest correlation with citation scores. A note of caution should be added here as this is not necessarily a causal effect. It might simply be that authors submit their best articles to high impact journals.

CHAPTER 7

Indicators

We will illustrate how most indicators introduced in the previous chapter can be applied to any set of articles, not just those published in the same journal. Also, collaboration indices are introduced. Moreover, some indicators which are less suitable for journals are discussed. We begin with a discussion of the h-index and h-type indices as these were originally introduced outside the context of journals. Among other things, we show how time series of indicators can be constructed.

7.1 INTRODUCTION

7.1.1 Definitions

Numerical data are facts expressed as numbers. Numerical data can be communicated and transformed into other data.

An indicator is a mathematical expression.

Applying this mathematical expression to numerical data leads to an *indicator value*.

Here is an example. The number of articles published by a university research group in a given year and the number of FTEs (full-time person equivalents) in that year are numerical data. Dividing the number of publications by the number of FTEs is an indicator (a mathematical expression). The resulting value of this indicator is the productivity of this research group in that year.

7.1.2 Some Remarks on Indicators

Although strictly speaking not correct, we will follow the general custom to consider the words index and indicator as synonyms. Moreover, people often refer to the value of an indicator or index as the indicator or the index, for instance one says: "This journal's h-index is 25," although strictly speaking they should say, "The value of this journal's h-index is 25." Although somewhat sloppy, we will often follow this habit.

Indicators are often used as proxy variables. This means that they are used for something else. The journal impact factor (JIF), for instance, is

Becoming Metric-Wise
DOI: http://dx.doi.org/10.1016/B978-0-08-102474-4.00007-8

often used, be it inappropriately, as a proxy for journal quality; similarly, the number of downloads is taken as a proxy for readership.

7.1.3 General Terminology: Validity, Fairness, Usefulness and Reliability

The term *validity* refers to whether or not the indicator measures what it claims to measure. An indicator is said to be *fair* if it is free of any kind of bias. It is *useful* if it provides essential information.

Finally, we consider *reliability* as a synonym of *reproducibility*. Calculation of an indicator in two similar circumstances should not lead to very different values, unless there is a clear explanation and then the circumstances were actually not similar.

Although fairness is a natural requirement, it is in practice probably impossible that an indicator is fair to everyone and in all circumstances.

7.1.4 Normalization

A normalized indicator is a ratio of an absolute indicator divided by a normalization parameter. This normalization parameter is either the maximum possible value, or an expected value. Normalization is usually applied to make results comparable over different, but similarly distributed, data sets. Normalization can be done in many ways. If indicator values are normally distributed, then z-values are used as normalized values. Unfortunately, few data sets or indicators in informetrics are normally distributed. If data are not normally distributed, but still more or less symmetric with respect to the median (which in this case coincides with the mean) one may divide by the mean or the median.

Of course, one may wonder why anyone would want to make the kind of comparisons alluded to above. Certainly such comparisons should not be made on an individual level i.e., one should not try to answer if geographer X is a better scientist than philosopher Y. Yet, we think that for a university leader it is a natural question to ask if the department of computer science is, compared with all other computer science departments in the country or in the world, better than the department of nanotechnology. By using an indicator and an appropriate normalization one may obtain an acceptable answer. Yet, one would not get an answer to the question which department performs the highest intellectual achievements, or the most useful results for society.

7.2 COLLABORATION AND COLLABORATION INDICES

Already in 1963, Price (1963) predicted that by 1980 the single author would be extinct. This prediction did not turn out to be correct, but the tendency of decreasing numbers of single-authored publications has continued since then. Although Price is best known for this prediction, he was not the first to notice the decrease in single-authored publications as Smith (1958) had already observed this trend in the field of psychology. Price further stated that the number of multiple authorship in a field reflects the financial support and the economic value attributed by society to that field. More recent information about multiple authorship can be found in Abramo et al. (2011).

Sonnenwald (2007) defines research collaboration as "the interaction taking place within a social context among two or more scientists that facilitates the sharing of meaning and completion of tasks with respect to a mutually shared, superordinate goal." Collaborative research leads to a combination of diverse perspectives, interpretations and models and avoids ignorance (about certain aspects of the topic of research, or about necessary technical skills) and lock-ins (doing what "everyone has always done").

7.2.1 Coauthorship Roles

Working together on a scientific project or during a scientific investigation does not automatically lead to coauthorship. This depends on the role a scientist plays during the investigation, and the "intensity" with which this role is played. Cosigning a project application is totally different from leading a team of six researchers with different and specific skills.

We reproduce (and slightly adapt) the taxonomy of Allen et al. (2014) which allows collaborators to describe their role(s) in a collaborative effort (Table 7.1). Deciding which contribution leads to (co-)authorship or maybe being the first author is another problem (see Subsection 2.3.4). In a study on marine biology it might be that the one thing everyone remembers is that fantastic picture that has been taken during the research. Yet, the photographer is probably not a coauthor of the associated publication. Note also that for each category in Table 7.1 there might be a leader and one or more scientists in a supporting role. It is also possible that some categories do not apply for certain investigations. This remark certainly applies for theoretical studies.

Table 7.1 Role categories of scientists during an investigation (Allen et al., 2014)

Category—role	Description
Conception of the study	Ideas; formulation of research question(s); statement of hypotheses
Methodology	Development or design of methodology; creation of models
Computation	Programming; software development; designing computer programs; implementation of computer code and supporting algorithms
Formal analysis	Application of statistical, mathematical or other formal techniques to analyze study data
Investigation; performing experiments	Conducting the research and investigation process, specifically performing experiments
Investigation; collecting data/evidence	Conducting the research and investigation process, specifically collecting data/evidence
Resources	Provision of study materials, reagents, materials, patients, laboratory samples, animals, instrumentation, or other tools
Data curation	Management activities to annotate and maintain research data for initial use and later re-use; producing metadata
Writing	Preparation, creation, presentation of the published work; providing critical review, comments, writing revisions
Manuscript preparation: visualization and data presentation	Preparation, creation, presentation of the published work, specifically taking care of data presentation in all possible forms
Supervision	Responsibility for supervising research; project orchestration; being the principal investigator
Project administration	Coordination or management of research activities leading to the publication
Funding	Acquisition of the financial support for the project, leading to the publication

Another important role is that of corresponding author. This role most often goes to the person in charge of supervision, which is usually the principal investigator (PI).

7.2.2 Forms of Collaboration

Excluding single-author publications, one can subdivide collaborative research into four types: Collaborations with colleagues from the same research group; collaboration with colleagues from the same institute, but at least some do not belong to the same research group; national collaboration: all authors belong to the same country but at least two institutions are involved; international collaboration: addresses in at least two countries are mentioned in the byline.

Similarly there are two types of sectorial collaborations, where sectors are university, health sector (mainly hospitals), companies, other, including public research centers, nonprofit organizations, and public administration. A collaboration may involve scientists from the same sector, or from at least two different sectors.

In gender studies one naturally studies if articles result from authors of the same gender, and which, or from mixed teams.

Finally we note that besides research collaboration, one may also distinguish publication collaboration. This happens when different teams decide, after the fact, to pool their results.

7.2.3 Measures of Collaboration (Egghe, 1991; Rousseau, 2011)

In this section we provide a review of measures that have been proposed to measure the collaboration intensity in a set of publications. Consider a set of N publications, none of which is written anonymously. We assume that in total A different scientists are author or coauthor of at least one of these papers. The number f_j denotes the number of papers with j (co)-authors. The index j belongs to the index set $I = \{1,2,....A\}$. In most practical cases, but not always, f_A will be zero, but it is certain that f_j, with $j > A$ is equal to 0.

We recall the following four collaboration indices, in order of sophistication.

1. The degree of collaboration (Subramanyam, 1983)

$$DC = 1 - \frac{f_1}{N} \tag{7.1}$$

This is nothing but the fraction of coauthored articles.

2. The collaborative index (Lawani, 1980)

$$CI = \frac{\sum_{j=1}^{A} j \, f_j}{N} \tag{7.2}$$

This is the average number of authors per publication.

3. The collaborative coefficient (Ajiferuke et al., 1988)

$$CC = 1 - \frac{\sum_{j=1}^{A} \frac{f_j}{j}}{N} \qquad (7.3)$$

The CC is one minus the average credit awarded to each author if complete–normalized fractional counting (5.6.3) is used.

4. The normalized CC (Egghe, 1991)

$$CC^* = \frac{A}{A-1}\left(1 - \frac{\sum_{j=1}^{A} \frac{f_j}{j}}{N}\right) \qquad (7.4)$$

Arguments can be put forward to conclude that CC is better than CC*, yet other arguments may lead to the conclusion that CC* is the better one (Rousseau, 2011). If A is large the difference between CC and CC* is in practice negligible.

Soon after the introduction of the CC Egghe (1991) and Englisch (1991) noted that this indicator does not provide detailed information and yields the same value in collaboration cases for which one would like to make a distinction. Consequently, Egghe proposed a list of eight principles which an acceptable collaboration measure should satisfy (one of these being normalization). Yet, he showed that CC* does not satisfy some of the other natural principles. After a thorough investigation he succeeded in finding a—rather sophisticated— measure, denoted as γ (gamma), which satisfies all his requirements. This measure, Egghe's gamma measure for collaboration, is defined as:

$$\gamma = \frac{s+t}{2} \quad \text{where} \qquad (7.5)$$

$$s = \frac{1}{A^2(A-1)^2 N}\left(\sum_{\substack{i,\,i'=1 \\ i \neq i'}}^{A} \sqrt{\sum_{j=1}^{q} x_{i,i'}^{(j)}}\,\right)^2 \qquad (7.6)$$

and

$$t = \frac{1}{A^2(A-1)^2 N k^2}\left(\sum_{i,i',j} \sqrt{x_{i,i'}^{(j)}}\,\right)^2 \qquad (7.7)$$

Here $x_{i,i'}^{(j)}$ denotes the number of times authors i and i' are coauthors in a paper with j authors in total. The number q is the largest natural number j such that $f_j \neq 0$, and the number k is equal to the number of elements in the set $K = \{j; j \geq 2, f_j \neq 0\}$.

The theory proposed by Egghe and English is the most refined approach known for the moment. Yet even within this approach open problems still exist, see the summary in (Egghe, 1991).

7.3 THE H-INDEX

7.3.1 Definition

Let us first recall the definition of the h-index as introduced by Hirsch (2005). Consider the list of articles (co-)authored by scientist S, ranked according to the number of citations each of these articles has received. Articles with the same number of citations are given different rankings (for the moment the exact order does not matter). Then the h-index of scientist S is h if the first h articles received each at least h citations, while the article ranked $h + 1$ received strictly less than $h + 1$ citations. Stated otherwise, scientist S' h-index is h if h is the largest natural number (representing a rank) such that the first h publications received each at least h citations.

The first h articles in such a ranked list form the h-core (Rousseau, 2006c). In case the articles themselves in the h-core are of importance in the study and the source at rank $h + 1$ has the same number of items as the source at rank h, then there are two options. The first is to restrict the h-core to exactly h elements. For this to happen one needs a second (or even tertiary) criterion to rank sources. We suggest using age as the secondary criterion and rank articles with the same number of citations in antichronological order i.e., the most recent article first. Indeed such articles have a higher number of citations per year than others with the same number of citations. A second option is to simply include all sources with the same number of items as the source on rank h. In that case an h-core can have any number of sources (but at least h). The resulting set is sometimes referred to as an extended h-core. Articles that do not belong to the h-core are said to belong to the h-tail. It is further noted that if the last article in the list occupies rank r and receives $c > r$ citations then this scientist's h-index is equal to r.

Consider, for example, Table 7.2 of publications and citations, ranked according to the number of received citations.

Table 7.2 Publication-citation (p-c) matrix of a fictitious scientist

Publication (date)	# citations
A (2010)	8
B (2013)	5
C (2011)	5
D (2011)	4
E (2008)	4
F (2014)	1
G (2010)	0

The scientist represented by Table 7.2 has h-index 4. Indeed, the first four publications have each at least 4 citations and four is the largest natural number for which this statement is true. Alternatively we may say that the first four publications have each at least 4 citations and the fifth ranked publication does not have $4 + 1 = 5$ citations. Using the convention to rank publications with an equal number of citations in antichronological order the h-core consists of articles A, B, C, and D. The extended h-core is {A,B,C,D,E}. When the context is clear, a scientist such as the one represented in Table 7.2 will be represented more succinctly by the array [8,5,5,4,4,1,0].

We note that citations are collected from some database, and hence a scientist's h-index depends on the used database or subdatabase. In practice a scientist can have a Web of Science (WoS) h-index (or a Social Science Citation Index h-index, when restricting the WoS to the part covering the social sciences), a Scopus h-index, a Google Scholar (GS) h-index and maybe also an h-index according to a local or other database.

What does the h-index measure? What type of measure is it? It is not an average, percentile or other basic statistical measure. It is another way of combining citation and publication counts. Almost overnight it became very popular, leading to its inclusion in the WoS, Scopus, and Publish or Perish, among others.

Before Hirsch most scientometricians agreed that scientometric indicators were not suitable for the evaluation of single scientists. In the introductory chapter of the *Handbook of Quantitative Science and Technology Research* (Moed et al., 2004) van Raan (2004a) wrote "the process of citation is a complex one, and it certainly does not provide an 'ideal' monitor on scientific performance. This is particularly the case at a statistically low aggregation level, e.g., the individual researcher." However, van Raan continues by stating that the application of citation analysis to the work of a group of researchers over a long period of time, does yield a strong indicator of scientific performance. This idea changed with the availability of the h-index which was precisely designed for the evaluation of individual scientists. Let us now have a look at some advantages and disadvantages of the h-index as an indicator for individuals. Such lists were presented for example in Glänzel (2006) and Liu & Rousseau (2007).

7.3.2 Advantages and Disadvantages of the h-index

Advantages of the h-index
- It is a mathematically simple index.
- As it combines two types of activity (in the original setting this is citation impact and publications) it can be argued that it is a better index than total number of publications or total number of citations alone.
- It encourages highly visible work.
- Increasing the number of publications alone does not have an immediate effect on this index.
- It is a robust indicator in the sense that small errors in data collection have no or little effect (Rousseau, 2007a; Vanclay, 2007)—but see the disambiguation problem in the next list.
- Single peaks (top publications) have no influence on the h-index.
- In principle, any document type can be included.
- In most cases publications that are hardly ever cited do not influence the h-index (an exception occurring when the h-index itself is very low).
- As the h-index is time-dependent it can be used as an indicator to study or evaluate a scientist's career.

Moreover, the h-index can be applied to any level of aggregation. This means that not only to scientists but also to different groups of scientists, such as all scientists belonging to a research institute, belonging to a university, or belonging to the same country. It can even be applied to most source-item systems (see Section 9.3) such as books per library classification category and loans (Liu & Rousseau, 2007, 2009). The value associated with a source such as an article, is in general referred to as its magnitude value, e.g., the number of received citations.

Disadvantages of the h-index

Yet, it is well-known that the h-index has several disadvantages. Some of these it shares with any other citation-based indicator.
- Like most citation measures it is field-dependent, database dependent, and may be influenced by self-citations.
- Highly cited work is not necessarily high quality work.

- There is a problem finding reference standards, leading to questions such as "What is a 'high' h-index in field F for a researcher who is active since 7 (or any other number of) years?"
- The number of coauthors may influence the number of citations received.
- It is rather difficult to collect all data necessary for the determination of the h-index. Often a scientist's complete publication list is necessary in order to discriminate between scientists with the same name and initial(s). We refer to this problem as the disambiguation problem.

Some other disadvantages are more specifically related to the h-index itself.

- The h-index is only useful for comparing the better scientists in a field. It does not discriminate among mediocre scientists. This follows from the facts that a) it is a rough indicator, always resulting in a slowly increasing, natural number; and b) when a scientist has just a few publications, say P, then the possible values of the corresponding h-index are restricted to the natural numbers in the interval [0, P].
- The h-index lacks sensitivity to performance changes: it can never decrease and is only weakly sensitive to the number of citations received. Concretely, once an article belongs to the h-core it does not matter anymore how many extra citations it receives. Conversely also for most articles in the tail the exact number of citations or increase in citations has no influence. In this context an article is called an h-critical publication (Rousseau and Ye, 2012) if one additional citation to this article would increase the h-index, and hence would let this article enter the h-core.
- The lack of sensitivity is the main reason for the introduction of most other h-type indices.
- From a purely logical point of view, the most important disadvantage of the h-index is the fact that it is not an independent indicator. This term and how it applies to the h-index is explained further on, see Subsection 7.3.3.

The following points have also been mentioned as disadvantages but we do not fully agree with this point of view.

- The h-index, in its original setting, puts newcomers at a disadvantage since both publication output and observed citation rates will be relatively low. In other words, it is based on long-term observations.

Although true, this disadvantage is easily removed by using publication and citation windows, in the same way as this is done for other citation-related indicators (Frandsen & Rousseau, 2005; Liang & Rousseau, 2009).

- The index allows scientists to rest on their laurels since the number of citations received may increase even if no new papers are published. Again, this is only a partial disadvantage. Indeed, if one would use the h-index for hiring decisions (we hope no one interprets this example as a serious suggestion) then one does not want to hire scientists that reached their h-index value by articles published a long time ago. Yet, if a person's h-index keeps increasing because of older articles that still receive citations, this points to the continuing influence of this scientist.

A remark. Consider the publication-citation matrix of scientist S in Table 7.3:

Determine the h-index of scientist S, denoted as h(S). Add now one more publication that received h(S) + 1 citations. What do you expect to happen to the h-index? And what happens in reality?

Answer to this problem: the h-index of S is 2. Hence we add a new article with 3 citations. Now the h-index of this new situation is still 2. This is rather surprising if we compare with the case that instead of the h-index we would use the average number of citations. Adding an article with above average citations leads to a higher new average or mean. This special behavior of the h-index has been observed by Woeginger (2008) when studying an axiomatization of the h-index.

Just as an observation we note that on July 1, 2017 the h-index of all articles in the WoS (since 1955) was 2703. This can easily be found by doing a search for all publication years and ranking the obtained publications in decreasing order of obtained citations. As there are more than 62 million articles in the WoS the corresponding h-core represents a tiny minority among all publications.

Table 7.3 A special example

Articles	Received citations
Art 1	4
Art 2	2
Art 3	2

7.3.3 Independence

The most significant disadvantage of the h-type index is that it is not independent in the sense of Bouyssou and Marchant (2011). If A and B represent sets of publications and citations, then strict independence for an indicator F means that if $F(A) < F(B)$ and one adds to A and to B the same publications (with the same number of received citations) then still $F(A) < F(B)$. This does not hold for the h-index. For instance:

$$A = [4, 4, 4, 4, 0], \text{ then } h(A) = 4$$

$$B = [5, 5, 5, 2, 1], \text{ then } h(B) = 3 \quad \text{and } h(B) < h(A)$$

Adding two publications with 5 citations (one may even assume that A and B were coauthors on these two publications) gives:

A′ (A with added publications) = [5, 5, 4, 4, 4, 4, 0], then $h(A') = 4$
B′ (B with added publications) = [5, 5, 5, 5, 5, 2, 1], then $h(B') = 5$
and consequently $h(A) < h(B)$.

This example is based on a similar one presented in (Waltman & van Eck, 2012a).

7.4 SIMPLE VARIATIONS ON THE H-INDEX

Besides using different publication and citation windows one may restrict publications to those where the scientist is either first author or corresponding author (Hu et al., 2010), or take only the first author into account. Note that we do not support the use of these two methods as they might not give credit to some collaborators. The first of these methods might, however, be used in addition to the standard h-index. Another simple variation is using complete-normalized fractional counting for citations (if an article is written with three authors, then each of them receives only one third of the citation credit), see Subsection 5.6.3.

The original h-index is a natural number, leading to many scientists with the same value for their h-index. Two proposals have been made to refine this.

7.4.1 The Rational h-index

The rational variant of the h-index, denoted as h_{rat}, was introduced by Ruane and Tol (2008) in the context of publications and citations (whole counting). It is defined as follows.

Definition: Consider a researcher with h–index h. Let n be the smallest possible number of citations necessary to reach an h-index equal to $h + 1$, then the rational h-index, denoted h_{rat}, is defined as:

$$h_{rat} = h + 1 - \frac{n}{2h + 1} \tag{7.8}$$

We next explain formula (7.8). If a researcher has h-index h, then one may ask about the minimum number of citations necessary to reach an h-index equal to $h + 1$. This number is denoted here as n. If, for instance, a scientist has the following series of citations [7, 4, 3, 1, 0] and hence has an h-index of 3, then she needs at least 4 more citations in order to reach an h-index of 4. Indeed the third article needs one more citation and the fourth needs 3 more. Of course, there is no guarantee that her next four citations are exactly for these two articles and with exactly these numbers of citations. If the next 4 citations go to the article ranked first then her h-index stays the same and if the "right" articles receive these four citations but equally (each two), then she is still one citation short. That is why we use the term "minimum." The next question is: If you only know that this scientist's h-index is 3, and no further details, what is then the largest possible value of this minimum? The answer is 7 which happens when the scientist has the following series of citations [3,3,3,0] (or with more uncited publications). In general, this largest minimum is 2h + 1 for a scientist with h-index h, corresponding with the "worst case scenario" that there are h publications with h citations each and the publication at rank $h + 1$ has 0 citations. This explains the occurrence of the factor 2h + 1 in the formula for the rational h-index.

Some examples: for [7,4,3,1,0] the rational h-index is $4 - 4/7 = 24/7 \approx 3.43$.

For [4,4,3,1,1,0] it is also $4 - 4/7 \approx 3.43$; while for [6,5,4,3,2,1,0] it is $4 - 1/7 \approx 3.86$. Finally for [10,3,3,0,0] it is $4 - 6/7 \approx 3.14$ and for [10, 2, 2, 2] (same number of citations and higher average number of citations as the previous case) it is $3 - 2/5 = 2.6$.

7.4.2 The Interpolated h-index

The interpolated h-index, denoted as h_{int}, was introduced by Rousseau (2006d) under the name of real-valued h-index. This variant of the h-index can be used in similar situations as the rational h-index, but when citation scores are not natural numbers then using this variant is, in our opinion, the method of choice. It is defined as follows:

Let $P(r)$ denote the magnitude value of the rth source and let $P(x)$ denote the piecewise linear interpolation of the sequence $(r, P(r))$, $r = 1, 2, \ldots$, then h_r is the abscissa of the intersection of the function $P(x)$ and the straight line $y = x$ (if this intersection exists). Its value is then given by:

$$h_{int} = \frac{(h+1)P(h) - hP(h+1)}{1 - P(h+1) + P(h)} \tag{7.9}$$

Clearly $h_{int} \geq h$ with equality sign only if $h = P(h)$.

Considering the previous examples we have:

For $[7,4,3,1,0]$ $h = 3$, $P(3) = 3$; $P(4) = 1$ and $h_{int} = (4{*}3-3{*} \ 1)/(1 - 1 + 3) = 9/3 = 3$. As long as the third publication receives exactly 3 citations h_{int} stays equal to 3. For $[6,5,4,3,2,1,0]$ we find $h_{int} = (4{*}4 - 3{*}3)/(1 - 3 + 4) = 7/2 = 3.5$. For $[10, 2, 2, 2]$ h_{int} is clearly 2. For $[10, 8, 1, 0]$ it is $(3{*}8 - 2{*}1)/(1 - 1 + 8) = 22/8 = 2.75$. In most cases, but not always, $h_{int} < h_{rat}$, see (Guns & Rousseau, 2009a).

It was mentioned that the interpolated h-index could also be used when citation values are not necessarily natural numbers, which happens e.g., when using fractional counting. It is then possible that the most-cited citation of a set of publications has a value of 0.5, in which case the line $y = x$ does not intersect $P(x)$. This explains the restriction in the definition (the part "if the intersection exists"). A solution for this problem has been suggested in (Rousseau, 2014c).

7.4.3 The m-quotient

It has been mentioned that in its original version the h-index favors scientists with a longer career. Hirsch (2005) provided a solution for this, namely by dividing the standard h-index by the length of a scientist's career expressed in years. We note that there is an unspoken assumption used in this proposal. This assumption is that in the "regular" case an h-index grows linearly over the years. If this regular growth were curved then either younger or older scientists would be favored by this correction. It has been observed that by and large the h-index of a scientist grows linearly, but, of course, there are many exceptions. Surely, the higher the h-index the more citations are needed (we remarked earlier that this number can be as high as $(2h + 1)$) to increase it by one unit. As many articles in the h-core tend to be older ones, for which it is less likely that they gain new citations, it seems that the m-quotient might disfavor older scientists. Yet, this has not been tested on a large scale.

7.4.4 Year-Based h-indices

In (Mahbuba & Rousseau, 2013, 2016) three groups of year-based h-indices were introduced. The first group of year-based h-type indices is defined as follows. We consider a scientist and all their articles published over some period of time (this can be their complete career). For each year we consider the number of publications, the total number of citations received by these publications during a given period (the citation window), and the average number of citations per year, leading to three variations of year-based h-indices. This citation window may be a fixed period or all years since publication.

Case 1: *Publications and publication years: the career years h-index by publications*

For each year we collect the number of publications of interest, e.g., by restricting to a certain database, a certain type of publications, a certain topic or some collaborations in terms of colleagues, institutions or countries. Then years are arranged in descending order of publications. This yields a typical h-type list. The career years publication h-index is then defined as the highest rank such that during the first h years (first in the list, not chronologically) at least h publications were written. A fictitious example is shown in Table 7.4.

Table 7.4 An author's career years h-index by publications

Rank	Publication Year	Number of publications
1	2009	15
2	2012	11
3	2011	7
4	2013	7
5	**2014**	**6**
6	2010	5
7	2008	3
8	2006	3
9	2007	0

The career years h-index by publications of the author in Table 7.4 is 5. The h-core consists of the years {2014, 2013, 2012, 2011, 2009}.

Meaning of this indicator

It is conceivable that two scientists have the same number of publications but that for one of them, publications are more or less evenly distributed over their career, while for the other publications are heavily concentrated (say, around the year of their doctoral dissertation). The career years h-index by publications makes a distinction between these two cases. The h-core of the career years h-index by publications brings together those years in which the scientist was—relatively speaking—the most active.

Case 2: *Citations and publication years: the career years h-index by citations*

For each year we determine the sum of all citations received by publications written in that year (note that we do not consider the year in which citations are received). Again, many variants are possible by restricting publications, similar to the career years h-index by publications. The years in this time series are arranged in descending order of citations. This again is a typical h-type list. The career years h-index by citations is then defined as the highest rank such that during the first h publication years (in the list, not chronologically) at least h citations were received. The corresponding h-core consists of the first h years, where in case of equality on rank h the most recent years are preferred. A fictitious example is shown in Table 7.5 for which the career years h-index by citations is 7.

Table 7.5 An author's career years h-index by citations

Rank	Publication year	Number of citations received
1	2001	29
2	2010	25
3	2011	19
4	1999	19
5	2000	15
6	2012	13
7	2008	11
8	2006	7
9	2005	7
10	2003	3

Meaning of this indicator

Similar to the previous case, it is conceivable that two scientists have the same total number of citations, but that for one of them citations are more or less evenly distributed over her career, while for the other citations are heavily concentrated (say, essentially for one top article). The career years h-index by citations makes a distinction between such cases. Also here the h-core of the career years h-index by citations is of importance. It brings together the years in which a scientist published their most-cited articles.

Case 3: *Citations and publication years: the career years h-index by citations (a variant)*

For each year we determine the sum of all citations received in that year. Again, many variants are possible by restricting publications, similar to the two previous cases. The years in this time series are arranged in descending order of citations, leading to a new h-type list. The corresponding citation-based h-index is then defined as the highest rank such that during the first h years (in the list, not chronologically) at least h citations were received.

Before discussing other h-type indices we note that a year-based h-index is not suited for cases where citations can easily be high such as e.g., for countries, as the number of years under consideration is always relatively small.

7.5 H-TYPE INDICES THAT TAKE THE NUMBER OF RECEIVED CITATIONS BY HIGHLY CITED PUBLICATIONS INTO ACCOUNT

7.5.1 The g-index

Perhaps the most famous variation on the h-index is the g-index, introduced by Egghe (2006a,b,c). It is defined as follows: As for the calculation of the h-index articles are ranked in decreasing order of received number of citations. Then the g-index of this set of articles is defined as the highest rank g such that the first g articles together received at least g^2 citations. This can be reformulated as follows: the g-index of a set of articles is the highest rank g such that the first g (>0) articles have an average number of citations equal to or higher than g. Indeed:

$$\sum_{j=1}^{g} c_j \geq g^2 \Leftrightarrow \frac{1}{g}\sum_{j=1}^{g} c_j \geq g \qquad (7.10)$$

Table 7.6 Calculation of a g-index

Rank	Publication (date)	# citations	Cumulative number of citations	Squared rank
1	A (2010)	8	8	1
2	B (2013)	5	13	4
3	C (2011)	5	18	9
4	D (2011)	4	22	16
5	E (2008)	4	26	25
6	F (2014)	1	27	36
7	G (2010)	0	27	49

An example. We consider again Table 7.2 and add the information necessary to determine its g-index, see Table 7.6.

As the articles ranked 1 to 5 have together at least $5^2 = 25$ citations, namely 26, and the articles ranked 1 to 6 have strictly less than $6^2 = 36$ citations (they have 27 citations), this set has a g-index equal to 5.

The use of a square in this definition is inspired by the fact that a set with h-index h has received together at least h^2 citations. Consider for instance [4, 4, 4, 4, 0, 0]. This set has h-index 4; the total number of citations is 16 and its g-index is also 4. From this it also follows that for a given set, we have $g \geq h$.

As for the h-index one may say that the first g articles form the g-core, again ranking in antichronological order if need be.

What happens if a list of T articles has together strictly more than T^2 citations? This is illustrated in Table 7.7. In this case one adds "fictitious" articles with zero citations until the g-index can be calculated. The fact that it is not bounded by the number of publications can be considered an advantage of the g-index (Glänzel, 2006).

Before discussing a few other h-type indices we consider the question: Which one of the two, the h-index or the g-index, is the best one? Egghe being the originator of the g-index naturally prefers the g-index. However, we leave it to the readers to make up their mind, or to decide whether this is a meaningless question. Either way, here are two examples, illustrating two opposite cases:

$X_1 = [15, 10, 5, 3]$ and $X_2 = [3,3,3,0,0,0]$ have the same h-index, namely 3, but different g-indices: $g(X_1) = 5$ while $g(X_2) = 3$.

Consider now $Y_1 = [60,4,0,0,0,0]$ and $Y_2 = [15,15,12,12,8,7,7,3,1]$. These scientists have the same g-index: $g(Y_1) = g(Y_2) = 8$, but different h-indices: $h(Y_1) = 2$ and $h(Y_2) = 7$.

Table 7.7 Determination of the g-index in a special case: 3 articles with a total number of $18 > 3^2 = 9$ citations. This set's g-index is 4

Rank	Article	# citations	Cumulative number of received citations	Rank^2
1	A	9	9	1
2	B	8	17	4
3	C	1	18	9
4	–	0	18	16
5	–	0	18	25

Bartolucci (2015) formulates the following answer to this question. If one believes that a good scientist is characterized by a reasonable number (not just a few) of highly cited articles, then the h-index is preferable to the g-index. If, however, one believes that even a single very highly cited article makes a good scientist, the g-index is preferable.

7.5.2 The R- and R^2-index

The R–index, introduced in Jin et al. (2007) has the same purpose as the g-index and is easier to determine. The R–index is defined as the square root of the sum of all citations received by the articles in the h-core. Omitting the square root yields the R^2-index.

Written as a formula we have:

$$R^2 = \sum_{i=1}^{h} c_i \tag{7.11}$$

where c_i denotes the number of citations received by the i-th publication (as always ranked according to received citations, from highest to lowest) and h is the corresponding h-index of this set of articles. This indicator takes citations in the h-core into account. The R^2-index of the articles represented in Table 7.2 is: $8 + 5 + 5 + 4 = 22$. In the extreme case that all articles in the h-core received h citations (the least possible number of citations) then $R^2 = h^2$ and $R = h = g$. Clearly $h \le R$ as all citation values in the h-core are at least equal to h.

There is, however, no direct inequality relation between g and R. Indeed if $X_0 = [7,1,1]$ then $h(X_0) = 1$, $g(X_0) = 3$ and $R(X_0) = \sqrt{7} \approx 2.65$, hence $R(X_0) < g(X_0)$. If, however, $Y_0 = [8,2,0]$, then $h(Y_0) = 2$, $g(Y_0) = 3$ and $R(X_0) = \sqrt{10} \approx 3.16$ and $g(Y_0) < R(Y_0)$.

7.6 SOME OTHER H-TYPE INDICES

7.6.1 Kosmulski's Index $h^{(2)}$

Kosmulski (2006) proposed the $h^{(2)}$-index in order to easily handle long lists. An example could be download lists as studied in Hua et al. (2009). The $h^{(2)}$-index is defined as follows: An author has a Kosmulski's index $h^{(2)}$ if $r = h^{(2)}$ is de highest rank such that the first $h^{(2)}$ articles have each at least $(h^{(2)})^2$ citations. The $h^{(2)}$-index for Table 7.2 is 2 as the first 2 articles each have at least 4 citations, while the third does not have 9 citations.

7.6.2 The AR-index

In an attempt to design an h-type indicator that can actually decrease over time and puts emphasis on recent publications Jin (2007) proposed the AR-index. She defines the AR-index as the square root of the sum of the average number of citations per year of articles included in the h-core. As a formula this is:

$$AR = \sqrt{\sum_{i=1}^{h} \frac{c_i}{a_i}} \qquad (7.12)$$

where a_i denotes the age (in years) of the i-th article. The AR-index is clearly inspired by the R-index.

7.6.3 The m-index

Bornmann et al. (2008) propose the m-index (not to be confused with Hirsch's m-quotient, see Subsection 7.4.3), which is the median of the items in the h-core. Being a median, it is less sensible to outliers than the g-index or the R-index.

7.6.4 The h-index of a Single Publication

Schubert (2009) proposes an h-index for a single publication (the source) as the h-index of the set of articles citing this source article. This means the h-index of the set of all forward first generation i.e., citing publications (actually, he does not consider all publications, but only those of article type).

We note that, when applied in a publication-citation context the h-index and similar indices can be considered to be an impact indicator as generally speaking many publications and many citations lead to a high value (many publications AND many citations = high impact). Much more h-type indicators have been introduced for which we refer the reader to the following reviews Alonso et al. (2009) and Egghe (2010c). Generally, one may say that only the h-index and the g-index are often applied.

7.7 A GENERAL IMPACT FACTOR

The term impact factor refers to a set of indicators originally introduced for journals as illustrated in the previous chapter. Yet, it is clear that these indicators can, at least theoretically, be applied to any set of articles if the data are of the required format. By this we mean that one needs at least one row in the citation part of the p-c matrix in order to calculate a synchronous impact factor, and at least one column for calculating a diachronous one.

One such set is the set of all articles (co-)authored by one scientist. Let us hasten to say that for scientists who do not publish many articles calculating any impact factor is utterly meaningless. Yet for very active researchers it might be of some interest to calculate author impact factors. Pan and Fortunato (2014) propose a 5-year synchronous author impact factor (SAIF). They show that this SAIF is capable to capture trends and variations in the impact of the scientific output of a researcher. Concretely the SAIF of a scholar in the year Y is defined as:

$$SAIF(Y) = \frac{\sum_{i=1}^{5} CIT(Y, Y - i)}{\sum_{i=1}^{5} PUB(Y - i)} \qquad (7.13)$$

Here $PUB(Y - i)$ denotes the number of publications coauthored by this scholar in the year $Y - i$, and $CIT(Y, Y - i)$ denotes the number of citations of articles published in the year $Y - i$ received in the year Y. Recall that publications and citations are those included in a chosen database such as WoS or Scopus. We note that Pan and Fortunato were certainly not the first to have the idea to apply the impact factor construction to a single author although we were not able to find the originator of this idea. However, they seem to be the first to study its behavior for a number of individuals (Nobel Prize winners) and this over a long period of time. They prove that, indeed, the SAIF is capable of showing the highlights in their career. The use of an author impact factor should not be seen as an element in a research evaluation, but rather as an element in the (historic) study of authors' careers and the response to their publications by colleagues.

According to Pan and Fortunato the SAIF has the following advantages:

- The SAIF is a dynamic index, showing the ups and downs in a person's career.
- The SAIF is an average so it is high if most papers published during the publication window are well cited, whereas low quality work (or not yet recognized work) keeps the score down. For this reason using the SAIF may be an incentive to focus on quality (or popularity?) instead of quantity.
- The SAIF is easy to calculate.

To this list we can add the following advantage: As the SAIF is an average, it may be influenced by one exceptionally highly cited publication. Yet, in this type of application this is an advantage as one wants to recognize this type of work.

At the same time, the SAIF also has some disadvantages:

- It makes no sense to calculate an SAIF for persons who rarely publish.
- Work published in a source outside the set covered by the used database has no influence on the SAIF (or any other general impact factor), while such work may have contributed to a Nobel Prize.

Another type of impact factor is the Web Impact Factor (WIF), introduced by Ingwersen (1998). The WIF of a web site or group of related websites such as all those with domain .dk (Denmark) is defined as the sum of the number of external inlinking pages plus the number of self-link web pages, divided by the number of web pages. External inlinking pages are webpages external to a given site (in the example: all those which do not carry the domain name .dk) which point at least once to that set of sites, e.g., a site with domain name .dk. Self-link web pages are websites which point at least once to the set of sites to which they themselves belong. The denominator consists of the number of websites (not the number of links) of the set under investigation. Although a clever idea it has turned out that it is almost impossible to determine the three numbers needed for its calculation. This explains why, after a short period of enthusiasm, use of the WIF is nowadays almost abandoned. Yet, total number of external inlinks plays a role in determining the Webometrics Ranking of World Universities (see Subsection 8.4.3).

7.8 SUCCESS INDICES AND SUCCESS MULTIPLIERS (ROUSSEAU & ROUSSEAU, 2016)

7.8.1 The Success Index

Kosmulski (2011) and Franceschini et al. (2012a) introduced the success index. This indicator, or actually family of indicators, is constructed as follows. One considers a set of articles and collects for each of these the number of citations received over a given citation window W. In a first step, a binary score (zero or one) is determined for each of these articles: the score is one if the citations received by a particular article reach a certain threshold value and it is zero otherwise. This threshold can be determined in a variety of ways (which is why we say that the success index is actually a family of indicators). In a next step the success index of this set of articles with respect to a particular threshold is defined as the number of publications that has reached the threshold, or stated otherwise: the sum of all binary scores. Among other proposals, the following thresholds could be used (Kosmulski, 2011; Franceschini et al., 2012a,b):

- The number of references (each publication's citations is compared with its own number of references). This is the original proposal by Kosmulski (2011).
- The mean or the median number of references in articles published in the same journal and year as the article under consideration.
- The mean or the median number of citations received by articles published in the same journal and year as the article under consideration, where citations are gathered over the same period W (Franceschini et al., 2012a,b). Kosmulski referred to this proposal as a modesty index, as it would reward publication of high-impact articles in lower impact journals (Kosmulski, 2012).

Clearly, the number of possible thresholds is limitless. One may, for instance, define a threshold by only considering citations in journals belonging to the first quartile in one of the JCR categories, or citations received from authors with a high h-index. Such approaches would operationalize the idea of "quality citations." Alternatively, one may consider only recent references.

In the beginning of this chapter we noted that an index can be defined as a number, derived from a mathematical expression, characterizing a property of a dataset. In the case of a success index, the data set is a set of articles and their citations, and its value is used as a proxy for the "success"— the term visibility or popularity would be more to the point—of this dataset and the corresponding entity (scientist, department, journal).

7.8.2 Payback Times: A Variation on the Success Index

Instead of determining whether a given article has reached a certain threshold, a more dynamic approach would be determining how long it takes for an article to reach the threshold. This idea precedes the concept of a success index. It was proposed by Liang and Rousseau (2008) for journals and is referred to as the yield period or the payback time. The term "payback time" refers to the idea that a journal uses resources from the science system (as shown by its lists of references) and that it takes a certain time to pay back (through received citations) to the science system what had been taken. Liang and Rousseau (2008) studied yearly issues of *Science* and *Nature*, leading to so-called yield sequences. They determined not only the time to reach a number of citations equal to the number of used references, but also the time to reach twice, thrice, ... this number. It was observed that at least for these journals, payback times tended to become shorter over the years. Another variation on the success index and the idea of a payback time would be to consider the percentage of articles in a given set that already reached the threshold after a given time *t*.

7.8.3 Success Multipliers (Rousseau & Rousseau, 2016)

Instead of a binary score leading to a success index, we can also determine the fraction of the threshold reached by an article at any given moment. For instance, if the threshold is 20 citations and an article has obtained 14 citations, a value 0.7 can be associated with it. Similarly, if an article received 30 citations, it receives a value of 1.5. The values 0.7 and 1.5 are then referred to as multipliers. An article's multiplier reflects the relative number of citations received by that article compared to the threshold value that is used.

The success multiplier of a set of articles is simply the sum of the scores of all articles in the set, generalizing the success index of a set of articles. When using success multipliers it is still possible to separate an elite set from the other ones, but this division is not as clear-cut as in the 0-1 case. Further, an average score is created by dividing this general score by the total number of articles. When the number of references is used as a threshold this leads to the formula:

$$\frac{1}{n}\sum_{j=1}^{n}\frac{c_j}{r_j} \tag{7.14}$$

Here n is the number of publications under consideration, c_j is the number of citations received by article j (over a given citation window) and r_j is the number of references of article j. In case all articles' citations are compared with the same threshold, say T, then formula (7.14) becomes:

$$\frac{1}{n * T} \sum_{j=1}^{n} c_j \tag{7.15}$$

This average score no longer has a theoretical upper limit. The multiplier idea has been proposed by Yanovsky (1981) and by Matsas (2012) for scientific leadership. Yanovsky's popularity factor is defined as (the number of received citations) divided by (the number of references given). Yanovsky proposed windows of equal length, but that is, of course not a necessary requirement. Matsas' indicator for scientific leadership is known under the name of Normalized Impact Factor (NIF). The NIF of scientist A in the sense of Matsas is defined as:

$$NIF(A) = \frac{\sum_{j=1}^{n} a_j c_j}{\sum_{j=1}^{n} b_j r_j} = \frac{\left(\sum_{j=1}^{n} a_j c_j\right)/n}{\left(\sum_{j=1}^{n} b_j r_j\right)/n} \tag{7.16}$$

Here n is the number of publications written by scientist A, during a given period; c_j is the number of citations received by article j (again over a given citation window) and r_j is the number of references of article j. The numbers a_j and b_j are weighting factors. In the simplest case they are all equal to one. In a somewhat more complex setup, one may take $a_j = b_j = 1/$ (the number of authors of article j); of course many other weighting factors are feasible. NIF(A) is the weighted average number of received citations divided by the weighted average number of references. Note that here we face the well-known ratio of averages versus average of ratios problem (Larivière & Gingras, 2011). In formula (7.14) we proposed an average of ratios (when dividing by the total number of articles in the set) while Matsas, formula (7.16), proposed a (weighted) ratio of averages.

7.9 PERCENTILE RANK SCORE AND THE INTEGRATED IMPACT INDICATOR (LEYDESDORFF & BORNMANN, 2011)

Suppose that articles in a reference set are subdivided in K disjoint classes. If an article belongs to class k it receives a score x_k. Let now A be a subset of this reference set, consisting of N documents and let $n_A(k)$ be the number of documents in A belonging to class k. Then the percentile rank score of A, denoted as $R(A)$, is defined as:

$$R(A) = \sum_{k=1}^{K} x_k \frac{n_A(k)}{N} \tag{7.17}$$

Proposition: The percentile rank score is a strict independent indicator for average performance.

Proof. Suppose that $R(A) = \sum_{k=1}^{K} x_k \frac{n_A(k)}{N} > R(B) = \sum_{k=1}^{K} x_k \frac{n_B(k)}{N}$ (for average performance the sets A and B must have an equal number of elements). We take a new element from class j and add it to A as well as to B, leading to sets A' and B'. Then $R(A') = \frac{N}{N+1} R(A) + x_j \frac{1}{N+1} > R(B') = \frac{N}{N+1} R(B) + x_j \frac{1}{N+1}$. This proves that R is a strict independent indicator for average performance.

We note that the independence property does not hold if sets A and B have a different number of elements. Indeed, let A consist of 2 elements, one with score 1 and one with score zero. Then its percentile rank score is ½. Let B consist of 10 elements, one with score 3, one with score 2, one with score 1 and 7 with score zero. Then its percentile rank score is 6/10, which is larger than A's. Now we add an element with score 1. This leads to a score of 2/3 for A' and for 7/11 for B', reversing the order of the scores for A and B.

Definition: The integrated impact indicator (I3) (Leydesdorff & Bornmann, 2011)

Leydesdorff and Bornmann argued that impact means: many publications *and* many citations. In this sense the term JIF is a misnomer. The nonnormalized percentile rank score, denoted $I3(A)$ (the integrated impact indicator) score satisfies this definition. Indeed, $I3(A)$ is defined as:

$$I3(A) = \sum_{k=1}^{K} x_k n_A(k) \tag{7.18}$$

Clearly, the $I3$ indicator too is a strict independent indicator, not only for average performance but even in general.

7.10 CITATION MERIT

It is always difficult to compare sets with a different number of elements. A proposal by Crespo et al. (2012) tries to remedy this. These colleagues propose the notion of merit, to be calculated as follows. We are given a (homogeneous) group of N articles, for instance all publications by research group G during the latest 5 years. Now, the evaluator must make two choices: the first is the indicator to be used, e.g., average number of received citations; total number of received citations, h-index, ..., and secondly a reference set. Next one determines the indicator value for group G. In a following step one determines a random set of N articles from the reference set and determines the indicator value for this random set. This procedure is repeated 1000 or more times. The merit of G is its percentile value among these 1000 or more indicator results. Clearly, a good choice of reference sets makes it possible to compare the merit of different research groups in a meaningful way.

7.11 TIME SERIES OF INDICATORS

In this Section, based on (Liu & Rousseau, 2008) we provide precise definitions of time series of indicators. Such definitions are necessary to avoid possible confusion as different time series may lead to different conclusions. We provide a general scheme for time series, using the terms *sequence* and *series* interchangeably. We only discuss time series for which terms—individual elements in the series—are obtained as sums (occasionally sums consisting of one element). Time series for which terms are averages can easily be derived from these.

7.11.1 The General Framework

We assume that the focus is on one set of articles. This set can be a scientist's research record, one specific journal, the set of all journals in one particular field, or even all journals in a database. For this set we intend to calculate a time series of indicators based on publication and citation data.

As a first example we consider how two simple time series can be derived from a given one. Assume we know the numbers of citations $c_0, c_1, \ldots, c_{10}$ received by a set of articles published in the year Y_0, where c_0 is received in the year Y_0, c_1 in the year $Y_0 + 1$ and so on. During an investigation one may be interested in a subsequence such as $s = (c_k)_{k=1,\ldots,10}$ (we are not interested in the number of citations received during the publication year). Similarly, we might be interested in the cumulative sequence $S = \left(\sum_{j=0}^{1} c_j, \sum_{j=0}^{2} c_j, ..., \sum_{j=0}^{10} c_j \right)$.

Next we come to the main point of this section starting from a general matrix of data, not a simple sequence. Consider a p-c matrix consisting of N publication years, from year Y to year $Y + N - 1$ (the columns) and M citation years, from year Y to year $Y + M - 1$ (the rows). Hence the p-c matrix is an $M \times N$-matrix. These N years form the publication window, while the M years form the citation window of interest. For specific terms in a sequence smaller windows will often be used. We, moreover assume that the number of columns is at most equal to the number of rows: $N \leq M$. We keep the p-c matrix fixed and study series of citation indicators derived from this set. We define general time series of indicators and characterize what they say about the set of publications.

Recall that citations are always drawn from a pool, such as the WoS, Scopus, a local database or subsets thereof. We will further assume that this pool is known and will not consider this aspect anymore.

7.11.2 Types of Time Series of Citation Indicators

We will explain the construction of different time series and their visualizations in p-c matrices. In these visualizations the shaded areas contain the citation data that are added in order to obtain one element in the time series. Series $(s_k)_k$ will be called *chronological* if the index k increases with time (years) and *antichronological* if it increases with decreasing years.

The first series is a citation cumulated, publication-chronological time series. The first term of this series is the sum of all citations received by publications of the year Y, during the period Y to $Y + M - 1$; the second term is the sum of all citations received by publications of the year $Y + 1$, during the period $Y + 1$ to $Y + M - 1$; and so on. This procedure leads to a series of diachronous indicators, making use of all data available in the p-c matrix. If year $Y + M - 1$ is the latest year for which data are available this is a natural approach, although publication years are treated unevenly (they contribute differently). Cells used in the calculation of one term of this series are shaded in Table 7.8. In this way the calculations of four terms are illustrated in Table 7.8, one below the other. For the p-c matrix shown in Table 7.8 the resulting series is: (22,13,23,19). This type of time series has been provided for the Hirsch index of the *Journal of the American Society for Information Science* in (Rousseau, 2006b). It was suggested that a normalization with respect to the number of published articles was preferable.

The second time series is a citation cumulated, publication cumulating chronological time series. It is similar to the first type but uses cumulative data. This time series, and also the previous one, was used in (Liu et al.,

Table 7.8 An illustration of the calculation of the first time series: a citation cumulated, publication-chronological time series, (case $M = 5$, $N = 4$)

Publication year (row) Citation year (column)	Y	Y+1	Y+2	Y+3
Y	2			
Y+1	3	4		
Y+2	4	4	7	
Y+3	5	3	7	9
Y+4	8	2	9	10
	Y	Y+1	Y+2	Y+3
Y	2			
Y+1	3	4		
Y+2	4	4	7	
Y+3	5	3	7	9
Y+4	8	2	9	10
	Y	Y+1	Y+2	Y+3
Y	2			
Y+1	3	4		
Y+2	4	4	7	
Y+3	5	3	7	9
Y+4	8	2	9	10
	Y	Y+1	Y+2	Y+3
Y	2			
Y+1	3	4		
Y+2	4	4	7	
Y+3	5	3	7	9
Y+4	8	2	9	10

2009) for the study of the field of horticulture (h–indices of journals). The third type is a citation-chronological time series with fixed-length publication window. In the illustration (Table 7.9) the length is 2 year, but in general the length can be any numbers of years. If a calculation cannot be performed then the series stops. This is illustrated by the lower right-hand part of Table 7.9. This case leads to the numerators in the calculation of a series of synchronous JIFs (a window of length two yields the standard Garfield-Sher impact factor). Time series of JIFs abound in the literature see e.g., López-Abente & Muñoz-Tinoco (2005).

Next we come to the fourth and fifth time series (Table 7.10). The fourth one is a citation-chronological, publication cumulated time series, while the fifth is a cumulating citation-chronological, publication

Table 7.9 An illustration of the calculation of the second (citation cumulated, publication cumulating chronological) time series and third (citation-chronological time series with fixed-length publication window) time series (case $M = 5$, $N = 4$)

Publication year (row) Citation year (column)	Y	Y+1	Y+2	Y+3	Publication year (row) Citation year (column)	Y	Y+1	Y+2	Y+3
Y					Y				
Y+1					Y+1				
Y+2					Y+2				
Y+3					Y+3				
Y+4					Y+4				
	Y	Y+1	Y+2	Y+3		Y	Y+1	Y+2	Y+3
Y					Y				
Y+1					Y+1				
Y+2					Y+2				
Y+3					Y+3				
Y+4					Y+4				
	Y	Y+1	Y+2	Y+3		Y	Y+1	Y+2	Y+3
Y					Y				
Y+1					Y+1				
Y+2					Y+2				
Y+3					Y+3				
Y+4					Y+4				
	Y	Y+1	Y+2	Y+3		Y	Y+1	Y+2	Y+3
Y					Y				
Y+1					Y+1				
Y+2					Y+2				
Y+3					Y+3				
Y+4					Y+4				

cumulated time series. This fourth type uses a general synchronous approach, making use of all data available in the p-c matrix, again, with the disadvantage that the first citation years are treated differently from the other ones. Yet, if $N << M$ then most indicators are based on the same number of data points, namely N. The fifth type is the cumulative case of the fourth. If one considers a scientist's set of publications then the h-index as proposed by Hirsch (the life-time achievement h-index) grows as this fifth type (at least if $M = N$). An example of this type of time series is presented in Rousseau & Jin (2008). See Table 7.10.

The sixth type is a publication age, chronological time series with a 1-year citation window similarly one may construct a time series in which

Table 7.10 An illustration of the calculation of the fourth (citation-chronological, publication cumulated) and fifth (cumulative, citation-chronological, publication cumulated) time series (case $M = 5$, $N = 4$)

Publication year (row) Citation year (column)	Y	Y+1	Y+2	Y+3		Publication year (row) Citation year (column)	Y	Y+1	Y+2	Y+3
Y						Y				
Y+1						Y+1				
Y+2						Y+2				
Y+3						Y+3				
Y+4						Y+4				
	Y	Y+1	Y+2	Y+3			Y	Y+1	Y+2	Y+3
Y						Y				
Y+1						Y+1				
Y+2						Y+2				
Y+3						Y+3				
Y+4						Y+4				
	Y	Y+1	Y+2	Y+3			Y	Y+1	Y+2	Y+3
Y						Y				
Y+1						Y+1				
Y+2						Y+2				
Y+3						Y+3				
Y+4						Y+4				
	Y	Y+1	Y+2	Y+3			Y	Y+1	Y+2	Y+3
Y						Y				
Y+1						Y+1				
Y+2						Y+2				
Y+3						Y+3				
Y+4						Y+4				
	Y	Y+1	Y+2	Y+3			Y	Y+1	Y+2	Y+3
Y						Y				
Y+1						Y+1				
Y+2						Y+2				
Y+3						Y+3				
Y+4						Y+4				

the citation window has a length of 2, 3 or more years. The term publication age refers to the fact that citations are collected for documents with increasing age. These sixth type time series are isochronous indicators as used, e.g., in Liang's theory on rhythm indicators (Liang, 2005; Egghe et al., 2008). The seventh type is then a cumulating publication age, chronological time series (Table 7.11).

Table 7.11 An illustration of the calculation of the sixth (publication age, chronological time series with a one-year citation window) and seventh (cumulating publication age, chronological) time series (case $M = 5$, $N = 4$)

Publication year (row) Citation year (column)	Y	Y+1	Y+2	Y+3
Y				
Y+1				
Y+2				
Y+3				
Y+4				

	Y	Y+1	Y+2	Y+3
Y				
Y+1				
Y+2				
Y+3				
Y+4				

	Y	Y+1	Y+2	Y+3
Y				
Y+1				
Y+2				
Y+3				
Y+4				

	Y	Y+1	Y+2	Y+3
Y				
Y+1				
Y+2				
Y+3				
Y+4				

	Y	Y+1	Y+2	Y+3
Y				
Y+1				
Y+2				
Y+3				
Y+4				

Publication year (row) Citation year (column)	Y	Y+1	Y+2	Y+3
Y				
Y+1				
Y+2				
Y+3				
Y+4				

	Y	Y+1	Y+2	Y+3
Y				
Y+1				
Y+2				
Y+3				
Y+4				

	Y	Y+1	Y+2	Y+3
Y				
Y+1				
Y+2				
Y+3				
Y+4				

	Y	Y+1	Y+2	Y+3
Y				
Y+1				
Y+2				
Y+3				
Y+4				

	Y	Y+1	Y+2	Y+3
Y				
Y+1				
Y+2				
Y+3				
Y+4				

Table 7.12 An illustration of the calculation of the eight type (publication-chronological time series with fixed citation window w), with w = 3; M = 5, N = 4; and the ninth type (publication-chronological time series with fixed, and equal, publication and citation windows w), with w = 3 and M = N = 5

Publication year (row) Citation year (column)	Y	Y+1	Y+2	Y+3		Publication year (row) Citation year (column)	Y	Y+1	Y+2	Y+3	Y+4
Y						Y					
Y+1						Y+1					
Y+2						Y+2					
Y+3						Y+3					
Y+4						Y+4					

	Y	Y+1	Y+2	Y+3			Y	Y+1	Y+2	Y+3	Y+4
Y						Y					
Y+1						Y+1					
Y+2						Y+2					
Y+3						Y+3					
Y+4						Y+4					

	Y	Y+1	Y+2	Y+3			Y	Y+1	Y+2	Y+3	Y+4
Y						Y					
Y+1						Y+1					
Y+2						Y+2					
Y+3						Y+3					
Y+4						Y+4					

	Y	Y+1	Y+2	Y+3			Y	Y+1	Y+2	Y+3	Y+4
Y						Y					
Y+1						Y+1					
Y+2						Y+2					
Y+3						Y+3					
Y+4						Y+4					

The eighth time series is a publication–chronological time series with fixed citation window (w). In Table 7.12 w = 3. It is a diachronous time series, similar to the first case, but now with a fixed window, so that publication years are treated in the same way. If w = 1 one obtains a series related to the immediacy index (if data refer to journal citations and publications). An example of this publication–chronological time series is presented in Gupta (1997) using a window of 5 years and steps of 10 years between publication years (and using percentages with respect to all citations). The ninth type is a publication–chronological time series with

Table 7.13 An illustration of the calculation of the tenth (citation-cumulated, publication-cumulated, publication-anti-chronological time series) time series ($M = N = 5$)

Publication year (row) / Citation year (column)	Y	Y+1	Y+2	Y+3	Y+4
Y					
Y+1					
Y+2					
Y+3					
Y+4					▓

	Y	Y+1	Y+2	Y+3	Y+4
Y					
Y+1					
Y+2					
Y+3				▓	
Y+4				▓	▓

	Y	Y+1	Y+2	Y+3	Y+4
Y					
Y+1					
Y+2			▓		
Y+3					
Y+4				▓	

	Y	Y+1	Y+2	Y+3	Y+4
Y					
Y+1		▓			
Y+2		▓	▓		
Y+3		▓		▓	
Y+4		▓	▓	▓	▓

	Y	Y+1	Y+2	Y+3	Y+4
Y	▓				
Y+1		▓			
Y+2	▓		▓		
Y+3	▓			▓	
Y+4	▓	▓	▓	▓	▓

fixed, and equal, publication and citation windows (w). This type can be considered a cumulative, truncated case of the previous one. It is used in the Essential Science Indicators (ESI) with w = 5.

The tenth time series, see Table 7.13, is a citation–cumulated, publication–cumulated, publication–anti-chronological time series. This type was used in Liang's backward looking approach to h–indices (Liang, 2006). In this case it seems natural to take $N = M$. Note that here the oldest publication year differs according to the term in the series.

7.11.3 Final Comments on Time Series

Clearly many more time series are possible, but we think these are the most interesting ones. In any case it must be made clear which type of time series is used in an investigation. Time series are used to study the dynamics of citation analysis, revealing trends and fluctuations. An interesting research question is to find the underlying mechanism that produces them. Such series may lead to (careful) predictions and hence can also be used in forecasting. This aspect is interesting in the framework of research evaluation: how will a scientist or research group most likely perform in the future?

A formal description of these time series is provided in Liu & Rousseau (2008), based on the notation introduced for impact factors in Frandsen & Rousseau (2005) see Subsection 6.6.1.

7.12 THE OUTGROW INDEX (CR INDEX) AND RELATED INDICES

7.12.1 Definitions

The outgrow or CR (citations of references) index was introduced by Rousseau and Hu (2010). It is defined as follows. Consider an article citation network and focus on one specific target article: the ego, as it is called in network theory (Wasserman & Faust, 1994). Let A denote this target article and consider A's reference list, denoted as $Ref(A)$. The length of A's reference list, i.e., its number of references, is denoted as $TRef(A)$. Article A and all articles in its reference list form a set, denoted as $ER(A) = Ref(A) \cup \{A\}$, where ER stands for the extended reference list. With each element of $ER(A)$ we associate a positive number, and this in different ways, leading to a family of indicators. These numbers lead to a ranking of the members $ER(A)$. The point is not so much this ranking (although interesting in its own right) but the position of article A in this ranked list.

As a first case we determine for each element of $ER(A)$ the number of articles by which it is cited. Next we rank all elements in $ER(A)$ according to its number of received citations. Finally the position of A in this list is characterized by its citations-of-references, or outgrow index defined as:

$$CR(A) = 1 - \frac{R(A)}{TRef(A) + 1} \tag{7.19}$$

Table 7.14 Determination of an outgrow or CR index

Rank	Article	Received citations
1	R5	56
2	R4	23
3	R7	10
4	A	9
5	R2	8
6	R1	2
7	R8	1
8	R3	0
9	R6	0

where $R(A)$ denotes the rank of A in this list. In case of ties we use an average rank.

An example of the calculation of a CR-index. Table 7.14 presents article A, its nine references (denoted as R followed by a number) and received citations at a given moment of time.

For this table the outgrow index of article A is equal to $1 - \dfrac{4}{10} = 0.6$. If A had received one more citation it would have ended at a joint third position and its outgrow index would have been $1 - \dfrac{3.5}{10} = 0.65$. The term "outgrow index" is used as it determines to which extent article A has outgrown, in terms of citations, its own references. Hence, this indicator is best seen in the context of a time series. Indeed, at the moment of its publication article a has zero citations while all its references have at least one. This means that at the moment of publication $CR(A) = 0$. The interesting question is then: will A rise in rank (will its CR-index increase) and maybe reach the number one position. It should be noted that when an article cites one or more 'classics' reaching the first position is highly improbable.

$CR(A)$ is always a number between zero (included) and one (not included). When A is ranked first its $CR(A)$ is equal to $1 - \dfrac{1}{TRef(A) + 1}$. This number is higher for long reference lists than for shorter ones. This implies that being the first among 100 is considered "better" than being the first among 10. Recall that articles that cite an article from A's reference list form the set of all articles which are bibliographically coupled with A.

Instead of considering the number of citations received by each element in $ER(A)$ we may also take the number of references in each of these articles. This is yet another number associated to $ER(A)$ (Hu et al., 2012). In this way we obtain another ranked list and we can determine a reference-reference index, $RR(A)$, defined as

$$RR(A) = 1 - \frac{R'(A)}{TRef(A) + 1} \tag{7.20}$$

where $R'(A)$ is the rank of A in the list determined by the number of references. This approach uses references of references, hence two generations of references as mentioned in Chapter 5, Publication and Citation Analysis.

Next we consider all articles that cite A and denote this set as $Cit(A)$. The number of elements in $Cit(A)$ is denoted as $TCit(A)$. This means that, taking A's point of view, we now follow the "is cited by" relation. Article A and all citing articles form a set, denoted as $EC(A) = Cit(A) \cup \{A\}$. Again we will attach a positive number to each element of $EC(A)$, leading to a ranking of the elements of $EC(A)$. As was the case for the "cites" relation, a number between zero and one will be used to characterize the relative position of A in this ranked list.

First we determine for each element in $EC(A)$ the number of articles by which it is cited. Next we rank each element in $EC(A)$ according to its number of received citations. Finally the position of A in this list is characterized by its citation-citation number

$$CC(A) = 1 - \frac{R''(A)}{TCit(A) + 1} \tag{7.21}$$

where $R''(A)$ denotes the rank of A in this new list. Again an average rank is used in the case of ties. Finally, instead of considering the number of citations received by each element in $EC(A)$ we can also take the number of references in each of these articles. In this way we obtain another ranked list and determine a reference-citation index $RC(A)$ using the relation

$$RC(A) = 1 - \frac{R'''(A)}{TCit(A) + 1} \tag{7.22}$$

where $R'''(A)$ is the rank of A in the list determined by the number of references. Articles that are cited by an article citing A form the set of all articles which are cocited with A. The meaning of these indicators has been discussed in (Hu et al., 2012).

We recall that the number of elements in $Ref(A)$ and in $EC(A)$ is fixed, while the number of elements in $Cit(A)$ and $EC(A)$ may—and usually does—increase. This implies that the denominator of the indica-tors $CC(A)$ and $RC(A)$ may increase. A software program to calculate these indices is described in (Rousseau & Rousseau, 2014) and is available at http://crindex.com.

7.12.2 Diffusion

Instead of different citing articles (usually referred to as number of cita-tions), one may count different citing authors, different citing journals, different citing institutions, countries, WoS categories, and similar enti-ties. Doing this, rankings, now based, e.g., on different WoS categories, and the resulting indices connect the approach presented in this section to diffusion theory (Liu & Rousseau, 2010; Liu et al., 2012) and the study of interdisciplinarity (Rafols & Meyer, 2010; Rousseau et al., 2018), as determined by references coming from different origins.

It is easy to see how this is done in the case of a diffusion outgrow or C-R index. One considers all elements in $ER(A)$ and determines for each article in this set the number of different authors citing it, the num-ber of different countries these authors belong to, the number of different journals, or, more generally, sources, in which citations occur and the WoS categories to which these sources belong.

In the case of the RR- index one again considers all elements in ER (A) and determines for each article the number of different cited authors, different cited sources and so on. For the CC index one considers the set $EC(A)$. For each of these elements one considers the number of different authors citing it, the number of different countries these authors come from (based on their institutional address or, maybe, their ethnicity), the number of different sources citing this document and so on. Finally, an RC diffusion index is determined by considering the set $EC(A)$ and for each of its elements the number of different cited authors, sources, coun-tries and so on.

7.13 SO'S OPENNESS AND AFFINITY INDICES (SO, 1990)
7.13.1 Openness Indices

A publication window is given. Then four indices for journal J in year Y are defined. These indicators are derived from three partial indicators A, B, and C. Publications are always taken from the given publication window. Fields are assumed to be disjoint: no article or journal belongs to two or more fields.

A is the number of references (not necessarily different ones) in journal J in year Y to articles published during the publication window in this journal (J).

B is the number of references in journal J in year Y to articles published, again during the publication window, in other journals, but in the same field as journal J.

C is the number of references in journal J in year Y to articles published during the publication window, in journals not belonging to J's field.

Hence $A + B + C$ is the total number of references in journal J in year Y to publications from the publication window.

The first index is the journal's self-citing rate in the year Y for a given publication window. It is defined as:

$$\frac{A}{A + B + C} \tag{7.23}$$

Own-field openness is defined as

$$\frac{B}{A + B} \tag{7.24}$$

It is the ratio of references to other journals in the field over the number of references to all journals in the field (including the journal J itself).

Other-field openness is defined as:

$$\frac{C}{A + B + C} \tag{7.25}$$

It is the ratio of references to journals not in J's field over the number of references to all journals.

Finally overall openness is defined as:

$$\frac{A + B}{A + B + C} \tag{7.26}$$

It is the ratio of references to journals in J's field over the number of references to all journals.

The self-citing rate expresses the degree of closeness of the journal to external input. If it is equal to one, all citations come from the journal itself. This is an extreme case of closeness. If it is zero, all citations come from other journals: it is an extreme case of openness.

Own field openness is zero if among all citations to the journal's own field, none is given to other journals in the field. It is one if all field citations are given to other journals in the field.

We note that instead of journals one may use an author or a group of authors. Similarly, instead of fields one may use country, institute, language, etc.

7.13.2 Affinity Indices

So (1990) further proposes the following affinity indices, constructed via partial indicators D, E, and F. Again a fixed publication window is used.

D is the number of citations received by journal J in year Y from itself (articles published in journal J) for articles published in J during the publication window.

E is the number of citations received by journal J in year Y from other journals in the same field as J, for articles published in J during the publication window.

F is the number of citations received by journal J in year Y from other journals from other fields as J's field, for articles published in J during the publication window.

Hence $D + E + F$ is the total number of citations received by journal J in year Y for publications published in J during the publication window.

The first affinity index is the journal's self-cited rate in the year Y for a given publication window. It is defined as:

$$\frac{D}{D + E + F} \qquad (7.27)$$

Own-field affinity is defined as

$$\frac{E}{D + E} \qquad (7.28)$$

It is the ratio of citations from other journals in the field over the number of citations from all journals in the field (including the journal J itself).

Other-field affinity is defined as:

$$\frac{F}{D + E + F} \qquad (7.29)$$

It is the ratio of citations from journals not in J's field over the number of citations from all journals (including the journal J itself).

Finally overall affinity is defined as:

$$\frac{D+E}{D+E+F} \tag{7.30}$$

It is the ratio of citations from journals in J's field over the total number of received citations.

The self-cited rate expresses the degree of narcissism of the journal (in terms of citations). If it is equal to one, all received citations come from the journal itself. This is an extreme case of narcissism. If it is zero, all citations come from other journals: it is the other extreme.

Own field affinity is zero if among all citations received from the journal's own field, none comes from other journals in the field. It is one if all field citations come from other journals in the field.

Again, instead of a journal one may use these indicators for an author or a group of authors; and instead of a field one may use a country, an institute, a language, and so forth.

7.13.3 Synchronous Impact Factors in So's Framework

Finally So (1990) also proposes the following synchronous impact factors, constructed via partial indicators D, E, F, and G. Again a fixed publication window is used. Partial indicators D, E, and F are already defined in Subsection 7.13.2. G is the number of articles published during the fixed publication window.

Self-directed impact, i.e., the self-cited rate, is defined as:

$$\frac{D}{G} \tag{7.31}$$

Own-field impact is defined as

$$\frac{D+E}{G} \tag{7.32}$$

Other-field impact is defined as:

$$\frac{F}{G} \tag{7.33}$$

Finally, overall synchronous impact is defined as:

$$\frac{D+E+F}{G} \tag{7.34}$$

7.14 PRATHAP'S THERMODYNAMIC INDICATORS

Prathap (2011a,b, 2014), proposed a series of indicators, which he describes in a thermodynamic framework. We will not go into details but just give their definitions.

Consider a set of P publications and their respective numbers of citations $(c_k)_{k=1,...,P}$ during a given citation window. Then the number of publications, P, can be written as:

$$P = \sum_{k=1}^{P} (c_k)^0 \tag{7.35}$$

The total number of received citations is then:

$$C = \sum_{k=1}^{P} (c_k)^1 \tag{7.36}$$

It is then natural to introduce a second-order indicator:

$$E = \sum_{k=1}^{P} (c_k)^2 \tag{7.37}$$

which is called the energy.

If the impact is denoted as i, then

$$i = \frac{C}{P} \tag{7.38}$$

Next Prathap introduces the so-called exergy, denoted as X, and defined as:

$$X = i^2 P = \frac{C^2}{P} = iC \tag{7.39}$$

The entropy of the system is then defined as $S = E - X$. Finally, he introduces the notion of consistency, denoted as ν, and defined as:

$$\nu = \frac{X}{E} \tag{7.40}$$

Prathap (2014) argues that besides quantity (P) and quality (C) a third attribute, namely consistency (7.40) must be considered for a complete three-dimensional evaluation of a research portfolio. Consistency can be interpreted as the variation in the quality of the portfolio. Indeed, if ν is equal to one, then $X = E$ and all papers in the set have the same number of citations.

7.15 CHARACTERISTIC SCORES AND SCALES

Characteristic scores and scales (CSS) were introduced in (Schubert et al., 1987; Glänzel & Schubert, 1988). CSS is a method for dividing a given set of numbers (in practice positive numbers) into classes without any fixed a priori thresholds. Consider a finite sequence of numbers $(x_1, \ldots, x_n)$, ranked in decreasing order:

$$x_1 \geq \ldots \geq x_n$$

In practice these numbers may represent the number of citations received by a set of n publications. For example, we have 20 publications that have obtained $(100, 50, 20, 4, 2, 2, 1, 1, 0, \ldots, 0)$ citations. We put $\beta_0 = 0$ and $\nu_0 = n$ (in the example $\nu_0 = 20$). The number β_1 is the mean, i.e.,

$$\beta_1 = \frac{1}{n} \sum_{i=1}^{n} x_i \tag{7.41}$$

For the example $\beta_1 = 180/20 = 9$. Then ν_1 is defined by the following equation: $x_{\nu_1} \geq \beta_1$ & $x_{\nu_1+1} < \beta_1$. In the example ν_1 is 3 as $x_3 = 20 \geq 9$ and $x_4 = 4 < 9$. Other β- and ν-values are defined recurrently by the relations:

$$\beta_k = \frac{1}{\nu_k - 1} \sum_{i=1}^{\nu_k - 1} x_i \quad \text{and} \quad x_{\nu_k} \geq \beta_k \ \& \ x_{\nu_k+1} < \beta_k \tag{7.42}$$

The procedure stops when $\nu_k = 1$ for some $k > 0$. The k-th group is defined by the pair of threshold values $\{\beta_{k-1}, \beta_k\}$. Its size is $\nu_{k-1} - \nu_k$. Clearly, each set determines its own thresholds and sizes. The β-values are called characteristic scores. The method itself is called the method of characteristic scales. For our example we have: $\beta_2 = 170/3 \approx 56.7$ and $\nu_2 = 1$.

Glänzel and Schubert add a category 0 of uncited papers. Articles in category 1, i.e., with citations in the interval $] 0, \beta_1 [$ are called poorly cited; those in category 2, with citations in the interval $[\beta_1, \beta_2 [$ are called fairly cited, those in category 3, with citations in the interval $[\beta_2, \beta_3 [$ are remarkably cited and finally those in category 4, with more than β_3 citations, i.e., with citations in $[\beta_3, \infty [$ are outstandingly cited. In this way any group of articles can be subdivided into five categories using the group itself as reference.

Egghe (2010b) used the idea of CSS to define a sequence of h-indices. Given a finite sequence of numbers $(x_1, \ldots, x_n)$, ranked in decreasing order, h_1 is the standard h-index. Then the first $h = h_1$ numbers are removed and one determines the h-index of the remaining $n - h_1$ items, leading to h_2. This process is continued until $h_k = 0$ or there are no more items in the remaining sequence. For our example (100, 50, 20, 4, 2, 2, 1, 1, 0, ..., 0) we find: $h = h_1 = 4$. The remaining sequence is (2, 2, 1, 1, 0, ..., 0). Hence $h_2 = 2$. This leaves the sequence (1, 1, 0, ..., 0). Hence $h_3 = 1$ and also $h_4 = 1$; finally the procedure stops with $h_5 = 0$. For the sequence (100, 50, 20, 4, 2) we find $h = h_1 = 4$; $h_2 = 1$ and the procedure stops because there are no more items in the sequence. Such a sequence of h-indices can be seen as a discrete characterization of a citation distribution.

7.16 CONCLUDING REMARKS

We end this chapter on indicators by referring the reader to a review of the literature on citation impact indicators by Waltman (2016). It provides an overview on bibliographic databases (WoS, Scopus, and GS) and further covers the selection of publications and citations to be included in the calculation of citation impact indicators, normalization issues related to citation impact indicators, counting methods and journal citation impact indicators. We especially draw attention to the four recommendations formulated in Waltman (2016).

- Do not introduce new citation impact indicators unless they have a clear added value relative to existing indicators.
- Pay more attention to the theoretical foundation of citation impact indicators.
- Pay more attention to the way in which citation impact indicators are being used in practice.
- Exploit new data sources to obtain more sophisticated measurements of citation impact.

Next we draw the readers' attention to the interesting opinion paper by Glänzel and Moed (2013), which discusses the following points: A deterministic versus a probabilistic approach to indicators, application related properties, time dependence of indicators, normalization issues, size dependence and the use of network indicators. Ding and Cronin (2011) point out the difference between popularity and prestige for authors, but the difference can also be made for journals. Although both can be considered to be measure of esteem, they are not the same. In their investigation they operationalize the notion of popularity as the number of times an author is cited and prestige as the number of times an author is cited in highly cited papers. In their work they compare 40 researchers in the field of information retrieval (IR) and indeed, find some remarkable differences between these two indicators. An extensive study of scientometric indicators and their application in research evaluation (for this aspect we refer the reader to Chapter 8: Research Evaluation) can be found in Vinkler (2010). *Scholarly Metrics under the Microscope* compiled by Blaise Cronin and Cassidy Sugimoto (2015) is a one-stop resource, as they call it, bringing together a collection of more than 60 articles, comments, editorials, letters and blog posts, written between 1955 and 2015, covering different concerns—theoretical, conceptual, methodological and ethical—related to performance metrics for scholarly research. In conclusion we recall that indicators lead to comparisons and open up expectations for improvements.

CHAPTER 8

Research Evaluation

In 1985 Garfield (1985) wrote:

> *By basing funding or even scholarly tenure and hiring decisions on quantitative bibliometric data, there is always the potential for making two serious mistakes: one, in believing that mere publication or citation counting is equivalent to citation analysis; and, two, in believing that citation analysis, even when carefully performed by experts, is sufficient by itself to ensure objectivity.*

This statement clearly determines the boundaries of this chapter, but we recall from Subsection 7.1.3 that indicators must be valid, fair, useful, and reliable.

Yet, since the time that Garfield wrote the above statement the world has become an audit society. Science has not escaped this evolution, maybe even on the contrary. The idea of a stable career in science has become blurred: scientists are in perpetual transition, have to prove their capability repeatedly, and, with the idea of tenure being questioned, are all the time at risk to be eliminated from the system or suffer burn-out (de Meis et al., 2003).

In this chapter on research evaluation, we discuss aspects related to measuring research impact, focusing on universities, research groups, and countries as main units. Less attention is given to individuals, while journals and their evaluation procedures and indicators have been discussed in Chapter 6, Journal Citation Analysis. Put differently, we focus on the macro (countries, regions, universities) and meso (departments, research groups) level and pay less attention to the micro (individuals) level. For completeness' sake we mention that it is also possible to perform studies on the nano level, i.e., the level of articles or parts thereof.

A notion that we will not try to define but that always hoovers around when talking about evaluations is the notion of "quality." We just recall Subsection 3.1.7 and mention the obvious, namely that quality is a relative concept determined by context, such as the field and goals of research.

Becoming Metric-Wise
DOI: http://dx.doi.org/10.1016/B978-0-08-102474-4.00008-X

8.1 INTRODUCTION

8.1.1 Measuring What we Know (van Raan, 1992)

The title of this section is also the title of the inaugural address of Professor Anthony van Raan upon becoming a full professor at Leiden University in 1992 (in Dutch: *Het meten van ons weten*).

Many people are fascinated by the idea of measuring science in all its aspects. They seem to forget that collecting and comparing specific data (e.g., counting numbers of publications) is *not* measuring science. That said, the research "business" has many stakeholders such as researchers, public and private funders, not-for-profit organizations, and policy makers. They all have an interest in auditing all aspects related to research in general. So, for instance, research councils of universities try to obtain a meaningful appreciation of the research conducted at their university. High values for indicators may lead to higher visibility, which in turn increases the probability for better and higher funding opportunities. Funding can be used for better equipped research facilities, reducing brain drain (top researchers staying at the university), and maybe even resulting in some brain gain: top researchers coming to work at the university or returning. The same reasoning applies at country level.

Trustees of research funds require researchers they support to publish the funded research in the most visible way possible. Besides placing their research results in public repositories, this also implies publishing in top journals, and preferably in Open Access. Publishing in top journals and with top publishers (for books) is one of the criteria of the Norwegian model for research funding see Subsection 8.9.1. Hence, it is no surprise that journal publishers and editors try to increase their journals' impact factors (Krell, 2010) and this not always in ethical ways.

8.1.2 Elements Used in Research Evaluation

Moed and Plume (2011) provide the following overview of elements that may play a role in research evaluation exercises.

Units of assessment: individuals, research groups, departments, institutions, research fields, countries, regions (e.g., the European Union).

Purpose: allocating resources, improving performance, increasing regional engagement, increasing visibility, stimulating (international) collaboration, promotion, hiring.

Output dimensions: research productivity, quality, scholarly impact, applications, innovation, social benefit, sustainability, research infrastructure.

Bibliometric indicators used: publications, citation impact, prestige, citations per publication.

Other indicators: peer review reports, patents, spin–offs, external research income, PhD completion rates, altmetric indicators.

Should one use integer counting or fractionalized counting in evaluations (cf. Subsection 5.6.3)? Both approaches have merit, but should be considered to be complementary. Integer counting of contributions of a unit (research group, university, country) indicates in how many publications the unit has participated. Fractionalized counting methods try to reflect the degree of participation.

8.1.3 Benefits Resulting From Research Evaluation

David Sweeney in Grayson (2015) described research impact on society as follows. Research impact on society at large is the demonstrable contribution that research makes to the economy, culture, national security, health, public policy or services, quality of life, and to the environment. If stakeholders (e.g., the taxpayers) want to be sure that these benefits actually occur, evaluation is a necessary step.

That said, research evaluation has different advantages to different parties.

Sarli et al. (2010) provide the following list of points related to research evaluation:

- It allows determining the exact number of publications and their impact.
- It helps in allocating funds to project submissions.
- It measures the output of funds.
- It helps to discover the use of research results.
- It may lead to the discovery of similar projects (involving other parties).
- It may lead to new collaborators.
- It plays a role in finding out if research results are confirmed, refined or rejected.
- It helps verifying if research results were applied in a new context.
- It makes it possible to verify if adequate credit has been given.
- It may lead to serendipitous findings that results have been used outside an academic context.
- It may be used in a dossier for possible promotion.
- It is a way to show that a person has met the minimum requirements for promotion.

8.1.4 Use of Citations for Research Evaluation

Basic Assumptions for the use of Citations in Evaluations (Smith, 1981)

Linda Smith stated the following four basic assumptions:

1. Citation of a document implies use of that document by the citing author.
2. Citations are positive and reflect merit quality, significance, impact.
3. The best possible works are cited.
4. If a document is cited, it is related in content with the citing document.

Some comments on these four assumptions.

Assumption 1: According to Smith (1981) assumption one has two parts:

1. Authors refer to all, or at least to the most important, documents used during the preparation of their work.
2. All documents listed are used, i.e., authors refer to a document only if its contents have contributed to their work.

Failure to meet this criterion for good citation behavior leads to "sins of omission and commission." It is, however, evident that what is cited is only a small percentage of what is read or what has in some way influenced the author. Moreover, a document is often cited because of the use of a small part of it, for instance one particular observation, theorem, or result.

Assumption 2: The underlying assumption in the use of citation counts as a kind of quality indicators is that there is a high positive correlation between the number of received citations and the quality of a document. Clearly, if most citations were made on the base of Thorne's list (Thorne, 1977), see Subsection 5.3.2, conclusions stemming from citation analysis would be invalid. Moreover, quality, impact and visibility are different notions and in practical applications a careful distinction should be made. Nevertheless, this second assumption has been tested and has found some support, see e.g., De Bellis (2009).

Assumption 3: If one assumes that citations are made to the best possible works, then one must imagine that authors sift through all the possible documents that could be cited and carefully select those judged the best. However, studies on referencing behavior suggested that, for instance accessibility is as important as quality as a factor in the selection of an information source. Soper (1976) found that the largest proportion of documents cited in authors' recent papers was located in personal collections, a smaller proportion was located in libraries in departments and institutions to which respondents belonged, and the smallest proportion was located in other cities and countries. This investigation clearly predates the Internet and the availability of journal collections on one's computer. Yet, we are convinced that availability, be it with a somewhat different meaning, still plays a major role in the selection of reading and citing material.

Assumption 4: The fact that the cited document is related in content to the citing document is supported by the use of citation databases as information retrieval tools. Successful applications of the notions of bibliographic coupling and cocitation are further testimony that this fourth assumption is often met in practice.

Overall, it seems likely that none of these four assumptions holds absolutely true in every single case, yet, as already mentioned, there is evidence that these assumptions are often met in practice. A typical case in which the cited document is not directly related to the actual contents of the citing article is a reference to a statistical test used in a medical article.

These four assumptions form the base for all evaluation studies using citation counts.

An older, but still interesting essay on the use of citations for the evaluation of scientists was written by Edward (1992). Edward, a Canadian professor in organic chemistry, takes a look at the most-cited scientists and most-cited papers in his field mostly during the 1960s and 1970s. He gives comments on the obliteration effect, notes that most articles are not or rarely cited and that often methods papers, such as the famous paper by Lowry et al. (1951), are more cited than theoretical breakthroughs. He concludes that citation counts give some indication of scientific excellence if one considers a whole corpus of papers, rather than individual papers. This idea can also be found in White (2001), where the author writes: "Within its limits, citation analysis works." Edward further observes that, besides for evaluative purposes, the Science Citation Index can be used to study the genealogy of ideas. By checking why papers are cited one may learn how others have developed one's ideas and by this, learn to become more alert oneself.

8.1.5 Criticism on Using Citations for Research Evaluations

Although indicators as presented in the previous sections and chapters are used on a large scale, not everyone is convinced about their validity. Let us say that we admit that each of these criticisms contains some truth, but it is our opinion that careful peers can, nevertheless, make sure that citation-based indicators are used during research evaluation exercises in a sensible way.

Schneider (2009), using among others work by Gläser and Laudel (2007), provides the following list of reasons why, according to him, citations can never lead to a valuable and generally useful measure for research quality. We added some comments to his list.

Citations do not Measure the Quality of an Article or a Set of Articles

Citations do not lead to a measure of quality but of visibility. Visibility depends on quality, but also on many other factors such as the publication language, the type of publication (article, review, contribution in an edited book, conference contribution), the scientific discipline, the publisher and its website, the prestige of author(s) or institute, the topicality of the contribution and pure luck.

Citation Statistics, Especially for Single Articles, do not Always Reflect Scientific Excellence

In order for scientometric indicators to yield reliable results (where we use "reliable" in the sense of "comparable with other ones") a large enough set of publications must be available. Sometimes a publication may receive quite a number of citations or sometimes it is barely cited, but little can be decided from this on statistical grounds. Only peer review may—perhaps—find out that an article which received just a few citations is the far higher intellectual achievement. This happened for instance with Nobel Prize winner Youyou Tu's article published in the Chinese Medical Journal (Tu, 1999). This is just one of the four articles she published which is included in the Web of Science. By the end of 2015 this article, strongly related to her Nobel Prize, had received (only) 19 citations. Yet, 8 articles citing (Tu, 1999) had already received more than 19 citations; the most cited one even more than 100. It is highly unlikely that these citing articles include more highly intellectual content than Tu's. Articles such as Tu's are referred to as under-cited influential articles (Hu & Rousseau, 2016, 2017).

No Database has Complete Coverage

Reliable conclusions about the work of a scientist or group of scientists can only be deduced if one has a good view on all scientific results of the research unit. Yet, the big international bibliographic databases do not have as their aim to cover all publications, let alone other scientific output.

Publication and Citation Windows Must Depend on the Field Being Evaluated

Using an adequate publication and/or citation window is of the utmost importance. Such windows differ between research fields. Moreover, some scientific domains depend on external circumstances on which they have no influence at all. An interesting case is the field of zero-gravity experiments. Researchers active in this field depend on space crafts. Room for their instruments must be reserved/negotiated years in advance; there are often delays, and sometimes failures (Challenger, Columbia). It is clear that these researchers cannot be evaluated using the same short-term windows as colleagues who perform experiments on earth (Nederhof et al., 2012).

Differences Between Scientific Disciplines

Not only time, in the case of publication and citation windows, plays a role when comparing different disciplines. Scientific domains often differ in the way reference lists are drawn. In some fields it is customary to include a short or sometimes long literature review, while in other fields one mainly cites what is actually used. Hence, it makes sense to normalize indicators based on disciplines. This is not a sinecure as even a small field such as library and information science has differences in citation potential: In recent years, articles dealing with networks (in LIS) or altmetric issues receive more citations than articles on librarianship. As a rule of thumb it may be said that it is best *not* to compare scientists active in different fields (why would one?). However, the question then becomes how fields and subfields should be delineated.

A balanced discussion on normalization is provided in Ioannidis et al. (2016). It covers normalization with respect to scientific fields, year of publication, document type and database coverage. The authors mention that all in all normalization is performed to correct for the imbalance of citation opportunity.

The Quality of the Used Database(s)

Only a few large, international databases exist: Clarivate Analytics' Web of Science and Elsevier's Scopus both belong to commercial enterprises and are not freely available. Only large research institutes or consortia can afford to buy them, or buy access to them. Yet, these databases are restricted e.g., qua language and subdomains. Freely available alternatives such as Google Scholar (GS) lack in quality or coverage.

Moreover, databases are not error-free: it is well-known that there are problems with inconsistent and erroneous spelling of author names, non-standardized journal names, wrong publication year, volume, pagination. According to Maydanchik (2007) a database (any, not just bibliographic databases) must have four basic qualities: accuracy, completeness, consistency and currency, with accuracy the key quality. Here the term accuracy refers to the degree to which data correctly reflects the real world object (a scientific publication in our case) or event being described. A bibliographic database cannot possibly be complete in the sense of containing a record of any document ever published, but it should be complete, and as current as possible, with respect to the set of publications it aims to cover. Consistency refers to the requirement that each record of the same type of publication should have the same fields, and, of course, no two different records should refer to the same original.

Emerging Fields

Leydesdorff (2008) warns against thoughtless use of citation indicators in case of emerging fields. Because of their heterogeneity it is difficult to delineate science domains. Hence, it is difficult to compare research outputs. This is, in particular, the case for researchers and research groups active in emerging fields. Their results are sometimes not accepted in traditional discipline-oriented journals and even if new, domain-specific journals exist, they are often not (yet) covered by the big databases. One may say that citations do not capture the aspect of opening up new perspectives, as by their nature new fields are peripheral and lowly cited. Even Nobel Prize winning work, such as Tu's, may receive less citations than those citing the original publication (Hu & Rousseau, 2016, 2017). Under such circumstances it is near-impossible to determine if research groups reach an international norm or benchmark.

8.2 THE LEIDEN MANIFESTO

Not everyone considers the use of metrics beneficial. A title such as *Metrics: a long-term threat to society* (Blicharska & Mikusinski, 2012) bears testimony of this feeling. Indeed, constant monitoring and evaluation may reduce long-term creativity and may lead to anxiety and in the worst case early burnout. Surely, such a climate works against mothers who try to combine a scientific career with caring for their child(ren) (Cameron et al., 2013). "Misuse of metrics" and "playing the game" are expressions which are all too familiar for those involved in evaluations based, or partially based, on bibliometric indicators. As a reaction a group of experienced colleagues composed the Leiden Manifesto (Hicks et al., 2015), named after the conference at which it crystallized. The authors presented it to the scientific community with the following words:

We offer this distillation of best practice in metrics-based research assessment so that researchers can hold evaluators to account, and evaluators can hold their indicators to account.

Irrespective of the metrics chosen, metrics–based evaluation should adhere to the following principles:

1. Quantitative evaluation should support qualitative, expert assessment.

    Metrics properly used support expert assessments; they do not substitute for judgment. Everyone must retain responsibility for their assessments.

2. Measure performance against the research missions of the institution, group or researcher.

    Metrics should align with strategic goals, maybe involving stakeholders, such as university leaders or those responsible for funding, in the process. Yet, if this is done, metrics cannot say anything about possible excellence of researchers, but only how their work relates to these goals.

3. Protect excellence in locally relevant research.

    This point relates to the mission of the university which should include locally relevant issues. This includes that research articles written in a local language, especially when the main target is a local audience, must be fully recognized. For this reason a local/regional database should belong to the set of tools of the trade.

4. Keep data collection and analytical processes open, transparent and simple.

Metrics should be transparent; the construction of the data should follow a clearly stated set of rules. Everyone should have access to the data.

5. Allow those evaluated to verify data and analysis.

Data should be verified by those evaluated, who should be offered the opportunity to provide corrections and contribute explanatory notes if they wish. It is easy to underestimate the difficulty of constructing accurate data. Evaluators must spend time and money to produce data of high quality. Those mandating the use of metrics should provide assurance that the data are accurate and hence budget for it.

6. Account for variation by field in publication and citation practices.

Sensitivity to field differences is important. Values of metrics differ by field and hence their interpretation must be adapted to the corresponding field or even subfield (Smolinsky & Lercher, 2012). Old and new fields may differ in growth rates, degree of interdisciplinarity and resources that are needed as inputs. This may affect the performance of scientists and the way in which scientists are best assessed. One way to take this aspect into account is by normalizing data based on variation in citation and publication rates by field and over time. Humanists will not be able to use citation counts; computer scientists will need to ensure conference papers are included. The state-of-the-art is to select a suite of possible indicators and allow fields to choose among them. Similarly, a disaggregated approach to research evaluation is always preferred to an aggregated one. This implies that research evaluation instruments should discard as little information (by not aggregating indicators or data) as possible. Even then, interdisciplinary research offers another challenge.

7. Base assessment of individual researchers on a qualitative judgement of their portfolio.

In other words: standard metrics have no bearing on individuals. We note that the h-index is invented for use on individuals. Following the Leiden Manifesto to the letter would exclude such use.

8. Avoid misplaced concreteness and false precision.

Providing journal impact factors with three decimals is a typical case of false precision.

9. Recognize the systemic effects of assessment and indicators.

Units under scrutiny will adapt their behavior and hence the use of indicators changes the system through the incentives they establish. In this context one refers sometimes to Goodhart's Law (Goodhart, 1975). which states that that when a feature is picked as an indicator it ceases to function as an indicator because people start to game it. These effects should be anticipated. One way to do this is by using a suite of indicators and not a single one.

10. Scrutinize indicators regularly and update them.

In order to perform acceptable research evaluation exercises bibliometricians should work on definitions, reproducibility, validation and compatibility (Glänzel, 1996) of existing and newly developed indicators. Such indicators should not be a hinder to the development of science worldwide but a help to better performance.

8.3 UNIVERSITY EVALUATION

8.3.1 A University's Mission

Evaluation of universities or its subunits should first and above all take the mission of the university into account. Nowadays universities have three major roles to play: research, education and community services i.e., playing a socio-economic role. All three contribute to the definition of the mission of a university and distinguish it from other institutions. The third role includes contributing to the economic development and to the social and intellectual welfare of the region to which the university belongs. The university's economic role has led to the idea of a triple helix (Etzkowitz & Leydesdorff, 1995, 2000) of universities, industry and governments. From a more humanistic point of view the third mission includes reaching out to the society by actively contributing to the public debate on matters of importance to the society at large. Although all these aspects are expected from the university as an institute, it would be inhuman to expect that each member of the university plays these three roles to the full.

8.3.2 The Ideal University

Related to the mission of a university and the existence of university rankings, discussed further on, we already note that university evaluation exercises and rankings are based at least partly on indicators. These indicators and the weights accorded to them should correctly reflect the essential functions of a university. Among these functions we mention teaching purely professional skills (typically in engineering studies, medicine, education, etc.) but also training the future political, social, economic and cultural leaders of the country, and of the world. Nowadays teaching is not restricted anymore to one's class room, but may include the whole world via so-called MOOCs (Massive Open Online Courses). Public engagement of academics should be rewarded with recognition and support. The best university is certainly not an institute directed only at certain "professions," say in the medical field, but an institute that is large enough to cover a broad variety of fields. Such a university also reaches a balance between the sexes and between different layers of the population (Van Parijs, 2009).

8.4 UNIVERSITY RANKINGS

A special phenomenon related to university evaluation is the occurrence of world-wide university rankings and the related phenomenon of world-class universities. This section is partially based on a review published in Rousseau (2009b).

8.4.1 University Rankings: an Introduction

Ranking universities and research institutions, and this on a world-wide scale, is a rather recent phenomenon. Yet, it has captured the whole scientific world. In 1983 Bob Morse from *U.S. News and World Reports* started the yearly publication of *America's Best Colleges*. Since then many other magazines all over the world followed his example. However, since 2003 a new phenomenon occurred: that of worldwide rankings. The Institute of Higher Education of Shanghai Jiao Tong University in China was the first to publish such a ranking. Soon the Times Higher Education Supplement (THES), and the World Universities' Ranking on the Web (http://www.webometrics.info) followed. Such lists have given rise to so-called world-class universities, namely those universities topping these lists (Deem et al., 2008; Ortega & Aguillo, 2009). Each country, and especially the new scientific tigers (say the BRICKS countries, i.e., the group of upcoming countries consisting of Brazil, Russia, India, China, (South) Korea, and South Africa), wants to have one or more world-class universities on its territory (Ngok & Guo, 2008). Nowadays the notion of a world-class university is discussed in hundreds of blogs on the Internet. Clearly, the notion of a world-class university is strongly linked to the mission of the university. In the next sections we will briefly discuss the methods used to derive these rankings and present the Van Parijs typology of worldwide university rankings (Van Parijs, 2009). Finally, following Van Parijs (2009) and Loobuyck (2009) we put the ranking phenomenon in an ethical perspective. A strong relation between the mission of a university, the idea of an ideal university and its ranking according to certain indicators is put forward.

8.4.2 The Main Worldwide University Rankings

Although more and more rankings are published, we just mention some of the more important ones.

- The Academic Ranking of World Universities (ARWU), informally known as the Shanghai ranking. This is the ranking drawn since 2003 by the Institute of Higher Education of Shanghai Jiao Tong University: http://www.arwu.org/
- The World University Ranking of the Times Higher Education (THE), formerly the THES, drawn since 2004 in collaboration with a private company QS (Quacquarelli Symonds). In November 2009 this collaboration has been stopped. Since then THE collaborated with Thomson Reuters, but switched to Scopus in 2015. The ranking can be found at: http://www.topuniversities.com/. QS has now its own QS World University Rankings to be found at: https://www.topuniversities.com/university-rankings.
- The Leiden Ranking: CWTS' rankings (note the plural) available since 2008 at http://www.cwts.nl/ranking/
- A somewhat special case is the World Universities' Ranking on the Web. This list is based on Internet web presence. It is the result of investigations performed at the Cybermetrics Lab (Madrid, Spain) under the direction of Isidro Aguillo. This list exists since 2004 and is updated twice a year see http://www.webometrics.info/
- The Performance Ranking of Scientific Papers for World Universities, drawn since 2007 by the Higher Education Evaluation & Accreditation Council of Taiwan (HEEACT): http://ranking.heeact.edu.tw/
- Since September 2009 the SIR (SCImago Institutions Ranking) has joined the set of worldwide university rankings: http://www.scimagoir.com/. Their report ranks more than 5100 research institutions and organizations and this in different ways. It takes research performance,

innovation and web presence into account and provides rankings per sector: University Research Rankings, University Innovation Rankings; University Web Visibility Rankings; Government Research Rankings; Government Innovation Rankings; Government Web Visibility Rankings; Hospital Research Rankings; Hospital Innovation Rankings; Hospital Web Visibility Rankings; Company Research Rankings; Company Innovation Rankings; Company Web Visibility Rankings.

8.4.3 Criteria Used to Draw These Rankings

Using different criteria leads to different rankings. For this reason we give an overview of the criteria used by the main actors. Most university rankings use a composite indicator: different indicators are weighted and joined into one final ranking. Moed (2017) provides a recent critical overview and comparison of 5 rankings: ARWU, THE, QS, Leiden ranking, and U-Multirank. The U-Multirank is not discussed in this book; its results, however, can be found at: www.umultirank.org.

The Shanghai Jiao Tong University ranking (ARWU) was originally conceived as a way to assess the global performance of top universities. It takes into account all universities with top researchers (Nobel laureates, Fields medalists, or highly cited researchers according to the Web of Science (WoS) databases) or papers in *Nature* or *Science*. It is based on the following indicators (their weights in the total score are shown between brackets):

- Quality of education, measured by the number of alumni that received a Nobel Prize or a Fields Medal (10%).
- Quality of faculty, measured by the number of university members that have been granted a Nobel Prize or Fields medal (20%) and the number of highly cited researchers in 21 large fields (20%).
- Research output, measured by the number of articles published in the journals *Science* and *Nature* over the last 5 years, accounting for author order, (20%) and the total number of publications (article type) included in the Web of Science (SCI and Social Science Citation Index (SSCI)) (20%).
- A weighted sum of the abovementioned scores divided by the full-time person equivalent (FTE) number of academic staff (10%).

For institutions specializing in social sciences or humanities, articles in *Science* and *Nature* are not taken into account and the weight of this indicator is spread over the other ones. For each indicator the institution that obtained the highest value receives a score of 100 and other institutions' scores are a percentage thereof. Adding these scores a new normalization is applied in such a way that the university with the highest score receives a final normalized score of 100. Again other scores are assigned proportionally.

The World University Rankings (THE) (edition 2016−2017) use a set of 13 indicators, grouped into the following five categories:

- *Teaching* (30%). This category includes five indicators, including a reputation survey, staff-to-student ratio, and the ratio of doctorates awarded to academic staff.
- *Research* (30%). This category focuses on reputation based on a survey, income (scaled against number of academic staff), and productivity. The latter is measured by the number of papers in Scopus (prior to 2015: Web of Science), normalized for university size and subject.
- *Citations* (30%). Citations are collected from Scopus and based on a 5-year publication and 6-year citation window. The data are normalized to account for subject differences. Since papers with a very large number (over 1000) of authors distorted the citation counts of smaller institutions, these papers were excluded in the 2015−2016 edition. In 2016−2017 these papers are incorporated again but their scores have been fractionalized. Each participating university gets at least 5% of the paper's citation credit; universities that contribute more authors get a proportionately larger share.
- *International outlook* (7.5%). This category looks at a university's international orientation via share of international students, share of international staff, and international research collaboration.
- *Industry income* (2.5%). The income from industry is scaled against the number of academic staff of the university.

The QS World University Rankings are based on 6 indicators:

- Academic reputation, measured by a global survey of academics (40%).
- Employer reputation, measured by a global survey of employers (10%).
- Student-to-faculty ratio (20%).
- Citations per faculty (20%). Data are obtained from Scopus and since 2015−2016 normalized for subject, such that five broad disciplines of research each contribute 20% to the final indicator.
- International faculty ratio (5%).
- International student ratio (5%).

The CWTS Leiden Rankings are focused on research and do not include teaching or reputation. No composite indicator is provided; instead, users choose themselves which indicators fit best for their own purposes.

In the 2016 edition, two types of indicators are provided: indicators of research impact and indicators of research collaboration. The impact indicators can be divided into size-dependent and size-independent ones.

- Size-dependent impact indicators are the overall number of publications and the number of publications in the top $n\%$ ($n = 1$, 10 or 50) most frequently cited publications in the same year and same field.

- The size-independent impact indicators are the proportion of publications in the top $n\%$ ($n = 1$, 10 or 50) most frequently cited publications in the same year and same field. Before 2015, average-based indicators like MCS and MNCS were also included. Note that, contrary to several other university rankings, the Leiden ranking corrects for size by taking into account the number of publications rather than the number of academic staff.

The collaboration indicators can also be divided into size-dependent and size-independent ones. The size-dependent collaboration indicators are:

- Collaboration: number of publications written in collaboration with another institution.

- International collaboration: number of publications written in collaboration with an institution from another country.

- Short distance collaborations: number of publications written in collaboration with an institution located within 100 km.

- Long distance collaborations: number of publications written in collaboration with an institution located over 5000 km away.

The 4 size-independent collaboration indicators are based on the same data, but use the proportion instead of the number of collaborations.

Compared with other university rankings, the Leiden Ranking offers more advanced indicators of scientific impact and collaboration and uses a more transparent methodology. The Leiden Ranking does not rely on subjective data obtained from reputational surveys or on data provided by universities themselves. Also, the Leiden Ranking refrains from aggregating different dimensions of university performance into a single overall indicator. New in the 2016 edition is that, in addition to the classic list view, the indicators can also be visualized on a scatter plot (chart view) and on a geographic map (map view).

The Performance Ranking of Scientific Papers for World Universities, also known as the NTU Ranking uses the number of publications, the number of citations, the average number of citations, the h-index, the number of highly cited articles and the number of articles published in high-impact journals. The main data sources are the SCIE and SSCI.

The SIR provides a composite indicator, which combines 12 indicators from three domains:

- Research (50%) includes 8 indicators related to output, impact and collaboration. One of the indicators is the number of publications published in journals that are ranked in the first quartile of their category according to the SCImago Journal Ranking. Data in this domain comes from Scopus.
- Innovation (30%) accounts for the number and proportion of publication output that is cited in patents. This part is based on the PATSTAT database.
- Societal impact (20%) is operationalized using two web-based indicators: the number of web pages in Google and the number of inbound links to the university as counted by Ahrefs (https://ahrefs.com/).
  Finally, the Webometrics Ranking of World Universities uses:
- Total number of web pages including rich files such as PDF (10%).
- Number of external inlinks, as counted by Ahrefs and Majestic (the top 20 linking domains are excluded) (50%).
- GS Citations institutional profile (10%).
- Top 10% most cited publications per discipline based on SCImago data (30%).

It should be mentioned that none of the leading international lists takes the quality of education into account as a direct measure. Most indicators used for international ranking try to measure the quality of research and the prestige of the university.

8.4.4 Is it Really Possible to Measure "The Quality of Universities"? (Buela-Casal et al., 2007)

Once these lists became known and started attracting the attention of scientists, research policy makers and even newspapers, discussions emerged about the feasibility of such lists: do there really exist indicators that lead to a meaningful ranking of universities?

Clearly, no single indicator can lead to a ranking that takes all aspects of university education and research into account. Hence a better question might be: which indicators may contribute to an accurate measurement of the quality of universities? Which methodology should be used to attain the goals of such rankings? And what precisely are these goals? These questions led to several international conferences such as the UNESCO-CEPES conference (held in Warsaw, 2002) and the First International Conference on World-Class Universities, (held in Shanghai, 2005). An International Rankings Expert Group (IREG) was brought together consisting of top-level experts. IREG was involved in the Berlin Principles on Ranking of Higher Education Institutions (Institute for Higher Education Policy, 2006). This declaration was made in order to promote good ranking practices. Yet, one may still wonder: is it possible to compare universities on a world-wide scale, across continents, across cultural and educational traditions? The idea itself that such a ranking might be feasible can be considered as a consequence of the globalization of university and higher education.

8.4.5 The Van Parijs Typology of University Rankings

In an elegantly argued essay Van Parijs (2009) makes a distinction between three types of rankings.

The Market Model

According to this model the purpose of this type of list is to support the market for higher education. This was, indeed, the original purpose of the Shanghai Jiao Tong ranking. Its creators wanted to inform Chinese students about which universities were the best places for going abroad to study. In this model universities are ranked for the benefit of students, considered as consumers of educational services provided by universities and institutes of higher education. The market model type of list wants to fill an information gap. Clearly a "one size fits all" approach can never succeed. A solution for this problem is an interactive ranking in which customers (students) may adapt weights of different indicators. For some students the price of a university education must receive the highest weight, for others the standing of the physics department or any other department. Maybe even the "student life" in the neighboring city is an indicator that should be weighted high. Of course, the language in which the education is provided may be an indicator used to exclude certain universities: few international students want to study in Dutch, or few European students want to study in Chinese or Japanese. All this leads to a phenomenon referred to by Van Parijs as "my rankings," where each ranking corresponds to the personal preference of one person. In order to make "my rankings" available, data must be collected on departmental level (or a similar unit), as global data i.e., data referring to a university as a whole are too coarse. It is an open question where funds (for collecting those enormous amounts of data, in such a way that comparisons become meaningful) are to be found to realize this idea.

The Podium Model

In this model, ranking is the result of a yearly "World Championship." The "best university in the world" features at the top step while runners-up also have a place on the winners' podium. This approach is in an essential way different from the market model. Even if students had no choice at all, this model would still exist as university leaders want their university to be the best in the world. Of course, as in reality, students do have a choice (be it a restricted one), the podium value can be used as a sales argument for attracting prospective students. Obviously, no university leader can ignore this function of university rankings. Whatever one's feelings about such lists, it is vain hope to believe that they will disappear, if alone because of their role played in the podium model.

The Input-Output Model

However, those responsible for the resources devoted to universities and institutes of higher education need another type of list. They are not so much interested in an absolute scale of accomplishments but in the efficiency with which universities handle the means entrusted to them. Not all universities start on an equal footing: some have more supporting staff; some are situated in a more attractive part of the country (or of the world) and so on. Policy makers want to know how a university transforms means into relevant accomplishments. Allocating money to the best performers in this sense will lead to a better attainment of the objectives of educational authorities. Moreover, if one university performs significantly better than another, and this using the same amount of or even fewer resources, there might be good reasons to imitate the methods of the better performing one.

These three models are related. We already pointed out that a high rank according to the podium model can be used as an asset for the market model and the input-output model can only be applied if one starts from a version of the podium model. Indeed, efficiency can only be defined with respect to specific goals. This leads to the idea of the ideal university, already mentioned earlier in this chapter.

8.4.6 Do Rankings Lead to More Inequality? (Van Parijs, 2009)

Van Parijs (2009) further discusses the question if ranking leads to increased inequality. At first sight the answer seems to be "yes." Yet, this may depend on the point of view. The higher a university's score (especially from the point of view of the podium model) the bigger its attraction to potential students and to scientists that want to become a member of its academic teams. This results in increased money flows. The lower the ranking the less the university's attractiveness to students and potential professors. All this leads to a spiral of increasing inequality among universities.

What about the inequality between individuals? The more important the rankings the larger the inequality among professors, researchers and all scientific university members. The best researchers may move up to the best universities, possibly leading to higher salaries. Note though that this is not evident: it seems that in some of the best universities average salaries are somewhat lower than those at runners-up, as scientists want to "pay" for the privilege of working at a top university. Conversely, universities aspiring to reach the top are willing to pay higher salaries in order to keep their best scientific performers. It goes without saying that top universities are able to provide researchers with better research facilities. Yet, inequality may lead to more competition among scientists, hence weakening their bargaining power with respect to the university administration. Hence, for scientists rankings are a mixed blessing. Finally, the market model, especially the existence of "my rankings," may benefit less privileged students leading to reduced inequality, as these students do not have the kind of networks that richer students have.

8.4.7 Rankings and an Ideal University

Finding better rankings is not just a technical or informetric question (Van Raan, 2005), it is also an ethical question (Loobuyck, 2009; Van Parijs, 2009). When university policy makers have defined what they see as an ideal university (and their opinions may differ), universities can be ranked according to different views on this ideal. According to Loobuyck (2009) it would be better not to rank whole universities but disciplines, specialized research institutes or departments (including those especially fostering multidisciplinary research). This is actually done by the Leiden and the SCImago ranking.

8.4.8 Some Further Observations on Rankings

Some lists regularly change their methodology. For instance, they adapt the weights given to different indicators. In the past *U.S. News and World Reports* has often changed its methodology, leading to sudden changes in rankings between universities and colleges. Although there is nothing wrong with a change in methodology, on the condition that the new approach is a real improvement, it makes comparisons over time difficult or even impossible.

The phenomenon of world-wide university rankings has changed the political agenda of many national educational ministries and even of international educational institutions, cf. the involvement of UNESCO in the Berlin Principles (Institute for Higher Education Policy, 2006).

Aguillo et al. (2010) have tried to compare some rankings. As the main rankings use different criteria they tend to differ considerably. Only top universities (Harvard, Stanford, Yale, Oxford, Cambridge (UK)) stay top universities in each ranking. However, one may say that we do not need dedicated rankings to know that these institutions are top universities. For most other universities these rankings entail a large reproducibility question.

8.4.9 Conclusion on University Rankings

For decades informetricians have studied journal rankings. Nowadays another type of rankings has come to the fore, namely (world) university rankings. Although such rankings may be condemned as a kind of race based on narrowly defined parameters, making "big" even 'bigger," this does not necessarily have to be the case. We have shown that Van Parijs (2009) formulated a possible purpose of such rankings. According to him university rankings must be redesigned so that they provide institutions and policy makers the incentives to honor the highest intellectual and social values. Unfortunately, nowadays incentives are often more directed to publishing often rather than to publishing well. Numbers of publications on their own should never be decisive in tenure decisions or grant submissions.

Recall that most of these rankings neglect educational parameters. One of the few attempts to include educational parameters in the university performance measurement (just within one university) is due to Degraeve et al. (1996). These authors used Data Envelopment Analysis, a technique that enables the incorporation of inputs and outputs of different types. Using this technique a group (or university) may have a high total score without scoring high on every aspect. We think that the use of this technique may benefit existing university rankings.

8.5 EVALUATION OF RESEARCH GROUPS

In this section, we provide a short overview of indicators used for scientometric evaluations of research groups. This overview is largely based on work performed at CWTS (Leiden), see (Moed et al., 1983, 1985a; de Bruin et al., 1993; Wilsdon et al., 2015). We assume that the evaluation takes place based on publications during the period [Y − T, Y], a period of a discrete length of T + 1 years.

8.5.1 Evaluation Indicators

- Average number of FTEs for research (indicator a).

    In this expression FTE stands for full-time equivalent. If each collaborator worked full-time as a researcher the indicator FTE would be the number of personnel. Yet, some researchers work part-time or worked just for a few months in a particular year (end of contract; maternity leave, etc.). This leads to a fractional contribution to the research group. Finally, some scientists, although working full-time do not work full-time as a researcher: they have teaching and/or administrative duties. Taking all these effects into account leads to a yearly FTE. These numbers are averaged over the period of study (T + 1 years).

- The total number of publications during the period of investigation (indicator b).

    To determine this number all scientific publications (any type, any publication outlet) with at least one member of the group as contributor are included (published during the period of investigation). Sometimes working papers are included too, especially if they are published, after initial screening, in a numbered series of such papers.

- Total number of publications in journals (indicator c).

    This number is determined in the same way as indicator b but restricted to journal articles.

- Total number of publications in journals included in a designated set of databases (indicator d).

    Often one considers only one such database, namely the WoS and the Journal Citation Reports, and these journals are then said to be "journals with an impact factor." Of course, one may consider other or larger sets obtained by including journals covered by Scopus, or included in a specially constructed local database (as in the Norwegian or the Flemish model, discussed further on). Further on, the database(s) used in the evaluation exercise will be referred to as the designated database.

- Total number of publications in the designated database, using fractional count (indicator e).

    Any form of fractional counting, cf. Chapter 5, Publication and Citation Analysis, can be used. For example, if an article has 6 authors and only 2 belong to the research group under investigation, then this publication receives $2/6 = 1/3$ publication credits for the research group in question (assuming complete-normalized counting).

- The length of a citation window is chosen and for each publication the number of received citations during the citation window is determined (indicator f).

- Global productivity of the group (indicator g).

    This indicator is defined as indicator b divided by indicator a. It can be seen as a maximum productivity.

- Fractionalized designated database-productivity (indicator h).

    This is defined as indicator e divided by indicator a.

    The values of indicators g and h provide an upper bound and a lower bound for the productivity of the research group. If the group publishes mostly articles in journals covered by the designated database and rarely collaborate with other groups, this upper bound and lower bound will not differ much. Yet, in most realistic situations there may be a large difference between these two indicator values.

- Percentage journal articles published in journals covered by the designated database (indicator i).

    Indicator i is defined as indicator d divided by indicator c.

    A small value for indicator i may indicate one of three things, or a combination thereof: either the group published mostly articles of lower quality which were not accepted in the better journals, or coverage of this group's field by the designated database is not adequate, or the group deliberately chooses to support new journals which are not yet covered by the designated database.

- Percentage of journal contributions with respect to all publications (indicator j).

    Defined as indicator c divided by indicator b.

Publications included in the calculation of indicator b and not included for c are mostly contributions to edited books and separately published conference proceedings. In the humanities we may encounter quite some monographs here. For some fields, this group of publications also includes working papers.

- Total number of received citations (indicator k).

    This is the total number of citations received by all publications, as obtained from the designated database (but published anywhere), and received during the citation window.

- Total number of received citations by articles published in the designated database (indicator l).

    As the set of articles used is a subset of the set used by indicator (k) the number of received citations is obviously smaller.

- Percentage of citations received by indicator l (indicator m).

    Indicator m is defined as the ratio of indicator l over indicator k. If this ratio is much smaller than 1 it indicates that "other" publications receive a fair share of citations and should certainly not be ignored.

- Three indicators that do not take self-citations into account (indicated as k', l', m').

    These indicators are calculated by removing self-citations. Self-citations can be defined in many ways. Here it is most appropriate to define self-citations as research group self-citations. This means that if A and B are members of the same research group and A cites a publication coauthored by B (even if A is not an author of this publication) then this counts as a self-citation.

- Percentage self-citations in indicators k and l.

    This is especially helpful to detect research groups with an excessive percentage of self-citations.

- A sequence of indicators: total number of received citations for each publication year separately (sequence s).

    Again only citations received during the citation window are taken into account.

- A sequence similar to sequence s, but now only for articles published in the designated database (sequence t).
- Sequences s and t but without self-citations (sequences s' and t').
- The sequence of citations per publications (CpP) (sequences u and u').

    The values of sequences s and s' divided by the corresponding number of publications (differing by the year).

- Sequence of CpP in the designated database (sequence v and v′). The values of sequences t and t′ divided by the corresponding number of publications in the designated database (differing by the year).
- Weighted (by number of publications) average diachronous impact factor of journals used by the research group calculated over the same citation window (denoted as JCSm).
- World citation average in the field (denoted as FCSm) (with or without self-citations).

  One of the weaknesses of a designated database such as the Journal Citation Reports for evaluation purposes as well as for studies of the science of science, is the fact that many journals are not in the correct category. Moreover, there is no classification of articles, in the sense that articles are assigned to the category of the journals in which they are published. Consequently there is a need for a better, article-based, classification scheme, see e.g. (Waltman & van Eck, 2012b). In an attempt to produce such a scheme, Glänzel and Schubert (2003) note that the classification of the scientific literature into appropriate subject fields is one of the basic conditions for valid scientometric analysis.
- Ratio of average impact of the group and average impact of the journal package CpP/JCSm (or CexpP/JCSm).

  CexpP is CpP but with research group self-citations removed. JCSm is the journal citation average.

  In older publications one finds the so-called crown indicator, defined as the ratio of the impact of the research group and the world citation average CpP/FCSm. This indicator became known as the Leiden crown indicator, but was actually used earlier by the research group of the Hungarian Academy (Braun-Schubert-Glänzel). Because of problems with this indicator (it has namely been shown that it is not independent, see Subsection 7.3.3), it has been replaced by the mean normalized citation score (MNCS). This indicator can roughly be described as the average number of citations of the publications under investigation, normalized for field differences, publication year and differences between document types. An MNCS value 1 represents the world average. Hence, an MNCS value of 2, for instance, means that these publications have in total been cited twice above their field's world average.
- JCSm/FCSm.

This indicator shows if the research group is conservative in its publication attitude, in the sense of publishing in journals with a rather low impact (JCSm/FCSm < 1), or more daring (JCSm/FCSm > 1) in its submission policy.

8.5.2 The Ratio of Averages Versus the Average of Ratios Problem

A few years ago colleagues such as Lundberg (2007) and Opthof & Leydesdorff (2010) criticized the (meanwhile corrected) "Crown indicator" of CWTS stating that ratios of averages only make sense when applied on data that are normally distributed. A better approach would be to consider the average of the ratio of observed data (say number of received citations) and an expected value (such as the average number of citations in the field). However, this approach does not completely solve the problem as one must still define 'the field' and the proper citation window.

Ratios of averages and averages of ratios, in the context of impact factors, have been introduced by Egghe and Rousseau (1996a,b), see Subsection 6.7.3. Clearly, the average impact factor is an average of ratios (AoR), while the global impact factor is a RoA. In the context of research evaluation an AoR is the better approach. Yet, we claim that the impact of a field can best be described as an RoA. We recall that when geometric means are used instead of arithmetic ones, the AoR verus RoA problem disappears.

8.6 TOP X% PUBLICATIONS

According to CWTS the proportion of top 10% cited publications (also known as the T indicator) is the best, i.e., most robust and size-independent, indicator for the quality of an institute's publications. By the term "top 10% publications" CWTS means the top 10% most frequently cited among similar publications, i.e., published in the same field, the same publication year and being of article or review type (in the WoS). Dividing by 10 yields that 1.0 is the expected global norm and one can compare an institute's (or research group's) performance with this global norm. Concretely if 12% of an institute's publications belong to the top 10% of its field, then this institute is performing rather well, while if 6% of an institute's publications belong to the top 10% of their field, then this institute is performing rather poorly. Similarly one may consider top 5% or top 1% publications.

This approach eliminates the AoR versus RoA problem and is nowadays preferred by many colleagues.

We already mentioned that the approach presented here is based on the evaluation procedures used at CWTS (Leiden, the Netherlands). Another, excellent approach is that explained in the *Bibliometric Handbook for Karolinska Institutet* (Rehn et al., 2014).

8.7 COUNTRY STUDIES

Most indicators that can be applied to universities can also be applied to countries. However, some are (even) less suited for countries than for universities, the h-index being a typical example. This indicator depends too much on the number of publications, so that lists according to h-index are very similar to lists according to number of publications. For that reason Molinari & Molinari (2008) proposed a size-independent h-index, defined as $h/T^{0.4}$, where T denotes the number of publications. Yet, based on Mahbuba & Rousseau (2010) we suggest that this indicator overcompensates and hence favors countries with smaller numbers of publications. In this context we note that in Chapter 9 (The Informetric Laws) we will show that in a so-called Lotkaian framework with exponent alpha, $h/T^{1/\alpha} = 1$.

When performing a scientometric study of a country the final scientific output is what counts. Yet, results must be placed in context: a study of a developing country or one of the G7-countries (Canada, France, Germany, Italy, Japan, UK, USA) is a totally different matter. Hence such a study may start by the description of the country's educational system and its basic economic indicators such as GDP, GDP per capita, percentage of GDP spend on R&D, GERD, compounded annual growth rate, etc. Gantman (2012) for instance studied the influence of economic, linguistic and political factors on the scientific production of countries. Among these the size of the economy had the largest positive influence. International think tanks have constructed indicators, not scientometric ones, allowing comparisons between countries such as the Human Development Index and the Global Innovation Index.

Combining economic, demographic and scientometric indicators may lead to indicators such as "Research papers per GDP per capita" (Mashelkar, 2015).

8.8 SOME REMARKS ON EVALUATIONS OF INDIVIDUALS

8.8.1 General Remarks

Most, or probably all, bibliometric indicators should not be used on the individual level (cf. Leiden Manifesto, point 7). With Phelan (1999) and many other colleagues we stress that when making inferences about individual cases, considerable caution should be used. The two main reasons for this are that, most of the time, numbers are too small, and more importantly numbers of citations are highly skewed so that averages or even medians become virtually meaningless. Nevertheless, Wildgaard et al. (2014) have even collected and discussed 108 author-level indicators. Indeed, individual researchers must be evaluated and this for multiple reasons. Here is an incomplete list of such reasons:

• Recruitment
• Promotion
• Tenure
• Funding allocation
• Yearly (or, more generally, periodical) review answering questions such as: Is this doctoral student on the right track to get their degree during the available time span? Shall we extend this person's contract for another period?
• In centers of excellence, being among the top 5% may not be good enough so one wants to find answers to questions such as: does one expect this person to move up to the top 1% in the field?
• In mission-oriented institutes one wants to make sure that researchers perform investigations relevant to the mission of the institute.

All these questions leading to the stated aims must be answered by review committees.

8.8.2 Evaluation and Author Roles

One aspect of scientists' publication careers is the role they play in published research, more concretely: are they usually first author or usually the last one? In the experimental sciences the first and last positions in the byline of a publication are usually considered to be the most important ones. The scientist occupying the first position is then doing the bulk of the experimental work, while the colleague in the last position supervises the research. In a study on cooperation between scientists Wardil and Hauert (2015) refer to authors who contribute mostly as last authors as lairds, those that publish mostly as first authors as workers, and those that contribute equally as first and as last author as traders. Of course, such a classification is only valid when authors are ranked in order of actual contribution, except for the last author who is the leader of the group, maybe only contributing by providing funds, organizing the work and taking the main responsibility of the published result. It goes without saying that such a classification is very rough and most certainly does not apply in fields were authors are usually placed in alphabetical order.

Returning to the purpose of this chapter we refer to Smolinsky and Lercher (2012) who performed an evaluation study in the field of mathematics. As basic truth they took received prizes and grants and compared the results with citation counts. They concluded that citation counts are misleading because of the existing variation by subdisciplines (even within mathematics). Hence, although citation counts are an attempt to satisfy the needs of nonexperts, they conclude that this attempt is not successful. Institutional administrators are in an external position to any discipline and hence need to rely on the work of experts.

When discussing individuals we recall the fact that not every scientist writes articles. Some are famous for their communication skills (Maxmen, 2016), while others provide essential tools for their colleagues. Indeed, outcomes of research often include software programs written by scientists. These programs are of the utmost importance in fields such as evolutionary biology and the life sciences in general. Recognizing and citing software can nowadays be done via a digital object identifier assigned to code. Recently, platforms such as Depsy (http://depsy.org) have been built to track the impact of software built for academic use (Chawla, 2016).

Finally we recall that there even exists an h-index for an individual article A (Subsection 7.6.4), defined as the largest natural number h such that articles citing A, received at least h citations. This concept used citations of citations or a form of second-generation citations. Continuing on the topic of single article indicators we note that PLOS (Public Library of Science) provides article-level metrics, in short, ALMs (Fenner & Lin, 2014). These are a form of altmetrics and include download data, citation data, social network data, blog and media data. Fenner and Lin (who work for PLOS) claim that collecting these ALMs has potential for research assessment, research navigation and retrieval, and research monitoring and tracking, leading to a thorough study of the research process.

8.9 PAYING ATTENTION TO THE SOCIAL SCIENCES AND ARTS & HUMANITIES

In this section we pay special attention to the social sciences and the arts & humanities. We discuss the Norwegian and Flemish models as examples; similar databases exist in many other (European) countries as well (Sīle et al., 2017).

8.9.1 The Norwegian Model

The driving force behind the Norwegian model is Sivertsen (2008). The following description of the model is based on Schneider (2009) and Sivertsen (2010).

The Norwegian model started as an assignment from the Norwegian Ministry of Education. Its aim is to assign a share of basic funding among 6 universities and 40 other institutes of higher education. It was applied for the first time in 2006. In this way, 2% of the total science budget was relocated.

As the model is based on publications, a database has been developed containing all acceptable (see further) Norwegian publications. Data in this database are complete, correct and reliable. Counting is fractionalized according to institutes and weighted according to three levels.

According to its inventor the most innovative part of the model is the construction of a documentation system, CRIStin (Current Research Information System in Norway), to support the bibliometric indicator used in the model. All Norwegian publications are registered, validated and standardized. The system is public and transparent. It is enhanced with a structured set of metadata. A first condition to be acceptable is that an article is published in a journal with an ISSN and a book has an ISBN. Moreover, journals must be peer-reviewed and if two thirds or more of the authors of a journal belong to the same institute such journals are not accepted. In other words, journals that are "too local" are excluded. The Norwegian model combines production (quantity) and quality. Yet, no citations are used. Instead, field experts determine to which quality level a publication channel—a journal or publisher—belongs. Three types of publication channels are distinguished:

Level 0: Channels not accepted as being of scientific value.
Level 1: Channels accepted as scientific publication channels.
Level 2: Publication channels with extra-large scientific prestige.

Table 8.1 Publication scores in the Norwegian model

	Level 1	Level 2
Articles in journals	1	3
Articles in books	0.7	1
Books	5	8

In each field at most 20% of the channels accepted as being of scientific value (levels 1 and 2) belong to level 2.

The bibliometric indicator makes a distinction between three times two types of publications. Publications themselves are subdivided into journal articles, contributions in books and books themselves. Next, each category has two levels. Level 1 is the ordinary level, while level 2 contains the more selective journals and book publishers. These receive an extra weight. Different Norwegian research councils determine, each for their own field, the level of journals and publishers. A journal which is considered to be of level 2 by one research council is also of level 2 if used by a researcher of another research field. Finally, publication scores are distributed as shown in Table 8.1.

Scores are divided fractionally according to the institutes to which authors belong (or the author belongs). Fractionalization is considered to be essential in order to avoid an inexplicable increase in the number of authors. Since this model has been in use the number of Norwegian publications in the WoS has increased, but their impact has stayed the same. In other words: the model works as it is supposed to.

Although the Norwegian model is not especially made for the social sciences and humanities, it is constructed in such a way that all fields are treated equally. We further note that CRIStin is not unique as a CRIS: more and more countries (and fields) design and implement current research information systems (Giménez-Toledo et al., 2016; Sales & Sayao, 2015).

8.9.2 The Flemish Model

This section is based on Verleysen et al. (2014) and Ossenblok (2016) where more detailed information can be found. The Flemish model is inspired by the Norwegian one. In 2008 a decree of the Flemish Community in Belgium made it legally possible to construct the Flemish Academic Bibliographic Database of the Social Sciences and Humanities. Further on in the chapter we will use the official (Dutch) abbreviation VABB-SHW. Through this database it became possible for non-WoS publications in the social sciences and humanities to contribute to the system of output financing existing in Flanders for further details, see Debackere & Glänzel, 2004; Spruyt & Engels, 2013. In this way this financing scheme increased its value as an incentive for performing and communicating quality research, including that part that focuses on local aspects. As such we may say that the introduction of the VABB-SHW responded—*avant la lettre* to two points included in the Leiden Manifesto: (3) *Protect excellence in locally relevant research* and (6) *Account for variation by field in publication and citation practices*. The first version of the VABB-SHW was officially published on December 22, 2010. Since then it is updated on a yearly basis.

Next we describe how this database is constructed and which characteristics of the local, Flemish, research in the social sciences and humanities can be derived from it. In accordance with the regulations stipulated in the decree mentioned above, outputs eligible for inclusion must meet the following basic criteria:

1. to be publicly accessible, be it not necessarily free of charge.
2. to be unambiguously identifiable by an ISBN or ISSN.
3. to make a contribution to the development of new insights or to applications resulting from these insights.
4. to have been subjected—prior to publication—to a peer review process by independent scholars who are experts in the field to which the publication belongs. Peer review should be done by an editorial board, a permanent reading committee, external referees or a combination of these. Peer review should not be organized by the author.

The last stipulation means that, for instance journal editors may not organize peer review for their own submissions to the journal. This point was already mentioned in Subsection 3.1.4 when discussing the deontology of editors.

The following five publication types are eligible for inclusion in the VABB-SHW: journal articles (including reviews), monographs, edited books, book chapters and proceedings papers. The responsibility of deciding which publication channels meet the criteria mentioned above rests with an authoritative panel consisting of 18 members from all Flemish universities, covering all disciplines within the social sciences and humanities. An important task of this panel is to decide which publications and publication channels were peer-reviewed. As mentioned above, this database is used to decide which publications contribute to the Flemish allocation model. Other research-related parameters in the allocation model are the number of publications (of publication type article, letter, note or review) in the WoS as well as the number of citations in the WoS.

Publications in the VABB-SHW are assigned to one of seven disciplines in the social sciences and/or one of nine in the humanities, namely:

Social Sciences

- Criminology
- Economics, business and management (including library & information science)
- Educational sciences
- Political science
- Psychology
- Sociology
- Social health sciences

Humanities

- Archaeology
- Art history (including architecture and arts)
- Communication studies
- History
- Law
- Linguistics
- Literature
- Philosophy, ethics (including the history of ideas)
- Theology, religion

In addition, there are the general categories Social sciences general and Humanities general. The publication and updates of the VABB-SHW turned out to be a treasure trove for informetric research (Engels et al., 2012; Ossenblok et al., 2012, 2014; Verleysen & Engels, 2014a,b; Verleysen et al., 2014; Ossenblok & Engels, 2015; Ossenblok, 2016). Engels, Ossenblok, Verleysen, and colleagues were able, for the first time, to study the Flemish social sciences and humanities in more detail than had ever been possible. They documented the relative increase in the use of English and the corresponding decrease in the use of Dutch (the local language) and especially French and German (the other official national languages), with large differences between fields, see Engels et al. (2012) for more details. They also found that Flemish colleagues in the social sciences and humanities show a relatively high degree of research collaboration, again notwithstanding substantial disciplinary variations. One other result is the observation that, similar to the other sciences, scientific communication in the social sciences and the humanities is evolving at a fast rate. The existence of this database and its use in a funding formula makes it possible to study the influence of an incentive structure on the publication behavior of scientists (Guns & Engels, 2016). Moreover, the existence of a similar database in Norway has led to some inter-country comparisons (Ossenblok et al., 2012).

Clearly, these investigations made it overtly clear that for evaluations in the social sciences and humanities the use of the international databases alone does not suffice, and may lead to biased results: less than half (44%) of the publications in the VABB-SHW is also indexed in the WoS.

An important aspect of the VABB-SHW from a bibliometric point of view is the inclusion of monographs, edited books and chapters in edited books. These publication types are otherwise rarely studied. This led to the detection of a neglected form of research collaboration through coediting and between editors and contributing authors (Ossenblok & Engels, 2015; Ossenblok et al., 2015).

Further information and an analysis of the VABB-SHW database can be found in Engels et al. (2012).

8.10 HOW TO EVALUATE TOP LABS: AN EXAMPLE FROM CHINA

Research laboratories are larger units than research groups. Moreover, when evaluating labs one should not only take research output into account, but one must also consider the complete infrastructure and the level of the available personnel. As an example of factors that can be taken into account we discuss an approach applied in China for so-called Key Labs. More details can be found in Jin et al. (2005, 2006) and Ahlgren et al. (2017).

The evaluation procedure is mainly qualitative and is performed by experts according to a set of predefined quality indicators. These are subdivided into three groups:

Research level and contributions.

Increasing scientific capacity (including training).

Open communication and management structure.

Each of these topics includes several subaspects.

8.10.1 Research Level and Contributions

Under this heading the following points are considered: Orientation, tasks and key results. Orientation and task: the lab is classified as a basic research lab or an applied research lab. It has a clear statement of goals and means, and knows its priorities. It is capable of taking on major tasks for the government and has high productivity.

Key results: the lab presents five research results which fall within the scope of the lab's (scientific and/or technological) orientation and goals. These results are the best ones obtained over the latest five years. Basic research and applied research labs are evaluated according to different standards.

For basic research the requirements include:
- doing research on the frontier of science.
- publishing original articles in international journals with high impact.
- publishing monographs.
- giving keynote speeches at important international conferences.
  For applied research the corresponding requirements are:
- developing new methods and ideas of importance for the national economy, social development or national safety.
- making considerable progress in experimentation.
- doing innovative work, especially in key technologies.
- obtaining patents.
- building up a repertoire of new techniques with high potential for industrial applications.

8.10.2 Increasing Scientific Capacity

This point refers to the research capacity of individual scientists as well as the lab as a whole. It is subdivided into three sets of requirements. The first relates to the lab director and upper-level researchers. Here the CVs of the top persons are presented. The reason for including these in the evaluation is that labs should be directed by top-level scientists and academic leaders, not by mediocre scientists, administrators or politicians. The director must have the intellectual capacity and the time to work in their lab as a scientist (not just as an administrator), and play a central scientific role. The upper-level researchers must be researchers with a known reputation in the field. The second point relates to the personnel structure and aspects of team-building. Here the internal structure and collaboration (teamwork) are evaluated. This structure should be such that it leads to the best possible scientific research. The lab should neither be too fragmented into small units, nor be a huge mastodon with little internal structure. Researchers are encouraged to take upon them leading duties in academic organizations at the national and international level. Leading scientists from all over the world should be invited to participate in the lab's work. Teamwork in a spirit of cooperation should be encouraged. Moreover, teams should consist of scientists of all ages, but be dominated by younger and middle-aged colleagues. The lab is to be characterized by an intellectual and science friendly atmosphere. Finally the lab must provide training for young talented students. It provides Master and PhD education for national (Chinese) and foreign students.

8.10.3 Open Communication and Management

This point also consists of three parts.

- Publicly shared facilities and instruments. Does the lab have all the research facilities and instruments necessary for research at the forefront of science? The lab should develop its own instruments for leading-edge experiments and share the use of big expensive instruments with other labs.
- Open academic communication. The lab must have an open communication structure, internally as well as with the outside world, in particular with fellow scientists all over the world. Open communication also implies sharing the use of costly instruments (see above). The lab always has a group of temporary and visiting scholars. Its openness is also characterized by participation in international events, and the organization of international, national, regional and local conferences and symposia.
- Management. Clear management guidelines must exist, so that each member knows their duties and all operations are performed smoothly. The lab has access to all necessary research materials. Academic committees are present and play a role in the organization and management of the lab. Financial conditions are adequate and the lab receives the necessary support from an affiliated institute.

As with all evaluation procedures these indicators also have a prescriptive function: they tell lab directors what they should certainly do, namely activities that are explicitly mentioned in the evaluation procedures and what is of less importance, namely activities that are not evaluated.

Each research-intensive institution has a unique and characteristic profile with respect to the research that is performed in this institute. This should be taken into consideration during institutional and lab evaluation exercises.

The previous example illustrated the evaluation procedure for research institutes and laboratories. A totally different approach was provided some years ago by Noyons, Moed, and Luwel (1999) who combined a structural analysis, via mapping techniques, and a research performance assessment to place a micro-electronics institute in an international context.

8.11 THE NATURE INDEX

The Nature Index is a database compiled by the Nature Publishing Group (NPG) in collaboration with Digital Science, a sister company of NPG, focusing on providing software for scientific purposes. It is based on papers from so-called high-quality journals, independently chosen by a committee of active researchers. The Nature Index is used to discuss institutions, countries and articles and leads, as such, to a form of evaluation. It provides three indices: article count (AC), a complete count measure; fractional count (FC), under the assumption that each author contributes equally (complete normalized counting), and weighted fractional count, which is FC but weighted to compensate for the overrepresentation of papers in astronomy and astrophysics. It also provides a collaboration score. These scores are derived from 68 journals and shown depending on four fields: chemistry, earth & environmental sciences, life sciences and physical sciences. From 2016 on it includes clinical sciences.

Results using the Nature Index have been published in several supplementary issues of the journal. These include e.g., comparative data about continents or subcontinents and cities in China.

8.12 REFLECTIONS AND COMMENTS

8.12.1 Professional Evaluation Versus Amateur Bibliometrics

Francis Narin founded Computer Horizons Inc. in 1968, a company devoted to the analysis of science and technology. As such, he and his team were the first professional bibliometricians. In the early 80s similar groups, but more directly connected to academia, such as SPRU (Brighton, UK) under de guidance of Ben Martin; CWTS (Leiden, the Netherlands) under de guidance of Ton van Raan and Henk Moed; ISSRU (Budapest, Hungary) under the guidance of Tibor Braun, and FHG-ISI (Fraunhofer,

Karlsruhe, Germany) under the guidance of Hariolf Grupp, initiated more studies and evaluations of science and technology performances.

Since those days two tendencies related to research evaluation have developed. One is the professionalization of the field leading to expert organizations such as CWTS, Science Metrix (Montréal, Canada) and many other local ones, such as ECOOM in Flanders. The other is the fact that Thomson Reuters and Elsevier (Scopus) provided web-based software tools (InCites and SciVal) so that nonexperts can generate institutional metrics (and other ones). The use of such ready-made indicators without thorough reflection on their meaning is sometimes referred to as amateur bibliometrics. Basically, the data presented in the Web of Science or Scopus must be seen as raw data. From these data professional experts build their own databases, which are cleaned (most errors are removed), in which name disambiguation has been performed and in which searches can be performed which are not possible in the WoS or Scopus.

8.12.2 Focusing on a Small Set of Top Journals

In some fields there is a tendency to evaluate scholars exclusively by the number of publications in a small set of top or premier journals. In our opinion this is a practice that should be banned. Indeed, not all influential articles are published in this limited set of journals and not all articles published in a top journal are top articles. Moreover, this practice discourages publishing in journals outside the field. Using informetric indicators shifts the focus from the venue of publication to the use of publications. Note that the Nature Index uses a similarly problematic system.

It is essential that, if tenure or evaluation committees want to consider all publications, they dispose of a complete list of the candidates' publications, preferably provided by the candidate, and checked by the committee (the candidate might omit articles that were later shown to contain errors).

8.12.3 Lists and Some Reflections on the Compilation and Use of Lists

Continuing the previous section we note that, when evaluating scientific performance in disciplines or languages that are not adequately represented in the major international databases, one tends to draw lists of "best" journals. The field of management is an example of a field that often uses such lists (Xu et al., 2015). Using such lists is not necessarily a bad habit, especially when large groups reach a consensus. Yet, such an approach also entails some problems. Even in the exact sciences, where there is a large consensus about the list of journals included in the Journal Citation Reports some problems may occur.

- how to compare related subdisciplines?
- what is the relation between a journal and the articles included in it?

It has been shown (Seglen, 1989, 1992, 1994, 1997; Milojević, et al., 2017) that there is only a weak correlation between the impact factor of a journal (basically a measure for the visibility or popularity of a journal) and the actual impact of an article published in this journal. Yet, among factors determining impact the JIF_2 seems to be the one with the highest correlation (Bornmann & Leydesdorff, 2017). The main reason for this is the skewness of citation results, which implies that a few heavily cited articles determine the average i.e., the impact factor (Rousseau, 2014b). Lowly cited articles—the majority—are then "rewarded" for the citations received by a few other ones. This may happen to articles dealing with "fancy" topics which are easily accepted but are not necessarily of high quality and may not receive a lot of citations. Drawing lists of "top journals" for a field is often done in the social sciences or the humanities and, it seems, particularly often in business schools, for which Steward and Lewis (2010) report that nearly 40% used an internally developed list. Van Fleet et al. (2000) provide a table of advantages and disadvantages of drawing such lists.

Disadvantages
- Drawing a list is often difficult and it may take a long time before a consensus is reached.
- It may lead to stereotypical publication behavior.
- It may harm scientists' careers if such lists are very local.
- May harm colleagues active in a small, specialized domain.
- It discourages launching new journals.
- It provides more power to editors whose journal is included in the list.

Advantages
- It provides explicit targets.
- It reduces the time needed to perform evaluations.
- Such lists are useful for benchmarking.

An important practical problem is that scientists, especially in the social sciences and the humanities, have a tendency to consider those (local) journals used by themselves as those of importance. This makes it difficult to reach a consensus. A practical solution consists then in extending the list so that it is not a "quality" list anymore. In a study of management departments Van Fleet et al. (2000) found strong empirical evidence that there is an inverse correlation between the quality of a department and the probability of adopting a list (the better ones not adopting such a list).

8.12.4 Strategic Behavior and Goal Displacement

De Rijcke et al. (2016) point out that any assessment system tends to change the behavior of researchers – see also the Leiden Manifesto, point 9 (Section 8.2). This mainly happens in two distinct ways. The first one is described as goal displacement: the goal of research is not contributing significantly to increasing human knowledge and while doing so reaching certain performance levels, but increasing the value(s) on assessment indicators. The second one is even worse for science: because of assessments scientists become (even more) risk averse, which influences the topics that are investigated.

8.12.5 Another Look at the Importance and Visibility of Books

White et al. (2009) formulated the interesting idea of libcitations. Libcitations, as suggested by its name, is the number of times a book is bought by libraries contributing to OCLC's WorldCat. This approach would, in particular, be useful in the humanities. Clearly this idea is mainly applicable in the Anglophone part of the world, more precisely those libraries (countries) contributing to WorldCat. Yet, the idea of considering purchases of books as a kind of analogue of article citations is generally applicable.

Zuccala et al. (2015) compare the ranking of book publishers by their libcitations with a ranking by the number of citations in Scopus from journals in the field of history and find that "books by a certain publisher that are catalogued frequently in international libraries tend to receive higher citation rates in the journal literature." In today's terminology one could consider libcitations as a form of altmetrics.

8.12.6 International Prizes

Sometimes receiving international scientific prizes, typically Nobel Prizes or the Fields Medal are part of evaluations and rankings, such as in the

Shanghai (ARWU) Ranking. Of course when scientists receive such a prize while they are still young this has a huge influence on their further career.

Of much less notoriety we have the Derek J. de Solla Price Award for scientometrics. A list of those colleagues who obtained this award is included in the appendix.

8.13 FURTHER REMARKS

In this Section we bring together some further remarks and observations related to different aspects of research evaluation.

8.13.1 Single Metrics Versus Summary Metrics

A single metric can mislead (and often will) and when it leads to decisions about individuals or project, it may misdirect. When using a single metric, all too often one ignores its shortcomings. This may lead to a distortion of reality and to scientists paying only attention to what is measured.

Hence a whole battery of indicators, should be made available for peer review, taking into account that one metric among other ones can provide essential information. As a general rule one should discard as little information as possible when performing evaluations.

Composite indicators may be useful as summary measures, but, in our opinion, depend too much on the weights assigned to each component. Values and rankings based on such composite metrics are difficult to interpret and conceal trade-offs that should be made open.

8.13.2 Reputation

In a study on determinants of scholarly reputation in the field of management Dewett and Denisi (2004) found that quality of research (as measured by the proportion of refereed articles in premier journals, editorial activity and received awards), and in particular perceived creativity, is the main determinant for reputation. When determining reputation this variable is more important than sheer quantity of output.

8.13.3 Short-Term Versus Long-Term Objectives

Nowadays societal problems tend to favor short-term, goal-oriented projects over long-term basic research. "*Scientists have to describe in advance all their research steps, to detail milestones and to account for all changes in direction. This approach, if extended too far, is not only detrimental to curiosity-driven research. It is also counterproductive for applied research, as most practical devices come from breakthroughs in basic research and would never have been developed out of the blue,"* writes Nobel Prize winner Serge Haroche in *Nature* (Haroche, 2012). He adds that there is too much bureaucratic hassle for scientists, having to spend a great deal of time writing reports instead of doing research. Consequently, he concludes that the system cries out for simplification.

8.13.4 Data and Data Citations

Not all scientific results lead to publications. In some fields—space science and epidemiology are obvious examples—collecting the data is a big enterprise on its own. These data are then made available in research data repositories and are sources of citations. Huggett (2014) mentions an exponential growth of data citations. The topics covered by papers citing data deposited in data repositories seem nowadays to be centered on health-related issues. The most important challenges for retrieving such citations lie in unique identification of data and datasets.

8.13.5 Issues Related to Gender and Minority Groups

The role played by personal features such as gender and age on productivity and research impact and their relation with career success has been the topic of quite some published research (e.g., Costas et al., 2010; Bozeman & Gaughan, 2011; Costas & Bordons, 2011; Abramo et al., 2014).

Science is an institution with an immense inequality in career attainments. This statement holds for all aspects related to science and careers in science (position, publications, citations, recognition). It is well-known that minority groups, such as women in science, face an even harder battle than members of the majority (Etzkowitz et al., 1994). Many studies have found that female scientists publish at lower rates than male ones. Yet, Xie and Shauman (1998) found that the sex difference in research productivity declined from the early 1960s till the 1990s. They attributed remaining differences to structural positions (their rank within the hierarchy of the scientific community), marital status and motherhood and personal characteristics (collaboration network, choice of research topics). More than 10 years later, Larivière et al. (2011) observed the same differences in Québec universities. They moreover noted that women received less funding than men and were at a slight disadvantage in terms of scientific impact as measured by citations. Similar disadvantages with respect to women scientists were observed among Spanish Ph.D holders (Borrego et al., 2010). Yet these colleagues found one remarkable difference, namely that female Ph.D. holders were cited significantly more often. Kretschmer et al. (2012) found that in a group of German medical researchers male scientists were more prolific and received more citations than female scientists. Removing, however, the top performers (male and female) removed this difference. Yet, recently Larivière et al. (2013), Zeng et al. (2016), and Wagner (2016) found that women are still under-represented in terms of authorship, coauthorship, and being granted scientific prizes.

Bias with respect to female students still exists as shown in (Moss-Racusin et al., 2012). In a randomized double-blind study science faculty rated the application materials of a student for a laboratory manager position. This student was randomly assigned a male or female name. The "female" student was less likely to be hired while "male" applicants were offered a higher starting salary and better career mentoring.

Van den Besselaar and Sandström (2016) followed a group of male and female researchers over a period of 10 years. Differences in performance were not present at the start of their career and after 10 years field normalized citation impact indicators remained about equal for male and female researchers. Yet, productivity of male researchers had grown faster as did their careers. They concluded that the process of hiring academic staff is still biased against women.

Finally, we note the hopeful contribution by Campbell et al. (2013) who found that gender-heterogeneous teams produced journal articles that were perceived to be of higher quality by peers than those written by teams of the same gender. They concluded that promoting gender diversity not only promotes fairness but may also lead to better science.

It is clear that research evaluation should be unbiased with respect to women and all minority groups.

8.13.6 Age

It is generally accepted that genius and productivity decline with age. It seems indeed to be the case that for the majority of Nobel laureates the most significant scientific contribution in their career—usually the discovery or research for which they won the Nobel Prize—occurred early in their life. In a study by Kanazawa (2003) the author found that nearly a quarter of all scientists makes their most significant contribution of their career during the 5 years around age 30. A similar observation had been made 20 years earlier by Zhao and Jiang (1986). In collaboration with Liang et al. (1996) Zhao found that these peak achievements (1928 major scientific and technological inventions from the year 1500 to the year 1960) follow a Weibull distribution. In this set of major achievements the peak occurred between the ages of 31 and 40.

There is, however, a difference between good, even eminent work and peak performances. Dennis (1956), who studied 156 19th century scientists who lived at least till the age of 70, already found that, on the whole, there was little change in mean output of scientific articles between the ages of 30 and 60. Cole (1979) in a study of the number of published articles in a 25-year period and the number of received citations found that researchers who received professional recognition, namely citations, for their earlier work had the greatest inclination to be productive at a later stage. In this way productivity at later age was linked to a form of cumulative advantage. Kyvik (1990) studied more recent data and found a productivity peak among Norwegian scientists in the 45−49 age group (applying a kind of fractionalization and considering books as an equivalent of 2 to 6 articles, depending on the type and number of pages). This was, however, just an average over all fields. He found that e.g., in the social sciences productivity remained more or less at the same level for all age groups, while in the natural sciences productivity continually decreased with increasing age.

Costas et al. (2010) divided scientists working at the Spanish National Research Council (CSIC) into three professional categories: tenured scientists, research scientists and research professors. In each professional category and for each field studied they found that the younger scientists performed best as measured by productivity, received citations and impact-based indicators.

When studying the possible decline in intellectual powers or originality over the years, biological age is used. Yet, when the relation between age and one's career is the topic of study, it is better to consider career age, usually counted from the year a Ph.D is obtained.

8.13.7 Alberts's Warning Against "me-too science" (Alberts, 2013)

Bruce Alberts, former president of the National Academy of Sciences of the USA and former Editor-in-Chief of the journal *Science*, wrote in an editorial supporting the DORA declaration:

> ... *perhaps the most destructive result of any automated scoring of a researcher's quality is that it encourages "me-too science". Any evaluation system in which the mere number of a researcher's publications increases his or her score creates a strong disincentive to pursue risky and potentially groundbreaking work, because it takes years to create a new approach in a new experimental context, during which no publications should be expected. Such metrics further block innovation because they encourage scientists to work in areas of science that are already highly populated, as it is only in these fields that large numbers of scientists can be expected to reference one's work, ... only the very bravest of young scientists can be expected to venture into such a poorly populated research area, unless automated numerical evaluations of individuals are eliminated.*
>
> *The leaders of the scientific enterprise must accept full responsibility for thoughtfully analyzing the scientific contributions of other researchers. To do so in a meaningful way requires the actual reading of a small selected set of each researcher's publications, a task that must not be passed by default to journal editors.*

We fully agree with these thoughtful observations and note that they are not in disagreement with the contents of the Leiden Manifesto (Hicks et al., 2015).

8.14 CONCLUSION

Although research evaluation should be performed by peers, bibliometric expertise is needed and counting is a necessity. Because of differences in research aims such evaluations are not context-free, reflection is needed and one should realize that the research environment changes because it is measured.

Perutz (2002), with Cambridge University in mind, wrote that creativity in science, as in the arts, cannot really be organized. It arises spontaneously from individual talent. Well-run laboratories can foster it, but bureaucrats organizing research evaluations based on self-evaluation reports, lots of numbers (purely number-crunching scientometrics) and expensive site visitations by so-called experts can kill it. All too often scientists complain about hierarchical organizations, inflexible, bureaucratic rules, and mountains of futile paperwork. We hope that our book does not contribute to such barriers for creative science.

Yet, the research environment also changes because of external factors. Digitization has led to new data and corresponding opportunities for visualizations, data mining, and altmetric evaluation methods. In this way research evaluation has moved from a data poor to a data rich enterprise, increasing the opportunities for commercialization. All these developments are influencing scientists, university administrators and indirectly society at large and politicians. We note, moreover, that for science policy purposes research evaluation is not what really matters. For policy development it is better to focus on the mechanism than on the outcome.

We like to end this chapter with a remark on the social aspects of the work environment. Any kind of work-related evaluation, be it in a factory or at a university, tends to stress work-related performance. Evaluations rarely take the work-life balance into account. Yet, it is well-known that recreational pursuits such as sports, music, art or just relaxing with one's family are positively correlated with creativity and quality of life (Overbaugh, 2011). Too much emphasis on quantitative measures of sheer productivity instead of quality and originality of work, places an unfair burden on scientists and their families (Harvey, 2015). These points are not the purpose of this book, but they, nevertheless, deserve to be mentioned.

CHAPTER 9

The Informetric Laws

9.1 INTRODUCTION

In this chapter we focus on a set of statistical regularities occurring in the field of information science. We will show that these regularities do not only occur in the information sciences: they are ubiquitous. These regularities are mathematical formulae related to groups such as authors, journals, symbols in texts, and so forth.

Informetric theory can be seen as an attempt to connect empirical techniques to an empirical science. The relation between informetrics and the information sciences can be compared with the relation between econometrics and economy, or biometrics and general biology.

The number of "information theoretical" properties (to be understood in a very general sense) that can be studied is almost limitless. In this context, Egghe (1990) introduced the notions of one-dimensional, two-dimensional and three-dimensional informetrics, depending on the number of informetric objects one studies simultaneously, see further in this Chapter for one- and two-dimensional informetrics. These investigations can be performed at a specific moment in time (a static view), or as a function of time (a dynamic view).

9.2 ONE-DIMENSIONAL INFORMETRICS

9.2.1 Examples

We present here some examples of informetric objects that are the topic of investigation in one-dimensional informetric studies. Such studies are the result of elementary data collections, becoming more interesting when performed as time studies, leading to functions which have, hopefully, a more than local or single-use importance. Examples of one-dimensional informetric studies, among others, are:
- The number of authors active in a given domain.
- The number of journals published in a given domain.
- The number of journals in a given domain, covered by a specific database.

Becoming Metric-Wise
DOI: http://dx.doi.org/10.1016/B978-0-08-102474-4.00009-1

- The number of articles published in a given domain.
- The number of references of articles in a journal.
- The number of loans in a library.
- The number of websites related to a given topic (webmetrics).
- The number of downloads of an e-article.

In time-dependent studies one may investigate the growth in the number of published articles per year, or the obsolescence and growth of the literature on a topic. Note also that most examples in this list must be made more precise and for some this is utterly impossible on a large scale. For example, one must specify if a renewal of a loan counts as a loan or not. All problems related to scientific domains are impossible to answer precisely as the notion of a "domain" is a fuzzy concept. In such cases, one operationalizes the vague notion, here a domain, by another related notion that is precise. For example, the set of all horticultural articles of the year Y can be operationalized as all articles, published in the year Y, in journals included in the Web of Science category *Horticulture*. We do not claim that this is the best possible way of operationalization, nor do we claim that such an absolute best way exists.

9.2.2 Obsolescence

Aging of literature (i.e., the decline in the use of certain literature) is often described by the term obsolescence. There are different forms of obsolescence, or, viewed from another angle, one may say that obsolescence is operationalized and measured in different ways.

- Studying the use of a specific literature through reference lists in articles. This is a synchronous study when one studies only recent articles. The arrow of time goes from the present to the past.
- Studying the use of an article or set of articles through received citations. This is a diachronous study. The time arrow goes from the present to the future (or at least in the direction of the future).
- Studying the use of a particular type of books or objects in a library in a diachronous way.

The first two examples are examples of studies related to global (worldwide) obsolescence. The third one is an example of a study related to local obsolescence. Yet, all these types of studies can be performed using the same or very similar methods. The first two can be said to be each other's dual as they just transpose the notions of *to cite* and *to be cited*.

In practice, worldwide studies do not exist but are replaced by (large) database-dependent studies.

Next we provide an example of a synchronous study, recalling that other studies are performed in a similar way. Decreasing use over time or obsolescence can be measured as follows. Consider a set of articles published in the year Y e.g., published in the same journal. We consider their references and determine the age of each item, where a reference published in the year Y-3 has age 3. The number of references of age t is denoted as $c(t)$. Consider now the ratio

$$a(t) = \frac{c(t+1)}{c(t)} \tag{9.1}$$

If we assume that $a(t)$ is a constant function: $a(t) = a$, then $c(1)/c(0) = a$, hence $c(1) = c(0)a$. Now, $c(2)/c(1) = a$ and hence $c(2) = c(1)a = c(0)a^2$. Continuing in this way we find that for each t:

$$c(t) = c(0)a^t \tag{9.2}$$

where $c(0) = c$ is constant. This function is an exponential function. Note that decrease in use only occurs if $0 < a < 1$. If $a = 1$ then use stays constant, while for $a > 1$ we have an increasing exponential function. The general form of an exponential function with $0 < a < 1$ is shown in Fig. 9.1.

The parameter a is called the aging rate. When a is small, aging goes fast and when a is larger (but strictly smaller than 1), aging goes slow.

Note that we will always use the form a^t for an exponential function, but remark that a^t may also be written in the form $e^{kt} = \exp(kt)$, with

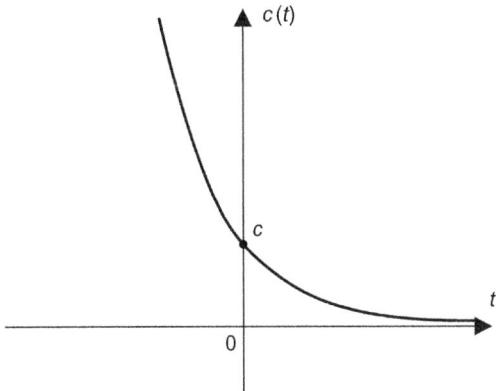

Figure 9.1 Graph of an exponential function $(0 < a < 1)$.

$k = \ln(a)$. We further note that an exponential function may not be confused with a power function, which is a function of the form t^b (with t the variable and b a constant).

In the previous example we assumed that $a(t)$ is a constant. This assumption does not always hold, of course, as a synchronous citation curve often has the form shown in Fig. 6.1. Citation curves can be described approximately as a fast increasing function, followed by a decreasing function which can—from a certain point on be approximated by an exponential function. In the informetric literature, such citation curves have been described by lognormal functions, see Matricciani (1991) and Egghe and Rao (1992a,b) for a complete explanation. Fig. 9.2 shows a lognormal function.

Although not correct for citations, the exponential function provides an acceptable description of download times (Moed, 2005b). Indeed, most downloads, either in a repository or from an e-journal's website, occur immediately when an article is made available, after which the number of downloads decreases.

The half-life time (named after the half-life time in radioactive decay) is the moment in the past (at least for synchronous studies) such that half of the references are younger. This means that a half-time is actually a median. In case formula (9.2) is valid the half-time t_0 is:

$$t_0 = -\frac{\log(2)}{\log(a)} \qquad (9.3)$$

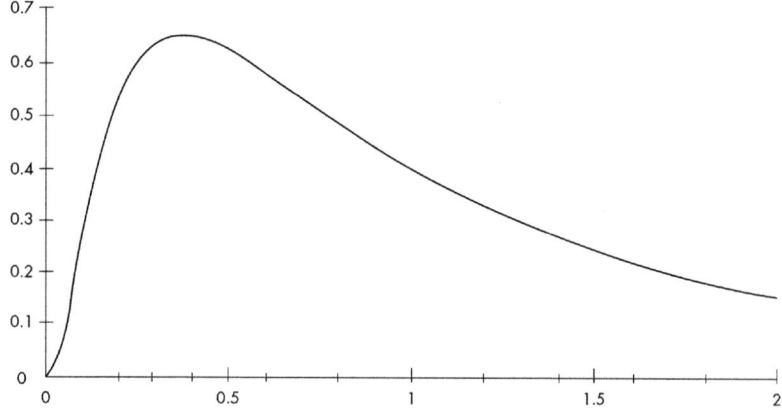

Figure 9.2 Graph of a lognormal function.

Note that (logically!) $t_0 > 0$ as $0 < a < 1$. Moreover, t_0 does not dependent on the type of logarithm used to perform the calculation.

9.2.3 Growth

At first sight, it seems that the growth of the literature has nothing to do with obsolescence. Yet, already many years ago Brookes (1970) wrote that the methodology to study these two phenomena is the same.

One may study yearly growth, comparing occurrences in one year with occurrences during the next one, or cumulative growth. The methodology is again essentially the same. The simplest, and most used, growth curve is exponential growth. If $g(t)$ denotes the number of documents in year t, then exponential growth is expressed as:

$$g(t) = ga^t \qquad (9.4)$$

where $a > 1$ and g is the original value, i.e., the value at time zero. This increasing function has the shape shown in Fig. 9.3.

In this context, the parameter a is called the growth factor. This parameter is always strictly larger than one for cumulative exponential growth. If growth is not exponential, one may again compare the value at time $t + 1$ with that at time t:

$$a(t) = \frac{g(t + 1)}{g(t)} \qquad (9.5)$$

This function $a(t)$ is always larger than one for cumulative growth. This fact, of course, does not necessarily hold for yearly growth. The use of a

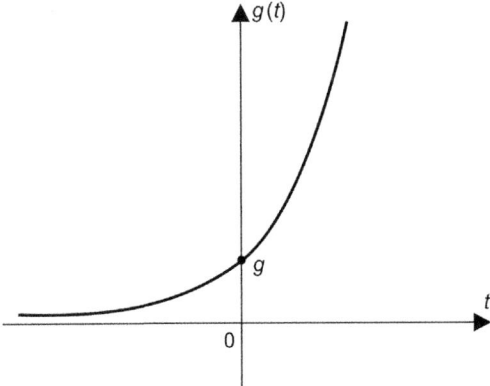

Figure 9.3 Graph of an exponential function ($a > 1$).

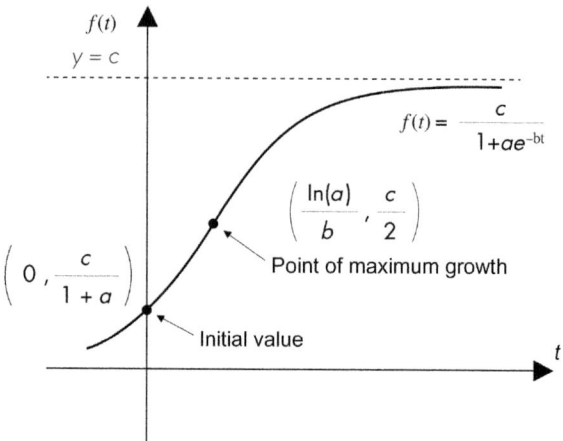

Figure 9.4 Graph of a logistic curve or Verhulst curve.

source during a particular year may be smaller than during the previous year. If $a(t)$ increases for a number of years and then starts to decrease year by year, the resulting cumulative growth curve has an S-shape, see Fig. 9.4.

A well-known S-curve is the logistic or Verhulst curve. A general rule is that new phenomena, if successful, grow at an exponential rate, yearly and cumulatively, while older, established phenomena have an S-shaped cumulative growth, see also (Price, 1963). The early Internet had an exponential growth in servers, see Adamic and Huberman (2001). On the website of the Internet Systems Consortium (2016) https://www.isc. org/network/survey/ we see that the number of hosts (computers connected to the Internet), nowadays has an S-shape, see Fig. 9.5.

In a similar vein, we note that for many years the number of publications with at least one Chinese address has been growing exponentially see e.g. Jin and Rousseau (2005).

9.2.4 The Influence of Growth on Obsolescence

We already mentioned that in many cases growth and obsolescence can be studied using the same methods. Yet, one has observed that there is a mutual influence between growth and obsolescence. The larger the growth, the more articles that can be cited and, relatively speaking, the smaller the probability that a particular article is cited, suggesting a faster obsolescence, but as there are more articles there are more references (suggesting a slower obsolescence). Hence the combined effect of growth and obsolescence is not immediately obvious. It has been shown, see

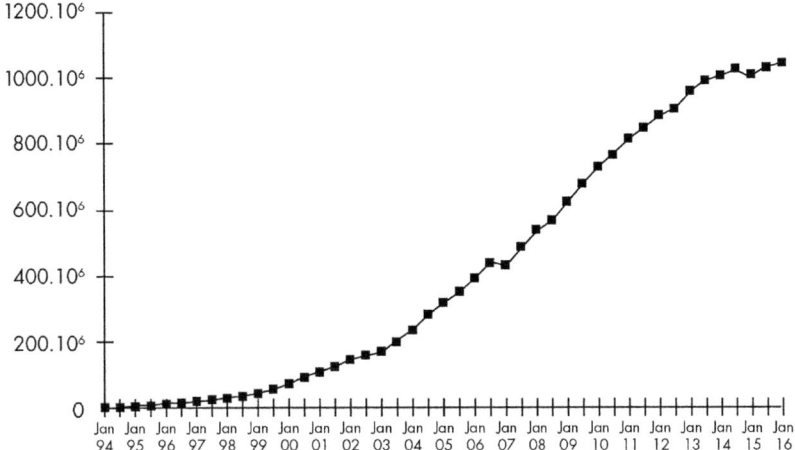

Figure 9.5 Growth of the number of Internet hosts. *Origin: www.isc.org; redrawn with permission.*

Egghe (1993a), Egghe, Rao, and Rousseau (1995), and Egghe and Rousseau (2000), that growth increases synchronous obsolescence, but decreases the diachronous one.

We finally note that general growth, aging and production models, described via differential equations, are presented in Vitanov (2016).

9.3 TWO-DIMENSIONAL INFORMETRICS

9.3.1 General IPPs

Two-dimensional informetrics studies the relation between two of the "informetric objects" mentioned in the part on one-dimensional informetrics. In this context these things are referred to as sources and items: sources "produce" or "have" items. Egghe (1990, 2005) refers to such relations as Information Production Processes, in short IPPs. For example, authors, as sources, and the number of articles (co)-authored by them as items. Usually one restricts investigations to a given domain and sometimes also to a specific time period. An IPP can be represented as in Fig. 9.6: S represents the set of sources; I represents the set of items; s_j represents source j connected via function f to its set of items I_j.

Examples of IPPs
- Authors and their articles.
- Journals and their articles.

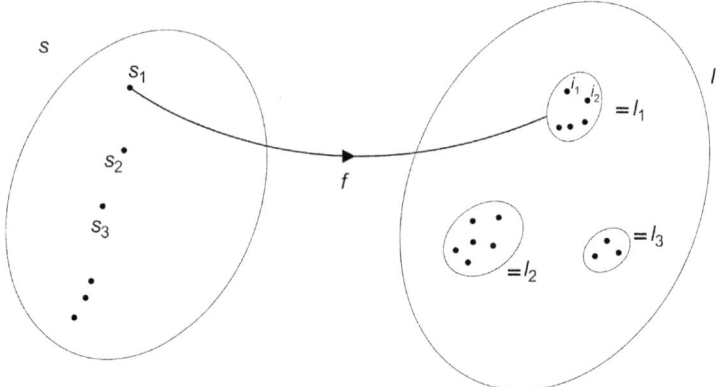

Figure 9.6 A representation of an IPP.

- Articles and received citations.
- Articles and their references.
- Articles and their author(s).
- Books and their loans.
- Words and their uses in a text. In linguistics the terminology types and tokens is often used in this context.
- Websites and incoming links.
- Websites and outgoing links.
- Websites and webpages belonging to them.
- Cities and inhabitants (demography).
- Employees and their production (economics).
- Employees and their salaries (economics).

All social, communication, and biological networks are examples of IPPs with nodes as sources e.g., persons in a friendship or authors in a authorship network, and linked nodes as items, e.g., friends or co-authors (see Chapter 10: Networks).

Clearly, as follows from the above examples, the notion of an IPP is very general. It can be interpreted in, and applied to, many domains not just the information sciences. The regularities we mention further on are, in many cases, also valid and have applications in these other domains.

9.3.2 The Classical Informetric Laws

The classical informetric laws describe source–items relations of IPPs. They all express that few sources have many items and many sources have few items. It can be said that the classical informetric laws describe an elitist situation. We feel it is important to point out that these regularities are not laws in the sense of the natural sciences, but just explainable probabilistic regularities that are in practice more or less valid. Yet we will follow the tradition and use the term "informetric laws" (actually, the traditional terminology is "bibliometric laws"). These remarks are valid whenever these "laws" are applicable, whatever the field of application (economy, demography, biology, etc.)

The first function we will discuss is the *size-frequency* function f. For each natural number $n = 1, 2, 3, \ldots$ $f(n)$ denotes the number of sources with n items, e.g., the number of authors who wrote n articles. The next function is the *rank-frequency* function g. A rank-frequency function is obtained as follows: rank sources decreasingly according to the number of items. The resulting ranks are $r = 1, 2, 3, \ldots$. Then $g(r)$ denotes the number of items of the source at rank r. Functions f and g of a given IPP are said to be dual functions. Their relation is given by formula (9.6):

$$r = g^{-1}(n) = \sum_{k=n}^{\infty} f(k) \qquad (9.6)$$

The function g^{-1} is the inverse function of the function g (assumed to be injective): If g maps the point x to the point y, then g^{-1} maps y to x. Formula (9.6) expresses the relation between the variables r and n, through the functions f and g. It further shows that if the function f is known, also g^{-1} is known and hence g itself. Theoretical work using discrete sums is difficult and often not possible. For this reason one makes models in which f and g are continuous functions: they can take any positive real value (sometimes restricted to a certain, possibly infinitely long, interval). In this continuous model the function f is obtained from the function g by taking the derivative of g^{-1} (Egghe, 2005). The use of continuous models to describe real life phenomena are standard techniques in probability theory, the most classical example being the Gauss curve, also known as the bell curve.

The term Lotkaian informetrics (Egghe, 2005) refers to those models and their application in which one assumes that the size-frequency function f is a power function, which in the field of informetrics is often referred to as Lotka's law. Concretely we have

$$f(n) = \frac{C}{n^{\alpha}} \qquad (9.7)$$

with $C > 0$ and $\alpha > 1$. When referring to observed data the variable n is a strictly positive natural number, while in models n is a real number usually larger than or equal to 1. This power law is called Lotka's law because the mathematician, physical chemist and specialist in population dynamics Alfred Lotka first formulated this law in 1926 in the context of authors (considering only first authors) and the number of articles they had written (Lotka, 1926). More precisely, Lotka used two data sets. One consisted of the publication of authors whose name began with A or B and whose publications were included in Chemical Abstracts (1907–1916); the other one were articles by physicists included in Auerbach's *Geschichtstafeln der Physik* of 1910. Using an estimation procedure based on linear regression on log-log scale (and after removing some outliers) he obtained an α value of 2.02 for Auerbach's data and an α value of 1.89 for the Chemical Abstracts data. As a first approximation one may say that at least for his data $\alpha \approx 2$. Consequently, in many modelling exercises one takes $\alpha = 2$. This value is also of interest for another reason. Experience has shown that $\alpha = 2$ is a real turning point for several Lotkaian properties. Examples of such phenomena—of a more advanced nature—can be found in (Egghe, 2005) and further in Subsection 9.4.2.

The Lotka function (9.7) describes a highly elitarian situation. Indeed, $f(1) = C$, and if $\alpha = 2$ it can be shown that the percentage of authors with just one article is equal to 60.79%. This result clearly illustrates that "many sources have few items."

The rank-frequency function corresponding with the Lotka function is a function known as Zipf's law:

$$g(r) = \frac{B}{r^\beta} \tag{9.8}$$

$(B, \beta > 0)$. This function too is a power function, but note that here the variable, r, denotes a rank. Observe that this function is injective as required in formula (9.6). Indeed, the inverse of g, denoted as g^{-1} is $g^{-1}(s) = \left(\frac{B}{s}\right)^{1/\beta}$. If one applies a function and then its inverse then one must obtain the identity function. Using the mathematical standard notation $\circ$ to denote the composition of functions (applying one function after the other), we check:

$$(g^{-1} \circ g)(r) = g^{-1}(g(r)) = \frac{B^{1/\beta}}{(g(r))^{1/\beta}} = \frac{B^{1/\beta}}{(B.r^{-\beta})^{1/\beta}} = \frac{B^{1/\beta}}{B^{1/\beta}.r^{-1}} = r \tag{9.9}$$

If $\beta = 1$, Zipf's law can be formulated as: The product of the rank order of an author (originally: word type) and his number of articles (originally, number of occurrences or tokens) is a constant for a given database (originally, a given text). It has been shown (Egghe, 2005) that Lotka's law and Zipf's law are equivalent: mathematically one follows from the other and vice versa, using formula (9.6) or its continuous version. The corresponding relation between the exponents α and β is given by formula (9.10):

$$\beta = \frac{1}{\alpha - 1} \qquad (9.10)$$

Note that by formula (9.10) $\alpha = 2$ corresponds with $\beta = 1$. The so-called law of Zipf in linguistics (sources are word types, and items are occurrences of these words in a text) was promoted and made popular by him (Zipf, 1949), but he was not the first to note this regularity: in linguistics Estoup (1916) and Condon (1928) were precursors. Moreover, this same relation had already been observed earlier by Auerbach (1913) in the context of cities and inhabitants. More information about Zipf's life can be found in Rousseau (2002a).

The same regularity was also observed by Pareto (1895) in the context of income inequalities. These facts show that for many years different fields have found the same regularities without realizing this.

Mandelbrot (1967) formulated a generalization of Zipf's law, consequently known as Mandelbrot's law, in the context of fractal theory. Mandelbrot's law has the form:

$$g(r) = \frac{D}{(1 + Er)^{\beta}} \qquad (9.11)$$

This function has one parameter more than Zipf's and hence fits observed data easier. We recall that fractals are mathematical objects that represent the limit of infinitely many iterations. An interesting aspect of fractals is that they are often self-similar. This means that a part of the fractal is identical to the entire fractal itself. Fractal dimensions, related to the exponent β in Mandelbrot's law, are used to measure the complexity of objects. For more on fractals, see Mandelbrot (1977), Feder (1988), and Egghe (2005).

Besides the functions f and g and the related laws of Lotka and Zipf, also the laws of Bradford (1934) and Leimkuhler (1967) belong to the group of informetric laws. It can be shown that they correspond to the special case that $\alpha = 2$, or $\beta = 1$.

Bradford's law was observed in the context of journals and the number of articles they published on a given topic (historically Bradford studied the topics *Lubrication* and *Applied Geophysics*). It is formulated as follows.

Consider a rank-frequency list or IPP subdivided into p groups, each producing the same number of items. Then there exist numbers s_0 and $k > 1$ such that the first group (containing the most productive sources) consists of s_0 sources, the second group consists of $s_0 k$ sources, the third one of $s_0 k^2$ sources and, generally, the ith group contains $s_0 k^{i-1}$ sources.

In the original formulation (Bradford, 1934) $p = 3$. This is the smallest possible number to observe a regularity. Indeed, the first group always contains a certain number of sources and the second group contains more, expressed by the number $k > 1$. The observation that the third group contains precisely $s_0 k^2$ sources points to a regularity. Table 9.1 illustrates this formalism. It shows 7 journals and the number of articles they published on a given topic. Groups (shown in the right column) have 10 published items. The first group contains one journal ($s_0 = 1$); the second group two, hence $k = 2$. Now, this set of journals follows Bradford's law if the third group contains $s_0 k^2 = 4$ journals.

Later Leimkuhler (1967) showed that Bradford's law could be reformulated using the cumulative rank-frequency function R, known as Leimkuhler's function,

$$R(r) = a \ln(1 + br) \qquad (9.12)$$

where r denotes a rank and a and b are positive real numbers. Formula (9.12) is the cumulative form of the rank-frequency function g.

The general (i.e., not only corresponding to $\alpha = 2$) cumulative rank frequency form has no name, but was first formulated by Rousseau (1988b), see also Egghe (2005). Egghe was the first to prove the mathematical equivalence of all informetric laws (Egghe, 1985, 1990, 2005) although partial proofs and a hypothesis about their equivalence can be

Table 9.1 An illustration of Bradford's law

Ranked journals	Number of published articles	Number of journals in each group
1	10	1
2	6	2
3	4	
4	3	4
5	3	
6	2	
7	2	

found in Fairthorne (1969), Yablonsky (1980), and Bookstein (1976, 1979, 1984, 1990).

Egghe, (2005, see Chapter 1: Introduction) describes a large number of situations in which Lotka's and Zipf's law are applied. Zipf's law is often illustrated on a log-log scale. The reason is that a power function, represented on a log-log scale, is seen as a straight line. Indeed, on a log-log scale the function $g(r) = \frac{B}{r^\beta}$, $\beta > 0$, becomes

$$\log g(r) = \log B - \beta \log r \qquad (9.13)$$

Equation (9.13), being of the general form $y(x) = a - bx$, represents a decreasing straight line with slope—β. Examples in terms of Internet links can be found, e.g., in Adamic and Huberman (2001, 2002) and Lin (2011).

The ubiquity of these regularities has given rise to several attempts at explaining them and to corresponding models. The standard explanation in the field of informetrics is the so-called "Success-Breeds-Success" principle, also referred to as cumulative advantage, see Simon (1957) and Price (1976) for the original formulations, and Egghe (2005) for a discussion in the context of Lotkaian informetrics. Cumulative advantage is related to the Matthew Effect (Merton, 1968, 1988) and goes actually back to Yule (1925). The Matthew Effect is a socio-psychological phenomenon that got its name from the Gospel according to St. Matthew:

For unto everyone that hath shall be given, and he shall have abundance;

But from him that hath not shall be taken away even that which he hath.

The Matthew Effect as introduced by Merton refers to the habit people have of giving credit to already famous people and minimizing or withholding recognition for scientists who have not (yet) made their mark.

Assuming exponential growth of sources and items, an explanation has been proposed by Naranan (1970), see also Egghe (2010d) for a short proof and the related fractal theory (Egghe, 2005). These explanations were re-invented in the context of networks by Barabási and Albert (1999) who refer to it as preferential attachment.

Sometimes there is a so-called King Effect. This expression refers to the phenomenon where the top one (or two) members of a ranked set show up as outliers. Such an outlier is then referred to as the Dragon King (Cerqueti & Ausloos, 2015; Yukalov & Sornette, 2012). This means that they do not conform to the statistical regularity one observes for the other members of the dataset. The King effect has been observed for Chinese character use with respect to Zipf's law, the possessive 的 = de (in pinyin) = of (in English) being the Dragon King (Rousseau & Zhang, 1992) and for French cities (Paris as King) and country population sizes (China and India being the Dragon Kings) in the case of a so-called stretched exponential, another distribution with a fat tail (Laherrère & Sornette, 1998). In the case of a Zipf rank-frequency relation and a unique Dragon King the Leimkuhler form can be written as $R(r) = k + a \ln (1 + br)$.

9.4 TWO APPLICATIONS OF LOTKA'S LAW

In this section, we provide two applications of Lotka's law. The first gives a model for the h-index. The second deals with the first-citation function.

9.4.1 The h-index in a Lotkaian Framework (Egghe & Rousseau, 2006a)

In this framework we consider the continuous Lotka size-frequency function $f: [1, \infty[\rightarrow]0, C]$ of the form

$$f(j) = \frac{C}{j^{\alpha}} \tag{9.14}$$

where $C > 0$ and $\alpha > 1$ (Egghe, 2005) to describe the citation function. In a discrete setting $f(j)$ denotes the number of sources, here articles, with production j, here with j citations. We will describe the h-index, h, as a function of the exponent α and the total number of sources T. First we note that, with $g(r)$ the number of citations of the source at rank, the h-index is characterized as the rank r such that $g(r) = r$, see Fig. 9.7. Indeed, in its discrete interpretation, this equality states that there are r sources with r or more items while the other have no more than r items.

Theorem

Suppose that a Lotkaian system with T sources and parameter α is given. Then the h-index is:

$$h = T^{1/\alpha} \tag{9.15}$$

Readers who are not familiar with integrals can safely skip this proof.

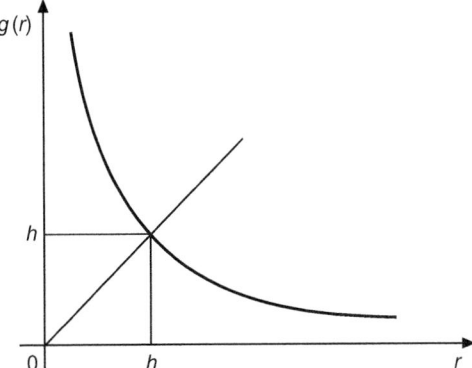

Figure 9.7 Illustration of the h-index in a continuous model.

Proof. In this framework the total number of sources with n or more items equals

$\sum_{k=n}^{+\infty} f(k)$. Now, as already mentioned before, we use a continuous framework to facilitate calculations. This leads to:

$$\sum_{k=n}^{+\infty} f(k) \approx \int_n^\infty f(j)\, dj = \int_n^\infty \frac{C}{j^\alpha}\, dj = \frac{C}{\alpha - 1}\, n^{1-\alpha} \qquad (9.16)$$

where $\alpha > 1$ (otherwise this integral makes no sense). The total number of sources, T, is equal to

$$T = \int_1^\infty f(j)dj = \frac{C}{\alpha - 1} \qquad (9.17)$$

Combining Eqs. (9.16) and (9.17) yields that the number of sources with n or more items is equal to $T n^{1-\alpha}$. We conclude that the h-index h is equal to that number n such that $T n^{1-\alpha} = n$. Consequently: $T . h^{1-\alpha} = h$ or $T = h^\alpha$, leading to the expression $h = T^{1/\alpha}$.

This is the expression of the h-index in a Lotkaian framework. Note that in its original context of publications and citations formula (9.15) includes the number of publications and the citation curve, through its parameter α. If this parameter is known also the number of citations is known, but clearly knowing that the citation curve has a Lotka distribution with exponent α contains more information. Of course, if data do not satisfy Lotka's distribution then this expression for the h-index cannot be applied. Schubert and Glänzel (2007) proposed the following relation between the h-index, the number of publications (*T*) and the total number of received citations, denoted as CIT:

$$h = c \left(\frac{(CIT)^2}{T} \right)^{1/3} \tag{9.18}$$

where *c* is a constant. We note that the fact that the variable *T* appears in the denominator of Eq. (9.18) does not contradict Eq. (9.15); Eq. (9.18) also increases in *T* since the variable CIT is increasingly dependent on *T*.

9.4.2 A Combination of One and Two-Dimensional Informetrics: the Cumulative First-Citation Distribution

Consider a bibliography, i.e., a set of related articles. For each article one determines the time when it received its first citation and the time between publication and the moment of first citation (in days, months or years, in practice depending on the availability of data). Rousseau (1994) noted that one may distinguish two types of cumulative first–citation curves: a concave increasing curve and an increasing S-shaped curve.

Occurrence of these two types of curves was explained by Egghe (2000). In this explanation he used the exponential obsolescence function and Lotka's law. Let Eq. (9.2) represent the distribution of all citations received *t* years after publication and let Eq. (9.7) represent the number of articles with *n* citations. If we denote the cumulative first-citation curve by $\Phi(t_1)$, i.e., the cumulative fraction of all articles which received at least one citation at time t_1, then Egghe (2000) showed that, with γ the fraction of cited articles (ever, not at time t_1) that

$$\Phi(t_1) = \gamma \left(1 - a^{t_1} \right)^{\alpha - 1} k \tag{9.19}$$

He further proved that Φ is concave for $1 < \alpha \le 2$ and that it is S-shaped for $\alpha > 2$. We note the special role played by $\alpha = 2$. Figs. 9.8 and 9.9 show examples of the two types of curves.

9.5 MEASURING INEQUALITY

Garfield (1972) showed that at that time the top 152 journals in the SCI accounted for 50% of all references to journals. It is, moreover, clear that the informetric laws describe situations in which a large inequality is present. This leads to the problem of how to measure this inequality. The

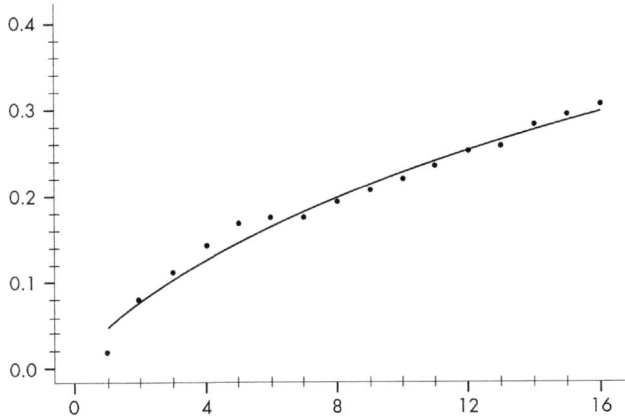

Figure 9.8 Motylev (1994) data (citations of Russian library journals): $a = 0.956$, $\alpha = 1.745 < 2$ (hence Φ is concave), $\gamma = 0.486$. *Redrawn with permission from SPRINGER based on (Rousseau, 1994).*

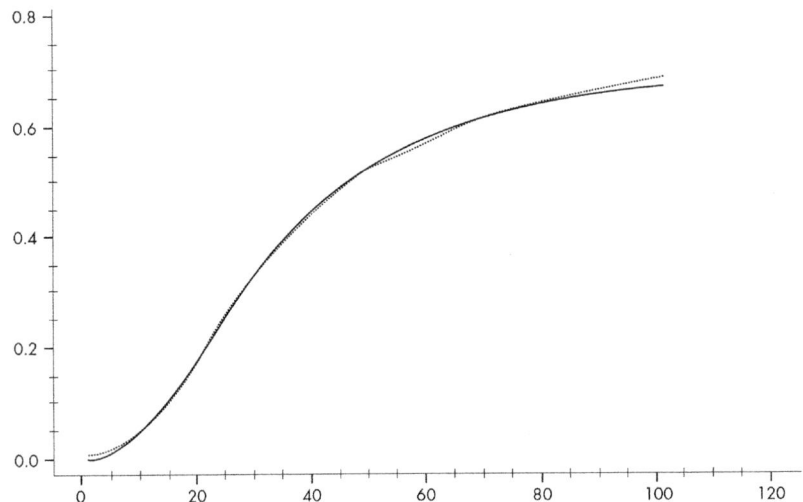

Figure 9.9 Journal self-citations in the Journal of the American Chemical Society; time unit equal to 2 weeks: $a = 0.955$, $\alpha = 3.641 > 2$ (hence Φ has an S-shape), $\gamma = 0.676$. Full line represents fitted curve; dotted line represents data. *Redrawn with permission from SPRINGER based on (Rousseau, 1994).*

problem we deal with in this section is the proper definition of measures of inequality, also described as concentration measures.

The 80/20-rule is a traditional way of describing the inequality in the production of sources. This rule states that the 20% most productive sources have or produce 80% of all items. Of course, this is just a rule of thumb. More generally one may have a $100y/100x$ rule, where $y > x$, i.e., $100x\%$ of the most productive sources have $100y\%$ of all items. In (Egghe, 1993b) it is shown that, if Lotka's law is valid then

$$y = x^{\frac{1}{\mu}} \tag{9.20}$$

where μ denotes the average number of items per source. Eq. (9.20) shows that y depends on x but not only on x.

A consequence: Assume that we have two IPPs following Lotka's law (9.7). If $\mu_1 < \mu_2$ and $y_1 = y_2$ then $x_1 > x_2$.

Proof. The equality $y_1 = y_2$ implies: $x_1^{(1/\mu_1)} = x_2^{(1/\mu_2)}$

Taking the logarithm of both sides yields: $\dfrac{\ln(x_1)}{\mu_1} = \dfrac{\ln(x_2)}{\mu_2}$

and thus: $\dfrac{\ln(x_1)}{\ln(x_2)} = \dfrac{\mu_1}{\mu_2} < 1$

From this inequality we derive that $\ln(x_1) > \ln(x_2)$, using the fact that x_1 and x_2 are smaller than 1 and hence their logs are negative. Consequently: $x_1 > x_2$ (as a logarithmic function is increasing).

This result shows that the higher the average production per source, the smaller the fraction needed to obtain a fixed percentage of items.

We recall from Chapter 4, Statistics that Lorenz curves can be seen as graphical representations of the generalized 80/20-rule: For each percentage $100x$ of most productive sources they show the corresponding percentage $100y$ of items. Lorenz curves are the basis of a concentration theory and related acceptable measures of concentration. We explain this.

Assume that an array of N nonnegative numbers is given. Which requirement should one impose for an acceptable measure of concentration? For the moment we keep N fixed. A first requirement is that the measure should not depend on the order in which the numbers are given.

As this function, denoted by F, must measure inequality another requirement is that if all values are equal the resulting concentration is zero:

$$F(x, x, \ldots, x) = 0 \tag{9.21}$$

If all values are zero except one then F must attain its highest value (given N). Further, we consider concentration as a relative property, hence the value of F for $(x_1, \ldots, x_N)$ must be the same as for $(cx_1, \ldots, cx_N)$, with $c > 0$.

Finally, we come to the most important requirement, known as Dalton's transfer principle (Dalton, 1920). In terms of monetary values this requirement states that if one takes money from a poorer person and gives it to a richer one (a so-called elementary transfer) then the concentration of richness increases. Mathematically this requirement can be expressed as follows:

If $x_i \leq x_j$ and $0 < k \leq x_i$ then

$$F\left(x_1, \ldots, x_i, \ldots, x_j, \ldots, x_N\right) < F\left(x_1, \ldots, x_i - k, \ldots, x_j + k, \ldots, x_N\right)$$

$$(9.22)$$

The transformation from the left-hand side of (9.22) to the right-hand side is called an elementary transfer. The fact that the Lorenz curve is the correct tool to describe concentration follows from the following theorem.

Theorem

(Muirhead, 1903): Let $X = (x_1, \ldots, x_N)$ and $Y = (y_1, \ldots, y_N)$ be decreasing arrays and let $L(X)$ and $L(Y)$ be their corresponding Lorenz curves. If $L(X)$ is situated above $L(Y)$ (but not coinciding) then X can be generated from Y by a finite number of elementary transfers. The reverse is also true.

Besides the Gini index (see Subsection 4.10.3) also the coefficient of variation defined as the standard deviation divided by the arithmetic mean is a measure which, for fixed N, satisfies all the requirements mentioned above. Another one is the Simpson index, also known as the Hirschmann-Herfindahl index. This measure, denoted as λ, is defined as:

$$\lambda(X) = \sum_{i=1}^{N} \left(\frac{x_i}{M}\right)^2 = \sum_{i=1}^{N} p_i^2 \text{ with } M = \sum_{i=1}^{N} x_i \text{ (the total number of items)}$$

$$(9.23)$$

9.6 MEASURING DIVERSITY FOR A VARIABLE NUMBER OF CELLS

If F is an acceptable measure of concentration which never takes the value 0, then $G = 1/F$ is an acceptable measure of diversity. Similarly, if F is an acceptable measure of concentration, bounded by 1, then $G = 1 - F$ is an acceptable measure of diversity.

The theory proposed above is just the basic theory for fixed N. When N is variable things become much more complicated and divergent opinions exist. As these aspects are mostly studied in a diversity context we continue using the terminology of diversity measures.

Stirling (2007) and Leinster and Cobbold (2012) have pointed out that the notion of diversity has three components variety, balance, and disparity. Each of them, considered separately, is necessary, but not sufficient, to measure diversity in an adequate manner.

Variety is the number of nonempty categories to which system elements are assigned. In particular, it is the answer to the question: how many types of things do we have? In information science it may be the answer to the question: In how many different journals has this author published? Assuming that all things are equal, the greater the variety, the greater the diversity. In the previous section variety was kept fixed and equal to N.

Balance is a function of the pattern of the assignment of elements across categories. It is the answer to the question: What is the relative number of items of each type? Balance is also called evenness (in ecology) and concentration (in economics and the information sciences). Evenness can be represented by the Lorenz curve (Nijssen et al., 1998): it is the theory explained in Chapter 4, Statistics. In information science one may consider, for instance, how many articles an author has published in each journal. All else being equal, the more balanced the distribution, the larger the diversity.

Disparity refers to the manner and the degree in which things may be distinguished. It is the answer to the question: How different from each other are the types of things that we observe? For instance, publishing only in LIS journals shows less disparity than publishing in LIS and management and economics journals. All else being equal, the higher the disparity, the greater the diversity.

Mathematically speaking, variety is a positive natural number as categories are numbered in sequence, balance is a function of fractions summing up to one, and disparity is a function of a matrix of distances (or dissimilarities). Sometimes one starts from a matrix of similarities or proximities, which are then converted to a matrix of disparities.

The problem now is how to find a single index that can aggregate properties of variety, balance and disparity in a meaningful way and without much loss of information. The term *meaningful* includes, among others, notions such as sensitivity to changes, perspective and context.

Clearly, it is impossible for one function, one candidate diversity measure, to satisfy all "reasonable" requirements. It seems though that a very good choice is given by Leinster and Cobbold (2012) and Zhang et al. (2016):

$$\frac{1}{1 - D} \tag{9.24}$$

where D is Rao's quadratic entropy measure (Rao, 1982) defined as:

$$D = \sum_{\substack{i,j=1 \\ i \neq j}}^{N} d_{ij}\ p_i p_j \tag{9.25}$$

Rao describes this index as the expected dissimilarity between two individuals selected randomly with replacement, where d_{ij} is the dissimilarity between species i and j and p_i (p_j) is the proportion of species i (j). If there is only one cell, D is set equal to zero. Rao's quadratic entropy measure is a generalization of the Simpson index, formula (9.23).

CHAPTER 10

Networks

Networks can be seen as abstractions of complex systems of interacting entities (Newman, 2010). Network analysis is a scientific method based on links and nodes as fundamental units. It originates from Euler's famous example in graph theory about the seven bridges of Königsberg (nowadays Kaliningrad). Königsberg is crossed by the river Pregel and had seven bridges connecting both sides and two islands. Leonhard Euler was the first to prove that it is not possible to take a walk through the city and cross each bridge exactly once. In order to prove this, he abstracted the problem to what is nowadays called a graph. Important applications in informetrics are networks of collaborating authors, citing journals and related entities showing the organization of science.

10.1 BASIC NETWORK THEORY

10.1.1 Definitions and Representations

A network or graph, G, is a pair of two related sets: $G = (V,E)$ consisting of a set V of vertices or nodes (used as synonyms) and a set E of edges, links or arcs (also used as synonyms). Edges are ordered pairs of nodes, representing a connection between these two nodes. We will use the terms network and graph interchangeably. In sociological research nodes are often referred to as *actors*. If W is a subset of V and if F is a subset of E, then $G_s = (W,F)$ is a subgraph of G. Of course, each of the edges in F must connect nodes that belong to W. Although they are theoretically subgraphs of $G = (V,E)$, the cases $(\emptyset,\emptyset)$ and $G = (V,E)$ will not be considered when talking about subgraphs of G.

Networks can be represented in different ways, including the following three, (see Chapter 3: Publishing in Scientific Journals, where we introduced these methods in the context of citation networks).

1. Two-dimensional graphs. By this we mean a two-dimensional figure consisting of dots, representing nodes, and lines connecting dots, representing the links. When lines intersect, this has no graph-theoretical meaning in the sense that the intersection is not a new node.

Becoming Metric-Wise
DOI: http://dx.doi.org/10.1016/B978-0-08-102474-4.00010-8

2. Adjacency matrices. These are square matrices for which the number of rows, and hence of columns, is equal to the number of nodes. The cell (i,j) contains a 1 if node i is connected to node j and a 0 if this is not the case.

3. Adjacency lists. This is just a list of pairs (i,j) where only pairs that are linked to each other are mentioned. This representation is very useful if the matrix contains many zeros.

Examples of two-dimensional representations and their corresponding adjacency matrices can be found in Fig. 10.1 and Table 10.2.

If j is a node then the nodes linked to j are called the neighbors of j.

10.1.2 Social Networks

When networks deal directly or indirectly with persons, such as authors, friends (directly), or their papers (indirectly) one uses the term social networks and their study is then referred to as social network analysis (in short: SNA), see Scott (1991), Wasserman and Faust (1994), and Otte and Rousseau (2002). In social network analysis, one makes a distinction between two types of analysis: the study of ego-networks, and global studies. Ego-networks study the network originating from one actor referred to as the ego. The ego network is the subgraph consisting of the ego and all nodes linked directly (neighbors) or indirectly (neighbors of neighbors) to the ego, and the corresponding links. Sometimes an ego network is restricted to the ego and its neighbors. An example in the information sciences is Howard White's description of Eugene Garfield's research network (White, 2000). When performing a global analysis, one tries to map all relations of all actors belonging to the network.

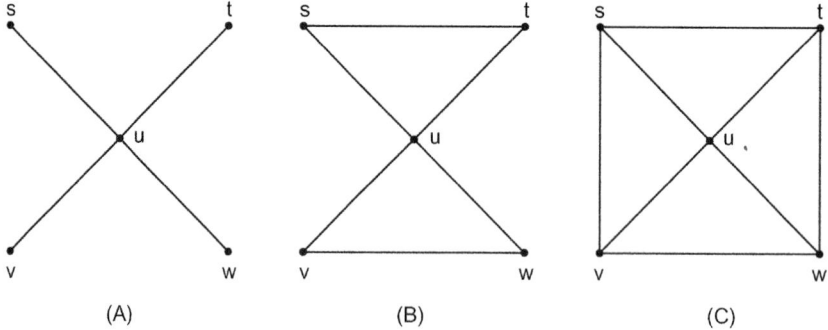

Figure 10.1 Three simple networks with five nodes: (A), (B), and (C), from left to right.

10.1.3 Types of Networks: Directed or not; Weighted (Valued) or not

Directed and Undirected Networks

A link e is an ordered pair (i,j) representing a link from node i to node j. Node i is called the initial node of link e, while node j is called its terminal node. If a link has no direction we say that this network is undirected. A coauthorship network is an example of an undirected graph if author A coauthored an article with author B, automatically author B coauthored an article with A. An undirected graph can be represented by a symmetric matrix $M = (m_{ij})$, where $m_{ij} = m_{ji}$ is equal to 1 if there is an edge between nodes i and j, and m_{ij} is zero otherwise. Two-dimensional representations of directed networks often have arrows on the links, pointing from the initial to the terminal node.

Weighted and Unweighted Networks

In a weighted or valued network a weight function w: $E \rightarrow \mathbf{R}_0^+$ (the positive real numbers, except zero) is given. In a so-called unweighted graph all edges have weight one. Two types of weights can be distinguished: those expressing a similarity or proximity, such as the number of times A addresses B in an observation study in a friendship network, and those expressing a dissimilarity or distance such as time to travel (by car or train) from point P to point Q in a route map. In the adjacency matrix of a weighted network the weight of edge $e = (i,j)$ is placed in cell (i,j).

Bringing these considerations together we see that there exist four types of networks. They result from a double binary classification: directed or not and weighted (or valued) or not. Table 10.1 provides some informetric examples.

Each weighted network can be considered an unweighted one by setting all weights equal to 1. Similarly each directed network can be considered an undirected one by ignoring directions. This network is called the underlying undirected network.

A path in a network from $s \in V$ to $t \in V$ is a sequence alternating between vertices and edges, starting with s, ending with t such that each edge connects a vertex in the sequence to the succeeding one. The length of a path is the sum of the weights of its edges. In an unweighted graph the length is simply the number of edges. The length of a shortest path (or geodesic) between vertices s and t is called the distance between s and t, denoted $d_G(s,t)$ (Brandes, 2001). In particular, $d_G(s,s)$ is set equal to 0 for each $s \in V$ and if there is no path from s to t we say that their distance

Table 10.1 Types of networks and some examples

	Directed	Nondirected
Unweighted (0-1)	Nodes: articles Links: direct citations Nodes: scientists Links: from supervisor to (former) Ph.D student	Nodes: scientific journals Links: having the same publisher Nodes: articles Links: bibliographically coupled or not
Valued or weighted	Nodes: scientists Links: citations given, weighted by number of citations Nodes: articles Links: citations, weighted by the time between publication and citation	Nodes: authors Links: being coauthors, weighted by the number of coauthorships Nodes: journals or articles Links: being cocited, weighted by the number of times

is equal to infinity (∞). In undirected networks $d_G(s,t) = d_G(t,s)$, for every s and t in V.

One may distinguish two types of directed networks: one in which cycles do not occur i.e., if there is a path from u to v, then there certainly isn't a path from v to u, and a second type for which this restriction does not play. "Normal" citations between articles are of the first type: If article a cites article b, then normally article b does not cite article a. If it does happen that a is linked to b, b is linked to c, and so on ending with a node that is linked to a, this construction is called an Escher staircase, because of its resemblance to the famous Escher lithograph "Ascending and descending." Such an Escher staircase is relatively easy to find between sites on the Internet (Rousseau & Thelwall, 2004), but Rousseau and Small (2005) even provide an example of a giant Escher staircase for article citations.

10.1.4 Definition of Cliques and Components

Cliques: A clique in a graph is a subgraph in which any node is directly connected to every other node of the subgraph.

Components: A component of a graph is a subgraph with the characteristic that there is a path between any two nodes in the subgraph and there is no path between a node in the component and any node not in the component. If the whole graph forms one component it is said to be totally connected. Otherwise it is said to be unconnected.

In directed networks, one makes a distinction between strongly connected components and weakly connected ones. A strongly connected component is a subgraph such that it satisfies the definition of a component using only directed paths. If a subgraph in a directed network is a component when ignoring directions one says that it is a weakly connected component.

10.2 NETWORK INDICATORS (WASSERMAN & FAUST, 1994)

Next we define some indicators describing the structure (cohesion) of networks and the role played by particular nodes. Many more are described in the literature, but we will restrict ourselves to the following elementary ones.

10.2.1 Density

Definition: density (D)

The density is an indicator for the general level of connectedness of the graph. If every node is directly connected to every other node, we have a complete graph. The density of a graph is defined as the number of links divided by the number of vertices in a complete graph with the same number of nodes. For a complete, undirected graph G with N nodes, the number of links is equal to $\binom{N}{2} = \dfrac{N(N-1)}{2}$. Hence the density D of an undirected network is defined as:

$$D = \frac{2 \cdot (\#E)}{N(N-1)} \tag{10.1}$$

where E denotes the set of edges or links in the graph and $\#$ means "the number of elements in."

In a directed network D is defined as

$$D = \frac{\#E}{N(N-1)} \tag{10.2}$$

10.2.2 Centrality Indicators

The use of centrality measures, originating from social network analysis (Scott, 1991; Wasserman & Faust, 1994) has led to valuable methods in all types of networks (Bollen et al., 2009; Borgatti et al., 2009; Otte &

Rousseau, 2002). Although all these measures are applied to identify and characterize key nodes in a network, various centrality measures focus on different roles played by nodes in a network. The most important centrality measures are degree centrality, closeness centrality, and betweenness centrality. They can all be interpreted as measuring aspects of leadership. Degree centrality refers to activity, closeness centrality to efficiency, while betweenness refers to control over the flow in the network.

Degree centrality of a node is defined as the number of neighbors this node has (in graph-theoretical terminology: the number of edges adjacent to this node). It is the most basic indicator of a node in a network. In mathematical terms degree centrality, $d(i)$, of node i is defined as:

$$\deg(i) = \sum_j m_{ij} \qquad (10.3)$$

where $m_{ij} = 1$ if there is a link between nodes i and j, and $m_{ij} = 0$ if there is no such link. In this context $m_{ii} = 0$ for all i. In a coauthor graph the degree centrality of an author is just the number of authors in the graph with whom they have coauthored at least one article. The degree centrality in an N-node network can be standardized (Freeman, 1979) by dividing by $N - 1$: $\deg_S(i) = d(i)/(N - 1)$.

The distribution of degree centralities (or, in short, degrees) of the nodes in a network is often examined when studying networks; for many real-world networks this degree distribution is highly skewed.

Many other parameters such as those based on shortest paths and fundamental properties of networks such as scale-free phenomena (Barabási & Albert, 1999; Barabási et al., 2000) are based on the notion of a degree. In a directed network one makes a distinction between the in-degree and the out-degree of a network.

The following measures make use of the distance function.

Closeness centrality of a node (Sabidussi, 1966) is equal to the total distance (in the graph) of this node from all other nodes. As a mathematical formula closeness centrality, $c(i)$, of node i can be written as:

$$c(i) = \sum_{t \in V} d_G(i, t) \qquad (10.4)$$

where $d_G(i,t)$ is the distance from node i to node t. In this form closeness is an inverse measure of centrality in that a larger value indicates a less central actor while a smaller value indicates a more central actor. For this reason closeness is usually defined as $c'(i) = \dfrac{N-1}{\sum_{t \in V} d_G(i,t)}$, making $c'(i)$ a direct measure of centrality. In an unconnected network the closeness centrality of any vertex is zero. Yet, a solution for this unfortunate state of affairs is to define closeness centrality for nodes in disconnected graphs as

$c''(i) = (N-1) \sum_{\substack{t \in V; \\ t \neq i}} \dfrac{1}{d_G(i,t)}$ (Opsahl et al., 2010). Of course, this has

the disadvantage of introducing two types of closeness.

Graph centrality (Hage & Harary, 1995) is defined as

$C_G(v) = \dfrac{1}{\max_{t \in V}(d_G(v,t))}$. This measure too is zero in an unconnected network.

Let σ_{st} denote the number of shortest paths between s and t, where σ_{ss} is set equal to 1. In an undirected, unweighted network we always have $\sigma_{st} = \sigma_{ts}$ but this equality does not have to hold in general. Let $\sigma_{st}(v)$ be the number of shortest paths between s and t, passing through v. Next we consider a centrality measure that makes use of the σ-function.

Betweenness Centrality

Betweenness centrality may be defined loosely as the number of times a node needs a given node to reach another node. Stated otherwise: it is the number of shortest paths that pass through a given node. As a mathematical formula the betweenness centrality of node v (Anthonisse, 1971; Bavelas, 1948; Freeman, 1977) is defined as $b(v) = \sum_{\substack{s \neq v; \\ t \neq v}} \dfrac{\sigma_{st}(v)}{\sigma_{st}}$. If v is a singleton then its betweenness centrality is equal to zero. According to Borgatti (1995), the purpose of measuring betweenness is to provide a weighting system so that node i is given a full centrality credit only when it lies along all shortest paths between s and t. Betweenness gauges the extent to which a node facilitates the network flow. It can be shown that for an N-node network the maximum value for $b(v)$ is $(N^2 - 3N + 2)/2$. Hence standardized betweenness centrality is:

$$b_S(v) = \frac{2b(v)}{N^2 - 3N + 2} \tag{10.5}$$

Leydesdorff (2007) used centrality measures when studying interdisciplinarity. He claims that betweenness can be used as a valid local measure for interdisciplinarity.

Fig. 10.1 presents three simple examples of undirected networks and differences in their characteristics. All networks have five nodes. We use adjacency matrices (Table 10.2) to describe the networks. Density and centrality measures are given in Table 10.3

The density index, D, of this example indicates that the networks (a), (b), and (c) (considered in this order) become increasingly dense. All centrality measures show that node u is the center, and that the other nodes become increasingly central (this is have a larger centrality value) when considering graphs (a), (b), and (c) (in this order). The relative values also illustrate the difference between the three centrality measures considered here.

Eigenvector Centrality

Already in 1972, Bonacich (1972) proposed the notion of eigenvector centrality. Especially during the latest two decades this measure has gained in popularity, mainly because of its close relation with Google's PageRank. Eigenvector centrality values of nodes are obtained as the components of the principal eigenvector, v, of the adjacency matrix, A, of the network. Mathematically, eigenvector values are found as the components of the vector v, the solution of the vector equation: $Av = \lambda v$, where the matrix A is the adjacency matrix of the network, λ (the Greek letter *lambda*) is the largest eigenvalue of the network and v is the corresponding eigenvector. If v is an eigenvector corresponding to the eigenvalue λ, then cv, with c a positive number is also an eigenvector. Hence one has to normalize the eigenvector, usually in such a way that the sum of the components is one. If a node has a high eigenvector centrality value this usually points to the fact that it is situated close to other nodes with high eigenvector centrality values. The eigenvector centrality value can be interpreted as a measure for the influence of a node. If, for example, node w influences only one other node, but this node has a very high influence, then also the influence of node w is high.

The Gefura Measure

There exist centrality measures that take preexisting groupings in a network into account. One of these is the so-called gefura or Q-measure (Flom et al., 2004; Guns & Rousseau, 2015). The value of this measure reflects the importance of a node as a bridge between different groups.

Definition: gefura measure for two groups in an undirected network should better be placed below the Tables 10.2 and 10.3, preceding the part in which the definition is actually given.

Table 10.2 Adjacency matrices for the networks shown in Fig. 10.1

Network (a)

	s	t	u	v	w
s	0	0	1	0	0
t	0	0	1	0	0
u	1	1	0	1	1
v	0	0	1	0	0
w	0	0	1	0	0

Network (b)

	s	t	u	v	w
s	0	1	1	0	0
t	1	0	1	0	0
u	1	1	0	1	1
v	0	0	1	0	1
w	0	0	1	1	0

Network (c)

	s	t	u	v	w
s	0	1	1	0	1
t	1	0	1	1	0
u	1	1	0	1	1
v	0	1	1	0	1
w	1	0	1	1	0

Table 10.3 Density and centrality measures for the networks shown in Fig. 10.1 and Table 10.1

Network characteristic		Network (a)	Network (b)	Network (c)
Density	D	$(2*4)/(5*4) = 0.4$	$(2*6)/(5*4) = 0.6$	$(2*8)/(5*4) = 0.8$
Degree centrality	$\deg(s)=\deg(t)$ $=\deg(v)$ $=\deg(w)$	$1/4 = 0.25$	$2/4 = 0.5$	$3/4 = 0.75$
	$\deg(u)$	$4/4 = 1$	$4/4 = 1$	$4/4 = 1$
Closeness centrality	$l'(s)=l'(t)$ $=l'(v)=l'(w)$	$4/7 = 0.571$	$4/6 = 0.667$	$4/5 = 0.8$
	$l'(u)$	$4/4 = 1$	$4/4 = 1$	$4/4 = 1$
Betweenness centrality	$b(s)=b(t)$ $b(v)=b(w)$	0	0	$1/3 = 0.333$
	$b(u);\ b_s(u)$	$6;\ 1$	$4;\ 0.667$	$0.667;\ 0.111$

We assume that we have a network $N = (V, E)$, consisting of a set V of nodes or vertices and a set E of links or edges. If a network consists of two groups G (consisting of m nodes) and H (consisting of n nodes), then the gefura measure of node a is defined as:

$$\Gamma(a) = \sum_{\substack{g \in G \\ h \in H}} \frac{\sigma_{g,h}(a)}{\sigma_{g,h}} \tag{10.6}$$

Definition: the gefura measure for a finite number of groups in an undirected network

Guns and Rousseau (2009b, 2015) expanded the definition for two groups to directed networks with any finite number of groups and showed that one can define a global, a local and an external variant. We restrict ourselves to the definition of the global gefura measure in an undirected network.

Assume that there are S groups ($2 \le S < +\infty$): $G_1, \ldots, G_S$; the number of nodes in group G_i is denoted as m_i. The global gefura measure of node a is then defined as:

$$\Gamma_G(a) = \sum_{k,l} \left(\sum_{\substack{g \in G_k \\ h \in G_l}} \frac{\sigma_{g,h}(a)}{\sigma_{g,h}} \right) \tag{10.7}$$

where k takes all values from 1 to S and l takes all values strictly larger than k. Clearly, if S = 2, formula (10.7) reduces to formula (10.6).

An example.

Consider the example in Fig. 10.2. The network consists of three node groups $\{a_1, a_2, a_3\}$, $\{b_1, b_2, b_3\}$, and $\{c_1, c_2\}$. To illustrate the procedure we calculate the (unnormalized) gefura measure for node b_1. This node is part of the following shortest paths between different groups:

- Between a_1 and b_2: $a_1 - b_1 - b_2$
- Between a_2 and b_2: $a_2 - b_1 - b_2$
- Between b_2 and c_2. In this case there are two possible shortest paths, namely $b_2 - b_1 - a_2 - c_2$ and $b_2 - a_3 - c_1 - c_2$.

Hence, we have $\Gamma(b_1) = 1 + 1 + 0.5 = 2.5$. Using similar reasoning we find the following results: $\Gamma(a_1) = 0.5$; $\Gamma(a_2) = 1.5$; $\Gamma(a_3) = 2$; $\Gamma(b_2) = 0$; $\Gamma(b_3) = 0$; $\Gamma(c_1) = 4.5$; $\Gamma(c_2) = 5$. This result shows that node c_2 has the highest gefura-value, which means that it has the most important bridging function in this network.

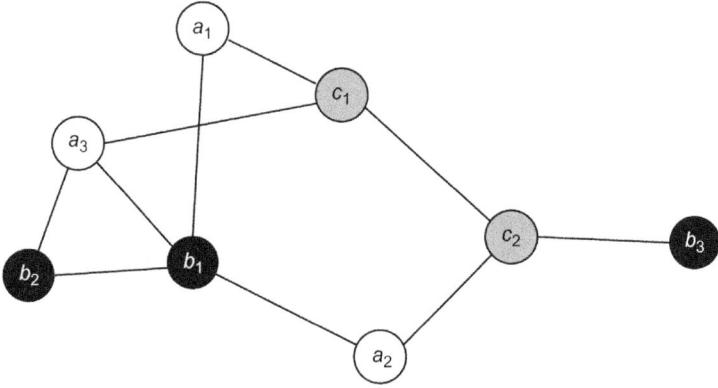

Figure 10.2 Example network with three groups.

10.2.3 Clustering Coefficients

It may happen that if node a is connected to node b and node b is connected to node c, then also nodes a and c are connected, as in the saying "a friend of a friend is a friend." How often this happens in a given network can be measured by the clustering coefficient $C^{(1)}$, defined by (Newman, 2003):

$$C^{(1)} = \frac{3 \cdot (\text{number of triangles in the network})}{\text{number of connected triples of vertices}} \tag{10.8}$$

Here a triangle is a set of three vertices each of which is connected to the other two and a connected triple is a set of three vertices such that one vertex is connected to the other two (whether or not these other two are connected). It can be shown that $0 \le C^{(1)} \le 1$. This clustering coefficient is also known as the fraction of transitive triples. Yet, there exists another clustering coefficient which will be denoted as $C^{(2)}$. Its definition starts from a local clustering coefficient, denoted as C_j, where

$$C_j = \frac{\text{number of triangles connected to node } j}{\text{number of triples centered on node } j} \tag{10.9}$$

If a vertex has degree zero or one, C_j is set equal to zero. Then the clustering coefficient $C^{(2)}$ is the average value of all C_j:

$$C^{(2)} = \frac{1}{N} \sum_j C_j \tag{10.10}$$

Here we assumed that the network has N nodes. Clearly the difference between these two clustering coefficients is that of an average of ratios versus a ratio of averages.

10.2.4 Modularity

Many networks divide naturally into modules or communities. Roughly speaking, communities are characterized by the fact that within a community network connections are dense, but between communities connections are sparse. Fig. 10.3 shows a network with three communities.

The notion of modularity is defined (Newman, 2006; Newman & Girvan, 2004) as follows. Consider a particular division of a network into k communities. Then a symmetric $k \times k$ matrix $E = (e_{ij})_{ij}$ is defined. The cell e_{ij} contains the fraction of all edges in the network that link vertices in community i to vertices in community j. The sum of the elements on the diagonal $\sum_{j=1}^{k} e_{jj}$, known as the trace of the matrix, gives the fraction of edges in the network that connect vertices in the same community. Clearly, if we have a good division into communities then the ratio $\sum_{j=1}^{k} e_{jj} / \sum_{i,j} e_{ij}$ should be close to one. The trace on its own, however, is

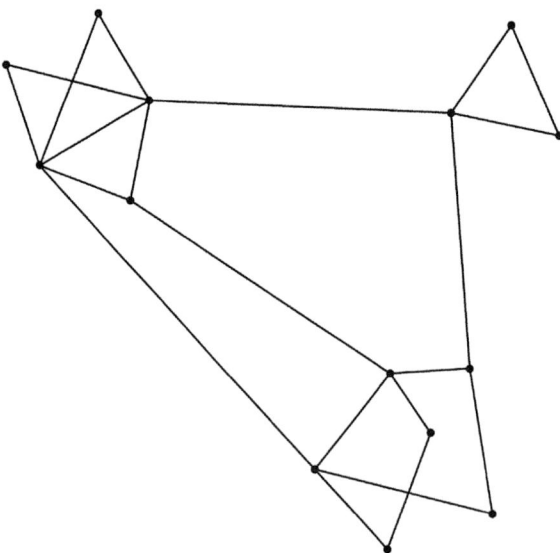

Figure 10.3 A network with three communities.

not a good indicator of the quality of the division since placing all vertices in a single community would give the value one while giving no information about community structure at all. For this reason, Newman and Girvan proceed as follows. Let $a_i = \sum_j e_{ij}$; this number represents the fraction of edges that connect to vertices in community i. In a network in which edges connect vertices without taking community structure into account one would have the independence relation: $e_{ij} = a_i a_j$. This leads to the notion of modularity Q, as defined by Newman and Girvan (2004),

$$Q = \sum_i \left(e_{ii} - a_i^2 \right) \tag{10.11}$$

Modularity Q measures the fraction of the edges in the network that connect vertices of the same type i.e., within-community edges, minus the expected value of the same quantity in a network with the same community divisions but random connections between the vertices. If the number of within-community edges is no better than random, we have $Q = 0$. Modularity values lie in the range $[-1/2, 1)$. They are positive if the number of edges within groups exceeds the number expected on the basis of chance. The higher the modularity value the stronger the community structure.

Algorithms to find the best division in communities try to maximize the modularity value. Although Newman and Girvan (2004) propose such an algorithm the most widely used method today for detecting communities in large networks is the Louvain method (Blondel et al., 2008). This is a simple, efficient and easy-to-implement method for identifying communities in large networks. It has been used with success for networks of many different types and for sizes up to 100 million nodes and billions of links. The Louvain method unveils hierarchies of communities and allows zooming in within communities to discover subcommunities. Once communities have been determined it makes sense to apply the gefura measure and determine the bridging roles of nodes in the network.

We finally mention the term *homophilous networks* (McPherson et al., 2001). Networks are homophilous if people, or generally actors, sharing similar characteristics establish more edges between them than with others. This means that they tend to lead to well-defined communities. In this context one uses the saying, "Birds of a feather flock together." (see e.g., Kretschmer, 2002).

10.2.5 Reciprocity

In a directed unweighted network, reciprocity is defined as the observed probability that if node i points to node j, also j points also to node i. A friendship network is a typical case for which it makes sense to calculate a reciprocity value.

In weighted networks such as journal citation networks reciprocity is defined as follows (Squartini et al., 2013):

Let w_{ij} be the weight of the link between node i and node j, in that order, where $w_{ii} = 0$ for all i. Let $rw_{ij} = rw_{ji} = \min(w_{ij}, w_{ji})$ denote the reciprocated weight between nodes i and j. Then the reciprocity value W for the network is:

$$W = \frac{\sum_i \sum_j rw_{ij}}{\sum_i \sum_j w_{ij}} \tag{10.12}$$

10.2.6 Complex Networks and the Small-World Phenomenon

The term *complex networks* is not precisely defined, but usually refers to large networks which are neither regular nor completely random. One may say that the citation network is a complex network. Two well-known and much studied classes of complex networks are scale-free networks and small-world networks. The term scale-free network is used for networks that have a degree distribution following a power law. Size and rank frequency of hyperlinks between websites follow—approximately a power law as was observed by Rousseau (1997b) for a small sample and by Faloutsos et al. (1999) for a much larger set. Also the network of protein interactions has a power law distribution (Jeong et al., 2001). A small-world network is characterized as a network exhibiting a high degree of clustering and having at the same time a small average distance between nodes. These characteristics distinguish small-world networks from random networks which also have a small average distance between nodes, but a much smaller degree of clustering. The small-world phenomenon is related to the notion of *six degrees of separation* (Kochen, 1989; Milgram, 1967; Newman & Watts, 1999). The concept that all persons on earth are linked through friendship or acquaintanceship in at most six steps was first proposed in 1929 by the Hungarian writer Frigyes Karinthy in a short story called "Chains" (Braun, 2004). This idea is a practical expression of the concept that such networks tend to grow exponentially. A related concept is the Erdős number. The Erdős number, named after the famous Hungarian mathematician Paul (Pál) Erdős, is a way of describing the collaboration distance in scientific articles between an author and Erdős. Erdős himself has an Erdős number zero. Those who have collaborated with Erdős have an Erdős number equal to one (more than 500 persons), those that have collaborated with a person who has Erdős number one have Erdős number two, and so on. Of course, scientists active in fields far away from mathematics have no Erdős number (or one may say that their Erdős number is infinity). Glänzel and Rousseau showed that many informetricians have a finite Erdős number (Glänzel & Rousseau, 2005).

A review on complex networks is provided in Newman (2003). In this work the author pays attention to three main aspects in the study of complex networks: statistical properties such as path lengths and degree distributions, creating models for networks, and the effects of structure on system behavior. He points out that much progress has been made on the first two aspects, but that less in known about the third. Another review of network science can be found in (Watts, 2004).

Motifs

Barabási and Oltvai (2004) pointed out that the occurrence of motifs seems to be a general property of all real networks. Motifs are small, local patterns of interactions that occur in complex networks and that are characterized by the fact that they occur significantly more than expected (Milo et al., 2002). To be precise, a motif M is a pattern (such as a triangle) that reoccurs in a network. Mathematically, a motif can be said to be the name of the equivalence class of a set of isomorphic subgraphs. Motifs have been shown to occur in transcription networks, signaling and neuronal networks, economics, information and social networks and other types of networks (Krumov et al., 2011; Sporns & Kötter, 2004; Zhang et al., 2014). In all these networks motifs serve as basic building blocks. Although in Milo et al. (2002) a set of three criteria is proposed for a subgraph to be a motif, these criteria can only be described as "ad hoc." At the moment there does not seem to exist a precise mathematical definition of a motif.

10.3 H-INDICES IN NETWORKS

10.3.1 The Lobby Index and the h-index of a Network

Schubert, Korn and Telcs (Korn et al., 2009; Schubert et al., 2009) introduced the lobby index as a centrality parameter for nodes, while Schubert and Soos (Schubert & Soos, 2010) defined the h-index of a network as an indicator for complete networks. The lobby index of node n in an unweighted network is defined as the largest integer k such that n has at least k neighbors with a degree, $d(n)$, at least k. The degree h-index of a network is defined as, "A network's degree h-index is h if not more than h of its nodes have a degree not less than h" (Schubert et al., 2009).

10.3.2 The h-degree (Zhao et al., 2011)

In many real networks, the strength or weight of a link is an important parameter, leading to the notion of weighted (or valued) networks. We define the node strength of a node in a weighted network as the sum of the strengths (or weights) of all its links (Barrat et al., 2004). In weighted networks, we use the term node strength, denoted as $d_s(n)$, not to be confused with the term node degree which we only use in unweighted networks (or for the underlying unweighted network where each weight is equal to one).

The lobby index mentioned in Section 10.3.1 can be adapted to a weighted network as follows, the w-lobby index (weighted network lobby index) of node n is defined as the largest integer k such that node n has at least k neighbors with node strength at least k. Next we define the h-degree of a node in a weighted network.

Definition: The h-degree (Zhao et al., 2011)

The h-degree (d_h) of node n in a weighted network is equal to $d_h(n)$, if $d_h(n)$ is the largest natural number such that n has $d_h(n)$ links each with strength at least equal to $d_h(n)$.

Properties
- In directed weighted networks, one can define an in-h-degree and an out-h-degree.
- In a weighted network with N nodes, the highest possible h-degree is $N-1$. This happens in a star network where the center is linked to the other nodes with a weight equal to (at least) $N-1$.
- In a ring where each weight is at least 2, each node has h-degree 2.
- In unweighted networks, the h-degree of a node is either 1 (a nonisolated node) or 0 (an isolated node). Also in weighted networks isolated nodes have $d_h = 0$.

Schubert introduced the coauthor partnership ability (2012), which is a special case of the h-degree (Rousseau, 2012). Indeed, when considering a coauthorship network, then Schubert's coauthor partnership ability index is exactly the h-degree in this network, where weights are the number of coauthorships between authors. The application of this index to movie actor networks and sexual encounter networks all lead to special cases of the h-degree.

10.4 SOFTWARE FOR NETWORK ANALYSIS

Practical work with networks can be done using software packages such as UCINET (Borgatti et al., 2002), Pajek (Batagelj & Mrvar, 1998; de Nooy et al., 2005) or VOSviewer (van Eck & Waltman, 2007, 2010, 2011, 2014). Finally, we mention that Bibexcel is a freely available biblio-metric toolbox which, among other things, prepares data for introducing them for mapping with Pajek (Persson et al., 2009).

CHAPTER 11

Timeline of Informetrics

In this chapter, we provide a timeline showing important steps in the history of scientific communication, publication analysis, citation analysis and science policy (Hertzel, 1987; de Bellis, 2009).

1665 (5 January): Publication of the first issue of the *Journal des Sçavans* (Paris), the first ever academic journal, established by Denis de Sallo.

1665 (6 March): Publication of the first issue of the *Philosophical Transactions of the Royal Society* (London) under the editorship of Henry Oldenburg.

1869: Publication of the first issue of the journal *Nature* (November 4).

1873: Alphonse de Candolle publishes *Histoire des Sciences et des Savants depuis deux Siècles,* which includes a description of the scientific strength of countries.

1877: Francis Galton publishes *English Men of Science: Their Nature and Nurture.*

1880: Foundation of the journal *Science* by John Michels with financial support from Thomas Edison.

1895: Vilfredo Pareto: The first power law, formulated in a context of income distribution (Pareto, 1895).

1906: J. McKeen Cattell publishes the first edition of *American Men of Science.*

1913: Felix Auerbach finds a hyperbolic relationship between the rank and the size of German cities (what we nowadays call Zipf's law) (Auerbach, 1913).

1916: Hyperbolic nature of word use (Zipf's law): Estoup (1916).

1917: The article "The history of comparative anatomy" by F.J. Cole and Nellie B. Eales includes publication counts and graphical representations (Cole & Eales, 1917).

1922: The term *statistical bibliography* was introduced by Wyndham Hulme. These lectures were published 1 year later (Hulme, 1923).

1922: Arnold Dresden's work on the publications of the Chicago section of the American Mathematical Society: a Lotka type presentation (Dresden, 1922).

Becoming Metric-Wise
DOI: http://dx.doi.org/10.1016/B978-0-08-102474-4.00011-X

1925: G. Udny Yule proposes the process named (afterward) after him and which is the basis for the explanation of the informetric laws (Yule, 1925).

1926: Alfred Lotka writes "Frequency distribution of scientific productivity" in which his famous law was formulated (Lotka, 1926).

1927: First article using citation analysis (Gross & Gross, 1927).

1928: Hyperbolic nature of word use (Condon, 1928).

1932: Selected studies of the principle of relative frequency by George K. Zipf. This book includes a size-frequency study of Chinese words (Zipf, 1932).

1934: Samuel C. Bradford publishes "Sources of information on specific subjects" about the scattering of the literature on a topic, later referred to as Bradford's law (Bradford, 1934).

1934: Paul Otlet uses the term "bibliométrie" in his *Traité de Documentation* (Otlet, 1934).

1935: Publication of "The psychobiology of language." This book contains the first clear formulation of "Zipf's law" by Zipf himself, (Zipf, 1935).

1936: The first journal-to-journal cross-citation network (psychological journals) presented by Hulsey Cason & Marcella Lubotsky (Cason & Lubotsky, 1936).

1939: John Desmond Bernal published "The Social Function of Science" the earliest text on the sociology of science (Bernal, 1939).

1945: Vannevar Bush publishes "As we may think," a visionary text anticipating the information society, including the idea of a memex (sometimes seen as a precursor of the Internet) that would transform the information explosion into a knowledge explosion (Bush, 1945a).

1945: Vannevar Bush's *Science: The Endless Frontier* marking the beginning of modern science policy (Bush, 1945b).

1948: Samuel Bradford publishes his main book: *Documentation* (Bradford, 1948).

1948: Claude Shannon publishes his mathematical theory of communication (Shannon, 1948a,b).

1948: The term *librametrics* is proposed by S.R. Ranganathan (but not published).

1949: Study of the characteristics of the literature of chemistry and physics; use of "key journals" by Herman Fussler (Fussler, 1949).

1949: George K. Zipf published his book *Human Behavior and the Principle of Least Effort* which summarizes his main ideas (Zipf, 1949).

1954: Publication of *Structure formelle des texts et communication*, including Mandelbrot's law (Mandelbrot, 1954).

1955: Eugene Garfield proposes the idea of a citation index (Garfield, 1955).

1956: Bibliographic coupling idea: Fano (1956).

1960: Index of realized research potential: A first type of impact factor (Raisig, 1960).

1960: R.E. Burton & R.W. Kebler introduce the notion of *half-life* in the literature of the information sciences (Burton & Kebler, 1960).

1962–1963: Michael M. Kessler introduces the idea of *bibliographic coupling* (Kessler, 1962, 1963).

1963: The first *Science Citation Index* (Garfield, 1963).

1963: Derek J. de Solla Price publishes *Little science, big science* (Price, 1963).

1963: Definition of the standard Journal Impact Factor by Garfield & Sher (1963).

1963: First version of the Frascati Manual, or officially *The Proposed Standard Practice for Surveys of Research and Experimental Development*.

1964: William Goffman and colleagues introduce disease epidemiology concepts to model the spread of knowledge including the dynamics of scientific discovery (Goffman & Newill, 1964).

1965: "Networks of scientific papers" by Price (1965) the most influential paper introducing the network idea in citation analysis.

1966: Vassily V. Nalimov proposes the term *naukometria = scientometrics* (Nalimov & Mul'chenko, 1969).

1966–1968: K.E. Rosengren introduces the idea of comentioning (in literary reviews), which is conceptually the same as the cocitation idea (Rosengren, 1966, 1968).

1967: The Leimkuhler function: a continuous description of Bradford's law (Leimkuhler, 1967).

1968: Robert Merton popularizes the term Matthew effect (Merton, 1968).

1968: Francis Narin founds Computer Horizons Inc.

1969: Alan Pritchard re-invents the term *bibliometrics* (Pritchard, 1969).

1969: Equivalence of bibliometric laws (strongly suggested) by Robert Fairthorne (Fairthorne, 1969).

1972: The Coles disprove the Ortega hypothesis which states that every scientist contributes to the progress of science. They claim that primarily elite scientists contribute to scientific progress (Cole & Cole, 1972).

1973: First U.S. National Science Board's *Science Indicators* (covering the year 1972).

1973: The first *Social Science Citation Index*.

1973: Henry Small (USA) and Irina Marshakova (USSR) independently introduce the notion of *cocitation* (Small, 1973; Marshakova, 1973).

1975: Michael J. Moravcsik and Poovanalingam Murugesan propose a classification scheme for citations (Moravcsik & Murugesan, 1975).

1975: First International Research Forum in Information Science (IRFIS): London, organized by B.C. Brookes.

1975: Benoît Mandelbrot publishes *Les objets fractals: forme, hasard, et dimension* (Mandelbrot, 1975), translated as: *Fractals: Form, Chance and Dimension* (Mandelbrot, 1977) later reworked to *The Fractal Geometry of Nature* (Mandelbrot, 1982), his main work on fractals, including an explanation of Zipf's law.

1976: Derek J. de Solla Price models the informetric laws using the success-breeds-success or cumulative advantage principle (based on the work of H. Simon), (Price, 1976).

1976: The first *Journal Citation Reports*.

1976: Gabriel Pinski and Francis Narin propose a citation influence measure, the precursor of Google's PageRank (Pinski & Narin, 1976).

1977: Nigel Gilbert claims that persuasiveness is the main reason for citing (Gilbert, 1977).

1978: Journal *Scientometrics* founded under the editorship of Tibor Braun.

1978: *Arts & Humanities Citation Index* launched.

1979: Term "informetrics" proposed by Nacke (1979) and by Blackert and Siegel (1979).

1979: Coword analysis introduced as a bibliometric technique (Callon, Courtial, Turner, 1979).

1981: Evaluation of big science and the idea of converging partial indicators: Martin & Irvine (1981, 1983).

1983: Anthony van Raan, Henk Moed and their team from Leiden (the Netherlands) perform evaluations of university research groups (Moed et al., 1983, 1985a,b).

1984: Eugene Garfield receives the first Derek J. de Solla Price medal.

1984: Abraham Bookstein's heuristic argument for the ubiquity of Lotka's law (Bookstein, 1984, 1990).

1985: Miranda Pao published a fitting procedure for Lotka's law based on ordinary least-squares (Pao, 1985).

1985: First study of citer motivations: Brooks (1985).

1985–1990: Leo Egghe proves formally the mathematical equivalence of the bibliometric laws (Egghe, 1985, 1990, 2005).

1987: Paul Nicholls proposes a fitting procedure for Lotka's law using a maximum likelihood approach (Nicholls, 1987).

1987: First International Conference on bibliometrics and informetrics, held in Diepenbeek (Belgium) (later known as the ISSI conferences) (Egghe & Rousseau, 1988).

1988: First Science & Technology Indicators (STI) Conference (the "Leiden" conferences).

1988–1992: First regional large-scale citation indexes (China).

1995: Henry Etzkowitz & Loet Leydesdorff (1995) propose the term Triple Helix to study University-Government-Industry relations.

1997: Tomas Almind and Peter Ingwersen introduce the term *web(o) metrics* (Almind & Ingwersen, 1997).

1997: Ronald Rousseau shows that inlinks on the Internet follow a power law (small sample) (Rousseau, 1997b).

1998: Sergey Brin and Lawrence Page introduce PageRank (Brin & Page, 1998).

1999: Inlinks on the Internet follow a power law (large-scale investigation) (Faloutsos et al., 1999).

1999: Albert-László Barabási and Réka Albert introduce the term *preferential attachment* (for what was already known as cumulative advantage, success-breeds-success or the Yule process).

2004: Elsevier launches Scopus.

2004: Google Scholar becomes available.

2005: First global Map of Science at the journal level by Boyack, Klavans, and Börner (2005).

2005: Jorge Hirsch defines the h-index (Hirsch, 2005).

2005: Thomson Reuters launches the *Century of Science* database which includes publications and citations since the year 1900.

2006: Leo Egghe defines the g-index (Egghe, 2006a,b,c).

2007: *Journal of Informetrics* founded by Elsevier with Leo Egghe as first Editor-in-Chief.

2008: The Louvain method for community detection (Blondel et al., 2008).

2010: Jason Priem, Dario Taraborelli, Paul Groth and Cameron Neylon post the Altmetrics manifesto (Priem et al., 2010).

2012: DORA declaration against misuse of the JIF (DORA, 2012).

2015: Leiden Manifesto (Hicks et al., 2015).

2015. Metric Tide (Wilsdon et al., 2015).

2015: Sandra and Ronald Rousseau propose the term *metric-wiseness* (Rousseau & Rousseau, 2015).

Recipients of the Derek J. de Solla Price Award

1984	Eugene Garfield
1985	Michael J. Moravcsik
1986	Tibor Braun
1987	Vasiliy V. Nalimov and Henry Small
1988	Francis Narin
1989	Bertram C. Brookes and Jan Vlachý
1993	András Schubert
1995	Anthony F.J. van Raan and Robert K. Merton
1997	John Irvine & Ben Martin (jointly) and Belver C. Griffith
1999	Wolfgang Glänzel and Henk F. Moed
2001	Leo Egghe and Ronald Rousseau
2003	Loet Leydesdorff
2005	Peter Ingwersen and Howard D. White
2007	Kate McCain
2009	Michel Zitt and Péter Vinkler
2011	Olle Persson
2013	Blaise Cronin
2015	Mike Thelwall
2017	Judit Bar-Ilan

BIBLIOGRAPHY

Aad, G., et al. (ATLAS Collaboration, CMS Collaboration). (2015). Combined measurement of the Higgs boson mass in pp collisions at $\sqrt{s} = 7$ and 8 TeV with the ATLAS and CMS experiments. *Physical Review Letters, 114*(19), 191803.

Abramo, G., D'Angelo, C. A., & Rosati, F. (2014). Relatives in the same university faculty: Nepotism or merit? *Scientometrics, 101*(1), 737–749.

Abramo, G., D'Angelo, C. A., & Solazzi, M. (2011). The relationship between scientists' research performance and the degree of internationalization of their research. *Scientometrics, 86*(3), 629–643.

Adamic, L. A., & Huberman, B. A. (2001). The Web's hidden order. *Communications of the ACM, 44*(9), 55–60.

Adamic, L. A., & Huberman, B. A. (2002). Zipf's law and the internet. *Glottometrics, 3*(1), 143–150.

Adams, J., & Testa, J. (2011). Thomson reuters book citation index. In E. Noyons, P. Ngulube, & J. Leta (Eds.), *Proceedings of the ISSI 2011 conference* (pp. 13–18). Durban: ISSI, Leiden University & University of Zululand.

Aguillo, I., Bar-Ilan, J., Levene, M., & Ortega, J. L. (2010). Comparing university rankings. *Scientometrics, 85*(1), 243–256.

Ahlgren, P., Jarneving, B., & Rousseau, R. (2003). Requirements for a cocitation similarity measure, with special reference to Pearson's correlation coefficient. *Journal of the American Society for Information Science & Technology, 54*(6), 550–560.

Ahlgren, P., Yue, T., Rousseau, R., & Yang, LY. (2017). The role of the Chinese Key Labs in the international and national scientific arena revisited. *Research Evaluation, 26*(2), 132–143.

Ajiferuke, I., Burrell, Q., & Tague, J. (1988). Collaborative coefficient: A single measure of the degree of collaboration in research. *Scientometrics, 14*(5–6), 421–433.

Alberts, B. (2013). Impact factor distortions. *Science, 340*(6134), 787–787.

Allen, L., Brand, A., Scott, J., Altman, M., & Hlava, M. (2014). Credit where credit is due. *Nature, 508*(7496), 312–313.

Almind, T. C., & Ingwersen, P. (1997). Informetric analyses on the world wide web: Methodological approaches to 'webometrics'. *Journal of Documentation, 53*(4), 404–426.

Alonso, S., Cabrerizo, F. J., Herrera-Viedma, E., & Herrera, F. (2009). H-index: A review focused in its variants, computation and standardization for different scientific fields. *Journal of Informetrics, 3*(4), 273–289.

Amara, N., & Landry, R. (2012). Counting citations in the field of business and management: Why use Google Scholar rather than the Web of Science. *Scientometrics, 93*(3), 553–581.

Amos, K. A. (2014). The ethics of scholarly publishing: Exploring differences in plagiarism and duplicate publication across nations. *Journal of the Medical Library Association, 102*(2), 87–91.

Anonymous. (2016). On impact. *Nature, 535*(7613), 466–466.

Antelman, K. (2004). Do open-access articles have a greater research impact? *College & Research Libraries, 65*(5), 372–382.

Anthonisse, J. M. (1971). *The rush in a graph.* Amsterdam: Mathematisch Centrum.

Anuradha, K., & Urs, S. (2007). Bibliometric indicators of Indian research collaboration patterns. A correspondence analysis. *Scientometrics, 71*(2), 179–189.

Archambault, E., & Larivière, V. (2007). Origins of measures of journal impact: Historical contingencies and their consequences on current use. In D. Torres-Salinas, & H. F. Moed (Eds.), *Proceedings of ISSI 2007* (pp. 45−51). Madrid: CINDOC-CSIC.

Arunachalam, S. (2002). Reaching the unreached: How can we use information and communication technologies to empower the rural poor in the developing world through enhanced access to relevant information? *Journal of Information Science, 28*(6), 513−522.

Åström, F., & Hansson, J. (2013). How implementation of bibliometric practice affects the role of academic libraries. *Journal of Librarianship and Information Science, 45*(4), 316−322.

Auerbach, F. (1913). Das Gesetz der Bevölkerungskonzentration. *Petermanns Mitteilungen, 59*(1), 74−76.

Balaram, P. (2008). Scientometrics: A dismal science. *Current Science, 95*(4), 431−432.

Baldi, S. (1998). Normative versus social constructivist processes in the allocations of citations: A network-analytical model. *American Sociological Review, 63*(6), 829−846.

Barabási, A.-L. (2003). *Linked: How everything is connected to everything else and what it means for business, science, and everyday life.* Cambridge (MA): Plume.

Barabási, A.-L., & Albert, R. (1999). Emergence of scaling in random networks. *Science, 286*(5439), 509−512.

Barabási, A.-L., Albert, R., & Jeong, H. (2000). Scale-free characteristics of random networks: The topology of the world-wide web. *Physica A, 281*(1−4), 69−77.

Barabási, A. L., & Oltvai, Z. N. (2004). Network biology: Understanding the cell's functional organization. *Nature Reviews Genetics, 5*(2), 101−113.

Bar-Ilan, J. (2008). Informetrics at the beginning of the 21st century − a review. *Journal of Informetrics, 2*(1), 1−52.

Bar-Ilan, J. (2010). Citations to the "Introduction to Informetrics" indexed by WOS, Scopus and Google Scholar. *Scientometrics, 82*(3), 495−506.

Bar-Ilan, J. (2012). Journal report card. *Scientometrics, 92*(2), 249−260. Erratum to: Journal report card, 261−261.

Barrat, A., Barthélemy, M., Pastor-Satorras, R., & Vespignani, A. (2004). The architecture of complex weighted networks. *Proceedings of the National Academy of Sciences of the United States of America, 101*(11), 3747−3752.

Bartolucci, F. (2015). A comparison between the g-Index and the h-Index based on concentration. *Journal of the Association for Information Science and Technology, 66*(12), 2708−2710.

Batagelj, V., & Mrvar, A. (1998). Pajek − program for large network analysis. *Connections, 21*(2), 47−57.

Baumgartner, H., & Pieters, R. (2003). The structural influence of marketing journals: A citation analysis of the discipline and its subareas over time. *Journal of Marketing, 67*(2), 123−139.

Bavelas, A. (1948). A mathematical model for small group structures. *Human Organization, 7*(3), 16−30.

Bavelas, J. B. (1978). The social psychology of citations. *Canadian Psychological Review, 19* (2), 158−163.

Begley, C. G., & Ellis, L. M. (2012). Raise standards for preclinical cancer research. *Nature, 483*(7391), 531−533.

Behrens, H., & Luksch, P. (2011). Mathematics 1868−2008: A bibliometric analysis. *Scientometrics, 86*(1), 179−194.

Bergstrom, C. T. (2007). Eigenfactor: Measuring the value and prestige of scholarly journals. *College & Research Libraries News, 68*(5), 314−316.

Bergstrom, C. T., West, J. D., & Wiseman, M. A. (2008). The eigenfactor metrics. *Journal of Neuroscience, 28*(45), 11433−11434.

Bernal, J. D. (1939). *The social function of science*. London: Routledge.

Bernstein, S., Lebow, R. N., Stein, J. G., & Weber, S. (2000). God gave physics the easy problems: Adapting social science to an unpredictable world. *European Journal of International Relations*, 6(1), 43—76.

Blackert, L., & Siegel, S. (1979). Ist in der wissenschaftlich-technischen Information Platz für die Informetrie? *Wissenschaftliches Zeitschrift TH Ilmenau*, 25(6), 187—199.

Blicharska, M., & Mikusinski, G. (2012). Metrics: A long-term threat to society. *Nature*, 490(7420), 343—343.

Blondel, V. D., Guillaume, J. L., Lambiotte, R., & Lefebvre, E. (2008). Fast unfolding of communities in large networks. *Journal of Statistical Mechanics: Theory and Experiment*, 10, P10008.

BOAI (2002). Budapest Open Access Initiative. Available at <http://www.budapestope naccessinitiative.org/>.

Bohannon, J. (2013). Who's afraid of peer review? *Science*, 342(6154), 60—65.

Bollen, J., Rodriguez, M. A., & Van de Sompel, H. (2006). Journal status. *Scientometrics*, 69(3), 669—687.

Bollen, J., Van de Sompel, H., Hagberg, A., & Chute, R. (2009). A principal component analysis of 39 scientific impact measures. *PLOS ONE*, 4(6), e6022.

Bollen, J., Van de Sompel, H., Smith, J., & Luce, R. (2005). Toward alternative metrics of journal impact: A comparison of download and citation data. *Information Processing and Management*, 41(6), 1419—1440.

Bonacich, P. (1972). Factoring and weighting approaches to clique identification. *Journal of Mathematical Sociology*, 2(1), 113—120.

Bonacich, P. (1987). Power and centrality: A family of measures. *American Journal of Sociology*, 92(5), 1170—1182.

Bonitz, M. (1997). The scientific talents of nations. *Libri*, 47(4), 206—213.

Bonitz, M., Bruckner, E., & Scharnhorst, A. (1997). Characteristics and impact of the Matthew effect for countries. *Scientometrics*, 40(3), 407—422.

Bontis, N., & Serenko, A. (2009). A follow-up ranking of academic journals. *Journal of Knowledge Management*, 13(1), 16—26.

Bookstein, A. (1976). The bibliometric distributions. *The Library Quarterly*, 46(4), 416—423.

Bookstein, A. (1979). Explanations of the bibliometric laws. *Collection Management*, 3(2/3), 151—162.

Bookstein, A. (1984). Robustness properties of the bibliometric distributions. Unpublished manuscript. Partially published as (Bookstein, 1990).

Bookstein, A. (1990). Informetric distributions, Part I: Unified overview. *Journal of the American Society for Information Science*, 41(5), 368—375.

Borgatti, S. P. (1995). Centrality and AIDS. *Connections*, 18(1), 112—115.

Borgatti, S. P., Everett, M. G., & Freeman, L. C. (2002). *Ucinet for Windows: Software for social network analysis*. Harvard, MA: Analytic Technologies.

Borgatti, S. P., Mehra, A., Brass, D., & Labianca, G. (2009). Network analysis in the social sciences. *Science*, 323(5916), 892—895.

Bornmann, L. (2010). Does the journal peer review select the "best" from the work submitted? The state of empirical research. *IETE Technical Review*, 27(2), 93—96.

Bornmann, L. (2011). Scientific peer review. In B. Cronin (Ed.), *Annual Review in information science and technology* (45, pp. 199—245). Medford (NJ): Information Today, Inc.

Bornmann, L., & Daniel, H.-D. (2005). Selection of research fellowship recipients by committee peer review. Reliability, fairness and predictive validity of Board of Trustees' decisions. *Scientometrics*, 63(2), 297—320.

Bornmann, L., & Daniel, H.-D. (2008). What do citation counts measure? A review of studies on citing behavior. *Journal of Documentation*, 64(1), 45—80.

Bornmann, L., & Daniel, H.-D. (2009a). Extent of type I and type II errors in editorial decisions: A case study on *Angewandte Chemie International Edition*. *Journal of Informetrics*, *3*(4), 348—352.

Bornmann, L., & Daniel, H.-D. (2009b). The luck of the referee draw: The effect of exchanging reviews. *Learned Publishing*, *22*(2), 117—125.

Bornmann, L., & Leydesdorff, L. (2017). Skewness of citation impact data and covariates of citation distributions: A large-scale empirical analysis based on Web of Science data. *Journal of Informetrics*, *11*(1), 164—175.

Bornmann, L., Mutz, R., & Daniel, H.-D. (2008). Are there better indices for evaluation purposes than the h-index? A comparison of nine different variants of the h-index using data from biomedicine. *Journal of the American Society for Information Science and Technology*, *59*(5), 830—837.

Borrego, A., Barrios, M., Villaroya, A., & Ollé, C. (2010). Scientific output and impact of postdoctoral scientists: A gender perspective. *Scientometrics*, *83*(1), 93—101.

Bouyssou, D., & Marchant, T. (2011). Ranking scientists and departments in a consistent manner. *Journal of the American Society for Information Science and Technology*, *62*(9), 1761—1769.

Boyack, K., Klavans, R., & Börner, K. (2005). Mapping the backbone of science. *Scientometrics*, *64*(3), 351—374.

Boyack, K., Klavans, R., Paley, W. B., & Börner. (2006). A map of science, as part of: 2006 gallery: Brilliant display. *Nature*, *444*(7122), 985—985.

Bozeman, B., & Gaughan, M. (2011). How do men and women differ in research collaborations? An analysis of the collaborative motives and strategies of academic researchers. *Research Policy*, *40*(10), 1393—1402.

Bradford, S. C. (1934). Sources of information on specific subjects. *Engineering*, *137*, 85—86, reprinted in *Journal of Information Science*, 10(4), 176—180 (1985).

Bradford, S. C. (1948). *Documentation*. London: Crosby Lockwood.

Brandes, U. (2001). A faster algorithm for betweenness centrality. *Journal of Mathematical Sociology*, *25*(2), 163—177.

Braun, T. (2004). Hungarian priority in network theory. *Science*, *304*(5678), 1745—1745.

Braun, T., & Glänzel, W. (1990). United Germany: The new scientific superpower? *Scientometrics*, *19*(5—6), 513—521.

Braun, T., Glänzel, W., & Schubert, A. (2005). A Hirsch-type index for journals. *The Scientist*, *19*(22), 8—8.

Braun, T., Glänzel, W., & Schubert, A. (2010). On sleeping beauties, princes and other tales of citation distributions . . .. *Research Evaluation*, *19*(3), 195—202.

Brin, S., & Page, L. (1998). The anatomy of a large-scale hypertextual web search engine. *Computer Networks and ISDN Systems*, *30*(1—7), 107—117.

Broadus, R. N. (1953). The literature of educational research. *School and Society*, 77, 8—10.

Brody, T., Harnad, S., & Carr, L. (2006). Earlier web usage statistics as predictors of later citation impact. *Journal of the American Society for Information Science and Technology*, 57 (8), 1060—1072.

Brookes, B. C. (1970). The growth, utility, and obsolescence of scientific periodical literature. *Journal of Documentation*, *26*(4), 283—294.

Brooks, T. A. (1985). Private acts and public objects: An investigation of citer motivations. *Journal of the American Society for Information Science*, *36*(4), 223—229.

Brown, L. D. (2003). Ranking journals using Social Science Research Network downloads. *Review of Quantitative Finance and Accounting*, *20*(3), 291—307.

Brown, T. (2004). *Peer Review and the Acceptance of New Scientific Ideas*. Discussion paper from a Working Party on equipping the public with an understanding of peer review. London: Sense About Science.

Buela-Casal, G., Gutiérrez-Martínez, O., Bermúdez-Sánchez, M. P., & Vadillo-Muñoz, O. (2007). Comparative study of international academic rankings of universities. *Scientometrics*, *71*(3), 349−365.

Burrell, Q. L. (2003). Age-specific citation rates and the Egghe-Rao function. *Information Processing and Management*, *39*(5), 761−770.

Burton, R. E., & Kebler, R. W. (1960). The "half-life" of some scientific and technical literatures. *American Documentation*, *11*(1), 18−22.

Bush, V. (1945a). As we may think. *The Atlantic Monthly*, *July*, 101−108.

Bush, V. (1945b). *Science, the endless frontier: A report to the President*. Washington, D.C.: U.S. Government Printing Office.

Butler, D. (2013). The dark side of publishing. *Nature*, *495*(7442), 433−435.

Callaway, E. (2016). Reviews open up. *Nature*, *539*(7629), 343−343.

Callon, M., Courtial, J.-P., & Turner, W.A. (1979). *L'Action Concertée Chimie Macromoléculaire: Socio-logique d'une Agence de Traduction*. Centre Sociologie de l'Innovation Paris/Strasbourg, Groupe d'Étude sur la Recherche Scientifique Université Louis Pasteur.

Cameron, E. Z., Gray, M. E., & White, A. M. (2013). Is publication rate an equal opportunity metric? *Trends in Ecology & Evolution*, *28*(1), 7−8.

Campanario, J. M. (2009). Rejecting and resisting Nobel class discoveries: Accounts by Nobel laureates. *Scientometrics*, *81*(2), 549−565.

Campanario, J. M. (2011). Empirical study of journal impact factors obtained using the classical two-year citation window versus a five-year citation window. *Scientometrics*, *87*(1), 189−204.

Campanario, J. M., & Acedo, E. (2007). Rejecting highly cited papers: The views of scientists who encounter resistance to their discoveries from other scientists. *Journal of the American Society for Information Science and Technology*, *58*(5), 734−743.

Campbell, L. G., Mehtani, S., Dozier, M. E., & Rinehart, J. (2013). Gender-heterogeneous working groups produce higher quality science. *PLOS ONE*, *8*(10), e79147.

Case, D. O., & Miller, J. B. (2011). Do bibliometricians cite differently from other scholars? *Journal of the American Society for Information Science and Technology*, *62*(3), 421−432.

Cason, H., & Lubotsky, M. (1936). The influence and dependence of psychological journals on each other. *Psychological Bulletin*, *33*(2), 95−103.

Cawkell, A. E. (1974). Search strategy, construction and use of citation networks, within a socio-scientific example: "Amorphous semi-conductors and S.R. Ovshinsky". *Journal of the American Society for Information Science*, *25*(2), 123−130.

Cerqueti, R., & Ausloos, M. (2015). Evidence of economic regularities and disparities of Italian regions from aggregated tax income size data. *Physica A − Statistical Mechanics and its Applications*, *421*(1), 187−207.

Chaddah, P. (2014). Not all plagiarism requires a retraction. *Nature*, *511*(7508), 127−127.

Chandy, P. R., Ganesh, G. K., & Henderson, G. V. (1991). Awareness and evaluation of selected accounting journals inside and outside the discipline: An empirical study. *Akron Business and Economic Review*, *22*(2), 214−226.

Chawla, D. S. (2016). The unsung heroes of scientific software. *Nature*, *529*(7584), 115−116.

Chen, CM. (1999). *Information visualisation and virtual environments*. London: Springer-Verlag.

Chen, CM. (2003). *Mapping scientific frontiers: The quest for knowledge visualization*. London: Springer-Verlag.

Chen, CM. (2004). Searching for intellectual turning points: Progressive knowledge domain visualization. *Proceedings of the National Academy of Sciences of the United States of America*, *101*(Suppl. 1), 5303−5310.

Chen, XT. (2015). Questionable university-sponsored supplements in high-impact journals. *Scientometrics, 105*(3), 1985−1995.

Christenson, J. A., & Sigelman, L. (1985). Accrediting knowledge: Journal stature and citation impact in social science. *Social Science Quarterly, 66*(4), 964−975.

Chrousos, G. P., Kalantaridou, S. N., Margioris, A. N., & Gravanis, A. (2012). The 'self-plagiarism' oxymoron: Can one steal from oneself? *European Journal of Clinical Investigation, 42*(3), 231−232.

Chubin, D. E., & Moitra, S. D. (1975). Content analysis of references: Adjunct or alternative to citation counting? *Social Studies of Science, 5*(4), 423−441.

CIBER Research Ltd. (2011). The journal usage factor: Exploratory data analysis. Stage 2 Final Report, 27 May 2011. Available at <http://www.uksg.org/sites/uksg.org/files/JournalUsageFactorReportAppendix080711.pdf>.

Cole, F. J., & Eales, M. B. (1917). The history of comparative anatomy. Part I: A statistical analysis of the literature. *Science Progress, 11*, 578−596.

Cole, J. R., & Cole, S. (1972). The Ortega hypothesis. *Science, 178*(4059), 368−375.

Cole, S. (1979). Age and scientific performance. *American Journal of Sociology, 84*(4), 958−977.

Colebunders, R., Kenyon, K., & Rousseau, R. (2014). Increase in numbers and proportions of review articles in tropical medicine, infectious diseases and oncology. *Journal of the Association for Information Science and Technology, 65*(1), 201−205.

Colebunders, R., & Rousseau, R. (2013). On the definition of a review, and does it matter? In J. Gorraiz, E. Schiebel, C. Gumpenberger, M. Hörlesberger, & H. F. Moed (Eds.), *Proceedings of ISSI 2013, Vienna* (pp. 2072−2074). Vienna: AIT Austrian Institute of Technology.

Condon, E. U. (1928). Statistics of vocabulary. *Science, 67*(1733), 300−300.

Conrad, J. (2015). Don't cry wolf. *Nature, 523*(7558), 27−28.

Conyers, A. (2006). Building on sand? Using statistical measures to assess the impact of electronic services. *Performance Measurement and Metrics, 7*(1), 37−44.

Cornell, L. L. (1982). Duplication of Japanese names: A problem in citations and bibliographies. *Journal of the American Society for Information Science, 33*(2), 102−104.

Costas, R., & Bordons, M. (2011). Do age and professional rank influence the order of authorship in scientific publications? Some evidence from a micro-level perspective. *Scientometrics, 88*(1), 145−161.

Costas, R., van Leeuwen, T. N., & Bordons, M. (2010). A bibliometric classificatory approach for the study and assessment of research performance at the individual level: The effects of age on productivity and impact. *Journal of the American Society for Information Science and Technology, 61*(8), 1564−1581.

Cozzens, S. E. (1982). Split citation identity: A case study from economics. *Journal of the American Society for Information Science, 33*(4), 233−236.

Cozzens, S. E. (1985). Comparing the sciences: Citation context analysis of papers from neuropharmacology and the sociology of science. *Social Studies of Science, 15*(1), 127−153.

Craig, I. D., Plume, A. M., McVeigh, M. E., Pringle, J., & Amin, M. (2007). Do open access articles have greater citation impact? A critical review of the literature. *Journal of Informetrics, 1*(3), 239−248.

Crespo, J. A., Ortuño-Ortín, I., & Ruiz-Castillo, J. (2012). The citation merit of scientific publications. *PLOS ONE, 7*(11), e49156.

Cronin, B. (1981). Transatlantic citation patterns in educational psychology. *Education Libraries Bulletin, 24*(2), 48−51.

Cronin, B. (2001). Hyperauthorship: A postmodern perversion or evidence of a structural shift in scholarly communication practices? *Journal of the American Society for Information Science and Technology, 52*(7), 558−569.

Cronin, B. (2012). The resilience of rejected manuscripts. *Journal of the American Society for Information Science and Technology, 63*(10), 1903−1904.

Cronin, B. (2013). Self-plagiarism: An odious oxymoron. *Journal of the American Society for Information Science and Technology, 64*(5), 873−873.

Cronin, B., & Sugimoto, C. R. (2015). *Scholarly metrics under the microscope.* Medford (NJ): Information Today.

Csiszar, A. (2016). Troubled from the start. *Nature, 532*(7599), 306−309.

Cummings, L. J., & Fox, D. A. (1973). Some mathematical properties of cycling strategies using citation indexes. *Information Storage and Retrieval, 9*(12), 713−719.

Cyranoski, D. (2014). Cell-induced stress. *Nature, 511*(7508), 140−143.

Dalton, H. (1920). The measurement of the inequality of incomes. *The Economic Journal, 30*(119), 348−361.

Danell, R. (2014). The contribution of authors: A study of the relationship between the size and composition of author teams. In E. Noyons (Ed.), *Proceedings of the STI Conference 2014 Leiden: "Context counts: Pathways to master Big and Little Data"* (pp. 123−131). Leiden: Universiteit Leiden, CWTS.

Davenport, E., & Cronin, B. (2001). Who dunnit it? Metatags and hyperauthorship. *Journal of the American Society for Information Science and Technology, 52*(9), 770−773.

Davis, P. M. (2009). Reward or persuasion? The battle to define the meaning of a citation. *Learned Publishing, 22*(1), 5−11.

Davis, P. M. (2011). Open access, readership, citations: A randomized controlled trial of scientific journal publishing. *The FASEB Journal, 25*(7), 2129−2134.

Davis, P.M. (2012). The emergence of a citation cartel. *Scholarly Kitchen.* <http://scholarly kitchen.sspnet.org/2012/04/10/emergence-of-a-citation-cartel/>.

Davis, P. M., Lewenstein, B. V., Simon, D. H., Booth, J. G., & Connolly, M. J. L. (2008). Open access publishing, article downloads, and citations: Randomised controlled trial. *BMJ, 337*(7665), 343−345.

Davis, P. M., & Price, J. S. (2006). eJournal interface can influence usage statistics: Implications for libraries, publishers and Project COUNTER. *Journal of the American Society for Information Science and Technology, 57*(9), 1243−1248.

De Bellis, N. (2009). *Bibliometrics and citation analysis. From the science citation index to cybermetrics.* Lanham (MD): Scarecrow Press.

de Bruin, R., Kint, A, Luwel, M., & Moed, H. F. (1993). A study of research evaluation and planning: The University of Ghent. *Research Evaluation, 3*(1), 25−41.

De George, R. T., & Woodward, F. (1994). Ethics and manuscript reviewing. *Journal of Scholarly Publishing, 25*(3), 133−145.

de Meis, L., do Carmo, M. S., & de Meis, C. (2003). Impact factors: Just part of a research treadmill. *Nature, 424*(6950), 723−723.

de Mesnard, L. (2010). On Hochberg et al.'s "Tragedy of the reviewer commons". *Scientometrics, 84*(3), 903−917.

de Nooy, W., Mrvar, A., & Batagelj, V. (2005). *Exploratory social network analysis with Pajek.* Cambridge: Cambridge University Press.

de Rijcke, S., Wouters, P. F., Rushforth, A. D., Franssen, T. P., & Hammarfelt, B. (2016). Evaluation practices and effects of indicator use − a literature review. *Research Evaluation, 25*(2), 161−169.

Debackere, K., & Glänzel, W. (2004). Using a bibliometric approach to support research policy making: The case of the Flemish BOF-key. *Scientometrics, 59*(2), 253−276.

Deem, R., Mok, KH, & Lucas, L. (2008). Transforming higher education in whose image? Exploring the concept of the 'world-class' university in Europe and Asia. *Higher Education Policy, 21*(1), 83−97.

Degraeve, Z., Lambrechts, M., & Van Puymbroeck, V. (1996). Een vergelijkende presta-tiestudie van de departementen van de Katholieke Universiteit Leuven (A comparative performance study of the departments of the Catholic University of Leuven). *Tijdschrift voor Economie en Management, 41*(2), 165−193.

Dennis, W. (1956). Age and productivity among scientists. *Science, 123*(3200), 724−725.

Dewett, T., & Denisi, A. S. (2004). Exploring scholarly reputation: It's more than just productivity. *Scientometrics, 60*(2), 249−272.

Dietz, E. J. (1989). Teaching regression in a nonparametric statistics course. *The American Statistician, 43*(1), 35−40.

Ding, Y., & Cronin, B. (2011). Popular and/or prestigious? Measures of scholarly esteem. *Information Processing and Management, 47*(1), 80−96.

Ding, Y., Rousseau, R., & Wolfram, D. (Eds.). (2014). *Measuring scholarly impact*. Cham: Springer.

DORA (2012). San Francisco declaration on research assessment. DORA − ASCB. Available from: <http://www.ascb.org/dora/>.

Doyle, J. R., & Arthurs, A. J. (1995). Judging the quality of research in business schools: The UK as a case study. *Omega, The International Journal of Management Science, 23*(3), 257−270.

Doyle, J. R., Arthurs, A. J., McAulay, L., & Osborne, P. G. (1996). Citation as effortful voting: A reply to Jones, Brinn and Pendlebury. *Omega, The International Journal of Management Science, 24*(5), 603−606.

Dresden, A. (1922). A report on the scientific work of the Chicago section, 1897-1922. *Bulletin of the American Mathematical Society, 28*(6), 303−307.

Drijvers, P., & Gravemeijer, K. (2004). Computer algebra as an instrument: Examples of algebraic schemes. In D. Guin, K. Ruthven, & L. Trouche (Eds.), *The didactical challenge of symbolic calculators: Turning a computational device into a mathematical instrument* (pp. 171−206). Dordrecht: Kluwer.

D'Souza, J. L., & Smalheiser, N. R. (2014). Three journal similarity metrics and their application to biomedical journals. *PLOS ONE, 9*(12), e115681.

Du, J., & Wu, YS. (2016). A bibliometric framework for identifying the *Princes* who wake up the *Sleeping Beauty* in challenge-type scientific discoveries. *Journal of Data and Information Science, 1*(1), 50−68.

Duesenberry, J. S. (1949). *Income, savings, and the theory of consumer behavior*. Cambridge (MA): Harvard University Press.

Edge, D. (1977). Why I am not a co-citationist. *Society for Social Studies in Science: Newsletter, 2*, 13−19.

Edge, D. (1979). Quantitative measures of communication in science: A critical review. *History of Science, 17*(2), 102−134.

Edward, J. T. (1992). Be cited or perish. *Chemtech, 22*(9), 534−539.

Egghe, L. (1985). Consequences of Lotka's law for the law of Bradford. *Journal of Documentation, 41*(3), 173−189.

Egghe, L. (1990). The duality of informetric systems with applications to the empirical laws. *Journal of Information Science, 16*(1), 17−27.

Egghe, L. (1991). Theory of collaboration and collaborative measures. *Information Processing and Management, 27*(2−3), 177−202.

Egghe, L. (1993a). On the influence of growth on obsolescence. *Scientometrics, 27*(2), 195−214.

Egghe, L. (1993b). Exact probabilistic and mathematical proofs of the relation between the mean and the generalized 80/20-rule. *Journal of the American Society for Information Science, 44*(7), 369−375.

Egghe, L. (2000). A heuristic study of the first-citation distribution. *Scientometrics, 48*(3), 345−359.

Egghe, L. (2005). *Power laws in the information production process: Lotkaian informetrics*. Amsterdam: Elsevier.

Egghe, L. (2006a). How to improve the h-index. *The Scientist, 20*(3), 14—14.

Egghe, L. (2006b). An improvement of the h-index: The g-index. *ISSI Newsletter, 2*(1), 8—9.

Egghe, L. (2006c). Theory and practise of the g-index. *Scientometrics, 69*(1), 131—152.

Egghe, L. (2010a). Study of some Editor-in-Chief decision schemes. *Annals of Library and Information Studies, 57*(3), 184—195.

Egghe, L. (2010b). Characteristic scores and scales based on *h*-type indices. *Journal of Informetrics, 4*(1), 14—22.

Egghe, L. (2010c). The Hirsch-index and related impact measures. In B. Cronin (Ed.), *Annual review in information science and technology* (Vol. 44, pp. 65—114). Medford (NJ): Information Today, Inc.

Egghe, L. (2010d). A new short proof of the Naranan's theorem, explaining Lotka's law and Zipf's law. *Journal of the American Society for Information Science and Technology, 61* (12), 2581—2583.

Egghe, L., Liang, LM., & Rousseau, R. (2008). Fundamental properties of rhythm sequences. *Journal of the American Society for Information Science and Technology, 59*(9), 1469—1478.

Egghe, L., & Michel, C. (2002). Strong similarity measures for ordered sets of documents in information retrieval. *Information Processing and Management, 38*(6), 823—848.

Egghe, L., & Rao, I. K. R. (1992a). Citation age data and the obsolescence function: Fits and explanations. *Information Processing and Management, 28*(2), 201—217.

Egghe, L., & Rao, I. K. R. (1992b). Classification of growth models based on growth rates and its applications. *Scientometrics, 25*(1), 5—46.

Egghe, L., Rao, I. K. R., & Rousseau, R. (1995). On the influence of production on utilization functions: Obsolescence or increased use? *Scientometrics, 34*(2), 285—315.

Egghe, L., & Rousseau, R. (Eds.), (1988). *Informetrics 87/88*. Amsterdam: Elsevier.

Egghe, L., & Rousseau, R. (Eds.), (1990). *Informetrics 89/90*. Amsterdam: Elsevier.

Egghe, L., & Rousseau, R. (1990). *Introduction to informetrics.* Quantitative methods in library, documentation and information science. Amsterdam: Elsevier, ISBN: 0 444 88493 9.

Egghe, L., & Rousseau, R. (1996a). Average and global impact of a set of journals. *Scientometrics, 36*(1), 97—107.

Egghe, L., & Rousseau, R. (1996b). Averaging and globalizing quotients of informetric and scientometric data. *Journal of Information Science, 22*(3), 165—170.

Egghe, L., & Rousseau, R. (2000). Aging, obsolescence, impact, growth and utilization: Definitions and relations. *Journal of the American Society for Information Science, 51*(11), 1004—1017.

Egghe, L., & Rousseau, R. (2001). *Elementary statistics for effective library and information service management.* London: Aslib-IMI.

Egghe, L., & Rousseau, R. (2002). A general framework for relative impact indicators. *Canadian Journal of Information and Library Science, 27*(1), 29—48.

Egghe, L., & Rousseau, R. (2006a). An informetric model for the Hirsch-index. *Scientometrics, 69*(1), 121—129.

Egghe, L., & Rousseau, R. (2006b). Classical retrieval and overlap measures satisfy the requirements for rankings based on a Lorenz curve. *Information Processing and Management, 42*(1), 106—120.

Engels, T. C. E., Ossenblok, T. L. B., & Spruyt, E. H. J. (2012). Changing publication patterns in the social sciences and humanities, 2000-2009. *Scientometrics, 93*(2), 373—390.

Englisch, H. (1991). Monotonous structure measures for social groups. *Scientometrics, 21* (2), 159—169.

Errami, M., & Garner, H. (2008). A tale of two citations. *Nature, 451*(7177), 397—399.

Estoup, J. B. (1916). *Gammes Sténographiques: Méthode et exercices pour l'acquisition de la vitesse* (4th ed.). Paris: Institut Sténographique de France.

Etzkowitz, H., Kemelgor, C., Neuschatz, M., Uzzi, B., & Alonzo, J. (1994). The paradox of critical mass for women in science. *Science*, *266*(5182), 51–54.

Etzkowitz, H., & Leydesdorff, L. (1995). The Triple Helix—University – Industry – Government Relations: A Laboratory for Knowledge-Based Economic Development. *EASST Review*, *14*(1), 14–19.

Etzkowitz, H., & Leydesdorff, L. (2000). The dynamics of innovation: From National Systems and "Mode 2" to a Triple Helix of University–Industry–Government Relations. *Research Policy*, *29*(2), 109–123.

Eysenbach, G. (2006). Citation advantage of open access articles. *PLOS Biology*, *4*(5), e157.

Fairthorne, R. A. (1969). Empirical hyperbolic distributions (Bradford-Zipf-Mandelbrot) for bibliometric description and prediction. *Journal of Documentation*, *25*(4), 319–343.

Faloutsos, M., Faloutsos, P., & Faloutsos, C. (1999). *On power-law relationships of the internet topology. Proceedings of the conference on applications, technologies, architectures, and protocols for computer communication* (pp. 251–262). New York (NY): ACM.

Fanelli, D. (2013). Redefine misconduct as distorted reporting. *Nature*, *494*(7436), 149–149.

Fanelli, D. (2014). Publishing: Rise in retractions is a signal of integrity. *Nature*, *509* (7498), 33–33.

Fanelli, D. (2016). Set up a 'self-retraction' system for honest errors. *Nature*, *531*(7595), 415–415.

Fano, R. M. (1956). Information theory and the retrieval of recorded information. In J. H. Shera, A. Kent, & J. W. Perry (Eds.), *Documentation in action* (pp. 238–241). New York: Reinhold Publ. Co.

Feder, J. (1988). *Fractals*. New York: Springer.

Fenner, M., & Lin, J. (2014). Novel research impact indicators. *Liber Quarterly*, *23*(4), 300–309.

Ferber, M. (1986). Citations: are they an objective measure of scholarly merit? *Signs: Journal of Women in Culture and Society*, *11*(2), 381–389.

Feynman, R. P. (1974). Cargo cult science. *Engineering and Science*, *37*(7), 10–13.

Flom, P. L., Friedman, S. R., Strauss, S., & Neaigus, A. (2004). A new measure of linkage between two sub-networks. *Connections*, *26*(1), 62–70.

Franceschet, M. (2010a). Journal influence factors. *Journal of Informetrics*, *4*(3), 239–248.

Franceschet, M. (2010b). Ten good reasons to use the Eigenfactor^{TM} metrics. *Information Processing and Management*, *46*(5), 555–558.

Franceschini, F., Galetto, M., Maisano, D., & Mastrogiacomo, L. (2012a). The success-index: An alternative approach to the h-index for evaluating an individual's research output. *Scientometrics*, *92*(3), 621–641.

Franceschini, F., Galetto, M., Maisano, D., & Mastrogiacomo, L. (2012b). Further clarifi-cations about the success-index. *Journal of Informetrics*, *6*(4), 669–673.

Frandsen, T. F., & Rousseau, R. (2005). Article impact calculated over arbitrary periods. *Journal of the American Society for Information Science & Technology*, *56*(1), 58–62.

Freeman, L. C. (1977). A set of measures of centrality based on betweenness. *Sociometry*, *40*(1), 35–41.

Freeman, L. C. (1979). Centrality in social networks: I. Conceptual clarification. *Social Networks*, *1*(3), 215–239.

Fussler, H. H. (1949). Characteristics of the research literature used by chemists and physi-cists in the United States. *The Library Quarterly*, *19*(1), 19–35; *19*(2), 119–143.

Gantman, E. R. (2012). Economic, linguistic, and political factors in the scientific pro-ductivity of countries. *Scientometrics*, *93*(3), 967–985.

Gao, X., & Guan, JC. (2009). Networks of scientific journals: An exploration of Chinese patent data. *Scientometrics*, *80*(1), 283–302.

Garfield, E. (1955). Citation indexes for science: A new dimension in documentation through association of ideas. *Science*, *122*(3159), 108–111.

Garfield, E. (1963). *Science citation index. An international interdisciplinary index to the literature of science*. Philadelphia: Institute for Scientific information.

Garfield, E. (1965). Can citation indexing be automated? In M. E. Stevens, V. E. Giuliano, & L. B. Heilprin (Eds.), *Statistical association methods for mechanized documentation, symposium proceedings, 1964* (pp. 189−1921). Washington: Nat. Bureau of Standards, Reprinted in: *Essays of an Information Scientist*, Vol.1 (1977), 84−90.

Garfield, E. (1970). Citation indexing, historio-bibliography, and the sociology of science. In K. E. Davis, & W. D. Sweeney (Eds.), *Proceedings of the third international congress of medical librarianship* (pp. 187−204). Amsterdam: Excerpta Medica, Reprinted in: *Essays of an Information Scientist, 1* (Philadelphia: ISI Press), 1977, 158-174.

Garfield, E. (1972). Citation analysis as a tool in journal evaluation. *Science, 178*(4060), 471−479.

Garfield, E. (1975). What's in a name? If it's a journal name, sometimes there's too much! *Current Contents*, November 17. Reprinted in: *Essays of an Information Scientist*, 2 (ISI Press, Philadelphia), 1977, 378−381.

Garfield, E. (1976). *Journal citation reports; a bibliometric analysis of references processed for the 1974 science citation index; Science Citation Index 1975, 9*. Philadelphia: Institute for Scientific Information.

Garfield, E. (1979). *Citation indexing: Its theory and application in science, technology, and humanities*. New York: Wiley.

Garfield, E. (1980). Premature discovery or delayed recognition − why? *Current Contents*, May 26, 1980. Reprinted in: *Essays of an Information Scientist*, 4 (ISI Press, Philadelphia), 1981, 488−493.

Garfield, E. (1982). More on the ethics of scientific publication: Abuses of authorship attribution and citation amnesia undermine the reward system of science. *Current Contents*, July 26, 1982. Reprinted in: *Essays of an Information Scientist*, 5 (ISI Press, Philadelphia), 1983, 621−626.

Garfield, E. (1985). Uses and misuses of citation frequency. *Current Contents*, October 28, 1985. Reprinted in: *Essays of an Information Scientist*, 8 (ISI Press, Philadelphia), 1985, 403−409.

Garfield, E. (1989). Delayed recognition in scientific discovery: Citation frequency aids the search for case studies. *Current Contents*, June 5. Reprinted in: *Essays of an Information Scientist*, 12 (ISI Press, Philadelphia), 1989, 154−160.

Garfield, E. (1998). Long-term vs. short-term journal impacts: Does it matter? *The Scientist, 12*(3), 10−12.

Garfield, E. (2009). From the science of science to Scientometrics: Visualizing the history of science with *HistCite* software. *Journal of Informetrics, 3*(3), 173−179.

Garfield, E., & Sher, I. H. (1963). New factors in the evaluation of scientific literature through citation indexing. *American Documentation, 14*(3), 195−201.

Gargouri, Y., Hajjem, C., Lariviére, V., Gingras, Y., Carr, L., Brody, T., & Harnad, S. (2010). Self-selected or mandated, open access increases citation impact for higher quality research. *PLOS ONE, 5*(10), e13636.

Garner, R. (1967). A computer oriented graph theoretic analysis of citation index structures. In B. Flood (Ed.), *Three Drexel information science studies* (pp. 3−46). Philadelphia: Drexel Institute of Technology.

Gattei, S. (2009). *Karl Popper's philosophy of science. Rationality without foundations*. New York: Routledge.

Gauffriau, M., & Larsen, P. O. (2005a). Counting methods are decisive for rankings based on publication and citation studies. *Scientometrics, 64*(1), 85−93.

Gauffriau, M., & Larsen, P. O. (2005b). Different outcomes of different counting methods for publications and citations. In P. Ingwersen, & B. Larsen (Eds.), *Proceedings of ISSI 2005* (pp. 242−246). Stockholm: Karolinska University Press.

Gilbert, G. N. (1977). Referencing as persuasion. *Social Studies of Science, 7*(1), 113–122.

Giménez-Toledo, E., Mañana-Rodríguez, J., Engels, T. C. E., Ingwersen, P., Pölönen, J., Sivertsen, G., Verleysen, F. T., & Zuccala, A. A. (2016). Taking scholarly books into account: Current developments in five European countries. *Scientometrics, 107*(2), 685–699.

Gini, C. (1909). Il diverso accrescimento delle classi sociali e la concentrazione della richezza. *Giornale degli Economisti, 38*, 69–83.

GL'99 Conference Program. (1999). Fourth International Conference on Grey Literature: New Frontiers in Grey Literature. GreyNet, Grey Literature Network Service. Washington D.C. USA: 4–5 October 1999.

Glänzel, W. (1996). The need for standards in bibliometric research and technology. *Scientometrics, 35*(2), 167–176.

Glänzel, W. (2006). On the opportunities and limitations of the H-index. *Science Focus, 1*(1), 10–11. [In Chinese]. An English translation can be found at E-LIS: http://hdl.handle.net/10760/9378.

Glänzel, W. (2009). The multi-dimensionality of journal impact. *Scientometrics, 78*(2), 355–374.

Glänzel, W. (2010). What is the impact of fraudulent literature? *ISSI Newsletter, 6*(2), 44–47.

Glänzel, W., & Gorraiz, J. (2015). Usage metrics versus altmetrics: Confusing terminology? *Scientometrics, 102*(3), 2161–2164.

Glänzel, W., & Moed, H. F. (2002). Journal impact measures in bibliometric research. *Scientometrics, 53*(2), 171–193.

Glänzel, W., & Moed, H. F. (2013). Opinion paper: Thoughts and facts on bibliometric indicators. *Scientometrics, 96*(1), 381–394.

Glänzel, W., & Rousseau, R. (2005). Erdős distance and general collaboration distance. *ISSI Newsletter, 1*(2), 4–5.

Glänzel, W., & Schubert, A. (1988). Characteristic scores and scales in assessing citation impact. *Journal of Information Science, 14*(2), 123–127.

Glänzel, W., & Schubert, A. (2003). A new classification scheme of science fields and subfields designed for scientometric evaluation purposes. *Scientometrics, 56*(3), 357–367.

Glänzel, W., Thijs, B., & Schlemmer, B. (2004). A bibliometric approach to the role of author self-citations in scientific communication. *Scientometrics, 59*(1), 63–77.

Gläser, J., & Laudel, G. (2007). The social construction of bibliometric evaluations. In R. Whitley, & J. Gläser (Eds.), *The changing governance of the sciences: The advent of research evaluation systems, sociology of sciences yearbook 26* (pp. 101–123). Dordrecht: Springer.

Goffman, W., & Newill, V. A. (1964). Generalization of epidemic theory: An application to the transmission of ideas. *Nature, 204*(4955), 225–228.

González-Pereira, B., Guerrero-Bote, V. P., & Moya-Anegón, F. (2010). A new approach to the metric of journals' scientific prestige: The SJR indicator. *Journal of Informetrics, 4*(3), 379–391.

Goodhart, C. A. E. (1975). Problems of monetary management: The U.K. Experience. *Papers in Monetary Economics* (Vol. I). Sydney: Reserve Bank of Australia.

Gordon, M. D. (1980). The role of referees in scientific communication. In J. Hartley (Ed.), *The psychology of written communication* (pp. 263–275). London: Kogan Page.

Gorkova, V. I. (1988). Informetria. *Reviews in Science and Technology*. Moscow: VINITI.

Grayson, M. (2015). Raising standards. *Nature, 520*(7549), S10–S12.

Gross, P. L. K., & Gross, E. M. (1927). College libraries and chemical education. *Science, 66*(1713), 385–389.

Guan, JC., & Gua, X. (2009). Exploring the h-index at patent level. *Journal of the American Society for Information Science and Technology, 60*(1), 35–40.

Guns, R. (2013). The three dimensions of informetrics: A conceptual view. *Journal of Documentation, 69*(2), 295−308.

Guns, R. & Engels, T.C.E. (2016). Effects of performance-based research funding on publication patterns in the social sciences and humanities. *Proceedings of the 21st International STI Conference (STI2016)*, València: September 14−16, 2016.

Guns, R., & Rousseau, R. (2009a). Real and rational variants of the h-index and the g-index. *Journal of Informetrics, 3*(1), 64−71.

Guns, R., & Rousseau, R. (2009b). Gauging the bridging function of nodes in a network: Q-measures for networks with a finite number of subgroups. In B. Larsen, & J. Leta (Eds.), *Proceedings of ISSI 2009 − the 12th International Conference on Scientometrics and Informetrics* (pp. 131−142). Rio de Janeiro: BIREME/PAHO/WHO and Federal University of Rio de Janeiro.

Guns, R., & Rousseau, R. (2015). Unnormalized and normalized forms of gefura measures in directed and undirected networks. *Frontiers of Information Technology & Electronic Engineering, 16*(4), 311−320.

Gupta, B. M. (1997). Analysis of distribution of the age of citations in theoretical population genetics. *Scientometrics, 40*(1), 139−162.

Hage, P., & Harary, F. (1995). Eccentricity and centrality in networks. *Social Networks, 17* (1), 57−63.

Hagen, N. T. (2008). Harmonic allocation of authorship credit: Source-level correction of bibliometric bias assures accurate publication and citation analysis. *PLOS ONE, 3* (12), e4021.

Hagen, N. T. (2010). Harmonic publication and citation counting: Sharing authorship credit equitably − not equally, geometrically or arithmetically. *Scientometrics, 84*(3), 785−793.

Halmos, P. (1960). *Naive set theory.* Princeton (NJ): Van Nostrand.

Hargens, L. L. (1988). Scholarly consensus and journal rejection rates. *American Sociological Review, 53*(1), 139−151.

Harnad, S., & Brody, T. (2004). Comparing the impact of open access (OA) vs. non-OA articles in the same journals. *D-Lib Magazine, 10*, 6.

Harnad, S., Brody, T., Vallières, F., Carr, L., Hitchcock, S., Gingras, Y., Oppenheim, C., Hajjem, C., & Hilf, E. (2008). The access/impact problem and the green and gold roads to open access: An update. *Serials Review, 34*(1), 36−40.

Haroche, S. (2012). The secrets of my prizewinning research. *Nature, 490*(7420), 311−311.

Harvey, S. C. (2015). Social impacts of science metrics. *Nature, 524*(7563), 35−35.

Harzing, A.-W. (2010). *The Publish or Perish Book.* Melbourne: Tarma Software Research.

Haustein, S. (2012). *Multidimensional journal evaluation. Analyzing scientific periodicals beyond the impact factor.* Berlin: De Gruyter Saur.

Haustein, S., Bowman, T.D., & Costas, R. (2015). When is an article actually published? An analysis of online availability, publication, and indexation dates. arXiv: 1505.00796.

Haustein, S., Costas, R., & Larivière, V. (2015). Characterizing social media metrics of scholarly papers: The effect of document properties and collaboration patterns. *PLOS ONE, 10*(3), e0120495.

Hernon, P., & Schwartz, C. (2002). The word "research": Having to live with a misunderstanding. *Library & Information Science Research, 24*(3), 207−208.

Hertzel, D. H. (1987). History of the development of ideas in bibliometrics. In A. Kent (Ed.), *Encyclopedia of library and information science.* (vol. 42 (Suppl. 7), pp. 144−219). New York (NY): Dekker.

Hicks, D., Wouters, P., Waltman, L., de Rijcke, S., & Rafols, I. (2015). The Leiden Manifesto for research metrics. *Nature, 520*(7548), 429−431.

Hirsch, J. E. (2005). An index to quantify an individual's scientific research output. *Proceedings of the National Academy of Sciences of the United States of America, 102*(46), 16569−16572.

Hirst, G. (1978). Discipline impact factors: A method for determining core journal lists. *Journal of the American Society for Information Science, 29*(4), 171−172.

Hochberg, M. E., Chase, J. M., Gotelli, N. J., Hastings, A., & Naeem, S. (2009). The tragedy of the reviewer commons. *Ecology Letters, 12*(1), 2−4.

Hodge, S. E., & Greenberg, D. A. (1981). Publication credit. *Science, 213*(4511), 950−950.

Holsapple, C. W. (2008). A publication power approach for identifying premier information systems journals. *Journal of the American Society for Information Science and Technology, 59*(2), 166−185.

Hu, XJ. (2009). Loads of special authorship functions: Linear growth in the percentage of 'equal first authors' and corresponding authors. *Journal of the American Society for Information Science and Technology, 60*(11), 2378−2381.

Hu, XJ., & Rousseau, R. (2013). Meeting abstracts: A waste of space? *Current Science, 105* (2), 150−151.

Hu, XJ., & Rousseau, R. (2016). Scientific influence is not always visible: The phenomenon of under-cited influential publications. *Journal of Informetrics, 10*(4), 1079−1091.

Hu, XJ., & Rousseau, R. (2017). Nobel Prize Winners 2016: Igniting or sparking foundational publications? *Scientometrics, 110*(2), 1053−1063.

Hu, XJ., Rousseau, R., & Chen, J. (2010). In those fields where multiple authorship is the rule, the h-index should be supplemented by a role-based h-index. *Journal of Information Science, 36*(1), 73−85.

Hu, XJ., Rousseau, R., & Chen, J. (2011). On the definition of forward and backward citation generations. *Journal of Informetrics, 5*(1), 27−36.

Hu, XJ., Rousseau, R., & Chen, J. (2012). Structural indicators in citation networks. *Scientometrics, 91*(2), 451−460.

Hua, PH., Rousseau, R., Sun, XK., & Wan, JK. (2009). A download $h^{(2)}$-index as a meaningful usage indicator of academic journals. In B. Larsen, & J. Leta (Eds.), *Proceedings of ISSI 2009 − the 12th international conference on scientometrics and informetrics* (pp. 587−596). Rio de Janeiro: BIREME/PAHO/WHO and Federal University of Rio de Janeiro.

Huber, J. C., & Wagner-Döbler, R. (2003). Using the Mann-Whitney test on informetric data. *Journal of the American Society for Information Science and Technology, 54*(8), 798−801.

Huggett, S. (2014). A quick look at references to research data repositories. *Research Trends, 38*, 19−21.

Hulme, E. W. (1923). *Statistical bibliography in relation to the growth of modern civilization. Two lectures delivered in the University of Cambridge in May* (p. 1922) London: Grafton.

Hyndman, R. J., & Fan, Y. (1996). Sample quantiles in statistical packages. *The American Statistician, 50*(4), 361−365.

Independent Expert Group on Open Innovation and Knowledge Transfer (K. Debackere, chair). (2014). *Boosting open innovation and knowledge transfer in the European Union.* Luxembourg: Publications Office of the European Union.

Ingwersen, P. (1998). The calculation of Web Impact Factors. *Journal of Documentation, 54* (2), 236−243.

Ingwersen, P., & Björneborn, L. (2004). Methodological issues of webometric studies. In H. F. Moed, W. Glänzel, & U. Schmoch (Eds.), *Handbook of quantitative science and technology research. The use of publication and patent statistics in studies of S&T systems* (pp. 339−369). Dordrecht: Kluwer.

Ingwersen, P., Larsen, B., Rousseau, R., & Russell, J. (2001). The publication-citation matrix and its derived quantities. *Chinese Science Bulletin, 46*(6), 524−528.

Ingwersen, P., Larsen, B., & Wormell, I. (2000). Applying diachronic citation analysis to ongoing research program evaluations. In B. Cronin, & H. B. Atkins (Eds.), *The Web of Knowledge: A Festschrift in Honor of Eugene Garfield* (pp. 373−387). Medford, N.J: Information Today, Inc. & American Society for Information Science.

Inhaber, H. (1974). Is there a pecking order in physics journals? *Physics Today, 27*(5), 39−43.

Institute for Higher Education Policy (2006). Berlin Principles on Ranking of Higher Education Institutions. <http://www.ihep.org/research/publications/berlin-principles-ranking-higher-education-institutions>.

Internet Systems Consortium (2016). Internet domain survey. Host Count <http://www.isc.org/solutions/survey>.

Ioannidis, J. P. A. (2005). Why most published research findings are false. *PLOS Med, 2*(8), e124.

Ioannidis, J. P. A., Boyack, K., & Wouters, P. F. (2016). Citation metrics: A primer on how (not) to normalize. *PLOS Biology, 14*(9), e1002542.

Jaccard, P. (1901). Étude comparative de la distribution florale dans une portion des Alpes et du Jura. *Bulletin de la Société Vaudoises des Sciences Naturelles, 37*(142), 547−579.

Jansz, C. N. M., & Le Pair, C. (1992). Bibliometric invisibility of technological advances. In P. Weingart, R. Sehringer, & M. Winterhager (Eds.), *Representations of science and technology. Proceedings of the International STI Conference* (pp. 315−326). Leiden: DSWO Press.

Jefferson, T., Alderson, P., Wager, E., & Davidoff, F. (2002). Effects of editorial peer review. *JAMA, 287*(21), 2784−2786.

Jeong, H., Mason, S. P., Barabási, A.-L., & Oltvai, Z. N. (2001). Lethality and centrality in protein networks. *Nature, 411*(6833), 41−42.

Jin, BH. (2007). The AR-index: Complementing the h-index. *ISSI Newsletter, 3*(1), 6−6.

Jin, BH., Liang, LM., Rousseau, R., & Egghe, L. (2007). The R- and AR-indices: Complementing the h-index. *Chinese Science Bulletin, 52*(6), 855−863.

Jin, BH., & Rousseau, R. (2005). China's quantitative expansion phase: Exponential growth but low impact. In P. Ingwersen, & B. Larsen (Eds.), *Proceedings of ISSI 2005* (pp. 362−370). Stockholm (Sweden): Karolinska University Press.

Jin, BH., & Rousseau, R. (2008). *Dust storms*. Available online at <eprints.rclis.org/12259>.

Jin, BH., Rousseau, R., & Sun, XX. (2005). Key labs and open labs in the Chinese scientific research system: Qualitative and quantitative evaluation indicators. *Research Evaluation, 14*(2), 103−109.

Jin, BH., Rousseau, R., & Sun, XX. (2006). Key labs and open labs in the Chinese scientific research system: Their role in the national and international scientific arena. *Scientometrics, 67*(1), 3−14.

Jin, BH., & Wang, B. (1999). Chinese science citation database: Its construction and application. *Scientometrics, 45*(2), 325−332.

Jin, BH., Zhang, JG., Chen, DQ., & Zhu, XY. (2002). Development of the Chinese Scientometric Indicators (CSI). *Scientometrics, 54*(1), 145−154.

Jouannaud, J.-P., & Lescanne, P. (1982). On multiset orderings. *Information Processing Letters, 15*(2), 57−63.

Kanazawa, S. (2003). Why productivity fades with age: The crime-genius connection. *Journal of Research in Personality, 37*(4), 257−272.

Kao, K. C., & Hockham, G. A. (1966). Dielectric-fibre surface waveguides for optical frequencies. *Proceedings of the Institution of Electrical Engineers, 113*(7), 1151−1158.

Ke, Q., Ferrara, E., Radicchi, F., & Flammini, A. (2015). Defining and identifying sleeping beauties in science. *Proceedings of the National Academy of Sciences of the United States of America, 112*(24), 7426–7431.

Kessler, M. M. (1962). *An experimental study of bibliographic coupling between technical papers.* M.I.T., Lincoln Laboratory.

Kessler, M. M. (1963). Bibliographic coupling between scientific papers. *American Documentation, 14*(1), 10–25.

Kim, J. (2011). Motivations of faculty self-archiving in institutional repositories. *Journal of Academic Librarianship, 37*(3), 246–254.

Kim, M. T. (1991). Ranking of journals in library and information science: A comparison of perceptual and citation-based measures. *College & Research Libraries, 52*(1), 24–37.

Klavans, R., & Boyack, K. W. (2009). Toward a consensus map of science. *Journal of the American Society for Information Science and Technology, 60*(3), 455–476.

Kochen, M. (1974). *Principles of information retrieval.* Los Angeles: Melville.

Kochen, M. (Ed.). (1989). *The small world.* Norwood (NJ): Ablex.

Korn, A., Schubert, A., & Telcs, A. (2009). Lobby index in networks. *Physica A-Statistical Mechanics and Its Applications, 388*(11), 2221–2226.

Koshland, D. E., Jr. (2007). The cha-cha-cha theory of scientific discovery. *Science, 317* (5839), 761–762.

Kosmulski, M. (2006). A new Hirsch-type index saves time and works equally well as the original index. *ISSI Newsletter, 2*(3), 4–6.

Kosmulski, M. (2011). Successful papers: A new idea in evaluation of scientific output. *Journal of Informetrics, 5*(3), 481–485.

Kosmulski, M. (2012). Modesty-index. *Journal of Informetrics, 6*(3), 368–369.

Kousha, K., & Thelwall, M. (2007). Google Scholar citations and Google Web/URL citations: A multi-discipline exploratory analysis. *Journal of the American Society for Information Science and Technology, 58*(7), 1055–1065.

Kousha, K., Thelwall, M., & Rezaie, S. (2011). Assessing the citation impact of books: The role of Google Books, Google Scholar, and Scopus. *Journal of the American Society for Information Science and Technology, 62*(11), 2147–2164.

Krauze, T. K., & McGinnis, R. (1979). A matrix analysis of scientific specialties and careers in science. *Scientometrics, 1*(5–6), 419–444.

Krell, F-T. (2010). Should editors influence journal impact factors? *Learned Publishing, 23* (1), 59–62.

Kretschmer, H. (2002). Similarities and dissimilarities in coauthorship networks: Gestalt theory as explanation for well-ordered collaboration structures and production of scientific literature. *Library Trends, 50*(3), 474–497.

Kretschmer, H., Pudovkin, A., & Stegmann, J. S. (2012). Research evaluation. Part II: Gender effects of evaluation: Are men more productive and more cited than women? *Scientometrics, 93*(1), 17–30.

Kretschmer, H., & Rousseau, R. (2001). Author inflation leads to a breakdown of Lotka's law. *Journal of the American Society for Information Science and Technology, 52*(8), 610–614.

Krumov, L., Fretter, C., Müller-Hannemann, M., Weihe, K., & Hütt, M. T. (2011). Motifs in co-authorship networks and their relation to the impact of scientific publications. *The European Physical Journal B, 84*(4), 535–540.

Kuhn, T. S. (1962). *The structure of scientific revolutions.* Chicago: University of Chicago Press.

Kurtz, M. J., Eichhorn, G., Accomazzi, A., Grant, C., Demleitner, M., Henneken, E., & Murray, S. S. (2005a). The effect of use and access on citations. *Information Processing and Management, 41*(6), 1395–1402.

Kurtz, M. J., Eichhorn, G., Accomazzi, A., Grant, C., Demleitner, M., Murray, S. S., Martimbeau, N., & Elwell, B. (2005b). The bibliometric properties of article readership information. *Journal of the American Society of Information Science and Technology, 56* (2), 111−128.

Kyvik, S. (1990). Age and scientific productivity. Differences between fields of learning. *Higher Education, 19*(1), 37−55.

Laakso, M., & Björk, B.-C. (2013). Delayed open access − an overlooked high-impact type of openly available scientific literature. *Journal of the American Society for Information Science and Technology, 64*(7), 1323−1329.

Labbé, C. (2010). Ike Antkare, one of the great stars in the scientific firmament. *ISSI Newsletter, 6*(2), 48−52.

Labbé, C., & Labbé, D. (2013). Duplicate and fake publications in the scientific literature: How many SCIgen papers in computer science? *Scientometrics, 94*(1), 379−396.

Laherrère, J., & Sornette, D. (1998). Stretched exponential distributions in nature and economy: "fat tails" with characteristic scales. *The European Physical Journal B − Condensed Matter and Complex Systems, 2*(4), 525−539.

Langfeldt, L. (2006). The policy challenges of peer review: Managing bias, conflict of interests and interdisciplinary assessments. *Research Evaluation, 15*(1), 31−41.

Langville, A. N., & Meyer, C. D. (2006). *Google's PageRank and beyond: The science of search engine rankings*. Princeton (NJ): Princeton University Press.

Larivière, V., & Gingras, Y. (2011). Averages of ratios vs. ratios of averages: An empirical analysis of four levels of aggregation. *Journal of Informetrics, 5*(3), 392−399.

Larivière, V., Ni, CQ., Gingras, Y., Cronin, B., & Sugimoto, C. R. (2013). Global gender disparities in science. *Nature, 504*(7479), 211−213.

Larivière, V., Vignola-Gagné, E., Villeneuve, C., Gélinas, P., & Gingras, Y. (2011). Sex differences in research funding, productivity and impact: An analysis of Québec university professors. *Scientometrics, 87*(3), 483−498.

Lawani, S.M. (1980). *Quality, collaboration and citations in cancer research: A bibliometric study*. Ph.D. Thesis, Florida State University, USA.

Lawani, S. M. (1982). On the heterogeneity and classification of author self-citations. *Journal of the American Society for Information Science, 33*(5), 281−284.

Lawrence, S. (2001). Free online availability substantially increases a paper's impact. *Nature, 411*(6837), 521−521.

Leimkuhler, F. F. (1967). The Bradford distribution. *Journal of Documentation, 23*(3), 197−207.

Leinster, T., & Cobbold, C. A. (2012). Measuring diversity: The importance of species similarity. *Ecology, 93*(3), 477−489.

Leydesdorff, L. (2007). Betweenness centrality as an indicator of interdisciplinarity of scientific journals. *Journal of the American Society for Information Science & Technology, 58*(9), 1303−1319.

Leydesdorff, L. (2008). *Caveats* for the use of citation indicators in research and journal evaluations. *Journal of the American Society for Information Science & Technology, 59*(2), 278−287.

Leydesdorff, L. (2009). How are new citation-based journal indicators adding to the bibliometric toolbox? *Journal of the American Society for Information Science & Technology, 60* (7), 1327−1336.

Leydesdorff, L. (2012). World shares of publications of the USA, EU-27, and China compared and predicted using the new Web of Science interface versus Scopus. *El Profesional de la Información, 21*(1), 43−49.

Leydesdorff, L., & Bornmann, L. (2011). Integrated impact indicators compared with impact factors: An alternative research design with policy implications. *Journal of the American Society for Information Science & Technology, 62*(11), 2133−2146.

Leydesdorff, L., & Jin, BH. (2005). Mapping the Chinese Science Citation Database in terms of aggregated journal-journal citation relations. *Journal of the American Society for Information Science & Technology, 56*(14), 1469−1479.

Leydesdorff, L., & Vaughan, L. (2006). Co-occurrence matrices and their applications in information science: Extending ACA to the Web environment. *Journal of the American Society for Information Science and Technology, 57*(12), 1616−1628.

Li, J., Shi, DB., Zhao, S. X., & Ye, F. Y. (2014). A study of the "heartbeat spectra" for "sleeping beauties". *Journal of Informetrics, 8*(3), 493−502.

Li, J., & Ye, F. Y. (2012). The phenomenon of all-elements-sleeping-beauties in scientific literature. *Scientometrics, 92*(3), 795−799.

Liang, LM. (2005). The R-sequence: A relative indicator for the rhythm of science. *Journal of the American Society for Information Science & Technology, 56*(10), 1045−1049.

Liang, LM. (2006). H-index sequence and h-index matrix: Constructions and applications. *Scientometrics, 69*(1), 153−159.

Liang, LM., & Rousseau, R. (2008). Yield sequences as journal attractivity indicators: Payback times for *Science* and *Nature*. *Journal of Documentation, 64*(2), 229−245.

Liang, LM., & Rousseau, R. (2009). A general approach to citation analysis and an h-index based on the standard impact factor framework. In B. Larsen, & J. Leta (Eds.), *Proceedings of ISSI 2009 − the 12th international conference on scientometrics and informetrics* (pp. 143−153). Rio de Janeiro: BIREME/PAHO/WHO and Federal University of Rio de Janeiro.

Liang, LM., Rousseau, R., & Zhong, Z. (2013). Non-English journals and papers in physics and chemistry: Bias in citations? *Scientometrics, 95*(1), 333−350.

Liang, LM., Zhao, HZ., Wang, Y., & Wu, YS. (1996). Distribution of major scientific and technological achievements in terms of age group − Weibull distribution. *Scientometrics, 36*(1), 3−18.

Liang, LM., Zhong, Z., & Rousseau, R. (2014). Scientists' referencing (mis)behavior revealed by the dissemination network of referencing errors. *Scientometrics, 101*(3), 1973−1986.

Liebowitz, S. J., & Palmer, J. P. (1984). Assessing the relative impacts of economics journals. *Journal of Economic Literature, 22*(1), 77−88.

Lin, F. (2011). A study on power-law distribution of hostnames in the URL references. *Scientometrics, 88*(1), 191−198.

Lin, J., & Fenner, M. (2013). Altmetrics in evolution: Defining and redefining the ontology of article-level metrics. *Information Standards Quarterly, 25*(2), 19−26.

Lindsey, D. (1980). Production and citation measures in the sociology of science: The problem of multiple authorship. *Social Studies of Science, 10*(2), 145−162.

Lipetz, B.-A. (1999). Aspects of *JASIS* authorship through five decades. *Journal of the American Society for Information Science, 50*(11), 994−1003.

Liu, MX. (1993). A study of citing motivation of Chinese scientists. *Journal of Information Science, 19*(1), 13−23.

Liu, YX. (2011). *The diffusion of scientific ideas in time and indicators for the description of this process*. Doctoral thesis: University of Antwerp.

Liu, YX., Rao, I. K. R., & Rousseau, R. (2009). Empirical series of journal h-indices: The JCR category Horticulture as a case study. *Scientometrics, 80*(1), 59−74.

Liu, YX., Rafols, I., & Rousseau, R. (2012). A framework for knowledge integration and diffusion. *Journal of Documentation, 68*(1), 31−44.

Liu, YX., & Rousseau, R. (2007). Hirsch-type indices and library management: The case of Tongji University Library. In D. Torres-Salinas, & H. F. Moed (Eds.), *Proceedings of ISSI 2007. 11th international conference of the international society for scientometrics and informetrics* (pp. 514−522). Madrid: CINDOC-CSIC.

Liu, YX., & Rousseau, R. (2008). Definitions of time series in citation analysis with special attention to the h-index. *Journal of Informetrics*, *2*(3), 202−210.

Liu, YX., & Rousseau, R. (2009). Properties of Hirsch-type indices: The case of library classification categories. *Scientometrics*, *79*(2), 235−248.

Liu, YX., & Rousseau, R. (2010). Knowledge diffusion through publications and citations: A case study using ESI-fields as unit of diffusion. *Journal of the American Society for Information Science and Technology*, *61*(2), 340−351.

Liu, YX., & Rousseau, R. (2012). Towards a representation of diffusion and interaction of scientific ideas: The case of fiber optics communication. *Information Processing and Management*, *48*(4), 791−801.

Liu, YX., & Rousseau, R. (2013). Interestingness and the essence of citation. *Journal of Documentation*, *69*(4), 580−589.

Loobuyck, P. (2009). What kind of university rankings do we want? *Ethical Perspectives*, *16*(2), 207−224.

López-Abente, G., & Muñoz-Tinoco, C. (2005). Time trends in the impact factor of public health journals. *BMC Public Health*, *5*, 24. Available at: <http://www.biomedcentral.com/1471-2458/5/24>.

Lorenz, M. O. (1905). Methods of measuring concentration of wealth. *Journal of the American Statistical Association*, *9*(70), 209−219.

Lotka, A. J. (1926). The frequency distribution of scientific productivity. *Journal of the Washington Academy of Sciences*, *16*(12), 317−323.

Lowry, O. H., Rosebrough, N. J., Farr, A. L., & Randall, R. J. (1951). Protein measurement with the Folin phenol reagent. *Journal of Biological Chemistry*, *193*(1), 265−275.

Lundberg, J. (2007). Lifting the crown − citation z-score. *Journal of Informetrics*, *1*(2), 145−154.

Luwel, M., & van Wijk, E. (2012). Publication delays revisited: 1998-2012. In E. Archambault, Y. Gingras, & V. Larivière (Eds.), *Proceedings of STI 2012 Montréal. 17th international conference on science and technology indicators* (pp. 567−577). Montréal: Science-Metrix.

Ma, F., & Wu, YS. (2009). A survey study on motivations for citation: A case study on periodicals research and library and information science community in China. *China Journal of Library and Information Science*, *2*(3), 28−43.

Macdonald, S. (2015). Emperor's new clothes: The reinvention of peer review as myth. *Journal of Management Inquiry*, *24*(3), 264−279.

Macrae, C. N., Bodenhausen, G. V., & Calvini, G. (1999). Contexts of cryptomnesia: May the source be with you. *Social Cognition*, *17*(3), 273−297.

MacRoberts, M. H., & MacRoberts, B. R. (1987). Testing the Ortega hypothesis: Facts and artifacts. *Scientometrics*, *12*(5−6), 293−295.

MacRoberts, M. H., & MacRoberts, B. R. (1989). Problems of citation analysis; a critical review. *Journal of the American Society for Information Science*, *40*(5), 342−349.

MacRoberts, M. H., & MacRoberts, B. R. (2010). Problems of citation analysis: A study of uncited and seldom-cited influences. *Journal of the American Society for Information Science & Technology*, *61*(1), 1−12.

Mahbuba, D., & Rousseau, R. (2010). Scientific research in the Indian subcontinent: Selected trends and indicators 1973−2007 comparing Bangladesh, Pakistan and Sri Lanka with India, the local giant. *Scientometrics*, *84*(2), 403−420.

Mahbuba, D., & Rousseau, R. (2013). Year-based h-type indicators. *Scientometrics*, *96*(3), 785−797.

Mahbuba, D., & Rousseau, R. (2016). New definitions and applications of year-based h-indices. *COLLNET Journal of Scientometrics and Information Management*, *10*(2), 321−332.

Mandavilli, A. (2011). Peer review: Trial by Twitter. *Nature, 469*(7330), 286–287.

Mandelbrot, B. B. (1954). Structure formelle des textes et communication (deux études). *Word, 10*(1), 1–27; 1955: Corrections: *Word,* 11, 424–424.

Mandelbrot, B. B. (1967). How long is the coast of Britain? Statistical self-similarity and fractional dimension. *Science, 156*(3775), 636–638.

Mandelbrot, B. B. (1975). *Les objets fractals: Forme, Hasard, et Dimension* (1e édition). Paris: Flammarion.

Mandelbrot, B. B. (1977). *Fractals: Form, chance and dimension.* San Francisco: Freeman.

Mandelbrot, B. B. (1982). *The fractal geometry of nature.* New York: Freeman.

Mann, H. B., & Whitney, D. R. (1947). On a test of whether one of two random variables is stochastically larger than the other. *Annals of Mathematical Statistics, 18*(1), 50–61.

Marion, L. S. (2002). A tricitation analysis exploring the image of Kurt Lewin. *Proceedings of the ASIST Annual Meeting, 39,* 3–13.

Marshakova, I. V. (1973). System of document connections based on references (in Russian). *Nauchno-Tekhnicheskaya Informatsiya, ser. 2*(6), 3–8.

Martin, B. R. (2013). Whither research integrity? Plagiarism, self-plagiarism and coercive citation in an age of research assessment. *Research Policy, 42*(5), 1005–1014.

Martin, B. R., & Irvine, J. (1981). Internal criteria for scientific choice – An evaluation of research in high-energy physics using electron-accelerators. *Minerva, 19*(3), 408–432.

Martin, B. R., & Irvine, J. (1983). Assessing basic research – Some partial indicators of scientific progress in radio astronomy. *Research Policy, 12*(2), 61–90.

Martyn, J. (1964). Bibliographic coupling. *Journal of Documentation, 20*(4), 236–236.

Marx, W., Bornmann, L., Barth, A., & Leydesdorff, L. (2014). Detecting the historical roots of research fields by reference publication year spectroscopy (RPYS). *Journal of the Association for Information Science and Technology, 65*(4), 751–764.

Mashelkar, R. A. (2015). What will it take for Indian science, technology and innovation to make global impact? *Current Science, 109*(6), 1021–1024.

Matsas, G. E. A. (2012). What are scientific leaders? The introduction of a normalized impact factor. *Brazilian Journal of Physics, 42*(5–6), 319–322.

Matricciani, E. (1991). The probability distribution of the age of references in engineering papers. *IEEE Transactions of Professional Communication, 34*(1), 7–12.

Maxmen, A. (2016). The myth buster. *Nature, 540*(7633), 330–333.

Maydanchik, A. (2007). *Data quality assessment.* Bradley Beach (NJ): Technics Publications.

McCain, K. W. (1990). Mapping authors in intellectual space: A technical overview. *Journal of the American Society for Information Science, 41*(6), 433–443.

McCain, K. W. (2009). Using tricitation to dissect the citation image: Conrad Hal Waddington and the rise of evolutionary developmental biology. *Journal of the American Society for Information Science and Technology, 60*(7), 1301–1319.

McCain, K. W. (2010). The view from Garfield's shoulders: Tri-citation mapping from Eugene Garfield's citation images over three successive decades. *Annals of Library and Information Studies, 57*(3), 261–270.

McCain, K. W. (2012). Assessing obliteration by incorporation: Issues and caveats. *Journal of the American Society for Information Science & Technology, 63*(11), 2129–2139.

McCook, A. (2006). Is peer review broken? *The Scientist, 20*(2), 26–34.

McPherson, M., Smith-Lovin, L., & Cook, J. M. (2001). Birds of a feather: Homophily in social networks. *Annual Review of Sociology, 27,* 415–444.

McVeigh, M. (2009). Citation indexes and the Web of Science. In: M.J. Bates & M.N. Maack (Eds.), *Encyclopedia of Library and Information Sciences* (3rd ed.), 1:1 (pp. 1027–1037).

Meho, L. I., & Yang, K. (2007). Impact of data sources on citation counts and rankings of LIS faculty: Web of science versus Scopus and Google Scholar. *Journal of the American Society for Information Science & Technology, 58*(13), 2105—2115.

Merton, R. K. (1942). The normative structure of science. In R. K. Merton (Ed.), *The sociology of science: Theoretical and empirical investigations* (p. 1973). Chicago (IL): University of Chicago Press.

Merton, R. K. (1968). The Matthew effect in science. *Science, 159*(3810), 56—63.

Merton, R. K. (1988). The Matthew effect in science II. Cumulative advantage and the symbolism of intellectual property. *Isis, 79*(4), 606—623.

Milgram, S. (1967). The small world problem. *Psychology Today, 1*(1), 61—67.

Milo, R., Shen-Orr, S., Itzkovitz, S., Kashtan, N., Chklovskii, D., & Alon, U. (2002). Network motifs: Simple building blocks of complex networks. *Science, 298*(5594), 824—827.

Milojević, S., Radicchi, F., & Bar-Ilan, J. (2017). Citation success index — An intuitive pair-wise journal comparison metric. *Journal of Informetrics, 11*(1), 223—231.

Mingers, J. (2014). Problems with the SNIP indicator. *Journal of Informetrics, 8*(4), 890—894.

Moed, H. F. (2005a). *Citation analysis in research evaluation.* Dordrecht (the Netherlands): Springer.

Moed, H. F. (2005b). Statistical relationships between downloads and citations at the level of individual documents within a single journal. *Journal of the American Society for Information Science and Technology, 56*(10), 1088—1097.

Moed, H. F. (2007). The effect of "Open Access" upon citation impact: An analysis of ArXiv's condensed matter section. *Journal of the American Society for Information Science and Technology, 58*(13), 2047—2054.

Moed, H. F. (2010). Measuring contextual citation impact of scientific journals. *Journal of Informetrics, 4*(3), 265—277.

Moed, H. F. (2012). Does open access publishing increase citation or download rates? *Research Trends, 28*, 3—4.

Moed, H. F. (2016). Comprehensive indicator comparisons intelligible to non-experts: The case of two SNIP versions. *Scientometrics, 106*(1), 51—65.

Moed, H. F. (2017). A critical comparative analysis of five world university rankings. *Scientometrics, 110*(2), 967—990.

Moed, H. F., Burger, W. J. M., Frankfort, J. G., & van Raan, A. F. J. (1983). *On the measurement of research performance: The use of bibliometric indicators.* University of Leiden, ISBN 90-9000552-8.

Moed, H. F., Burger, W. J. M., Frankfort, J. G., & van Raan, A. F. J. (1985a). The use of bibliometric data for the measurement of university research performance. *Research Policy, 14*(3), 131—149.

Moed, H. F., Burger, W. J. M., Frankfort, J. G., & van Raan, A. F. J. (1985b). A comparative-study of bibliometric past performance analysis and peer judgement. *Scientometrics, 8*(3—4), 149—159.

Moed, H. F., Glänzel, W., & Schmoch, U. (Eds.), (2004). Handbook of quantitative science and technology research. *The Use of Publication and Patent Statistics in Studies of S&T Systems.* Dordrecht: Kluwer.

Moed, H. F., & Plume, A. (2011). The multi-dimensional research assessment matrix. *Research Trends, 23*, 5—7.

Molinari, J.-F., & Molinari, A. (2008). A new methodology for ranking scientific institutions. *Scientometrics, 75*(1), 163—174.

Mongeon, P., & Larivière, V. (2014). The consequences of retractions for co-authors: Scientific fraud and error in biomedicine. In E. Noyons (Ed.), *Context counts: Pathways to master big and little data. Proceedings of the STI conference 2014 Leiden* (pp. 404—410). Leiden: Universiteit Leiden, CWTS.

Moravcsik, M. J., & Murugesan, P. (1975). Some results on the function and quality of citations. *Social Studies of Science, 5*(1), 86—92.

Morillo, F., Bordons, M., & Gomez, I. (2003). Interdisciplinarity in science: A tentative typology of disciplines and research areas. *Journal of the American Society for Information Science and Technology, 54*(13), 1237—1249.

Moss-Racusin, C. A., Dovidio, J. F., Brescoll, V. L., Graham, M. J., & Handelsman, J. (2012). Science faculty's subtle gender biases favor male students. *Proceedings of the National Academy of Sciences of the United States of America, 109*(41), 16474—16479.

Motylev, V. M. (1994). Study into the stochastic process of change in the literature citation pattern and possible approaches to literature obsolescence estimation. *International Forum on Information and Documentation, 6*(2), 3—12.

Muirhead, R. F. (1903). Some methods applicable to identities and inequalities of symmetric algebraic functions of n letters. *Proceedings of the Edinburgh Mathematical Society, 21*(February), 144—157.

Mullard, A. (2011). Reliability of 'new drug target' claims called into question. *Nature Reviews Drug Discovery, 10*(9), 643—644.

Mulligan, A., Hall, L., & Raphael, E. (2013). Peer review in a changing world: An international study measuring the attitudes of researchers. *Journal of the American Society for Information Science and Technology, 64*(1), 132—161.

Nacke, O. (1979). Informetrie. Ein neuer Name für eine neue Disziplin. *Nachrichten für Dokumentation, 30*(6), 219—226.

Nalimov, V. V., & Mul'chenko, Z. M. (1969). *Наукометрия, Изучение развития Науки как информационного процесса [Naukometriya, the Study of the Development of Science as an Information Process] (in Russian)*. Moscow: Nauka.

Naranan, S. (1970). Bradford's law of bibliography of science: An interpretation. *Nature, 227*(5258), 631—632.

Neale, A. V., Dailey, R. K., & Abrams, J. (2010). Analysis of citations to biomedical articles affected by scientific misconduct. *Science and Engineering Ethics, 16*(2), 251—261.

Nederhof, A. J., van Leeuwen, T. N., & Clancy, P. (2012). Calibration of bibliometric indicators in space exploration research: A comparison of citation impact measurement of the space and ground-based life and physical sciences. *Research Evaluation, 21*(1), 79—85.

Newman, M. E. J. (2003). The structure and function of complex networks. *SIAM Review, 45*(2), 167—256.

Newman, M. E. J. (2006). Modularity and community structure in networks. *Proceedings of the National Academy of Sciences of the United States of America, 103*(23), 8577—8582.

Newman, M. E. J. (2010). *Networks: An introduction*. Oxford: Oxford University Press.

Newman, M. E. J., & Girvan, M. (2004). Finding and evaluating community structure in networks. *Physical Review E, 69*(2), 026113.

Newman, M. E. J., & Watts, D. J. (1999). Scaling and percolation in the small-world network model. *Physical Review E, 60*(6), 7332—7342.

Ngok, KL., & Guo, WQ. (2008). The quest for world class universities in China: Critical reflections. *Policy Futures in Education, 6*(5), 545—557.

Nicholls, P. T. (1987). Estimation of Zipf parameters. *Journal of the American Society for Information Science, 38*(6), 443—445. Erratum: *Journal of the American Society for Information Science, 39*(4), 287 (1988).

Nickerson, R. S. (1998). Confirmation bias: A ubiquitous phenomenon in many guises. *Review of General Psychology, 2*(2), 175—220.

Nicolaisen, J. (2008). Citation analysis. *Annual Review of Information Science & Technology, 41*, 609—641.

Nijssen, D., Rousseau, R., & Van Hecke, P. (1998). The Lorenz curve: A graphical representation of evenness. *Coenoses, 13*(1), 33—38.

Noyons, E. C. M., Moed, H. F., & Luwel, M. (1999). Combining mapping and citation analysis for evaluative bibliometric purposes: A bibliometric study. *Journal of the American Society for Information Science, 50*(2), 115−131.

Ohba, N., & Nakao, K. (2012). Sleeping beauties in ophthalmology. *Scientometrics, 93*(2), 253−264.

Open Science Collaboration. (2015). Estimating the reproducibility of psychological science. *Science, 349*(6251), aac4716.

Opsahl, T., Agneessens, F., & Skvoretz, J. (2010). Node centrality in weighted networks: Generalizing degree and shortest paths. *Social Networks, 32*(3), 245−251.

Opthof, T., & Leydesdorff, L. (2010). Caveats for the journal and field normalizations in the CWTS ("Leiden") evaluations of research performance. *Journal of Informetrics, 4* (3), 423−430.

Oromaner, M. (1975). Collaboration and impact: The career of multi-authored publications. *Social Science Information/Information sur les Sciences Sociales, 14*(1), 147−155.

Ortega, J. L., & Aguillo, I. F. (2009). Mapping world-class universities on the web. *Information Processing and Management, 45*(2), 272−279.

Ossenblok, T. L. B. (2016). *Scientific communication in the social sciences and humanities: Analysis of publication and collaboration patterns in flanders.* Doctoral thesis University of Antwerp.

Ossenblok, T. L. B., & Engels, T. C. E. (2015). Edited books in the social sciences and humanities: Characteristics and collaboration analysis. *Scientometrics, 104*(1), 219−237.

Ossenblok, T. L. B., Engels, T. C. E., & Sivertsen, G. (2012). The representation of the social sciences and humanities in the Web of Science. A comparison of publication patterns and incentive structures in Flanders and Norway (2005-2009). *Research Evaluation, 21*(4), 280−290.

Ossenblok, T. L. B., Guns, R., & Thelwall, M. (2015). Book editors in the social sciences and humanities: An analysis of publication and collaboration patterns of established researchers in Flanders. *Learned Publishing, 28*(4), 261−273.

Ossenblok, T. L. B., Verleysen, F. T., & Engels, T. C. E. (2014). Co-authorship of journal articles and book chapters in the social sciences and humanities (2000−2010). *Journal of the American Society for Information Science and Technology, 65*(5), 882−897.

Otlet, P. (1934). *Traité de Documentation, le Livre sur le Livre.* Brussels: D. Van Keerberghen & Sons.

Otte, E., & Rousseau, R. (2002). Social network analysis: A powerful strategy, also for the information sciences. *Journal of Information Science, 28*(6), 441−453.

Overbaugh, J. (2011). A healthy work−life balance can enhance research. *Nature, 477* (7362), 27−28.

Palacios-Huerta, I., & Volij, O. (2004). The measurement of intellectual influence. *Econometrica, 72*(3), 963−977.

Pan, R. K., & Fortunato, S. (2014). Author impact factor: Tracking the dynamics of individual scientific impact. *Scientific Reports, 4*, 4880.

Pao, M. L. (1985). Lotka's law: A testing procedure. *Information Processing and Management, 21*(4), 305−320.

Paradigm. Wikipedia. <https://en.wikipedia.org/wiki/Paradigm>.

Pareto, V. (1895). La legge della domanda. *Giornale degli Economisti (2nd series), 10*, 59−68.

Pautasso, M. (2014). The jump in network ecology research between 1990 and 1991 is a Web of Science artefact. *Ecological Modelling, 286*, 11−12.

Pendlebury, D. A., & Adams, J. (2012). Comments on a critique of the Thomson Reuters journal impact factor. *Scientometrics, 92*(2), 395−401.

Perakakis, P., Taylor, M., Mazza, M., & Trachana, V. (2010). Natural selection of academic papers. *Scientometrics, 85*(2), 553−559.

Perneger, T. V. (2010). Citation analysis of identical consensus statements revealed journal-related bias. *Journal of Clinical Epidemiology, 63*(6), 660−664.

Persson, O., Danell, R., & Schneider, J. W. (2009). How to use Bibexcel for various types of bibliometric analysis. In F. Åström, R. Danell, B. Larsen, & J. W. Schneider (Eds.), *Celebrating Scholarly Communication Studies. A Festschrift for Olle Persson at his 60th Birthday* (pp. 9−24). Leuven: ISSI.

Perutz, M. (2002). *I wish I'd made you angry earlier. Essays on science, scientists and humanity.* Oxford: Oxford University Press.

Phelan, T. J. (1999). A compendium of issues for citation analysis. *Scientometrics, 45*(1), 117−136.

Pinski, G., & Narin, F. (1976). Citation influence for journal aggregates of scientific publications: Theory, with application to the literature of physics. *Information Processing and Management, 12*(5), 297−312.

Piternick, A. B. (1992). Name of an author. *The Indexer, 18*(2), 95−100.

Piwowar, H. (2013). Value all research products. *Nature, 493*(7431), 159−159.

Polanyi, M. (1966). *The tacit dimension.* London: Routledge & Kegan Paul.

Poole, H. L. (1985). *Theories of the middle range.* Norwood (NJ): Ablex.

Popper, K. (1959). *The logic of scientific discovery.* London: Hutchinson & Co.

Popper, K. (1972). *Objective knowledge: An evolutionary approach.* Oxford: Clarendon Press.

Porter, A. L. (1977). Citation analysis: Queries and caveats. *Social Studies of Science, 7*(2), 257−267.

Powell, K. (2016). The waiting game. *Nature, 530*(7589), 148−151.

Poynder, R. (2009). Open access: Whom would you back? See <http://poynder.blogspot.be/2009/03/open-access-who-would-you-back.html>.

Prathap, G. (2011a). A thermodynamic explanation for the Glänzel-Schubert model for the h-index. *Journal of the American Society for Information Science and Technology, 62*(5), 992−994.

Prathap, G. (2011b). The energy-exergy-entropy (or EEE) sequences in bibliometric assessment. *Scientometrics, 87*(3), 515−524.

Prathap, G. (2014). Quantity, quality, and consistency as bibliometric indicators. *Journal of the Association for Information Science and Technology, 65*(1), 214−214.

Price de Solla, D. J. (1963). *Little science, big science.* New York: Columbia University Press.

Price de Solla, D. J. (1965). Networks of scientific papers. *Science, 149*(3683), 510−515.

Price de Solla, D. J. (1970). Citation measures of hard science, soft science, technology, and nonscience. In C. E. Nelson, & D. K. Pollock (Eds.), *Communication among scientists and engineers* (pp. 3−22). Lexington (MA): Heath.

Price de Solla, D. J. (1976). A general theory of bibliometric and other cumulative advantage processes. *Journal of the American Society for Information Science, 27*(5), 292−306.

Price de Solla, D. J. (1986). *Little science, big science, . . . and beyond.* New York: Columbia University Press.

Priem, J., Taraborelli, D., Groth, P., Neylon, C. (2010). Alt-metrics: A manifesto. Available from <http://altmetrics.org/manifesto/>.

Pritchard, A. (1969). Statistical bibliography or bibliometrics? *Journal of Documentation, 25*(4), 348−349.

Rafols, I., & Meyer, M. (2010). Diversity and network coherence as indicators of interdisciplinarity: Case studies in bionanoscience. *Scientometrics, 82*(2), 263−287.

Rafols, I., Porter, A. L., & Leydesdorff, L. (2010). Science overlay maps: A new tool for research policy and library management. *Journal of the American Society for Information Science and Technology, 61*(9), 1871−1887.

Raisig, L. M. (1960). Mathematical evaluation of the scientific serial. *Science, 131*(3411), 1417−1419.

Ramanana-Rahary, S., Zitt, M., & Rousseau, R. (2009). Aggregation properties of relative impact and other classical indicators: Convexity issues and the Yule-Simpson paradox. *Scientometrics, 79*(2), 311−327.

Rao, C. R. (1982). Diversity and dissimilarity coefficients: A unified approach. *Theoretical Population Biology, 21*(1), 24–43.

Rehn, C., Gornitzki, C., Larsson, A., & Wadskog, D. (2014). *Bibliometric handbook for Karolinska Institutet*. Stockholm: Karolinska Institutet.

Reitz, J.M. (s.a). ODLIS. Online Dictionary for Library and Information Science <http://www.abc-clio.com/ODLIS/odlis_A.aspx>.

Rennie, D., & Yank, V. (1998). If authors became contributors, everyone would gain, especially the reader. *American Journal of Public Health, 88*(5), 828–830.

Rinia, E. J., Van Leeuwen, T. N., Bruins, E. E. W., Van Vuren, H. G., & Van Raan, A. F. J. (2002). Measuring knowledge transfer between fields of science. *Scientometrics, 54*(3), 347–362.

Rodrigues, R. S., & Abadal, E. (2014). Scientific journals in Brazil and Spain: Alternative publishing models. *Journal of the Association for Information Science and Technology, 65* (10), 2145–2151.

Ronald, P. (2016). Speed publication of self-corrections. *Nature, 533*(7603), 321–321.

Rosengren, K.E. (1966). *The literary system*. Master's thesis in sociology. Lund, Sweden.

Rosengren, K. E. (1968). *Sociological aspects of the literary system*. Stockholm: Natur och Kultur.

Rousseau, B., & Rousseau, R. (2014). Calculating the outgrow index and similar structural indicators: A simple software program for visualizing outcomes. *Collnet Journal of Scientometrics and Information Management, 8*(1), 31–40. Software is available at: http://crindex.com.

Rousseau, R. (1987). The Gozinto theorem: Using citations to determine influences on a scientific publication. *Scientometrics, 11*(3–4), 217–229.

Rousseau, R. (1988a). Citation distribution of pure mathematics journals. In L. Egghe, & R. Rousseau (Eds.), *Informetrics 87/88* (pp. 249–262). Amsterdam: Elsevier.

Rousseau, R. (1988b). Lotka's law and its Leimkuhler representation. *Library Science with a Slant to Documentation and Information Studies, 25*(3), 150–178.

Rousseau, R. (1994). Double exponential models for first-citation curves. *Scientometrics, 30*(1), 213–227.

Rousseau, R. (1997a). The proceedings of the first and second international conferences on bibliometrics, scientometrics and informetrics: A data analysis. In B. Peritz, & L. Egghe (Eds.), *Proceedings of the Sixth Conference of the International Society for Scientometrics and Informetrics* (pp. 371–380). Jerusalem: The Hebrew University of Jerusalem.

Rousseau, R. (1997b). Sitations: An exploratory study. *Cybermetrics, 1*(1). Available from http://www.cindoc.csic.es/cybermetrics/articles/v1i1p1.html.

Rousseau, R. (2002a). George Kingsley Zipf: Life, ideas, his law and informetrics. *Glottometrics, 3*, 11–18.

Rousseau, R. (2002b). *Journal evaluation: Technical and practical issues. Library Trends, 50*(3), 418–439.

Rousseau, R. (2005a). Median and percentile impact factors: A set of new indicators. *Scientometrics, 63*(3), 431–441.

Rousseau, R. (2005b). Impact factors and databases as instruments for research evaluation. In J. P. Qiu (Ed.), *University evaluation & research evaluation* (pp. 255–262). Beijing: Hua Xia Publishing House.

Rousseau, R. (2006a). Preference for the own group favours largest group most. *ISSI Newsletter, 2*(4), 5–5.

Rousseau, R. (2006b). Timelines in citation research. *Journal of the American Society for Information Science and Technology, 57*(10), 1404–1405.

Rousseau, R. (2006c). New developments related to the Hirsch index. *Science Focus, 1*(4), 23–25 [In Chinese]. An English translation can be found at: E-LIS, ID 6376.

Rousseau, R. (2006d). Simple models and the corresponding h- and g-index. Available at: E-LIS ID 6153.

Rousseau, R. (2006e). After the journal impact factor and the web impact factor a referee factor enters the fray: Some comments. *ISSI Newsletter*, *2*(2), 2–3.

Rousseau, R. (2007a). The influence of missing publications on the Hirsch index. *Journal of Informetrics*, *1*(1), 2–7.

Rousseau, R. (2007b). Cha-cha-cha in informetrics. *ISSI Newsletter*, *3*(3), 43–45.

Rousseau, R. (2008). Publication and citation analysis as a tool for information retrieval. In D. Goh, & S. Foo (Eds.), *Social information retrieval systems* (pp. 252–268). New York: IGI Global.

Rousseau, R. (2009a). What does the Web of Science five-year synchronous impact factor have to offer? *Chinese Journal of Library and Information Science*, *2*(3), 1–7.

Rousseau, R. (2009b). University rankings and the Van Parijs typology. *Zambia Library Association Journal*, *24*(1–2), 37–43.

Rousseau, R. (2009c). The most influential editorials. In: F. Åström, R. Danell, B. Larsen & J.W. Schneider (Eds.), *Celebrating Scholarly Communication Studies. A Festschrift for Olle Persson at his 60th Birthday* (pp. 47–53). Leuven, ISSI.

Rousseau, R. (2011). Comments on the modified collaborative coefficient. *Scientometrics*, *87*(1), 171–174.

Rousseau, R. (2012). Comments on "A Hirsch-type index of co-author partnership ability". *Scientometrics*, *91*(1), 309–310.

Rousseau, R. (2013). A discussion of some recently introduced indicators for research evaluation. *Documentation, Information & Knowledge*, *5*, 4–14.

Rousseau, R. (2014a). Advanced search in Thomson Reuters' Web of Science. *ISSI Newsletter*, *10*(2), 42–44.

Rousseau, R. (2014b). Skewness for journal citation curves. In E. Noyons (Ed.), *Proceedings of the science and technology indicators conference 2014 Leiden Context Counts: Pathways to master big and little data* (pp. 498–501). Leiden: Universiteit Leiden, CWTS.

Rousseau, R. (2014c). A note on the interpolated or real-valued h-index with a generalization for fractional counting. *ASLIB Journal of Information Management*, *66*(1), 2–12.

Rousseau, R. (2016). Citation data as a proxy for quality or scientific influence are at best PAC (Probably Approximately Correct). *Journal of the Association for Information Science and Technology*, *67*(12), 3092–3094.

Rousseau, R., García-Zorita, C., & Sanz-Casado, E. (2013). The h-bubble. *Journal of Informetrics*, *7*(2), 294–300.

Rousseau, R., & Hu, XJ. (2010). An outgrow index. *Annals of Library and Information Studies*, *57*(3), 287–290.

Rousseau, R., & Jin, BH. (2008). The age-dependent h-type AR^2-index: Basic properties and a case study. *Journal of the American Society for Information Science and Technology, 59* (14), 2305–2311.

Rousseau, R., Jin, BH., Yang, N., & Liu, X. (2001). Observations concerning the two- and three-year synchronous impact factor, based on the Chinese Science Citation Index. *Journal of Documentation*, *57*(3), 349–357.

Rousseau, R., & Leydesdorff, L. (2011). Simple arithmetic versus intuitive understanding: The case of the impact factor. *ISSI Newsletter*, *7*(1), 10–14.

Rousseau, R., & Rousseau, S. (2016). From a success index to a success multiplier. In C. R. Sugimoto (Ed.), *Theories of informetrics and scholarly communication* (pp. 148–164). Cham: de Gruyter.

Rousseau, R., & Small, H. (2005). Escher staircases dwarfed. *ISSI Newsletter*, *1*(4), 8–10.

Rousseau, R., & Spinak, E. (1996). Do a field list of internationally visible journals and its journal impact factors depend on the initial set of journals? A research proposal. *Journal of Documentation, 52*(4), 449−456.

Rousseau, R. & STIMULATE 8 Group. (2009). On the relation between the WoS impact factor, the eigenfactor, the SCImago journal rank, the article influence score and the journal h-index. Available at <http://eprints.rclis.org/13304>.

Rousseau, R., & Thelwall, M. (2004). Escher staircases on the World Wide Web. *First Monday, 9*(6−7). Available from http://firstmonday.org/ojs/index.php/fm/article/view/1152/1072.

Rousseau, R., Xu, F., & Liu, WB. (2015). Interpolated sub-impact factor (SIF) sequences for journal rankings. *Journal of Informetrics, 9*(4), 907−914.

Rousseau, R., & Ye, F. Y. (2012). Basic independence axioms for the publication-citation system. *Journal of Scientometric Research, 1*(1), 22−27.

Rousseau, R., & Ye, F. Y. (2013). A multi-metric approach for research evaluations. *Chinese Science Bulletin, 58*(26), 3288−3290.

Rousseau, R., Zhang, L., & Hu, XJ (2018). Knowledge Integration: Its meaning and measurement. In W. Glänzel, H. F. Moed, U. Schmoch, & M. Thelwall (Eds.), *Springer handbook of science and technology indicators*. Heidelberg: Springer (to appear).

Rousseau, R., & Zhang, QQ. (1992). Zipf's data on the frequency of Chinese words revisited. *Scientometrics, 24*(2), 201−220.

Rousseau, S., & Rousseau, R. (2012). Interactions between journal attributes and authors' willingness to wait for editorial decisions. *Journal of the American Society for Information Science and Technology, 63*(6), 1213−1225.

Rousseau, S., & Rousseau, R. (2015). Metric-wiseness. *Journal of the Association for Information Science and Technology, 66*(11), 2389−2389.

Rousseau, S., & Rousseau, R. (2017). Being metric-wise: Heterogeneity in bibliometric knowledge. *El Profesional de la Información, 26*(3), 480−487.

Ruane, F., & Tol, R. S. J. (2008). Rational (successive) h-indices: An application to economics in the Republic of Ireland. *Scientometrics, 75*(2), 395−405.

Russell, J. F. (2013). If a job is worth doing, it is worth doing twice. *Nature, 496*(7443), 7−7.

Sabidussi, G. (1966). The centrality index of a graph. *Psychometrika, 31*(4), 581−603.

Sales, L. F., & Sayao, L. F. (2015). Cyberinfrastructure and information for research: A proposal for architecture for integrating repositories and CRIS systems. *Informação & Sociedade − Estudos, 25*(3), 163−184.

Samuelson, P. (1994). Self-plagiarism or fair use? *Communications of the ACM, 37*(8), 21−25.

Sandström, U., & Hällsten, M. (2008). Persistent nepotism in peer-review. *Scientometrics, 74*(2), 175−189.

Santini, S. (2005). We are sorry to inform you.... *Computer, 38*(12), 126−128.

Sarli, C. C., Dubinsky, E. K., & Holmes, K. L. (2010). Beyond citation analysis: A model for assessment of research impact. *Journal of the Medical Library Association, 98*(1), 17−23.

Schiermeier, Q. (2008). Self-publishing editor set to retire. *Nature, 456*(7221), 432−432.

Schlögl, C., & Gorraiz, J. (2010). Comparison of citation and usage indicators: The case of oncology journals. *Scientometrics, 82*(3), 567−580.

Schneider, J. W. (2009). An outline of the bibliometric indicator used for performance-based funding of research institutions in Norway. *European Political Science, 8*(3), 364−378.

Schneider, J. W. (2012). Testing university rankings statistically: Why this perhaps is not such a good idea after all. Some reflections on statistical power, effect size, random sampling and imaginary populations. In E. Archambault, Y. Gingras, & V. Larivière

(Eds.), *Proceedings of the International STI Conference* (pp. 719—732). Montréal: Science-Metrix.

Schneider, J. W. (2013). Caveats for using statistical significance tests in research assessments. *Journal of Informetrics*, 7(1), 50—62.

Schneider, J. W. (2015). Null hypothesis significance tests. A mix-up of two different theories: The basis for widespread confusion and numerous misinterpretations. *Scientometrics*, 102(1), 411—432.

Schubert, A. (2002). The Web of Scientometrics. *Scientometrics*, 53(1), 3—20.

Schubert, A. (2009). Using the h-index for assessing single publications. *Scientometrics*, 78(3), 559—565.

Schubert, A. (2012). A Hirsch-type index of co-author partnership ability. *Scientometrics*, 91(1), 303—308.

Schubert, A., & Glänzel, W. (2007). A systematic analysis of Hirsch-type indices for journals. *Journal of Informetrics*, 1(3), 179—184.

Schubert, A., Glänzel, W., & Braun, T. (1987). Subject field characteristic citation scores and scales for assessing research performance. *Scientometrics*, 12(5—6), 267—291.

Schubert, A., Korn, A., & Telcs, A. (2009). Hirsch-type indices for characterizing networks. *Scientometrics*, 78(2), 375—382.

Schubert, A., & Soos, S. (2010). Mapping of science journals based on h-similarity. *Scientometrics*, 83(2), 589—600.

Schultz, D. M. (2010). Are three heads better than two? How the number of reviewers and editor behavior affect the rejection rate. *Scientometrics*, 84(2), 277—292.

Science. Wikipedia. <http://en.wikipedia.org/wiki/Science>.

SCImago. (2007). SJR — SCImago Journal & Country Rank. Retrieved January 6, 2017, from <http://www.scimagojr.com>.

Scott, J. (1991). *Social network analysis: A handbook*. London: Sage.

Seglen, P. O. (1989). From bad to worse: Evaluation by Journal Impact. *Trends in Biochemical Sciences*, 14(8), 326—327.

Seglen, P. O. (1992). The skewness of science. *Journal of the American Society for Information Science*, 43(9), 628—638.

Seglen, P. O. (1994). Causal relationship between article citedness and journal impact. *Journal of the American Society for Information Science*, 45(1), 1—11.

Seglen, P. O. (1997). Why the impact factor of journals should not be used for evaluating research. *BMJ*, 314(7079), 498—502.

Sen, B. K. (1997). Mega-authorship from a bibliometric point of view. *Malaysian Journal of Library and Information Science*, 2(2), 9—18.

Sen, S. K., & Gan, S. K. (1983). A mathematical extension of the idea of bibliographic coupling and its applications. *Annals of Library Science and Documentation*, 30(2), 78—82.

Serenko, A., & Bontis, N. (2009). A citation based ranking of the business ethics scholarly journals. *International Journal of Business Governance and Ethics*, 4(4), 390—399.

Serenko, A., & Bontis, N. (2013). Global ranking of knowledge management and intellectual capital academic journals: 2013 update. *Journal of Knowledge Management*, 17(2), 307—326.

Serenko, A., & Jiao, CQ. (2012). Investigating information systems research in Canada. *Canadian Journal of Administrative Sciences/Revue canadienne des Sciences de l'Administration*, 29(1), 3—24.

Shanahan, D. R. (2016). Auto-correlation of journal impact factor for consensus research reporting statements: A cohort study. *PeerJ*, 4, e1887.

Shannon, C. E. (1948a). A mathematical theory of communication. *Bell System Technical Journal*, 27(3), 379—423.

Shannon, C. E. (1948b). A mathematical theory of communication. *Bell System Technical Journal*, 27(4), 623—656.

Shepherd, P. T. (2006). COUNTER: Usage statistics for performance measurement. *Performance Measurement and Metrics, 7*(3), 142−152.

Shi, DB., Rousseau, R., Yang, L., & Li, J. (2017). A journal's impact factor is influenced by changes in publication delays of citing journals. *Journal of the Association for Information Science and Technology, 68*(3), 780−789.

Shneider, A. M. (2009). Four stages of a scientific discipline; four types of scientist. *Trends in Biochemical Sciences, 34*(5), 217−223.

Shotton, D. (2013). Open citations. *Nature, 502*(7471), 295−297.

Sîle, L., Guns, R., Sivertsen, G., & Engels, T. (2017). *European Databases and Repositories for Social Sciences and Humanities Research Output.* Antwerp: ENRESSH. Retrieved from https://doi.org/10.6084/m9.figshare.5172322.

Sills, J. (Ed.). (2014). Science ethics: Young scientists speak. *Science, 345*(6192), 24−27.

Simon, H.A. (1957). Models of man: Social and Rational. Chapter 9. *On a class of skew distribution functions.* New York: John Wiley & Sons.

Sivertsen, G. (2008). Experiences with a bibliometric model for performance based funding of research institutions. In J. Goriaz, & E. Schiebel (Eds.), *Book of abstracts, 10th international science and technology indicators conference* (pp. 126−128). Vienna: Univ. Vienna.

Sivertsen, G. (2010). A performance indicator based on complete data for the scientific publication output at research institutions. *ISSI Newsletter, 6*(1), 22−28.

Small, H. (1973). Co-citation in the scientific literature: A new measure of the relationship between two documents. *Journal of the American Society for Information Science, 24*(4), 265−269.

Small, H. (1974). Multiple citation patterns in scientific literature: The circle and hill models. *Information Storage and Retrieval, 10*(11−12), 393−402.

Small, H. (1978). Cited documents as concept symbols. *Social Studies of Science, 8*(3), 327−340.

Small, H. (1986). The synthesis of specialty narratives from co-citation clusters. *Journal of the American Society for Information Science, 37*(3), 97−110.

Small, H. (1993). Macro-level changes in the structure of co-citation clusters: 1983−1989. *Scientometrics, 26*(1), 5−20.

Smith, L. C. (1981). Citation analysis. *Library Trends, 30*(Summer), 83−106.

Smith, M. (1958). The trend toward multiple authorship in psychology. *American Psychologist, 13*(10), 596−599.

Smolinsky, L., & Lercher, A. (2012). Citation rates in mathematics: A study of variation by subdiscipline. *Scientometrics, 91*(3), 911−924.

So, C. Y. K. (1990). Openness index and affinity index: Two new citation indicators. *Scientometrics, 19*(1−2), 25−34.

Solomon, D. J., & Björk, B-C. (2012a). Publication fees in Open Access Publishing: Sources of funding and factors influencing choice of journals. *Journal of the American Society of Information Science and Technology, 63*(1), 98−107.

Solomon, D. J., & Björk, B-C. (2012b). A study of open access journals using article processing charges. *Journal of the American Society of Information Science and Technology, 63*(8), 1485−1495.

Sombatsompop, N., Markpin, T., & Premkamolnetr, N. (2004). A modified method for calculating the impact factors of journals in ISI Journal Citation Reports: Polymer science category in 1997−2001. *Scientometrics, 60*(2), 217−235.

Sonnenwald, D. H. (2007). Scientific collaboration. *Annual Review of Information Science and Technology, 41*, 643−681.

Soper, M. E. (1976). Characteristics and use of personal collections. *The Library Quarterly, 46*(4), 397−415.

Sporns, O., & Kötter, R. (2004). Motifs in brain networks. *PLOS Biology, 2*(11), e369.

Spruyt, E. H. J., & Engels, T. C. E. (2013). Nieuwe sleutel verdeling van middelen Bijzonder Onderzoeksfonds. *THeMA: Tijdschrift voor Hoger Onderwijs en Management*, *13*(3), 56−61.

Squartini, T., Picciolo, F., Ruzzenenti, F., & Garlaschelli, D. (2013). Reciprocity of weighted networks. *Scientific Reports*, *3*, 2729.

Stegmann, J. (1999). Building a list of journals with constructed impact factors. *Journal of Documentation*, *55*(3), 310−324.

Stern, A. M., Casadevall, A., Steen, R. G., & Fang, F. C. (2014). Financial costs and personal consequences of research misconduct resulting in retracted publications. *eLife*, *3*, e02956.

Steward, M. D., & Lewis, B. R. (2010). A comprehensive analysis of marketing journal rankings. *Journal of Marketing Education*, *32*(1), 75−92.

Stigbrand, T. (2017). Retraction note to multiple articles in Tumor Biology. *Tumor biology.* Available from http://dx.doi.org/10.1007/s13277-017-5487-6.

Stigler, S. M. (1980). Stigler's law of eponymy. *Transactions of the New York Academy of Sciences*, *39*, 147−158. (Merton Festschrift Volume, F. Gieryn (Ed)).

Stirling, A. (2007). A general framework for analysing diversity in science, technology and society. *Journal of the Royal Society Interface*, *4*(15), 707−719.

Stock, W. G. (2009). The inflation of impact factors of scientific journals. *ChemPhysChem*, *10*(13), 2193−2196.

Stokes, D. E. (1997). *Pasteur's quadrant − basic science and technological innovation.* Washington, D.C.: Brookings Institution Press.

Stokes, G. (1998). *Popper: Philosophy, politics and scientific method.* Cambridge: Polity Press.

Stremersch, S., Camacho, N., Vanneste, S., & Verniers, I. (2015). Unraveling scientific impact: Citation types in marketing journals. *International Journal of Research in Marketing*, *32*(1), 64−77.

Su, XN., Han, XM., & Han, XN. (2001). Developing the Chinese Social Science Citation Index. *Online Information Review*, *25*(6), 365−369.

Subramanyam, K. (1983). Bibliometric studies of research collaboration: A review. *Journal of Information Science*, *6*(1), 33−38.

Sugimoto, C. R., Larivière, V., Ni, CQ., & Cronin, B. (2013). Journal acceptance rates: A cross-disciplinary analysis of variability and relationships with journal measures. *Journal of Informetrics*, *7*(4), 897−906.

Száva-Kováts, E. (2002). Unfounded attribution of the "half-life" index-number of literature obsolescence to Burton and Kebler: A literature science study. *Journal of the American Society for Information Science and Technology*, *53*(13), 1098−1105.

Tagliacozzo, R. (1977). Self-citations in scientific literature. *Journal of Documentation*, *33* (4), 251−265.

Tague-Sutcliffe, J. (1992). An introduction to informetrics. *Information Processing and Management*, *28*(1), 1−3.

Tahai, A., & Meyer, M. J. (1999). A revealed preference study of management journals' direct influences. *Strategic Management Journal*, *20*(3), 279−296.

Taylor, M. (2013). The challenges of measuring social impact using altmetrics. *Research Trends*, *33*, 11−15.

The GUSTO investigators. (1993). An international randomized trial comparing four thrombolytic strategies for acute myocardial infarction. *New England Journal of Medicine*, *329*(10), 673−682.

Thelwall, M. (2004). *Link analysis: An information science approach.* San Diego: Academic Press.

Thelwall, M. (2017). *Web indicators for research evaluation: A practical guide.* San Rafael (CA): Morgan & Claypool.

Thelwall, M., & Fairclough, R. (2015). Geometric journal impact factors correcting for individual highly cited articles. *Journal of Informetrics*, *9*(2), 263−272.

Thorne, F. C. (1977). The citation index: Another case of spurious validity. *Journal of Clinical Psychology*, *33*(4), 1157−1161.

Todorov, R., & Glänzel, W. (1988). Journal citation measures: A concise review. *Journal of Information Science*, *14*(1), 47−56.

Trajtenberg, M. (1990). A penny for your quotes: Patent citations and the value of innovations. *The RAND Journal of Economics*, *21*(1), 172−187.

Trivers, R. L. (1971). The evolution of reciprocal altruism. *Quarterly Review of Biology*, *46* (1), 35−57.

Truex, D., Cuellar, M., & Takeda, H. (2008). Assessing scholarly influence: Using the Hirsch indices to reframe the discourse. *Journal of the Association for Information Systems*, *10*(7), 560−594.

Tu, YY. (1999). The development of new antimalarial drugs: Qinghaosu and Dihydro-Qinghaosu. *Chinese Medical Journal*, *112*(11), 976−977.

Valiant, L. (2013). *Probably approximately correct*. New York: Basic Books.

Van de Sompel, H., & Lagoze, C. (2000). The Santa Fe convention of the Open Archive Initiative. *D-Lib Magazine*, *6*(2). See http://www.dlib.org/dlib/february00/vandesompel-oai/02vandesompel-oai.html.

Van den Besselaar, P., & Sandström, U. (2016). Gender differences in research performance and its impact on careers: A longitudinal case study. *Scientometrics*, *106*(1), 143−162.

Van der Veer Martens, B., & Goodrum, A. A. (2006). The diffusion of theories: A functional approach. *Journal of the American Society for Information Science and Technology*, *57* (3), 330−341.

van Eck, N. J., & Waltman, L. (2007). VOS: A new method for visualizing similarities between objects. In R. Decker, & H.-J. Lenz (Eds.), *Advances in data analysis: Proceedings of the 30th Annual Conference of the German Classification Society* (pp. 299−306). Heidelberg: Springer.

van Eck, N. J., & Waltman, L. (2010). Software survey: VOSviewer, a computer program for bibliometric mapping. *Scientometrics*, *84*(2), 523−538.

van Eck, N. J., & Waltman, L. (2011). Text mining and visualization using VOSviewer. *ISSI Newsletter*, 7(3), 50−54.

van Eck, N. J., & Waltman, L. (2014). Visualizing bibliometric networks. In Y. Ding, R. Rousseau, & D. Wolfram (Eds.), *Measuring scholarly impact: Methods and practice* (pp. 285−320). Cham: Springer.

Van Fleet, D. D., McWilliams, A., & Siegel, D. S. (2000). A theoretical and empirical analysis of journal rankings: The case of formal lists. *Journal of Management*, *26*(5), 839−861.

Van Leeuwen, T. N., Visser, M. S., Moed, H. F., Nederhof, T. J., & van Raan, A. F. J. (2003). The Holy Grail of science policy: Exploring and combining bibliometric tools in search of scientific excellence. *Scientometrics*, *57*(2), 257−280.

Van Noorden, R. (2014). Publishers withdraw more than 120 gibberish papers. <http://www.nature.com/news/publishers-withdraw-more-than-120-gibberish-papers-1.14763>.

Van Parijs, P. (2009). European higher education under the spell of university rankings. *Ethical Perspectives*, *16*(2), 189−206.

van Raan, A. F. J. (1992). *Het Meten van ons Weten: Over de Kwantitatieve Bestudering van Wetenschap en Technologie*. Leiden: Rijksuniversiteit Leiden.

van Raan, A. F. J. (2004a). Measuring science. In H. F. Moed, W. Glänzel, & U. Schmoch (Eds.), *Handbook of quantitative science and technology research* (pp. 19−50). Dordrecht: Kluwer.

van Raan, A. F. J. (2004b). Sleeping beauties in science. *Scientometrics*, *59*(3), 467−472.

van Raan, A. F. J. (2005). Fatal attraction: Conceptual and methodological problems in the rankings of universities by bibliometric methods. *Scientometrics, 62*(1), 133−143.

Van Rijnsoever, F. J., & Hessels, L. K. (2011). Factors associated with disciplinary and interdisciplinary research collaboration. *Research Policy, 40*(3), 463−472.

van Rooyen, S., Black, N., & Godlee, F. (1999). Development of the review quality instrument (RQI) for assessing peer reviews of manuscripts. *Journal of Clinical Epidemiology, 52*(7), 625−629.

Vanclay, J. K. (2007). On the robustness of the h-index. *Journal of the American Society for Information Science and Technology, 58*(10), 1547−1550.

Vanclay, J. K. (2012). Impact factor: Outdated artifact or stepping-stone to journal certification? *Scientometrics, 92*(2), 211−238.

Varn, D.P. (2014). Comment posted at ASIS&T SIGMETRICS list on 22/07/2014.

Vaughan, L. (2001). *Statistical methods for the information professional: A practical, painless approach to understanding, using, and interpreting statistics.* Medford, NJ: Information Today.

Verleysen, F. T., & Engels, T. C. E. (2013). A label for peer-reviewed books. *Journal of the American Society for Information Science and Technology, 64*(2), 428−430.

Verleysen, F. T., & Engels, T. C. E. (2014a). Barycenter representation of book publishing internationalization in the Social Sciences and Humanities. *Journal of Informetrics, 8*(1), 234−240.

Verleysen, F. T., & Engels, T. C. E. (2014b). Internationalization of peer reviewed and non-peer reviewed book publications in the Social Sciences and Humanities. *Scientometrics, 101*(2), 1431−1444.

Verleysen, F. T., Ghesquière, P., & Engels, T. C. E. (2014). The objectives, design and selection process of the Flemish Academic Bibliographic Database for the Social Sciences and Humanities (VABB-SHW). In W. Blockmans, et al. (Eds.), *Bibliometrics: Use and abuse in the review of research performance* (pp. 115−125). London: Portland Press.

Vidgen, B., & Yasseri, T. (2016). P-values: Misunderstood and misused. *Frontiers in Physics, 4,* 6.

Vieira, E. S., & Gomes, J. A. N. F. (2009). A comparison of Scopus and Web of Science for a typical university. *Scientometrics, 81*(2), 587−600.

Vinkler, P. (2010). *The evaluation of research by scientometric indicators.* Oxford: Chandos Publishing.

Vitanov, N. K. (2016). *Science dynamics and research production: Indicators, indexes, statistical laws and mathematical models.* Switzerland: Springer International Publishing.

Vygotski, L. S. (1978). *Mind in society: The development of higher psychological processes.* Cambridge (MA): Harvard University Press.

Wager, E., Barbour, V., Yentis, S., & Kleinert, S. (2010). Retractions: Guidance from the Committee on Publication Ethics (COPE). *Obesity Reviews, 11*(1), 64−66.

Wagner, C. (2016). Rosalind's ghost: Biology, collaboration, and the female. *PLOS Biology, 14*(11), e2001003.

Walters, W. H. (2016). The research contribution of editorial board members in library and information science. *Journal of Scholarly Publishing, 47*(2), 121−146.

Waltman, L. (2016). A review of the literature on citation impact indicators. *Journal of Informetrics, 10*(2), 365−391.

Waltman, L., & van Eck, N. J. (2012a). The inconsistency of the h-index. *Journal of the American Society for Information Science and Technology, 63*(2), 406−415.

Waltman, L., & van Eck, N. J. (2012b). A new methodology for constructing a publication-level classification system of science. *Journal of the American Society for Information Science and Technology, 63*(12), 2378−2392.

Waltman, L., van Eck, N. J., van Leeuwen, T. N., & Visser, M. S. (2013). Some modifications to the SNIP journal impact indicator. *Journal of Informetrics, 7*(2), 272−285.

Waltman, L., van Eck, N. J., van Leeuwen, T. N., Visser, M. S., & van Raan, A. F. J. (2011a). Towards a new crown indicator: Some theoretical considerations. *Journal of Informetrics, 5*(1), 37−47.

Waltman, L., van Eck, N. J., van Leeuwen, T. N., Visser, M. S., & van Raan, A. F. J. (2011b). Towards a new crown indicator: An empirical analysis. *Scientometrics, 87*(3), 467−481.

Waltman, L., Tijssen, R., & van Eck, N. J. (2011). Globalisation of science in kilometres. *Journal of Informetrics, 5*(4), 574−582.

Wan, JK., Hua, PH., Rousseau, R., & Sun, XK. (2010). The journal download immediacy index (DII): Experiences using a Chinese full-text database. *Scientometrics, 82*(3), 555−566.

Wang, D., Song, CM., & Barabási, A.-L. (2013). Quantifying long-term scientific impact. *Science, 342*(6154), 127−132.

Wardil, L., & Hauert, C. (2015). Cooperation and coauthorship in scientific publishing. *Physical Review E, 91*, 012825.

Wasserman, S., & Faust, K. (1994). *Social network analysis: Methods and applications.* Cambridge: Cambridge University Press.

Watts, D. J. (2004). The "new" science of networks. *Annual Review of Sociology, 30*, 243−270.

Weller, A.C. (2001). *Editorial peer review. Its strengths and weaknesses.* ASIST Monograph Series. Medford (NJ): Information Today.

West, J., Bergstrom, T., & Bergstrom, C. T. (2010). Big Macs and eigenfactor scores: Don't let correlation coefficients fool you. *Journal of the American Society for Information Science and Technology, 61*(9), 1800−1807.

White, H. D. (2000). Toward ego-centered citation analysis. In B. Cronin, & H. B. Atkins (Eds.), *The Web of Knowledge. A Festschrift in Honor of Eugene Garfield* (pp. 475−496). Medford (NJ): Information Today.

White, H. D. (2001). Authors as citers over time. *Journal of the American Society for Information Science, 52*(2), 87−108.

White, H. D. (2004). Reward, persuasion, and the Sokal hoax: A study in citation identities. *Scientometrics, 60*(1), 93−120.

White, H. D., Boell, S. K., Yu, HR., Davis, M., Wilson, C. S., & Cole, F. T. H. (2009). Libcitations: A measure for comparative assessment of book publications in the humanities and social sciences. *Journal of the American Society for Information Science and Technology, 60*(6), 1083−1096.

White, H. D., & Griffith, B. C. (1981). Author cocitation: A literature measure of intellectual structure. *Journal of the American Society for Information Science, 32*(3), 163−171.

White, H. D., & McCain, K. W. (1998). Visualizing a discipline: An author co-citation analysis of information science, 1972−1995. *Journal of the American Society for Information Science, 49*(4), 327−355.

Wildgaard, L., Schneider, J. W., & Larsen, B. (2014). A review of the characteristics of 108 author-level bibliometric indicators. *Scientometrics, 101*(1), 125−158.

Wilhite, A. W., & Fong, E. A. (2012). Coercive citation in academic publishing. *Science, 335*(6068), 542−543.

Wilsdon, J., Allen, L., Belfiore, E, ..., Johnson, B. (2015). *The metric tide: Report of the independent review of the role of metrics in research assessment and management.* <http://dx.doi.org/10.13140/RG.2.1.4929.1363>.

Wilson, C. S. (1999). Informetrics. *Annual Review of Information Science and Technology, 34*, 107−247.

Wilson, R., & Lancaster, J. (2006). 'Referee factor' would reward a vital contribution. *Nature, 441*(7095), 812. Erratum in *Nature* (2006); 441(7097), 1048−1048.

Woeginger, G. J. (2008). An axiomatic characterization of the Hirsch-index. *Mathematical Social Sciences*, *56*(2), 224—232.

Woit, P. (2006). *Not even wrong: The failure of string theory and the continuing challenge to unify the laws of physics*. London: Jonathan Cape.

Wouters, P. (1999). *The citation culture*. Doctoral thesis Universiteit van Amsterdam.

Wu, XF., Fu, Q., & Rousseau, R. (2008). On indexing in the Web of Science and predicting journal impact factor. *Journal of Zhejiang University Science B*, *9*(7), 582—590.

Wu, YS., Pan, Y., Zhang, Y., Ma, Z., Pang, J., Guo, H., Xu, B., & Yang, Z. (2004). China Scientific and Technical Papers and Citations (CSTPC): History, impact and outlook. *Scientometrics*, *60*(3), 385—397.

Xhignesse, L. V., & Osgood, C. E. (1967). Bibliographical citation characteristics of the psychological journal network in 1950 and in 1960. *American Psychologist*, *22*(9), 778—791.

Xia, J., Myers, R. L., & Wilhoite, S. K. (2011). Multiple open access availability and citation impact. *Journal of Information Science*, *37*(1), 19—28.

Xie, Y., & Shauman, K. A. (1998). Sex differences in research community: New evidence about an old puzzle. *American Sociological Review*, *63*(6), 847—870.

Xu, F., Liu, WB., & Rousseau, R. (2015). Introducing Sub-Impact Factor (SIF) sequences and an aggregated SIF-indicator for journal ranking. *Scientometrics*, *102*(2), 1577—1593.

Yablonsky, A. I. (1980). On fundamental regularities of the distribution of scientific productivity. *Scientometrics*, *2*(1), 3—34.

Yang, LY., Morris, S. A., & Barden, E. M. (2009). Mapping institutions and their weak ties in a specialty: A case study of cystic fibrosis body composition research. *Scientometrics*, *79*(2), 421—434.

Yanovsky, V. I. (1981). Citation analysis significance of scientific journals. *Scientometrics*, *3*(3), 223—233.

Yong, E., Ledford, H., & Van Noorden, R. (2013). 3 Ways to blow the whistle. *Nature*, *503*(7477), 454—457.

Yukalov, V. I., & Sornette, D. (2012). Statistical outliers and dragon-kings as Bose-condensed droplets. *European Physical Journal — Special Topics*, *205*(1), 53—64.

Yule, G. U. (1925). A mathematical theory of evolution, based on the conclusions of Dr. J. C. Willis, F.R.S. *Philosophical Transactions of the Royal Society of London B*, *213*(403), 21—87.

Zeng, X. H. T., Duch, J., Sales-Pardo, M., Moreira, J. A. G., Radicchi, F., Ribeiro, H. V., Woodruff, T. K., & Amaral, L. A. N. (2016). Differences in collaboration patterns across discipline, career stage, and gender. *PLOS Biology*, *14*(11), e1002573.

Zhang, H. Y. (2010). CrossCheck: An effective tool for detecting plagiarism. *Learned Publishing*, *23*(1), 9—14.

Zhang, L., Rousseau, R., & Glänzel, W. (2016). Diversity of references as an indicator for interdisciplinarity of journals: Taking similarity between subject fields into account. *Journal of the Association for Information Science and Technology*, *67*(5), 1257—1265.

Zhang, L., Thijs, B., & Glänzel, W. (2013). What does scientometrics share with other "metrics" sciences? *Journal of the American Society for Information Science and Technology*, *64*(7), 1515—1518.

Zhang, X., Shao, S., Stanley, H. E., & Havlin, S. (2014). Dynamic motifs in socio-economic networks. *EPL (Europhysics Letters)*, *108*(5), 58001.

Zhang, Y. (2006). The effect of open access on citation impact: A comparison study based on web citation analysis. *Libri*, *56*(3), 145—156.

Zhang, Y. H. (2016). *Against plagiarism. A guide for editors and authors*. Switzerland: Springer International Publishing.

Zhang, YH., & Jia, XY. (2013). Republication of conference papers in journals? *Learned Publishing*, *26*(3), 189—196.

Zhao, DZ. (2005). Challenges of scholarly publications on the web to the evaluation of science — A comparison of author visibility on the web and in print journals. *Information Processing and Management*, *41*(6), 1403—1418.

Zhao, HZ., & Jiang, GH. (1986). Life-span and precocity of scientists. *Scientometrics*, *9* (1—2), 27—36.

Zhao, S. X., Rousseau, R., & Ye, F. Y. (2011). h-Degree as a basic measure in weighted network. *Journal of Informetrics*, *5*(4), 668—677.

Zhou, QJ., & Leydesdorff, L. (2016). The normalization of occurrence and co-occurrence matrices in bibliometrics using cosine similarities and Ochiai coefficients. *Journal of the Association for Information Science and Technology*, *67*(11), 2805—2814.

Zhu, XD., Turney, P., Lemire, D., & Vellino, A. (2015). Measuring academic influence: Not all citations are equal. *Journal of the Association for Information Science and Technology*, *66*(2), 408—427.

Zipf, G. K. (1932). *Selected studies of the principle of relative frequency in Language*. Cambridge (MA): Harvard University Press.

Zipf, G. K. (1935). *The Psycho-biology of Language*. Oxford: Houghton-Mifflin.

Zipf, G. K. (1949). *Human behavior and the principle of least effort*. Cambridge (MA): Addison-Wesley, reprinted: 1965: New York: Hafner.

Zitt, M., & Small, H. (2008). Modifying the journal impact factor by fractional citation weighting: The audience factor. *Journal of the American Society for Information Science and Technology*, *59*(11), 1856—1860.

Zuccala, A. (2006). Modeling the invisible college. *Journal of the American Society for Information Science and Technology*, *57*(2), 152—168.

Zuccala, A., Guns, R., Cornacchia, R., & Bod, R. (2015). Can we rank scholarly book publishers? A bibliometric experiment with the field of history. *Journal of the Association for Information Science and Technology*, *66*(7), 1333—1347.

Zuckerman, H. (1968). Patterns of name-ordering among authors of scientific papers: A study of social symbolism and its ambiguity. *American Journal of Sociology*, *74*(3), 276—291.

Zuckerman, H., & Merton, R. K. (1971). Patterns of evaluation in science: Institutionalisation, structure and functions of the referee system. *Minerva*, *9*(1), 66—100.

INDEX

Note: Page numbers followed by "*f*" and "*t*" refer to figures and tables, respectively.

CPI Antony Rowe
Eastbourne, UK
September 21, 2020